PREVENTIVE STRATEGIES ON SUICIDE

ADVANCES IN SUICIDOLOGY

VOLUME II

PREVENTIVE STRATEGIES ON SUICIDE

EDITED BY

RENÉ F. W. DIEKSTRA · WALTER GULBINAT
INEKE KIENHORST · DIEGO DE LEO

PUBLISHED UNDER THE AUSPICES OF
THE WORLD HEALTH ORGANIZATION

E. J. BRILL
LEIDEN · NEW YORK · KÖLN
1995

The paper in this book meets the guidelines for permanence and durability of the Committee on Production Guidelines for Book Longevity of the Council on Library Resources.

Library of Congress Cataloging-in-Publication Data

Preventive strategies on suicide / edited by René F.W. Diekstra ... [et al.].
p. cm. — (Advances in suicidology ; v. 2)
"Published under the auspices of the World Health Organization."
Includes index.
ISBN 9004103392 (pbk. : alk. paper)
1. Suicide—Prevention. 2. Suicidal behavior—Treatment.
I. Diekstra, R. F. W. II. Series.
HV6545.P73 1995
382.2'8—dc20 95-19665
CIP

Die Deutsche Bibliothek – CIP-Einheitsaufnahme

Preventive strategies on suicide / ed. by René F. W. Diekstra ... [et al.]. –
Leiden ; New York ; Köln : Brill, 1995
(Advances in suicidology ; Vol. 2)
ISBN 90-04-10339-2
NE: Diekstra, René F. W. [Hrsg.]; GT

ISSN 0922-3061
ISBN 90 04 10339 2

PRINTED IN THE NETHERLANDS

Contents

Preface

W. H. GULBINAT

Suicidal behaviour poses a considerable public health problem in many countries of the world. Suicide, as a cause of death, is included in the mortality statistics of most countries, and, in 1991, 56 of the 166 Member States of the World Health Organization (WHO) reported deaths from suicide into WHO's international mortality data bank. Based on these statistics it has been estimated that annually more than 200,000 people commit suicide. On the other hand, these 56 reporting countries represent less than one-third of the world population, and it is known that suicide is a frequent phenomenon in non- reporting countries as well. Selected studies in non-reporting countries carried out over the last two decades permit rough estimations of at least 8 suicides per 100,000 population in Africa and non-reporting countries in Asia and Latin America, adding another 600,000 deaths from suicide to the 200,000 reported deaths. It is therefore a conservative estimate that the annual death toll from suicide world-wide adds to 800,000 people.

Suicide ranges among the ten leading causes of death in many countries and is even among the five most frequent causes of death in the economically productive age group between 15 and 65 years, and, in some developed countries, suicide is even more frequent than deaths from traffic accidents. The World Development Report 1993 published by the World Bank and produced in close collaboration with WHO estimates that 2.0 % of the total burden caused by all diseases is due to suicide (as a comparison, all cerebrovascular conditions combined constitute 3.2 % of the total burden of disease).

Suicidal behaviour, however, includes also attempted suicide (or parasuicide). The data base for the epidemiology of parasuicide is less complete than for completed suicide, but selected studies in a great number of countries over many years provide convincing evidence that the incidence of parasuicide is at least ten times higher than that of suicide. Parasuicide affects not only the person who commits the suicidal act but also his or her relatives and, very often, the health and social services to which the patient is referred for treatment and help.

Repeatedly the question has been raised whether or to which extent a suicidal act represents a medical or a public health problem, as there are philosophical belief systems which see suicide as a valid option of a person's free will. Scientific evidence, however, shows that this issue has little practical relevance as there is overwhelming evidence that more than 95% of all people committing a suicidal act suffer, at the time of the act, from some form of clinically manifest mental disorder, very often depression, but also neurotic & personality disorders, or substance abuse including alcohol abuse.

Prevention, obviously, is the only public health measure to reduce suicide rates, and it is by far the most desirable option for dealing with non-fatal suicidal acts. In spite of this, there are surprisingly few agreed and proven methods for suicide prevention. At a first glance and in view of the above high correlation it seems that preventing suicide is synonymous with preventing psychiatric illness. While this is, theoretically, true there are considerable practical obstacles: Only a relatively small percentage of people suffering, at a given point in time, from a mental disorder are in contact with the health services; of those who are in such contact, many are not properly diagnosed and hence the mental disorder is not recognized; and for certain psychiatric conditions - even if recognized - there is no straightforward, short-term treatment. While research into diagnosis, control, treatment and prevention of mental disorders is progressing (more recently with remarkable and unexpected success) there is an urgent need to look into specific methods for suicide prevention. It is the intention of the present volume to summarize what is known in this field, but also to point to new and promising new approaches to the prevention of suicidal behaviour. By doing this the book also points to the limits of suicide prevention and to the need for and the directions of future research needs.

Introduction

The enigma that has confronted and haunted mankind for centuries is the realization that not all people wish to live. Life is pleasure above all else, and once rooted there is a tenacious attempt to hold on to it and to maintain it at all costs. This clinging to life in the face of tragedy, adversity, torture, anguish, humiliation, the ravages of old age—even in terminable pain when dead is manifestly imminent—is characteristic of the overwhelming majority of humanity. There are, however, those who elect to terminate their existence. These individuals, on a seemingly volitional basis, make a drastic irrevocable decision to divest themselves of life. The word self-destruction accurately describes this act.

There are then individuals who, under varying circumstances, perceive life as so ungratifying, so unfruitful, so futile and so meaningless as to cause them to end it by murdering themselves. Or to attempt to do so. These people choose to execute themselves on the basis of their own rationale and on their own terms rather than wait out the normal course of events that inevitably results in demise as the inexorable force of fate. Although there is a strong tendency to denial about such matters, most people have at one point or another encountered gigantic conflictual struggles and crises in their lives and have considered suicide as an option. The vast majority have resolved, reversed, or diverted these self-destructive temptations, impulses and urges. However, the very fact that such premeditation is too prevalent and that many people merely postpone their suicide only to reinitiate the attempt at a later date emphasizes the vast preoccupation with death in human society. On this basis alone, there is ample reason for scientists to investigate this form of lethality.

For centuries, speculation and superstition about suicide were largely interspersed with moral, religious and philosophical dogma. It was not until the end of the 19th century and the beginning of the 20th, when scientific methodology was well on its way, that Emile Durkheim and Sigmund Freud dispersed the archaic cobwebs and opened more objective avenues for the exploration and study of suicide. The panorama that was refilled encompassed every sphere of human relations, including public health and medicine as well as mental health. Epidemiologists, statisticians, sociologists, psychiatrists, psychologists, and physicians became increasingly aware of suicide as a leading cause of death and suicidal behavior in general as both a major public health problem and a clinical issue.

Since the preliminary works of Durkheim and Freud, their proponents and opponents alike have brought forth a multitude of additions, elaborations, new concepts, and hypothetical constructs. The world's most renounced theorists and mental health practitioners offered their contributions. And for a good reason. The magnitude and the complexity of the problem is such that it cannot be demarcated and limited to anyone's profession or discipline. Suicidal behavior is a biopsychosocial phenomenon, both in its genotypes as well as in its phenotypes, both in terms of etiology as well as with regard to intervention and prevention.

The complexity of causation of suicidal behavior indicates the necessity of a parallel complexity of solution. The call for complexity of solution has been heard before in a number of other areas, such as aggression reduction, from community psychologists, ecological psychologists, epidemiological psychiatrists, environmental designers, system analysts and health policy makers in international organizations such as the World Health Organization. It has, however, relatively seldom been heard yet in the area of suicidology, presumably because most of the work with regard to intervention and prevention of suicidal behavior has mainly remained within the realm of clinical settings. Although in recent years a number of authors have proposed to approach the problem of the prevention of suicidal behavior from a broad community perspective, most of the interventions are either clinical activities or prevention activities that usually have taken the form of rather isolated projects, such as curricula for suicide education in school.

The state of the art in suicidology indicates that to have even a most moderate chance of enduring success of prevention of self-destructive behavior, programmes and messages designed to reduce that behavior must be oriented not only to the individual but also to the levels of the family, school, workplace and other large-scale organizations and organizational structures as well as the larger community context. One ought to use a variety of modes and channels simultaneously. It may very well be that one of the reasons that intervention and prevention programmes that have been tried out over the past decades have not been able to stand up against empirical tests of their efficacy, is precisely that they have not been based on the complex cause-complex cure approach. Simply put, complex problems yield complex solutions.

The present volume brings together a wealth of important recent insights both on descriptive-epidemiological as well as analytic aspects of suicidal behavior, both fatal and non-fatal, as well as gamut of wisdom with regard to therapeutic and preventive strategies. As such it presents a clear picture of both the strengths and the weaknesses in this field. One of the most conspicuous strengths of this field is that the cartography of suicide behavior is almost as complete as one can imagine. This is true both in the area of population epidemiology as well as in the area of clinical or psychiatric research. At the same time, while we know much about the what and how of suicidal behavior, we still know relatively little of the why, and therefore our knowledge base for effective preventive activities is still relatively small.

It is exactly for this reason that every report of the state of the art is more than welcome, for it points out where the gaps in our knowledge are to be found and stimulates both researchers and clinicians to continue their important though difficult and complicated work. The present volume, therefore, is both a milestone as well as once again a proof of the fact that science only emits interim reports.

René F.W. Diekstra
Walter Gulbinat
Ineke Kienhorst
Diego De Leo

Thanks to Vivian Kraay for her invaluable support in producing this manuscript.

The Epidemiology of Suicide and Parasuicide

R.F.W. DIEKSTRA

Introduction

In the 1991 World Health Statistics Annual (WHO, 1992) only 56 of the 166 member states of the United Nations are listed as reporting data on mortality by suicide. Altogether these 56 countries report 154,514 suicidal deaths in one year.

Clearly this figure provides a disturbingly incomplete picture of the magnitude of the phenomenon at a global level. In all of the non-reporting countries suicide does occur and there is more than suggestive evidence that in some of these countries the suicide rate at times equals or even surpasses the highest rates reported officially. In addition, it has been established that in the reporting countries a considerable number of suicidal deaths, estimates vary from an underestimation of 30 to 200 percent, are not recorded as such. If one combines these observations with the fact that in most countries, based on whatever data that *are* available, suicide ranks among the top 10 causes of death for individuals of all ages and among the 2 or 3 leading causes of death for those aged 15-34 years, the inevitable conclusion is that mortality by suicide constitutes a very serious public health problem.

It is, however, also a problem that is grossly neglected or underplayed. This becomes apparent if, for example, one considers the fact that today in many industrialized countries the number of people dying through suicide is significantly higher than the number of people dying on the road through motor traffic accidents. Over the last two decades motor traffic mortality rates have been decreasing while at the same time suicide rates, particularly among adolescents and young adults, have been sharply increasing. But in all countries, without any single exception, the resources being made available for preventive interventions in the case of suicidal behaviour constitute only a very tiny fraction of what is available for the prevention of motor traffic deaths.

This situation cannot simply be explained by the fact that in the case of road traffic we are not only dealing with mortality but also with many non-fatal casualties, not seldomly of a very serious nature. In the case of suicidal behaviour we are also faced with the fact that, in addition to the number of suicidal deaths, at least 10 times as many persons make a non-fatal suicide attempt or deliberately harm themselves, often seriously enough to require some form of medical assistance. Our knowlegde of the 'true' magnitude of this phenomenon of parasuicide (a term preferred by many contemporary authors above attempted suicide or suicide attempt, see Kreitman, 1977) is, even when compared to the case of committed suicide, extremely deficient. National records on parasuicide are kept nowhere in the world. Health care institutions that treat parasuicidal persons may or may not register such cases. Those that routinely record cases show a wide variability in operational criteria for the classification of a behaviour as parasuicide. The few population sample surveys carried out in this area indicate that approximately only 1 in 4 cases of attempted or parasuicide that meet the definitions and criteria set in a recent publication under the auspices of the World Health Organization (WHO) (Diekstra et al., 1989) leads to contact with medical or other professional health services. Nevertheless, in several countries parasuicide today forms one of the most frequent reasons for hospital emergency admissions in young people. The majority of parasuicides are by persons below 35 years of age. They constitute a pool from which many of the future suicides are drawn.

In the remainder of this chapter we will give an overview of secular trends in suicidal behaviours, with the main emphasis on countries in the European region, as well as discuss some of the prevailing explanations for these trends.

Secular trends in suicidal behaviour.

Suicide: the validity and reliability of suicide statistics

Any discussion of secular trends in suicide has first to address the issue of how valid and reliable the available data for trend description and analysis, national suicide statistics, are. The salient question here is whether methods and criteria in identifying suicides vary so much among different populations that they may account for the differences in rates. Several authors have argued that cultural attitudes towards suicide so affect certification that official suicide statistics are valueless (see a.o. Douglas, 1967). In 1968 The World Health Organisation established a working group on the comparability of suicide statistics that in its report (WHO Chronicle, 1975) stated: "The inescapable conclusion is that the present official suicide statistics are only of limited value. Constructing epidemiological and socio-demographic theories about suicide, therefore, will remain harzardous" (o.c. p. 193). Seven years later another WHO working group (WHO, 1982) came to an almost opposite conclusion since it expressed "confidence in the use of official suicide statistics from European countries for trendanalysis" (o.c. p.19). This conclusion was reached on the base of a careful examination of whatever empirical evidence was available on the matter.

The review clearly indicated that differences in ascertainment procedures do not explain differences in suicide rates between populations. A number of studies reviewed showed (Sainsbury and Barraclough, 1968; Whitlock, 1971; Lester, 1972; Barraclough, 1973; Sainsbury et al., 1981) that differences in the rank order of suicide rates of countries or cultural groups are barely altered when the effects of varying methods of ascertainment are controlled for, implying that national suicide mortality statistics can be assumed to be a valuable source of data on which to base comparative epidemiological studies.

This conclusion is supported by the fact that consistent differences in rates between national, demographic and social groups have been recorded over very long periods, in several instances far more than one century, differences which persist despite political changes that in many countries have altered ascertainment procedures.

In summary, then, suicide is underreported for a number of reasons and the rates are subject to many errors of a kind encountered in reporting mortality figures in general. Nevertheless, the evidence from studies designed to settle this point clearly indicates that these errors are randomised, at least to an extent that allows epidemiologists profitably to compare rates between countries, within them and over time.

The epidemiology of suicide[1]

There are large international variations in death rates from suicide between countries in the European region (see table 1). Of the countries that report to WHO and whose suicide rates are published in the 1989 World Health Statistics Annual 1989 (WHO, 1989), the range of suicide rates spans from a low of 6 per million females in Malta to a high of 581 per million males in Hungary. For all the countries taken together there were around 120,000 suicidal deaths reported in a one year period.

An inspection of table 2 shows a discernible pattern. Southern European countries have the lowest suicide rates, followed by the countries in the north-west region (United Kingdom, The Netherlands) with somewhat higher rates. The Scandinavian countries form a third group with again higher rates, while a fourth group of countries, also with relatively high rates are located in Europe's 'belt' - starting with Belgium and France in the west and via Switzerland, Austria and Hungary ending, on the eastern front, with Russia. This geographical 'suicide-chart' has more or less been characteristic for the European Region over the course of this century.

For 16 of the countries listed in table 1 suicide rates have been recorded for at least one hundred years. This allows us to answer the question: what has been the trend in suicide in Europe over the course of the 20th century? Is suicide increasing? As table 2 shows, the answer depends on what countries one is looking at.

---

[1] (In many publications age-adjusted suicides rates for countries are used. When these rates are compared with the crude rates for population aged 15 and over, the correlation coefficients are of the order of 0.99. We therefore decided to work with the more extensively reported unadjusted figures when discussing total rates as well as using age and sex specific rates.)

Table 1: Suicide rates in European countries (per 100,000 of inhabitants)

Name	Males	Females	Total	M/F ratio
Austria 88	33.6	13.3	24.95	2.7
Belgium 86	30.9	14.1	22.5	2.1
Bulgaria 87	24	9.5	16.75	2.5
Czechoslovakia 88	26.4	9.5	17.95	2.7
Denmark 87	36.1	19.9	28	1.8
Finland 87	44.6	11.7	28.15	3.8
France 87	31.7	12.5	22.1	2.5
Germany 88	24	10.8	17.9	2.3
Hungary 88	58.1	25.6	41.85	2.2
Iceland 88	23.9	4	13.95	5.9
Ireland 87	10.4	3.4	6.9	3.0
Italy 86	11.8	4.7	8.25	2.5
Luxembourg 88	28.6	8.9	18.75	3.2
Malta 88	4.7	0.6	2.65	7.8
Netherlands 87	13.7	8.4	11.05	1.6
Norway 87	23.5	7.7	15.6	3.0
Poland 88	20.5	4.3	12.4	4.7
Portugal 88	12.5	3.7	8.1	3.3
Spain 85	9.7	3.5	6.6	2.7
Sweden 87	26	10.9	18.45	2.3
Switzerland 88	32.4	12.9	22.65	2.5
USSR 87	30.3	9.3	19.8	3.2
U. Kingdom 88	13	4.6	8.8	2.8
Yugoslavia 87	23.9	10.6	17.25	2.2
	M= 24.9 SD= 11.9 range= 4.7-58.1	M= 9.3 SD= 5.5 range= 0.6-25.6	M= 17.1 SD= 8.5 range= 2.6-41.8	M= 3.1 SD= 1.3 range= 1.6-7.8

Source: World Health Statistics Annual (1989).

Table 2: Suicide in Europe 1881 - 1988

COUNTRY	1881-1890	1921-1925	1951-1954	1961-1967	1972-1974	1982-1984	1987-1988
Austria	16.1	28.3	23	21.9	23.6	28	25
Belgium	11.4	13.4	13.6	14.1	15.5	23	22.5
Denmark	22.5	13.8	23.5	18.3	24.6	28.9	28
Finland	3.9	12.7	17.4	20.7	24.2	24.6	27.6
France	20.7	19.5	15.5	15.5	15.8	21.8	22.1
Germany	20.9	22.1	18.6	18.9	20.6	21.4	17.9
Ireland	2.3	2.8	2.3	2.5	3.4	7.5	6.9
Italy	4.9	8.8	6.5	5.4	5.6	5.3	8.3
Netherlands	5.5	6.2	6.3	6.5	8.7	11.6	11
Norway	6.8	5.8	7.1	7.5	9.4	14.4	15.5
Portugal		6.9	10.2		8.7	10.2	8.1
Spain	2.4	5.6	5.9	6	4.3	7.2	7.8
Sweden	10.7	14.4	17.2	18	20.4	19.4	18.5
Switzerland	22.7	23.1	21.8	18.1	19.6	24.7	22.7
England&Wales	7.7	10.1	10.6	11.8	7.8	8.7	8.5
Scotland	5.5	6.6	5.6	8.5	8.3	10.7	11.9

Rates per 100,000 of population
Data from Cavan, 1928, Moens, 1990, and WHO databank 1987/88 equals last year reported in World Health Statistics Annual, 1989. For some countries last year is 1986.

In 9 countries the national suicide rate reached an all time high during the last decade, whereas in 7 countries the century's suicide peak occurred earlier, in most instances in the first part of the century. (The latter development can also be observed in the United States where the rate at the beginning of the century was 10.2 per 100,000, increased to 16.2 by 1915, then decreased sharply to again 10.2 in 1920. After 1925 it climbed steadily upwards, to reach a maximum of 17.4 in 1932. Since then, the rate has stayed significantly below this level (with 13.3 in 1977 and 12.7 in 1987)).

Despite these differences in trends between countries, it is noteworthy that the per period averaged rate for the 16 countries taken together has gone up over the course of the century (see figure 1) significantly. What is even more noteworthy is that while the average rate for Europe has gone up, the variation around the European mean as well as the rankorder of the countries has stayed pretty similar.

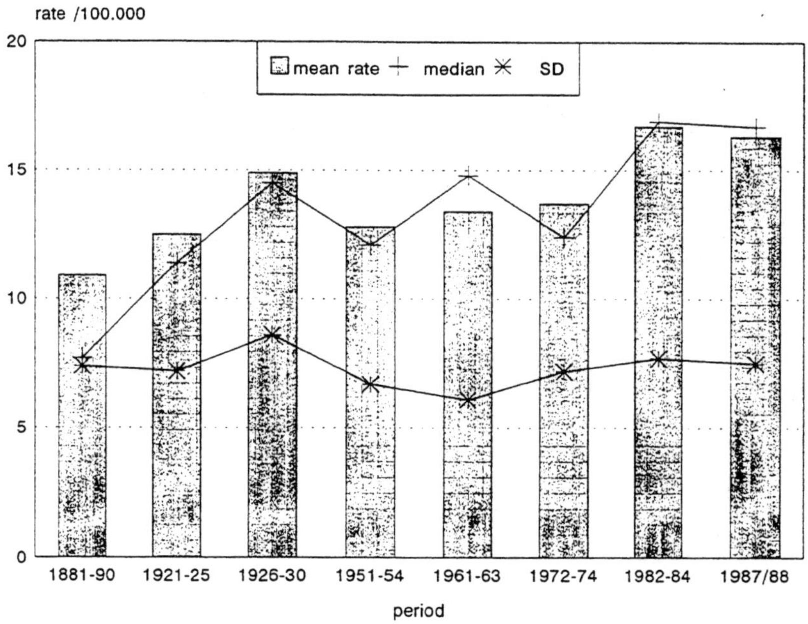

Fig. 1. Suicide rates in European countries, 1881-1988. Average rates for 16 countries, median rates, and standard deviations (SD).

This suggests that a) the prevalence of selfdestruction continues to vary in accordance with international differences in traditions, customs, religious convictions, social viewpoints, climactic conditions and other factors influencing human conduct while b) the strength of these international differences is decreasing. Apparently the countries in the European region are becoming more and more similar in many respects, including suicide mortality.

Age, gender and suicide

According to a multitude of authors (see Vaillant & Blumenthal, 1990) one of the most basic facts about suicide is that its risk increases as a function of age. Indeed, completed suicide is extremely rare in children under the age of twelve; becomes more common after puberty, with its incidence increasing in each of the adolescent years (Moens, 1990). From late adolescence/young adulthood onwards, however, the age-mortality relationship starts to diverge between countries and between the sexes within countries (see figures 2 to 4).

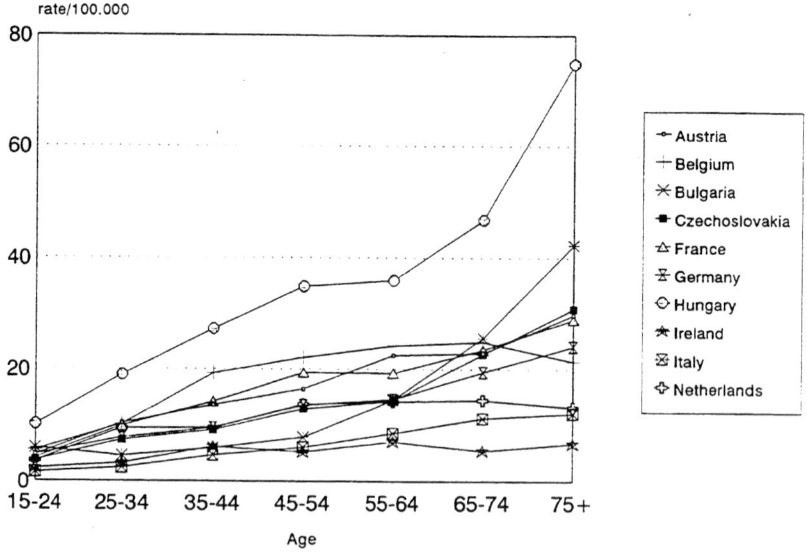

Fig. 2. Suicide and age: women in selected countries. Source: World health statistics annual (1989; 1992).

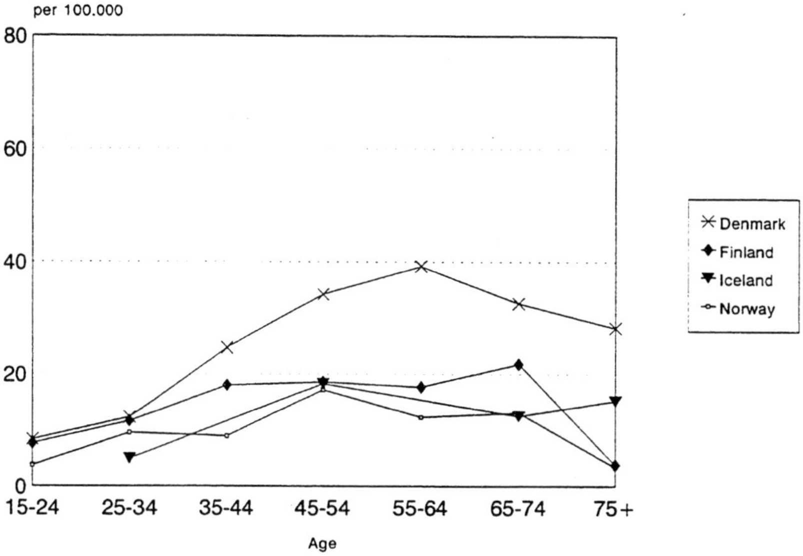

Fig. 3. Suicide and age: women in selcted countries. Source: World health statistics annual (1989; 1992).

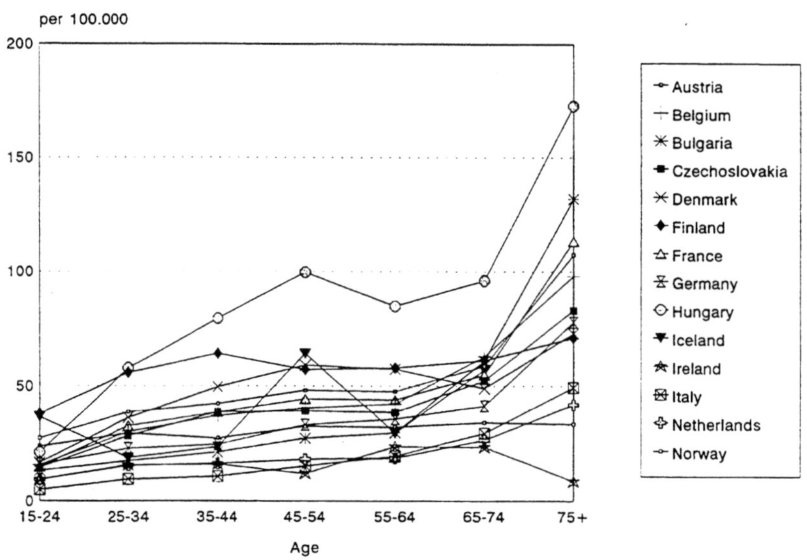

Fig. 4. Suicide and age: men in selcted countries. Source: World health statistics annual (1989; 1992).

In some countries we observe a first peak in the life cycle in that developmental period (roughly between 24 and 35 years of age, e.g. in males in Iceland, females in Norway, females in Bulgaria, in the United States for both sexes), whereas in other countries suicide rates continue to rise till midlife (roughly between 45 and 54 or 64 years of age, e.g. both sexes in Hungary and Denmark), after that stage a dip occurs. In almost all countries the highest suicide rates are among elderly men (age category 75+), but in quite a number of countries the highest suicide rates among females are found at a considerable younger age. As a comparison of figures 2, 3 and 4 shows, this is particularly the case among women in scandinavian countries (the peak age for women in Norway and Iceland is between 45-54 years of age and for Finnish women between 55-64).
Nevertheless, there is a high correlation between suicide and age in most of the countries. In 12 of the 14 countries for males the correlation between the suicide rate and age ranges from .78 to .91 (exceptions are Iceland (.51) and Ireland (.26)). In 11 countries for females the correlation ranges from .77 to .98 (the exceptions being Iceland (.59), Norway (.15) and Finland (.10)).
There is, however, another way of analyzing the relationship between suicide and age, namely using proportional mortality rates. If we relate the rank order of suicide in the hierarchy of causes of death to age, it appears that with increasing age the ranking of suicide in that hierarchy decreases (see figures 5 and 6).

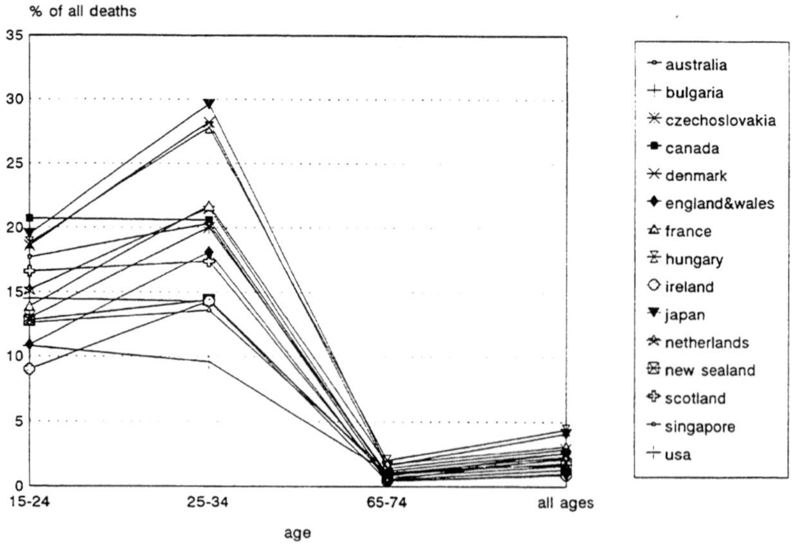

Fig. 5. Suicide as cause of death in men. Source: WHO Databank (years 1985/1988).

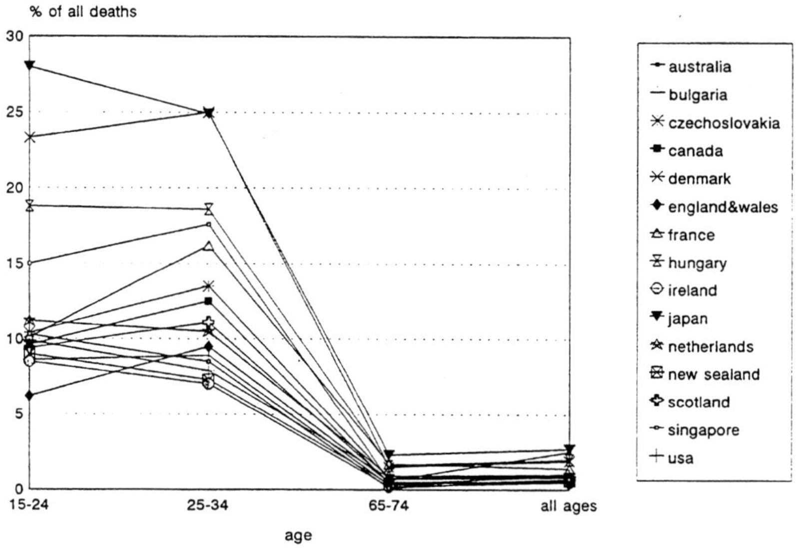

Fig. 6. Suicide as cause of death in women. Source: WHO Databank (years 1985/1988).

In most of the countries listed in figures 5 and 6 suicide ranks as the 9th or 10th cause of death all age groups taken together, accounting for sligthly more than (an averaged) 1% of all deaths in females and 2% in males. There are, however, substantial international differences. Some countries, such as Hungary, Japan and Denmark, have a suicide mortality three to five times as high as, for example, England & Wales and Ireland. There are also significant differences between age groups. In the age groups 15-34 years the percentage of all deaths caused by suicide is 15 to 20 times that percentage in the 65-74 age category. Among the former, suicide constitutes the second or third most important cause of death, accounting for 1 of every 8 deaths among females and 1 of every 6 among males. In some countries, such as Denmark and Japan, suicide is even the number one cause of death in the age group 25-34. Approximately 25% of all female deaths and 30% of all male deaths in this age category are by suicide. This hierarchical ranking is not simply a consequence of the fact that other causes of death, such as infectious and parasitic diseases, have to a large extent been brought under control or are almost completely eliminated, as we shall demonstrate in the following section.

Suicide: recent trends

There has been a real increase in suicide risk among adolescents and young adults over the past two decades in many European countries as well as in highly industrialized countries in other parts of the world. Figures 7 and 8 illustrate this by presenting age-specific suicide for the United States and The Netherlands as a percentage of total suicides in 5 year (USA) or 10 year (Netherlands) age groups, for the census years 1970 and 1987 (USA) or 1965-69 and 1985-87 (Netherlands). As can be seen, the rates of suicide in the younger age categories (approximately 15 to 30/34 years) are substantially lower around 1970 than around 1987. The trend is just the opposite for older age groups (45 and over).

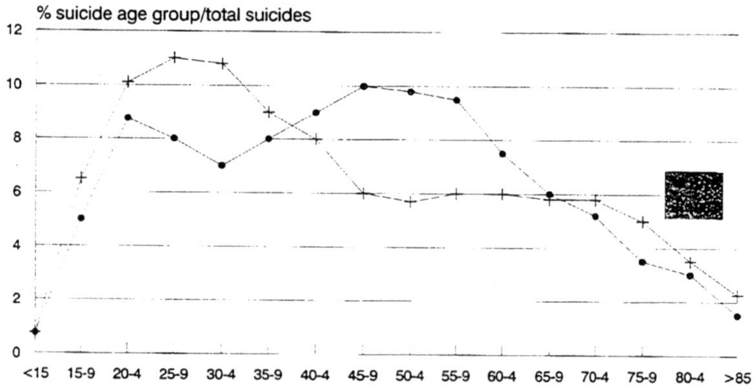

Fig. 7. Percentage of all suicides per age group: United States, 1970-1987. Data for USA, source: Buda & Tsuang, 5-year age groups.

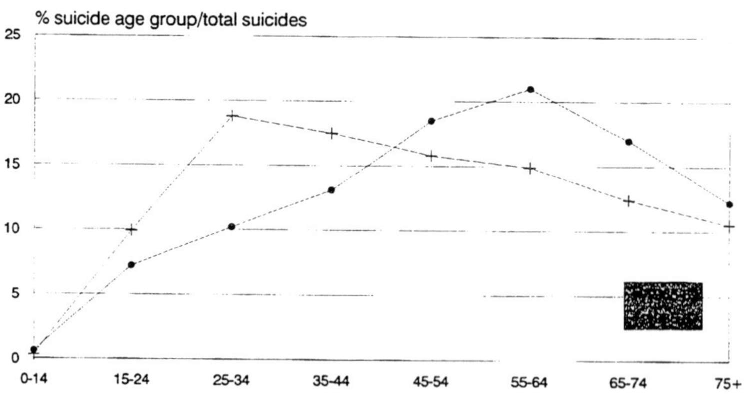

Fig. 8. Percentage of all suicides per age group: the Netherlands, 1965-1987. Source: WHO databank, 10-year age groups.

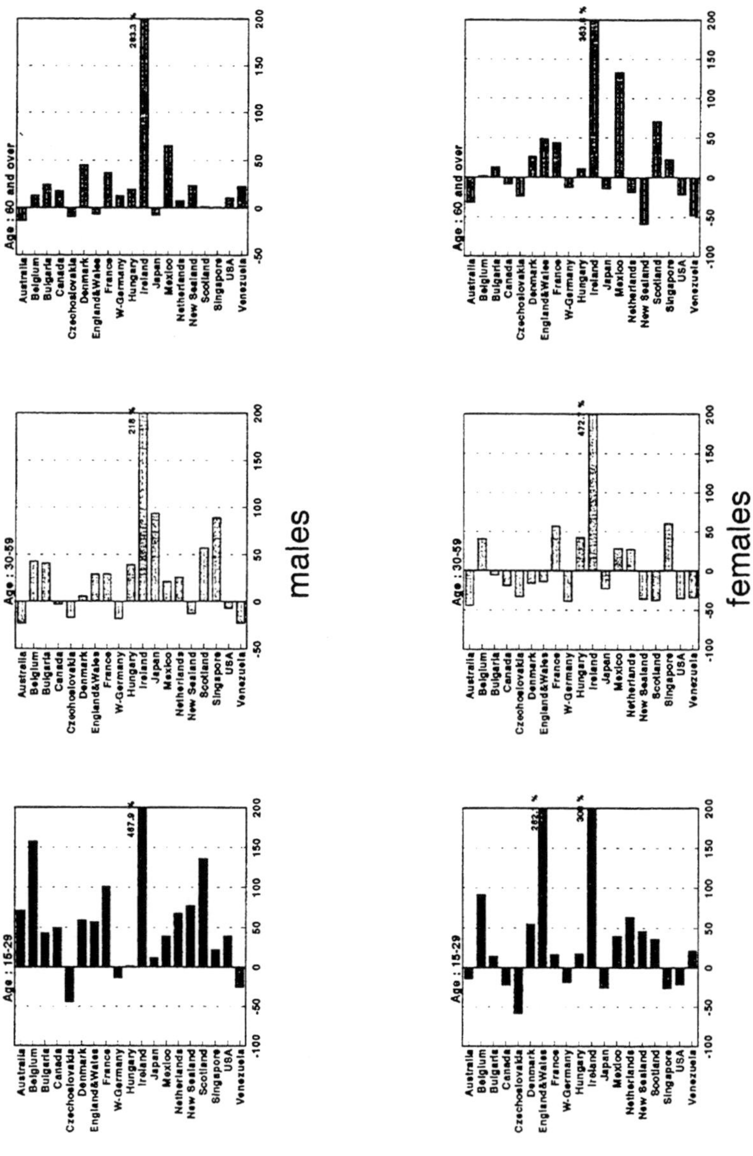

Fig. 9. Percentage change in suicide rates, 1970-1986. Source: WHO data bank.

As figure 9 shows for 19 selected countries throughout the world, there is a significant difference in trends between the sexes over the period 1970-1986. In the majority of the countries there is an increase in suicide among males in all age groups, be it that this trend is most pronounced in adolescents and young adults (a mean change of + 70%).
Among females the picture is clearly different. In the age group 15-29 years still the majority of countries shows an increase (a mean change of +40 %), but it is noteworthy that a number of countries with a significant increase in young males shows a decrease in young female suicides (e.g. Canada and the USA). For the age categories 30-59 years and 60 years and older only a minority of countries show a significant increase in suicide mortality among females.
A number of studies of suicide trends in countries like Canada (Solomon & Hellon, 1980; Reed et al., 1985; Barnes et al., 1986), the USA (Murphy & Wetzel, 1980; Lester, 1984), Australia (Goldney & Katsikitis, 1983), Germany (Häfner & Schmidtke, 1985), England & Wales (Murphy et al., 1986), Italy (La Vecchia et al., 1986), Belgium and the Netherlands (Moens, 1990) and Sweden (Asgard et al., 1987) all applying birth cohort methodologies, have confirmed this picture of a shift towards younger ages as well as a relatively greater risk increase among young males over the course of this century.

Suicide in adolescence and young adulthood: historical trends
From an epidemiological as well as theoretical point of view it is relevant to assess how recent or 'new' the observed upward trend as well as the present level of suicide mortality among adolescents and young adults, as described in the previous paragraph, is. A tentative answer to that question is given by the suicide rates (see figures 10 and 11) for the 15-24/29 years old over the whole of this century for two countries, the USA and The Netherlands. As figures 10 and 11 show, in both countries there are two conspicuous peak periods in youth suicide mortality over the course of this century - one starting around 1980 and another in the beginning of the century, around 1910. This pattern has been observed in other European countries as well. The first scientific meeting on suicide took place in Vienna in 1910 and was organised by the Viennese Psychoanalytic Society under the chairmanship of Alfred Adler and in the presence of Sigmund Freud. Most interestingly, suicide among high school students was the theme of the meeting, since increased rates in youth suicide in Austria and other middle European countries and

several so called 'school epidemics' had aroused public and professional concerns.

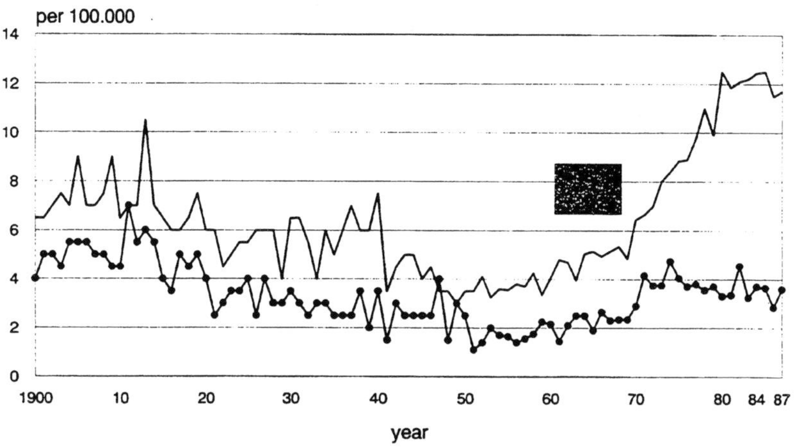

Fig.10. Suicide rates 1900-1987, the Netherlands. Source: Central bureau of Statistics. Until 1950, age groups are 16-20 and 21-29 years.

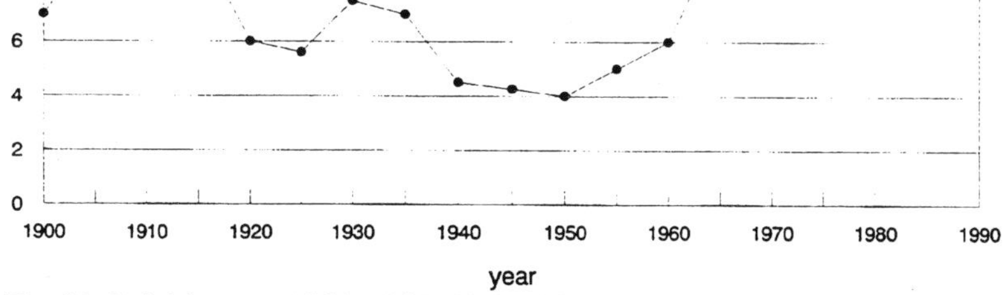

Fig.11. Suicide rates 1900-1987, United States. Source: Buda & Tsuang.

The remarkable thing about figures 10 and 11 is that the graphs for both the USA and the Netherlands are so strikingly similar. After an all time low around 1950, the rates rapidly rose till they reached around 1980 the level of the 1910 period but then broke through that 'barrier' to climb to all time highs. For The Netherlands, in contrast to the USA, this is only so for the age group 20-29 year old, both in males as well as in females. In the age group 15-19 the suicide rates remained below the level of the beginning of the century, although since 1950 we also observe a substantial increase in this age category.

The interaction between age and gender over time in overall suicide mortality appears to be different between the two countries. While in the Netherlands the increase of excess of young males to young females is accompanied by a decrease of excess in all age groups taken together, this is not so for the USA (see Tsuang and Buda, 1990).

The epidemiology of parasuicide

The fact that no country in the world collects official statistics on parasuicide makes it impossible to relate national trends in parasuicides to national trends in suicides. However, on the base of the data that are available it seems safe to assume that current trends in suicides and parasuicides are closely related. Data from special studies in centers with well-defined catchment areas collected over a number of years in several countries (Kreitman, 1977; Kreitman & Schreiber, 1979; Diekstra, 1982; Hawton & Goldacre, 1982; WHO, 1982) indicate that hospital discharge rates for parasuicide by adolescents and young adults rose sharply during the same period (1965-1980) in which their suicide rates were also rising. For two countries, Great Britain and The Netherlands, data from national hospital inpatient registers confirmed this observation (Diekstra, 1982).

In addition, numerous studies have shown that parasuicide is one of the most, if not the most powerful predictor of suicide (see the review by van Egmond et al., 1989). Many suicides (estimates range from about 30-60%) are the last in a series of attempts whose number can range from 1 to 20 or more. Follow-up studies show that 10-14 percent of the parasuicide eventually die through suicide, which is equal to a risk for suicide over 100 times that for the general population (Brent & Kolko, 1990).

Research has shown (Bancroft et al., 1979) that the motives for parasuicidal acts can be subsumed under three categories; cessation (stopping conscious experience forever = death); interruption (to interrupt conscious experience for a while, to sleep, not to feel anything for a while); and appeal (to mobilize others or change their behavior). Most parasuicides are motivated by a combination of interruption and appeal. For this reason it would be preferable to conceptualize such behavior as coping behavior that might or might not be appropriate or effective in a given context.

The question then arises as to our knowledge with regard to how common this coping behavior is in the world today. The answer to this question varies considerably according to the data source one uses, i.e. service utilization studies or population sample surveys.

With regard to the first category there are currently two international studies, one completed and one in progress, that shed some light on this issue. The former (Diekstra, 1982) was carried out in 1976 in seven of the nine countries that constituted the European Economic Community (EEC) at that time. Using data provided by centers with well-defined catchement areas it was extrapolated that for the whole of the EEC (comprising about 200 million inhabitants at the time) approximately 430,000 episodes of deliberate self-harm were treated in either in- or outpatient facilities. This equals an averaged rate of 215 cases per 100,000 persons aged 15 years and older (162 for males and 265 for females). Between countries or centers rates varied considerably (for males ranges from 26 to 353, for females from 82 to 527), a finding that can at least partially be explained by differences in referral and data recording procedures.

The other study in this category is currently in progress and is being carried out under the auspices of the World Health Organization (WHO Multicentre Study on Monitoring Trends in Parasuicide, see Platt et al., 1992). The first progress report, comprising data from 15 centers in 10 countries (Finland, France, Hungary, Italy, The Netherlands, Norway, Spain, Sweden, Germany, Denmark) indicates that parasuicide rates (based on admission to health facilities for the year 1989) vary widely between centers. With regard to parasuicide among males the highest rate (414 per 100,000) was found in Helsinki (Finland) and the lowest (61 per 100,000) in Leiden (The Netherlands), a ratio in excess of 7:1. For females the rate was highest (595 per 100,000) in Pontoise (France) and lowest (95 per 100,000) in Guipuzcoa (Spain).

Although in most centers the general picture of higher parasuicide rates among females than among males was confirmed, there was one notable exception to this rule, namely Helsinki where rates for males appeared to be remarkably higher.

From both studies it appears that peak ages for parasuicides, both in terms of absolute numbers and in rates per 100,000 of the particular age group, fall within the first half of the life cycle, i.e. between 15 and 44 years of age, although between countries and sexes there is considerable and unexplained variation in the age category (15-24, 25-34, 35-44) with the highest rate.
The results from studies in the second category, population sample surveys, shed considerable doubt upon the validity of the picture of magnitude and nature of the suicide attempt phenomenon that emerges from studies using service utilization data.

Table 3. Lifetime prevalence of parasuicide in the general population based on data of survey studies

STUDY	YEAR	PREVALENCE(%)	SUBJECTS
Mintz	1970	3.9	
Schwab et al.	1972	2.7	
Paykel et al.	1974	1.1	
Hallstrom	1977	4.5	women only
Diekstra et al.	1978	4.0	
Diekstra et al.	1980	5.0	
Ramsay et al.	1985	4.2	
Smith et al.	1986	10.5	adolescents
Moscicki et al.	1989	2.9	adolescents/ young adults
Dubow et al.	1989	7.0	adolescents
Rubinstein et al.	1989	20.0	adolescents
Andrews et al.	1990	6.8	adolescents
Kienhorst et al.	1990	2.2	adolescents
Nagy et al.	1990	12.1	adolescents
Pronovost et al.	1990	3.5	adolescents
Diekstra et al.	1991	4.6	adolescents

Estimates of the crude annual incidence of parasuicide (person rate) ranges from 300 to 800 per 100,000 of population aged 15 and over (Diekstra, 1985). On the one hand, the differences between studies in estimated incidence might be a valid reflection of differences between the respective countries or regions in parasuicide rates. On the other hand, however, there are differences in data collection between studies that certainly have had a strong impact on their findings. For example, Moscicki et al. (1989) simply asked their respondents the question 'have you ever attempted suicide?' (pp. 4-117). Diekstra et al. (1978; 1980) based their estimate on a specially designed Suicidal Behaviour Questionnaire in which the terms attempted suicide and suicide attempt were deliberately avoided. Instead they asked their respondents: 'Have you ever because of social, emotional or other problems: Tried to hang yourself? Taken an overdose of ...?' and eight other possible methods to attempting suicide. Whenever respondents ticked one or more of these (potentially) selfharming behaviors, they were asked to provide further details on each episode as well as circumstancial evidence. Only those episodes reported for which also a certain number of informational criteria were met, were then scored as suicide attempts. In one study (Diekstra et al., 1978) also data were collected on health care services contacts consequent upon the suicide attempt. It was found that 'only' one in every four attempts (24.3%) led to contact with professional health services, such as general hospitals and family physicians. A similar large 'tip of the iceberg' phenomenon has been reported in a recent study in the United States on parasuicide among high school students (CDC, 1991).

The question that still remains largely unanswered regards the similarities and dissimilarities between those parasuicides that are seen by health care services and those that are not. It can therefore not be excluded that preventive interventions (such as school programmes) or aftercare programs for parasuicides that are based on information from service utilization studies only, might not be adequately tailored to the characteristics and the needs of the majority of parasuicides.

Estimates of lifetime prevalence of parasuicide vary between approximately 1% (Paykel et al., 1974) and 20% (Rubinstein et al., 1989) for those aged 12/13 years and older (see table 3). A number of studies report lifetime prevalence rates for adolescents and young adults only. Given the reasonable expectation that life time prevalence rates should increase with age since time augments risk, it is surprising that the life time rates of parasuicide in general population studies do not exceed and sometimes even remain below the rates for adolescents (often defined as high school students). Assuming that recall of past episodes remains constant throughout the life span, one possible explanation for this finding is earlier age of 'first-ever' parasuicidal acts. Since parasuicide is an important, and presumably even the most important, precursor of suicide, a lowering of age for 'first-ever' parasuicides can be expected to have caused a lowering of age for suicides as well, a development that many authors have suspected to have occurred in the past decades but that has been difficult to document.

The role of depression

The fact that the population of persons engaging in a parasuicidal act forms a pool from which many of the future suicides are recruited, suggests that a gradient of severity is implied from parasuicide to suicide. It is also (see Moscicki et al., 1989) assumed that developmental pathways exist that sequentially link one to another, and there is some evidence to substantiate this, although little is known on the causes and patterns of recruitment from parasuicide to suicide and on the factors which precipitate or protect against these transformations.

In a meta-analysis of the relevant literature, Van Egmond and coworkers (1989) reviewed 81 published studies from a number of countries comprising 106 comparisons between clinical and nonclinical suicidal and nonsuicidal groups. Their findings on differential characteristics of suicides and parasuicides are the following: those prone to suicide are more likely to be older men, more often unmarried, divorced or widowed, living alone and unemployed or retired. The lethality of the method used in their previous (para)suicidal acts (previous to suicide) is often higher and suicide notes are more often present in these previous acts.

Other differences between the two groups are that suicides have a higher prevalence of long-term use of prescribed psychotropic drugs, and a higher prevalence of the psychiatric diagnoses of schizophrenia and depression. Furthermore, in the suicide group there are more persons with a criminal record, with repeated antisocial behavior and long-term alcohol and (nonprescribed or illicit) drug abuse, a history of psychiatric treatment and contact with medical services in the period just before their fatal act.

The findings also show that apart from the fact that suicides are more often older males and patients who are more likely to suffer severe psychiatric or personality disturbances, the differences in social circumstances between them and those individuals engaging in parasuicidal acts is often mainly a matter of degree, both in terms of duration and severity.

This becomes particularly apparent if one looks at the results of the meta-analysis of the 17 studies in Van Egmond's review concerning differential characteristics of persons who engage in parasuicides as compared to persons who never made a parasuicidal act: the parasuicides suffer more often from depressive disturbances and interpersonal conflicts. As far as depression symptomatology is concerned agitation, hostility and feelings of hopelessness and helplessness are most prevalent. Also, cognitive characteristics that are clearly associated with depressive disturbances, like a negative view of oneself, negative view of relationships with others and of the future are found much more often among the parasuicides. Their most common interpersonal conflicts are not limited to problems with partners, but extend to the majority of persons in their social networks. They also have much poorer employment records as well as more alcohol and drug abuse. In addition to their own history of suicidal behavior, there is a much greater incidence of suicide or deliberate acts of selfharm in the family of origin or among other significant others.

Consequently, although it appears that, demographically at least, completed suicides and parasuicides represent distinct though overlapping populations, the relationship between both categories can for many cases be represented by a stepwise hierarchy of suicidal actions with an underlying gradient of severity or fatality risk. The model finds support in the following replicated evidence/First, the most powerful predictors of suicide are (a) a history of parasuicidal act(s); (b) a history of alcohol/drug abuse; (c) suicide and parasuicide in the social network, and d) alcohol/drug abuse in next of kin (see also Gould et al., 1990). Second, depressive symptomatology is not more frequently observed in suicides than in parasuicides (there are even indications that the reverse might be the case), although depression in sensu strictu (such as bipolar depression, major depression disorder) is. Third, a dysphoric or depressive mood state (generalized sadness) does not necessarily implicate *suicidal* ideation (as distinct from death wishes). The latter is first and foremost dependent upon the availability of suicidal models (characteristic of (sub)culture, of next of kin, peers, 'celebrities' suicides in the media) and of means (availability of methods like guns, drugs, etc.).

Against the background of a hierarchical response model of suicidal behavior, the following findings on the epidemiology of depressive disturbances take on special significance for the explanation of the secular trends in suicide rates as they have been presented earlier. First, after puberty or mid-adolescence there is no increase in the prevalence of depressive disturbances with age (see Petersen et al., 1993). In fact, the highest prevalence of depressive disturbances today is among adolescents/young adults in many highly industrialized countries. Second, the age of onset for major depression has lowered over the last three to four decades. Some authors (Klerman et al, 1985; 1988) have put forward the hypothesis that the post world war II generation, the baby boomers that were coming to maturity in the period from 1960 to 1975, are particularly vulnerable to depressive disorders, although the question whether one deals here with a period or a cohort effect still remains unanswered. What has become clear, however, is that post-baby boom birth cohorts have prevalence rates at least equal, if not higher than the baby boomers.

Unfortunately, there are hardly any studies available on the general population level that have examined the relationship between suicide, parasuicide and depressive disturbance. An exception is a recent study in The Netherlands (Diekstra, 1990) in which the association between national suicide and parasuicide rates (hospital inpatient data), and depressive mood disturbance (point prevalence, based on population sample survey data) over the period 1975-1986 (1985 for parasuicide) was established. In this period The Netherlands like many other European countries experienced a strong increase in economic problems (in particular a sharp rise in (youth) unemployment), reaching a peak in 1983 (the 'crisis year') and thereafter levelling off somewhat. The findings showed that there is a clear association between the suicide rate, the parasuicide rate and depressive mood prevalence over the measurement period. The association is stronger for men than for women, which might indicate that depressed mood and (para)suicidal behaviour in men is more closely associated with adverse changes in economic and employment conditions than in women. Furthermore, although women may indeed more often experience dysphoric feelings (see Petersen et al., 1992), they may also be more inclined to communicate such feelings to others (even in the form of parasuicides), while men may be less inclined to do so and more often cope with them by substance (ab)use, therewith increasing the probability of not only worsening such feelings but also of more severe social, interpersonal and physical disruption, that in turn increases the risk for suicidal behaviour, when it occurs, to have more harmful or fatal consequences. It is relevant in this respect that the age of onset of substance (ab)use has lowered in the same period that the age of onset of depressive disturbances have (WHO, 1988). Against this background, the fact that the rising secular trends in suicide are particularly a (young) male phenomenon comes as no surprise.

Conclusions: images of the future

Not only in sheer numbers, as has been reviewed above, but also in terms of human suffering and economic terms the phenomenon of suicide and parasuicide is a public health problem of primordial importance, particularly among adolescents and young adults. Weinstein and Saturno (1989) calculated that each youth suicide (age group 15-24) in the United States results in the loss of 53 years of human life and US$ 432,000 of economic productivity, amounting to a total of national costs each year of 276,000 years of life lost, 217,000 years of productive life lost before the age of 65, and economic costs of 2,26 billion. With the costs of youth parasuicide added in, the figures rise to 262,000 years of productive life lost and economic costs of US$ 3,19 billion. If one adds in the costs associated with suicide and parasuicide in the age group 25-44 these figures more than double.

Applying Weinstein and Saturno's algorithm to the countries of the European Region these figures have to be multiplied by at least three and in the near future presumably more. While in most West-european countries national suicide rates seem to level off since 1982-83, it is probable that the countries in southern Europe with traditional low suicide rates will witness a considerable increase in suicide mortality as their political, economic and cultural ties with the countries in the north-west part of the region become closer and a number of developments that have been observed above as contributive to suicide, such as increase in divorce rate and diminution of church affiliation, will take effect. This development seems to be taking place already, as witnessed by the fact that in recent years the national suicide rate in a country like Spain seems to be rising rapidly.

Similar developments will a fortiori take place in the eastern European countries. The extremely rapid political, economic and cultural changes in eastern Europe have thrown several hundreds of millions of people in a state of economical malaise 'anomie' that unavoidably will lead to an increase in suicide rates for a considerable number of years.

But the most dramatic increase in suicide mortality in the next decades will be observed in the Third World countries. The most potent socioeconomic and behavioral factors of suicide risk as outlined in this chapter are already present in a degree considerably higher than in most developed countries and this discrepancy will in all probability only continue to grow. The accompanying toll in human suffering, the decrease in quality of life of those left behind, the loss in years of productive life and related economic and social costs will be beyond imagination.

But it is not only socioeconomic, cultural and behavioral developments that will push mortality by suicide on a global scale far beyond present limits. The strong increase in life expectancy in the majority of countries and the 'graying' of their populations will of necessity lead to an increase of national suicide rates given the strong correlation between suicide and age.

The grim bottom line therefore is that suicide, in a double sense, will prove to be the death of the future.

REFERENCES

Adler, R.S. & Jellinek, M.S. After teen suicide: Issues for pediatricians who are asked to consult to schools, *Pediatrics* 1990, 86 : 982-987.

Alcohol, Drug Abuse, and Mental Health Administration. *Report of the Secretary's Task Force on Youth Suicide. Volume 1: Overview and Recommendations.* (DHHS Publication No. ADM 89-1621). Washington, DC: U.S. Government Printing Office, 1989.

Alnaes, R., & Torgersen, S. Major depression, anxiety disorders and mixed conditions. *Acta Psychiatrica Scandinavica,* 1988, 78 : 632-638.

Andrews, J.A., Lewinsohn, P.M. *The prevalence, Lethality and Intent of Suicide Attempts among adolescents.* Paper presented at the 98th Annual Convention of the American Psychological Association, Boston, 1990.

Appelboom-Fondu, Kerkhofs, M., Mendlewicz, J. Depression in adolescents and young adults. *Journal of Affective Disorders,* 1988, 14 : 35-40.

Asgard, U., Nordström, P., Rabäck, G. Birth cohort analysis of changing suicide risk by sex and age in Sweden 1952-1981. *Acta Psychiatrica Scandinavica,* 1987, 76 : 456-463.

Bancroft, J.H.J., Skrimshire, A.M., Simkin, S. The reasons people give for taking overdoses. *British Journal of Psychiatry,* 1979, 128 : 538-548.

Barnes, R.A., Ennis, J., Schrober, R. Cohort analysis of Ontario suicide 1877-1976. *Canadian Journal of Psychiatry,* 1986, 31 : 208-213.

Barraclough, B. International variation in the suicide rate of 15-24 years olds. *Social Psychiatry,* 1988, 23 : 75-84.

Barraclough, B. Differences between national suicide rates. *British Journal of Psychiatry,* 1973, 122 : 95-96

Bayet, A. *Le suicide et la morale.* Paris, Alcon, 1922.

Berlin, I.N. Suicide among American Indian adolescents: An overview. *Suicide and Life Threatening Behavior,* 1987, 17 : 218-232.

Bertschy, G., Vandel, S., Volmat, R. Epidémiologie de la dépression: données récentes. I. Epidémiologie descriptive. *Psychiatrie et psychobiologie,* 1988, 3 : 149-158.

Blumenthal, S.J. Youth suicide: The physician's role in suicide prevention. *The Journal of the American Medical Association,* 1990, 264 : 3194-3196.

Blumenthal, S.J. Letter to the Editor. *JAMA,* 1991, 265 : 2806-2807.

Boor, M. Methods of suicide and implications for suicide prevention. *Journal of Clinical Psychology,* 1981, 37 : 70-75.

Bowles, J.R. Suicide in Western Samoa: An example of a suicide prevention program in a developing country. In Diekstra, R.F.W., (Ed.) *'Preventive strategies on Suicide'.* 1991, WHO, Brill, Leiden.

Boyd, J.H. The increasing rate of suicide by firearms. *New England Journal of Medicine,* 1983, 308 : 872-874.

Boyd, J.H. & Moscicki, E.K. Firearms and youth suicide. *American Journal of Public Health,* 1986, 76 : 1240-1242.

Brent, D.A., Kerr, M.M., Goldstein, C.,Bozigar, J., Wartell, M. & Allan, M.A. An outbreak of suicide and suicidal behavior in a high school. *Journal of the American Academy of Child and Adolescent Psychiatry,* 1989, 28 : 918-924.

Brent, D.A., Perper, J.A. & Allman, C.J. Alcohol, firearms and suicide among youth. *Journal of the American Medical Association,* 1987, 257 : 3369-3372.

Brent, D.A., Perper, J.A., Goldstein, C.E., Kolko, D.J., Allan, M.J., Allman, C.J. & Zelenak, J.P. Risk factors for adolescent suicide: A comparison of adolescent suicide victims with suicidal inpatients. *Archives of General Psychiatry,* 1988, 45 : 581-588.

Brent, D.A., Kolko, D.J. The assessment and treatment of children and adolescents at risk for suicide. In: Blumenthal, S.J., Kupfer, D.J. (Eds.) *Suicide over the Life Cycle.* Washington, 1990 APA Press, p. 253-302.

Brown, J.H. Suicide in Britain. *Archives of General Psychiatry,* 1979, 36 : 1119-1124.

Bush, J.A. Suicide and blacks. *Suicide and Life Threatening Behavior,* 1976, 6 : 216-222.

Cavan, P.S. *Suicide.* New York: Russell & Russell, 1928.

CDC-Centers of Disease Control. Attempted Suicide among high school students - United States 1990, leads from the Morbidity and Mortality Weekly Report. *JAMA,* 1991, 266 : 14, 911.

Choquet, M., Ledoux, S., Menke, H. Santé etcomportements à risque. *Rev. Franc.Aff.Soc.*, 41, 1947, No. hors-série, 21-42.

Davidson, F., Choquet, M. Le suicide de l'adolescent, *Etude épidémiologique,* Paris, ESF, 1981.

Deykin, E., Klerman, G.L. *Depression and suicide among college-age youth.* Roneot. doc; no date.

Diagnostic and Statistical Manual for Mental Disorders (DSM-III), 3rd edition, 1980, A.P.A., Washington, D.C. Traduction francaise, Pichot, R. (dir.) Massau, Paris, 1983.

Diekstra, R.F.W. & Loo, K.J.M., van de. Attitudes toward suicide and incidence of suicidal behaviour in a general population. In: H.Z. Winnik & L. Miller (Eds.) *Aspects of suicide in modern civilization.* Jerusalem: 1978. Jerusalem Academic Press, 1978, p. 79-85.

Diekstra, R.F.W. and Kerkhof, A.J.F.M. Hulp bij zelfdoding: opvattingen onder het publiek. In: Speijer, N. & Diekstra, R.F.W. (Eds.) *Hulp bij zelfdoding.* Deventer: Van Loghum Slaterus, 1980.

Diekstra, R.F.W. Epidemiology of attempted suicide in the EEC. In Wilmotte, J., Mendlewicz, J. (Eds.). *New trends in suicide prevention.* Bibliotheca Psychiatrica, Basel, Karger, 1982, 1-16.

Diekstra, R.F.W. Suicide and suicide attempts in the European Economic Community: an analysis of trends with special emphasis on trends among the young. *Suicide and Life-threatening Behavior,* 1985, 15 : 402-421.

Diekstra, R.F.W., et al. *Health Council of the Netherlands. Rapport inzake suicide (Report on Suicide),* December 1986, Health Council of the Netherlands, The Hague.

Diekstra, R.F.W., Hawton, K. *Suicide in Adolescence.* Dordrecht/New York: Kluwer, Academic Publishers, 1987.

Diekstra, R.F.W. The complex psychodynamics of suicide. In: Diekstra, R.F.W. & Hawton, K. (Eds.), *Suicide in Adolescence,* 1987, pp. 30-55, Nijhoff, Dordrecht/ Boston.

Diekstra, R.F.W., Moritz, B. Suicidal behaviour among adolescents. In: Diekstra, R.F.W. & Hawton, K. (Eds.), *Suicide in Adolescence,* 1987, pp. 7-24, Nijhoff, Dordrecht/Boston.

Diekstra, R.F.W. *City lifestyles.* World Health Organization, 1988; June: 18-19.

Diekstra, R.F.W., Maris, R., Platt, S., Schmidtke, A., Sonneck, G. *Suicide and its Prevention: the role of attitude and imitation.* Leiden: Canberra: Brill, 1989. A WHO co-publication.

Diekstra, R.F.W. Suicide, Unemployment and Economic recession. In: Veenhoven, R. (Ed.). *Did the crisis really hurt: effects after 1980-1982 economic recession on satisfaction, mental health and mortality.* Rotterdam, EUPR. 1989.

Diekstra, R.F.W. Suicide, Depression and Economic Conditions. In: D. Lester (ed.) *Current Concepts of Suicide.* Philadelphia, 1990, The Charles Press.

Diekstra, R.F.W., De Heus, P., Garnefski, N., de Zwart, R., Van Praag, B.M.S. *Monitoring the Future: Behavior and Health among high school students. The Hague:* NIBUD, 1991.

Douglas, J.D. *The social meanings of suicide,* Princeton University Press, 1967

Dubow, E.F., Kausch, D.F., Blum, M.C., Reed, J. Correlates of suicidal ideation and attempts in a community sample of junior high school students. *Journal of Clinical Child Psychology,* 1989, 18 : 158-166.

Durkheim, E. *Le Suicide,* 1987; Paris: Alcan.

Egmond, M. van, Diekstra, R.F.W. The predictability of suicidal behaviour: the results of a meta-analysis of published studies. In: Diekstra, R.F.W., Maris, R.A., Platt, S., Schmidtke, A., Sonneck, G. (Eds), *Suicide Prevention: The role of attitude and imitation,* Leiden, The Netherlands; Brill, 1989.

Egmond, M. van, Diekstra, R.F.W. The predictability of Suicidal Behaviour: The Results of a meta-Analysis of Published Studies. *Crisis,* 1990, 11/2 : 57-84.

Frazier, Sh. *US task force on youth suicide.* Paper read at WHO Meeting on Preventive Strategies in Suicidal Behaviour, 4 October 1986.

Garland, A. & Shaffer, D. School-based adolescent suicide prevention programs. In: M.J. Rotheram, J. Bradley & N. Obolensky (Eds.), *Planning to Live Evaluating and Treating Suicidal Teens in Community Settings.* Tulsa, OK : University of Oklahoma Press, 1990.

Garland, A., Shaffer, D. & Whittle, B. A national survey of adolescent suicide prevention programs. *Journal of the American Academy of Child and Adolescent Psychiatry,* 1989, 28 : 931-934.

Garrison, C.Z., Addy, C.L., Jackson, K.L., McKeown, R.E. & Waller, J.L. A longitudinal study of suicidal ideation in young adolescents. *Journal of the American Academy of Child and Adolescent Psychiatry,* 1991, 30 : 597-603.

Gallup Organization, Inc. *Teenage suicide study: Executive Summary.* (Available from the Gallup Organization, Inc.), 1991.

Gibbs, J.T. Conceptual, methodological, and sociocultural issues in black youth suicide: Implications for assessment and early intervention. *Suicide and Life Threatening Behavior,* 1988, 18 : 73-89.

Goldney, R.D., Katsikitis, M. Cohort analysis of suicide rates in Australia. *Archives of General Psychiatry.* 1983, 40 : 71-74.

Gould, M.S. & Shaffer, D. The impact of suicide in television movies. *New England Journal of Medicine,* 1986, 315 : 690-694.

Gould, M.S., Shaffer, D. & Kleinman, M. The impact of suicide in television movies: Replication and commentary. *Suicide and Life Threatening Behavior,* 1988, 18 : 90-99.

Gould, M.S., Shaffer, D. & Davies, M. Truncated pathways from childhood: attribution in follow-up studies due to death. In: Robins & Rutter (Eds.). *Straight and devious pathways to adulthood.* Cambridge: Cambridge University Press, 1990, 3-9.

Goldberg, D.P. Estimating the prevalence of psychiatric disorders from the results of a screening test. In: Wing, J., Bebbington, P., Robins, L.N. (Eds.). *What is a case?* Grant, McIntyre, London, 1981.

Greenley, J.R., Mechanic, D. Social selection in seeking help fro psychological problems. *Journal of Health and Social Behavior,* 1976; 17 : 249-262.

Häfner, H., Schmidtke, A. Do cohort effects influence suicide rates? *Archives of General Psychiatry,* 1985, 42 : 926-927.

Häfner, H., Schmidtke, A. *Suizid und Suizidversuche-Epidemiologie und aetologie.* Nervenheilkunde, 1987; 6 : 49-63.

Hallstrom,. T. Life-wearness, suicidal thoughts and suicidal attempts among women in Gothenburg, Sweden. *Acta Psychiatrica Scandinavica,* 1977, 56 : 15-20.

Harry, J. *Sexual identity issues. Report of the Secretary's Task Force on Youth Suicide. Volume 2: Risk Factors for Youth Suicide.* (DHHS Pub.No. ADM 89-1622). Washington, DC: U.S. Government Printing Office, 1989.

Hart, E.E., Williams, C.L., Davidson, J.A. Suicidal Behaviour, Social Networks and Psychiatric Diagnosis. *Social Psychiatry and Psychiatric Epidemiology,* 1988; 23 : 222-228.

Harter, S. & Marold, D. *A model of risk factors leading to adolescent suicidal ideation.* Paper presented to Society for Research in Child Development, 1989.

Hawton, K., Goldacre, M. Hospital admission for adverse effects on medical agents (mainly self-poisoning) among adolescents in the Oxford region. *British Journal of Psychiatry,* 1982, 141 : 166-170

Hawton, K. *Suicide and attempted suicide among children and adolescents.* Newbury Park, CA.:Sage Publications, Inc., 1986.

Headly, L.A. *Suicide in Asia and the Near East.* Los Angeles, U.S.A., Univ. Cal. Press, 1983.

Hendin, H. Youth suicide: A psychosocial perspective. *Suicide and Life Threatening Behavior,* 1987, 17 : 151-165.

Henry, A.F. & Short, J.F. *Suicide and homicide.* Glencoe, IL: Free Press, 1954.

Hoberman, H.M. & Garfinkel, B.D. Completed suicide in children and adolescents. *Journal of the American academy of Child and Adolescent Psychiatry,* 1988, 27 : 689-695.

Hodgman, C.H. & Roberts, F.N. Adolescents suicide and the pediatrician. *Adolescents Medicine,* 1982, 101 : 118-123.

Holden, R.R., Mendonca, J.D. & Serin, R.C. Suicide, hopelessness, and social desirability: A test of an interactive model. *Journal of Consulting and Clinical Psychology,* 1989, 57 : 500-504.

Holinger, P.C., Offer, D., Zola, M.A. A prediction model of suicide among youth. *Journ. Nrev. Ment.Disease,* 1988; 176 : 275-79.

Jobes, D.A., Berman, A.L. Josselsen, A.R. The impact of psychosocial autopsies on medical examiners' determination of manner of death. *J. Forensic Sci.,* 1986; 31(1) : 177-89.

Jones, D.K. & Jones, S.L. Lunar association with suicide. *Suicide and Life Threatening Behavior,* 1977, 7 : 31.

Kagan, S.L., Powell, D.R., Weissbourd, B. & Zigler, E.F. *America's family support programs.* New Haven: Yale University Press, 1987.

Kandel, D.B., Davies, M. Epidemiology of depressive mood in adolescents. *Arch. Gen. Psychiat.,* 1982; 39 : 1205-1212.

Kandel, D., Davies, M. Adult sequelae of adolescent depressive symptomatology. *Arch. Gen. Psychiat.*, 1986; 43 : 255-262.

Kaplan, S.L., Hong, G.K., Weinhold, C. Epidemiology of depressive symptomatology in adolescents. *J. Am. Acad. Child Psychiatry,* 1984; 23 : 91-98.

Kaufman, J. & Zigler, E. The intergenerational transmission of child abuse. In: D. Cicchetti & V. Carlson (Eds.) *Child maltreatment: Theory and research on the causes and consequences of child abuse and neglect* (pp. 129-150). New York: Cambridge University Press, 1989.

Kazdin, A.E., French, N.H., Unis, A.S., Esveldt-Dawson, K. & Sherick, R.B. Hopelessness, depression, and suicidal intent among psychiatrically disturbed inpatient children. *Journal of Consulting and Clinical Psychology,* 1983, 51 : 504-510.

Kelleher, M.J.. Daly, M. *Suicide in Cork and Ireland.* Paper 2nd European Conference of Suicide Research, Edinburgh, U.K., 1988.

Kienhorst, C.W.M. *Suicidaal Gedrag bij Jongeren (Suicidal Behaviour among Youth).* Doctoral Dissertation, University of Leiden, The Netherlands, 1988.

Kienhorst, C.W.M., de Wilde, E.J., van den Bout, J., Broese van Groenou, M.I., Diekstra, R.F.W., Woltus, W.H.G., Self-Reported Suicidal Behavior in Dutch Secondary Education Students. *Suicide and Life Threatening Behavior,* 1990, 20 : 101-112.

Kienhorst, C.W.M., de Wilde, E.J., Diekstra, R.F.W., Wolters, W.H.G. Construction of an index for prediction Suicide Attempts in Depressed Adolescents. *British Journal of Psychiatry,* 1991, 159 : 676-682.

King, G.D. An evaluation of the effectiveness of a telephone counselling center. *American Journal of Community Psychology,* 1977, 5 : 75-83.

Kleck, G. Miscounting suicides. *Suicide and Life Threatening Behavior,* 1988, 18 : 219-236.

Klerman, G.L., Lavori, P.W., Price, J. Birth-cohort trends in rates of Major Depressive Disorders among relatives of patients with affective disorders. *Archives of General Psychiatry,* 1985; 42 : 689-693.

Klerman, G. Post-WWII Generation faces rising rates of depression, PUK, 1988; 10-13.

Kogan, L.S. The short term case in a family agency. Social Casework, 1957, 38 : 296-302.

Kosky, R., Silburn, S. & Zubrick, S.R. Are children and adolescents who have suicidal thoughts different from those who attempt suicide? *Journal of Nervous and Mental Disease,* 1990, 178 : 38-43.

Kreitman, N.S. *Parasuicide.* Chichester, Wiley, 1977.

Kreitman, N., Schreiber, M. Parasuicide in young Edinburgh women, 1968-75. *Psychological Medicine,* 1979, 9 : 469-479.

Ladame, F. Quelques remarques sur l'adolescent dépressif et le médicin omnipraticien. *Rev.Méd. Suisse Romande,* 1983; 103 : 415-417.

Lester, D. *Why people kill themselves: a summary of research findings on suicidal behaviour.* Springfield, Ill.: Thomas, 1972, p. 5-12.

Lester, D. Suicide risk by birth cohort. *Suicide and Life Threatening Behaviour,* 1984, 14 : 132-136.

Lester, D. One theory of teenage suicide. *J. School Health,* May 1988a; 58, 5 : 193-194.

Lester, D. Gun control, gun ownership, and suicide prevention. *Suicide and Life Threatening Behaviour,* 1988b, 18 : 176-180.

Lester, D. & Frank, M.L. The use of motor vehicle exhaust for suicide and the availability of cars. *Acta Psychiatrica Scandinavica,* 1989, 79 : 238-240.

Lester, D. & Murrell, M.E. The influence of gun control laws on suicidal behavior. *American Journal of Psychiatry,* 1980, 137 : 121-122.

Lester, D. *Why people kill themselves: a summary of research findings on suicidal behaviour.* Springfield, Ill.: Thomas, 1972, p. 5-12.

Mahler, H. *Epidemiology, Health Promotion and Health for all by the year 2000.* Paper XI Scietific meeting Int. Epid. ASS, Helsinki, Finland, 1987.

McCarthy, P.D., Walsh, D. Suicide in Dublin: I The underreporting of suicide and the consequences for national suicide statistics. *British Journal of Psychiatry,* 1975, 126 : 301-308

McKenry, P.C., Tishler, C.L. & Kelley, C. The role of drugs in adolescent suicide attempts. *Suicide and Life Threatening Behavior,* 1983, 13 : 166-175.

Memory, J.M. Juvenile suicides in secure detention facilities: Correction of published rates. *Death Studies,* 1989, 13 : 455-463.

Merikangas, K.R., Leckman, J.F., Prusoff, B.A. Familial transmission of depression and alcoholism. *Archives of General Psychiatry,* 1985; 42 : 367-372.

Miller, H.L., Coombs, D.W. & Leeper, J.D. An analysis of the effects of suicide prevention facilities on suicide rates in the United States. *American Journal of Public Health,* 1984, 74 : 340-343.

Mintz, R.S. *Prevalence of Persons in the City of Los Angeles who have attempted suicide: a pilot study Bulletin of Suicidology,* 1970, 7 : 9-16.

Moens, G.F.G. *Aspects of the Epidemiology and Preventions of Suicide,* Leuvens: Leuven University Press, 1990.

Moscicki, E.K., O'Caroll, P.W., Rae, D.S., Roy, A.G., Locke, B.Z., Regier, D.A. Suicidal Ideation and Attempts: the epidemiological catchment area study. In: *Report of the Secretary's Task Force on Youth Suicide.* Department of Health and Human Services Publication: Rockville-USA, 1989; no. (ADM) 89-1264, p. 4-115/4-128.

Murphy, G.E. Clinical identification of suicidal risk. *Archives of General Psychiatry,* 1972, 27 : 356-359.

Murphy, G.E., Wetzel, R.D. Suicide risk by birth cohort in the United States, 1949 to 1974. *Archives of General Psychiatry,* 1980, 37 : 519-523.

Murphy, E., Lindesay, J., Grundy, E. 60 years of suicide in England and Wales. A cohort study. *Archives of General Psychiatry,* 1986, 42 : 969-976.

Nagy, S., Adcock, A. *The Alabama Adolescent Health Survey: Health Knowledge and Behaviors. Summary Report II.* Alabama, 1990. The University of Alabama and Troy State University.

National Center for Health Statistics. *Vital Statistics of the United States, 1966-1987 Inclusive, Vol. II, Mortality, Parts A.* U.S. Department of Health and Human

Services Publication Number (DSH) 9--1102. Public Health Service, Washington, D.C.: U.S. Government Printing Office, 1966-1990.

Nelson, F.L. Evaluation of a youth suicide prevention school program. *Adolescence,* 1987, 38 : 813-825.

Orvaschel, H., Weissman, M.M., Kidd, K.K. Children and Depression: The children of depressed parents, the childhood of depressed patients: depression in children. *J. Affective Disorders,* 1980; 2 : 1-16.

Overholser, J., Hemstreet, A.H., Spirito, A. & Vyse, S. Suicide awareness programs in the schools: Effects of gender and personal experience. *Journal of the American Academy of Child and Adolescent Psychiatry,* 1989, 28 : 925-930.

Paykel, E.S., Myers, J.K., Lindentall, J.J., Tanner, J. Suicidal feelings in the general population: a prevalence study. *British Journal of Psychiatry,* 1974, 124 : 460-469.

Petersen, A.C., Compas, B., Brooks-Gunn, J., Stemmler, M., Ey, S., Grant, K. Depression in adolescence. *American Psychologist,* 1993, 48: 155-168.

Pfeffer, C.R. *The suicidal child.* New York: Guilford Press, 1986.

Phillips, D.P. The influence of suggestion on suicide: Substantive and theoretical implication of the Werther effect. *American Sociology Review,* 1974, 39 : 340 - 354.

Phillips, D.P. & Carstenson, L.L. Clustering of teenage suicides after television news stories about suicide. *New England Journal of Medicine,* 1986, 315 : 685-689.

Platt, S. *Data from Royal Infirmary.* Edinburgh, Scotland, 1988.

Platt, S. Unemployment and suicidal behavior: A review of the literature. *Social Science and Medicine,* 1984, 19 : 93-115.

Platt, S., Bille-Brahe, U., Kerkhof, A.J.F.M. Parasuicide in Europe: the WHO/ EURO multicentre study on parasuicide. I. Introduction and preliminary analysis for 1989. *Acta Psychiatr. Scand.*, 1992, 85 : 97-104.

Price, R.H. Cowen, E.L., Lorion, R.P., Ramos-McKay, J. The search for effective prevention programs: What we learned along the way. *American Journal of Orthopsychiatry,* 1989, 59 : 49-58.

Pronovost, J., Cote, L., Ross, C. Epidemiological Study of suicidal behaviour among Secondary-school Students. *Canada's Mental Health,* 1990, 38 : 9-14.

Radloff, L.S. The CES-D Scale: a self-report depression scale for research in the general population. *Applied Psychological Measurement,* 1977; 1, 3 : 385-401.

Ramsay, B., Bagley, C. The prevalence of Suicidal Behaviors, attitudes and associated life experiences in an urban population. *Suicide Life-Threatening Behavior,* 1985; 15(3) : 151-167.

Reed, J., Camus, J., Last, J.M. Suicide in Canada: Birth-cohort analysis. *Canadian Journal of Public Health,* 1985, 76 : 43-47.

Reisman, B.A. & Scharfman, M.A. *Teenage Suicide Prevention Workshops for Guidance Counselors (Trainers Manual & Resource Materials)* Douglas, N.Y.: Pride of Judea Mental Health Center, 1991.

Richardson, J.L., Dwyer, K., McQuigan, K., Hansen, W.B., Dent, C., Johnson, C.A., Sussman, S.Y., Brannon, B. & Flay, B. Substance use among right-grade students who take care of themselves after school. *Pediatrics,* 1989, 84 : 556-566.

Ross, C.P. Mobilizing schools for suicide prevention. *Suicide and Life Threatening Behavior,* 1980, 10 : 239-243.

Rotheram, M.J. Evaluation of imminent danger for suicide among youth. *American Journal of Orthopsychiatry,* 1987, 57 : 102-110.

Roy, A. Genetic factors in suicide. *Psychopharmacology Bulletin,* 1986, 22 : 666-668.

Rubinstein, J.L., Heeren, T., Housman, D., Rubin, C. & Stechler, G. Suicidal behavior in "normal" adolescents: Risk and protective factors. *American Journal of Orthopsychiatry,* 1989, 59 : 59-71.

Rudd, M.D. The prevalence of suicidal ideation among college students. *Suicide and Life Threatening Behavior,* 1989, 19 : 173-183.

Sainsbury, P., Barraclough, B.M. Differences between Suicide Rates. *Nature,* 1968, 220 : 1252

Sainsbury, S., Jenkins, J., Baert, A.E. *Suicide Trends in Europe.* Copenhagen, World Health Organization, ICP/MNH 036, 1981.

Schoenbach, V.J., Kaplan, B.H., Wagner, R.C. et al. Depressive Symptoms in Young Adolescents. *American J. Epidemiology,* 1980; 112 : 440.

Schoenbach et al., Prevalence of Self-reported depressive symptoms in Young Adults. *A.J.P. Health,* 1983; 73 : 1281-1287.

Schwab, J.J., Warheit, G.J., Holzer, C.E. Suicidal Ideation in a general population. *Diseases of the Nervous System,* 1972; 33 : 745-748.

Seidman, E. & Rapkin, B. Economics and psychosocial dysfunction: Toward a conceptual framework and prevention strategies. In: R.D. Flener, L.A. Moritsugu & S.S. Farber (Eds.), *Preventive psychology* (pp. 175-198). New York: Pergamon Press, 1983.

Seitz, V., Rosenbaum, L. & Apfel, N. Effects of family support intervention: A ten-year follow-up. *Child Development,* 1985, 54 : 376-391.

Shaffer, D. Suicide in childhood and early adolescence. *Journal of Child Psychology and Psychiatry,* 1974, 45 : 406-451.

Shaffer, D., Schonfeld, I., O'Conner, P.A. et al. Neurological Soft Signs. *Archive of General Psychiatry,* 1985; 42, 3: 342-353.

Shaffer, D. The epidemiology of teen suicide: An examination of risk factors. *Journal of Clinical Psychiatry,* 1988, 49 : 36-41.

Shaffer, D. & Fisher, P. *Commentary and discussion: Research on completed suicides.* (DHHS Publication No. ADM 278-0026). Washington, DC: U.S. Government Printing Officie, 1987.

Shaffer, D., Garland, A., Fisher, P., Bacon, K. & Vieland, V. Suicide Crisis Centers: A critical reappraisal with special reference to the prevention of youth suicide. In: F.E. Golston, C.M. Heinicke, R.S. Pynoos & J. Yager (Eds.). *Prevention of mental health disturbance in childhood.* (pp. 135-166). Washington: APA Press, 1990.

Shaffer, D., Garland, A., Gould, M., Fisher, P. & Trautman, P. Preventing teenage suicide: A critical review. *Journal of the American Academy of Child and Adolescent Psychiatry,* 1988, 27 : 675-687.

Shaffer, D., Garland, A., Vieland, V., Underwood, M. & Busner, C. The impact of curriculum-based suicide prevention programs for teenagers. *Journal of the American Academy of Child and Adolescent Psychiatry,* 1991, 30 : 588-596.

Shaffer, D., Garland, A., Whittle, B. & Underwood, M. *An evaluation of three adolescent suicide prevention programs.* (Contract No. 50013). Trenton, NJ: New Jersey Governor's Council Adolescent Suicide, 1988.

Shaffer, D. & Gould, M.S. *Progress Report: Study of completed and attempted suicides in adolescents.* (Contract No., R01-MH-38198). Bethesda, MD: National Institute of Mental Health, 1987.

Shaffer, D., Vieland, V., Garland, A., Rojas, M., Underwood, M. & Busner, C. Adolescent suicide attempters: Response to suicide prevention programs. *JAMA,* 1990, 264 : 3151-3155.

Shaffi, M., Carrigan, S., Whittinghill, J.R. & Derrick, A. Psychological autopsy of completed suicide in children and adolescebts. *American Journal of Psychiatry,* 1985, 142 : 1061-1064.

Shneidman, E.S. & Farberow, N.L. *Clues to suicide.* New York: Blakison, 1957.

Simmons, K. Task force to make recommendations for adolescents in terms of Suicide Risk. *Jauna,* 1987, 257 : 24 pp. 3330-3332.

Small, S. *Preventive programs that support families with adolescents.* (Available from Carnegie Council on Adolescent Development), 1990.

Smith, K., Crawford, S. Suicidal behavior among 'normal' high school students. *Suicide and Life Threatening Behavior,* 1986, 16 : 313-325.

Snelling, L.K. Letter to the editor. *JAMA,* 1991, 265 : 2806.

Solomon, M.I., Hellon, C.P. Suicide and age in Alberta, Canada: 1951 to 1977. *Archives of General Psychiatry,* 1980, 37 : 511-513.

Speijer, N., Diekstra, R.F.W. *Hulp bij zelfdoding: een onderzoek naar problemen rondom hulpverlening bij de zelfgekozen dood.* Deventer, 1980, Van Loghum Slaterus.

Spirito, A., Brown, L., Overholser, J. & Fritz, G. Attempted suicide in adolescence: A review and critique of the literature. *Clinical Psychology Review,* 1989, 9 : 335-363.

Spirito, A., Overholser, J., Ashworth, S., Morgan, J. & Benedict-Drew, C. Evaluation of a suicide awareness curriculum for high school students, *Journal of the American Academy of Child and Adolescent Psychiatry,* 1988, 27 : 705-711.

Stack, S. The effect of strikes on suicide: A cross national analysis. *Sociological Focus,* 1982, 15 : 135-146.

Stiffman, A.R. Suicide attempts in runaway youths. *Suicide and Life Threatening Behavior,* 1989, 19 : 147-159.

Stoudemire, A., Frank, R., Hedemark, N., Kamlet, M., Blazer, D. The economic burden of depression. *General Hospital Psychiatry,* 1986; 8: 387-394.

Syer-Soloursh, D. *Personal communications,* 1986.

Tsuang, M.T. & Buda, M. In: Blumental, S. & Kupfer, D. (Eds.) *Suicide over the Lifecycle.* APA-Press, 1990.

Vaillant, G.E., Blumental, S.J. Introduction: Suicide over the lifecycle-riser factors and lifespan development. In: Blumenthal, S.J., Kupfer, D.J. (eds) *Suicide over the life cycle. Washington* D.C.: American Psychiatric Press, 1990, p. 1-16.

Vecchia, C. la, Bollini, P., Imazio, C. Age, period of death and birth cohort effects on suicide mortality in Italy, 1955-1979. *Acta Psychiatrica Scandinavica,* 1986, 74 : 137-143.

Wass, H., Miller, M.D. & Stevenson, R.G. Factors affecting adolescents' behavior and attitudes toward destructive rock lyrics. *Death Studies,* 1989, 13 : 287-303.

Weinstein, M., Saturno, P. *Economic Impact of Youth Suicides and Attempted Suicides.* Department of Health and Human Services Publication: Rockville-USA, 1989; no. (ADM) 89-1264, p. 4-/82/4-89.

Weiss, H.B. State family support and education programs: Lessons from the pioneers. *American Journal of Orthopsychiatry,* 1989, 59 : 32-48.

Weissman, M.M. The epidemiology of suicide attempts. *Archives of General Psychiatry,* 1974, 30 : 737-746.

Weissman, M.M., Merikangas, K.R., Prusoff, B.A. Depressed Parents and their Children. *American J. Dis. Children,* 1986; 140 : 801-805.

Whitlock, F.A. Migration and Suicide. *Medical Journal of Australia,* 1971, 2 : 840-848

WHO: *Changing patterns in suicide behaviour.* Copenhagen, Denmark, WHO/Euro, reports and studies, 74, 1982.

WHO: *World Health Statistics Annual.* Geneva, World Health Organization, 1987, 1988, 1989, 1992.

WHO: *Correlates of youth suicide.* Division of Mental Health, World Health Organization, Geneva, tech. doc., 1988.

WHO: *Multi Centre Study on Monitoring Trends in Parasuicide,* 1989, Geneva: WHO

WHO: *Suicide statistics: the problem of comparability,* 1975, WHO Chronicle 29 188-193

Winnefield, A.H., Tiggeman, M., Goldney, R.D. Psychological Concomitants of Satisfactory Employment and Unemployment in Young People. *Social Psychiatry and Psychiatric Epidemiology,* 1988; 23 : 149-157.

Wisse, N. *Selbstmord und Todesfurcht bei den Naturvölkern.* Zutphen, The Netherlands, Thieme, 1933.

Zigler, E.F. Addressing the nation's child care crisis: The school of the twenty-first century. *American Journal of Orthopsychiatry,* 1989, 59 : 484-491.

Zigler, E.F. & Black, K. America's family support movement: Strengths and limitations. *American Journal of Orthopsychiatry,* 1989, 59 : 6-19.

Zigler, E.F. & Ennis, P. Child care: A new role for tomorrow's schools. *Principal,* 1988, 68 : 10-13.

Zivi, A. Les facteurs des tentatives de suicide de l'enfant et de l'adolescent. *Ann. Pédiatr.* (Paris), 1986; 33, 6 : 503-506.

The Epidemiology of Suicide in Old Age

W. GULBINAT

1. The WHO Data Bank on Suicide

The World Health Organization maintains a data bank on suicide mortality into which 97 of the Organization's 166 Member States report data in accordance with the International Classification of Diseases (ICD) (WHO, 1977). This data bank was established in the early 1950-ties. Annual incidence of suicide and suicide rates are reported in the World Health Statistics Annual (WHO, 1991). Such statistics are available by sex and by age groups.

The 58% of the WHO Member States reporting into the suicide data bank must not be interpreted as a representative sample of all countries or of all Member States. Furthermore, not all reporting countries report annually or even periodically. Table 1 (next page) shows the list of reporting countries by continent. Reporting coverage is very high in Europe and the American continent; the coverage is quite incomplete in Asia, and it is practically non-existent in Africa.

The question of reporting reliability has been raised repeatedly (Brugha & Walsh, 1978; WHO, 1982; Sainsbury, 1983). There cannot be any doubt that quality and reliability of official mortality reporting varies tremendously among countries. A direct comparison of suicide rates among countries may hence be interpreted with care, and additional information on the quality of reporting should be sought. The analysis of trends over time, however, or the presentation of ratios of suicide rates (such as male/female or old/young) may be less sensitive to different reporting patterns among countries.

In the following sections epidemiological data of suicide in old age are presented. Old age is defined as 75 years and above.[1] Whenever data are given for a whole continent it is understood that reference is made to those countries only which are listed in Table 1. Unless otherwise stated the latest available data are quoted.

Table 1. Countries reporting suicide into WHO's mortality data base

Africa	Americas	Asia	Australia	Europa
Cape Verde	Argentina	Hong Kong	Australia	Austria
Egypt	Canada	Israel	Fiji	Belgium
Mauritius	Chile	Japan	New Zealand	Bulgaria
Seychelle	Colombia	Korea (R.of)		Cz.slovakia
	Cuba	Singapore		Denmark
	Mexico	Sri Lanka		Finland
	Peru	Thailand		France
	Puerto Rico			Germany
	Uruguay			Greece
	USA			Hungary
	Venezuela			Iceland
				Ireland
				Italy
				Luxembourg
				Netherlands
				Norway
				Poland
				Portugal
				Spain
				Sweden
				Switzerland
				USSR
				UK
				Yugoslavia

---

[1] Analyses were also carried out for the age group 65 - 74 years. Trends for the age group 75^+ were similar, but often more pronounced. For that reason presentation is restricted to the high age group only.

2. Rates of Suicide in Old Age in Four Continents

It is well-known that suicide behavior of men and women differs sharply: attempted suicide, on the average, is at least ten times more frequent in women than in men (Schmidtke et al., 1988), while *successful* suicide is 2 - 3 times higher in men than in women (Leenaars, 1988). These figures indicate orders of magnitude, averaged over all age groups. Figure 1 shows that such sex differences are even more pronounced in old age, and that they depict a consistent pattern across continents: male suicide expressed in terms of suicide rates per 100,000 population is 5 times higher than for females, with the exception of Asia, where the male/female ratio is 3:1. This lower ratio in Asia is a result of relatively higher suicide rates in old women rather than a lower rate in men. Figure 1 also shows that there is a west-east gradient of increasing suicide rates for old men starting on the American continent.

Figure 1. Medians of suicide rates in four continents (rates per 100,000 population, 75⁺ years)

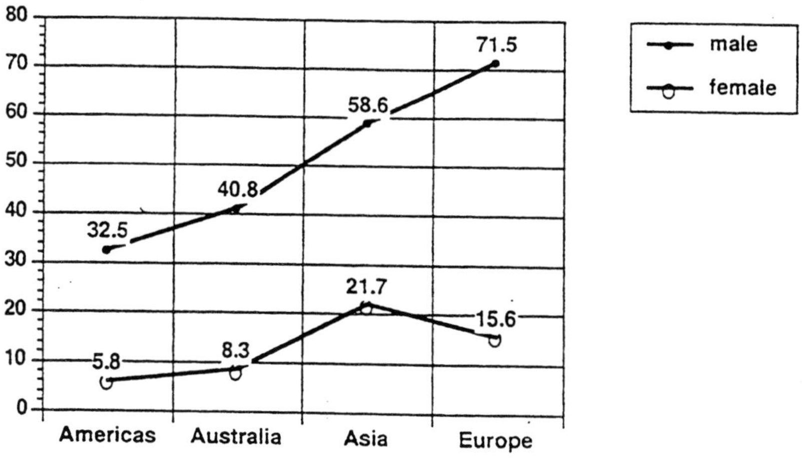

Within continents the variation of reported suicide rates in old age is tremendous, ranging, for males, in the Americas from 4 (Peru) to 105 (Cuba), in Asia from 17 (Thailand) to 104 (Sri Lanka), in Europe from 12 (Ireland) to 186 (Hungary), and in Australia from 38 to 43 (Figures 2 - 4).

Figure 2. Suicide rates per 100,000 population for selected countries in the Americas, 75⁺ years, male

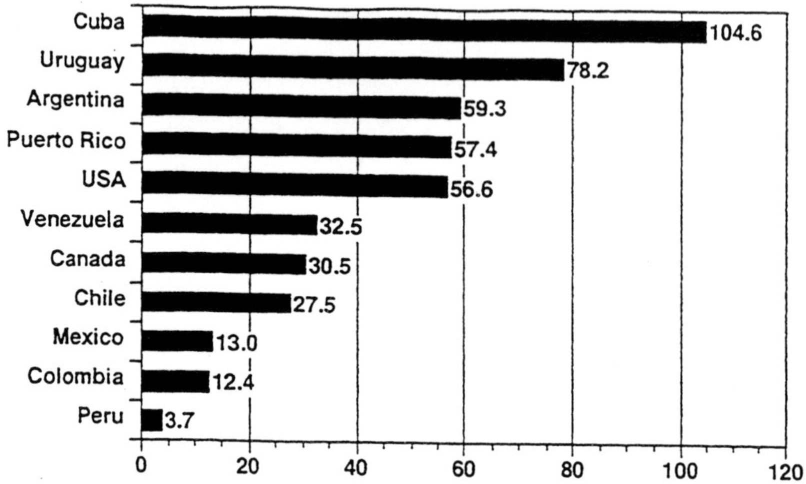

Figure 3. Suicide rates per 100,000 population for selected countries in Asia, 75⁺ years, male

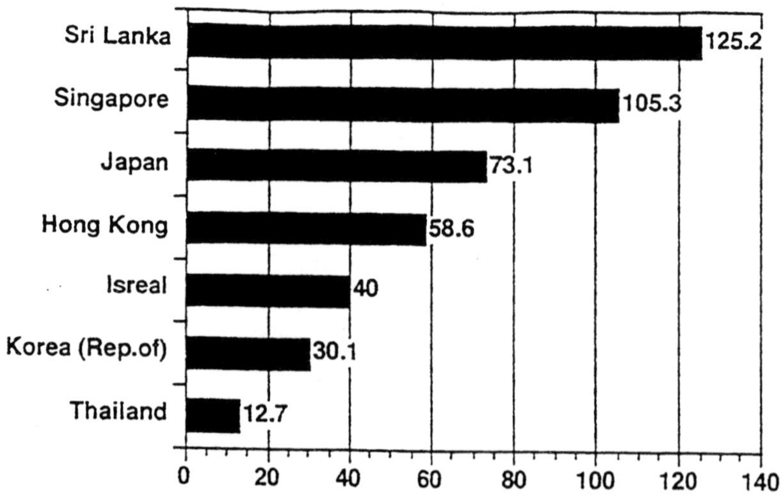

Figure 4. Suicide rates per 100,000 population for selected countries in Europe, 75+ years, male

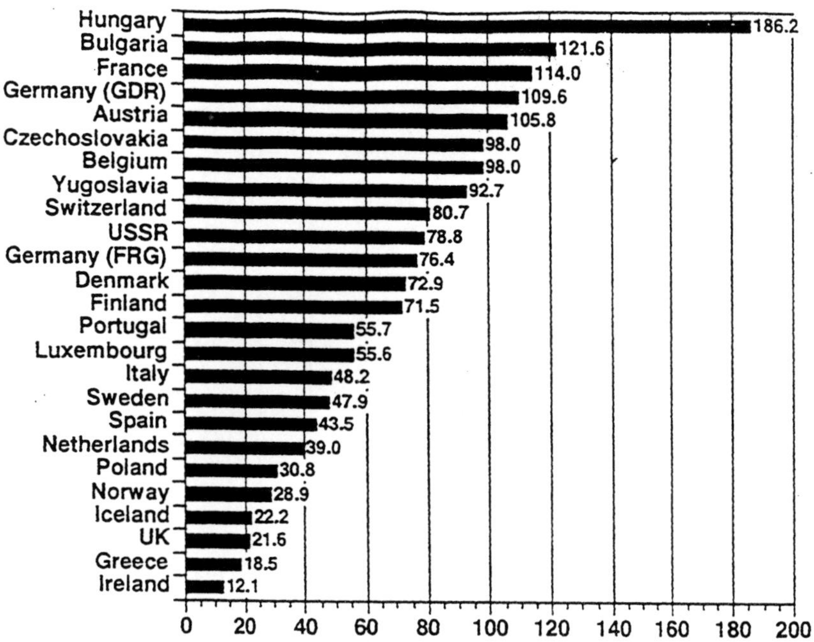

Countries with very high and very low suicide rates for elderly men are not restricted to particular continents. This is confirmed by listing the countries with highest suicide rates world-wide and noting that countries from all continents (except Australia) are represented (Figure 5). It should be noted, however, that the Australian continent is only represented by two countries, Australia and New Zealand.

Figure 5. Countries with highest suicide rates (per 100,000 population) in old age (male only, 75^{+} years) and in adolescence (male only, 15-24 years)

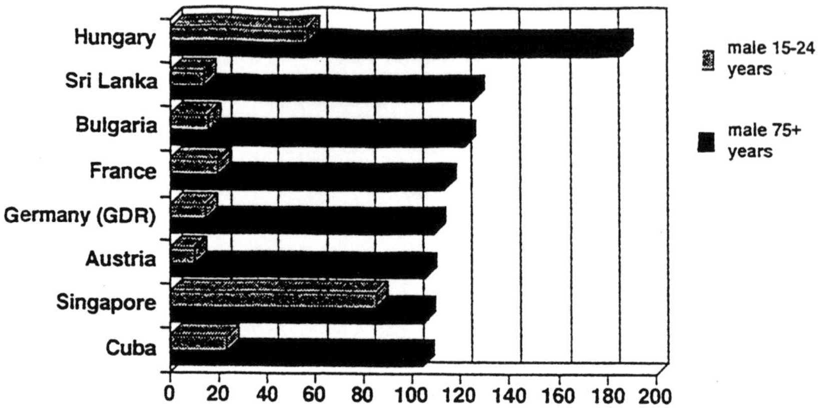

Figure 5 also shows that the suicide pattern in old age is very different from that of adolescents (age 15 - 24 years). Countries with high rates for the older population do not necessarily have high rates for adolescents. In fact, Spearman's rank correlation coefficient of -0.143 is negative, but does not differ significantly from 0.

3. Suicide Trends in Old Age over Time

Many countries report into WHO's suicide data base since 1955, others started later, but for most countries trend data are available for several decades. It is, hence, useful to study changes of suicide rates in old age over a time period of approximately 30 years. Figures 6 - 8 show the percentage changes of suicide rates (per 100,000 population) for selected countries in the Americas, Asia and Europe. The corresponding changes for Australia and New Zealand are -14% and -3.4% respectively.

Figure 6. Changes of male suicide rates in old age over the last 30 years - selected countries in the Americas (male, 75$^+$ years)

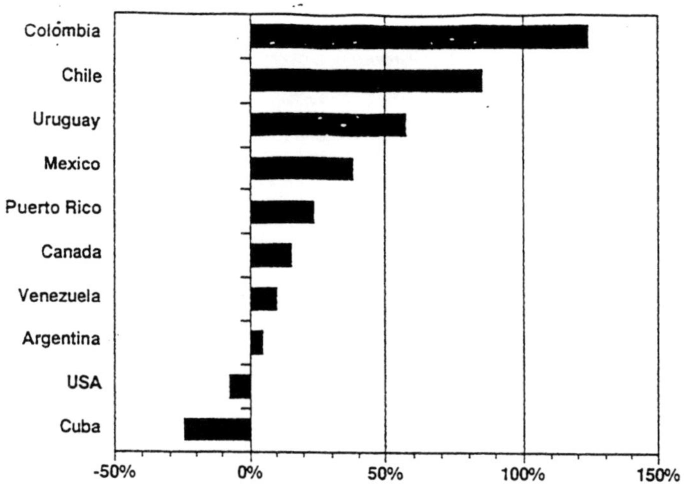

Figure 7. Changes of male suicide rates in old age over the last 30 years - selected countries in Asia (male, 75$^+$ years)

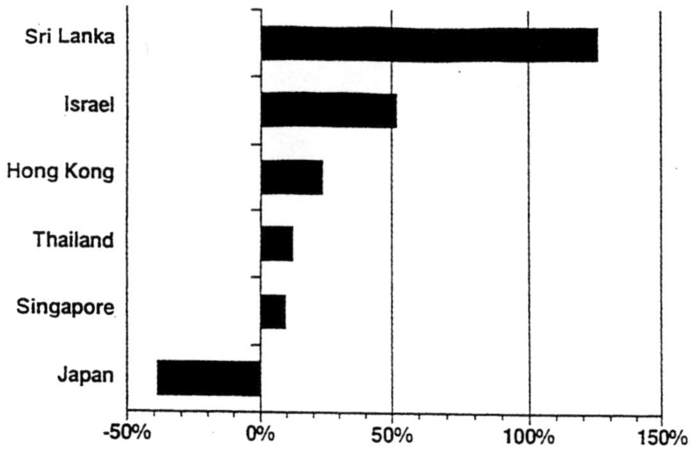

Figure 8. Changes of male suicide rates in old age over the last 30 years - selected countries in Europe (male, 75⁺ years)

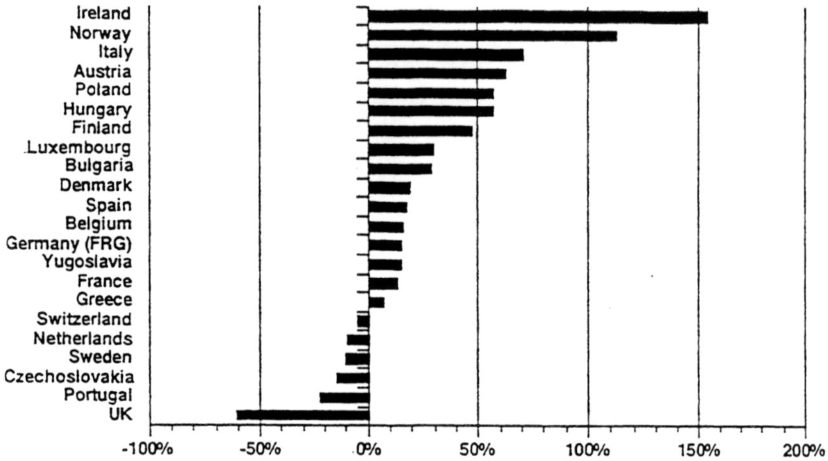

The following may be concluded:

- Suicide trends vary tremendously among countries; there are countries reporting sharp increases of male suicide over the last three decades, and there are countries with a clear decline in such rates.

- Countries with an increase in old age suicide outnumber those with a decrease by ratios between 2:1 (Europe) and 5:1 (Asia).

- Increases in old age suicide are much more pronounced than decreases (up to 150% increases, but not more than 60% decreases).

- The above phenomena can be observed in all three continents (i.e. Americas, Asia and Europe).

It is well-known that suicide reporting varies between countries in terms of coverage (Monk, 1987), definition (Diekstra, 1986), and reliability (Sainsbury, 1983). But it is widely accepted that reporting of suicide trends is much more reliable (WHO, 1982).

It is interesting to identify those countries with the most striking declining suicide rates (Figure 9a) as well as the countries with the most significant increases of old age suicide over the most recent decades for which data are available (Figure 9b). In Cuba (for which data are available only until 1979), Japan and the United Kingdom reported suicide in old men declined 20%, 35% and 48% respectively; it is to be noted, however, that Cuba and Japan started out at considerably higher rates (132.1 and 112.7) than the United Kingdom (with a rate of 41.4 per 100,000 population in the early 1950-ties). On the other hand, the increase in old age suicide was 53% in Ireland, 26% in Sri Lanka, 23% in Colombia, and 13% in Norway.

Figure 9a. Countries with declining suicide rates in old age (male, 75+ years)

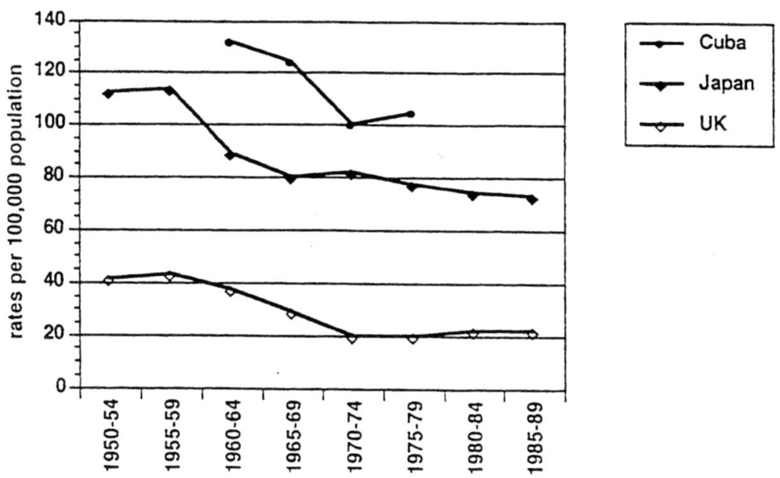

Figure 9b. Countries with increasing trends in suicide rates in old age (male, 75+ years)

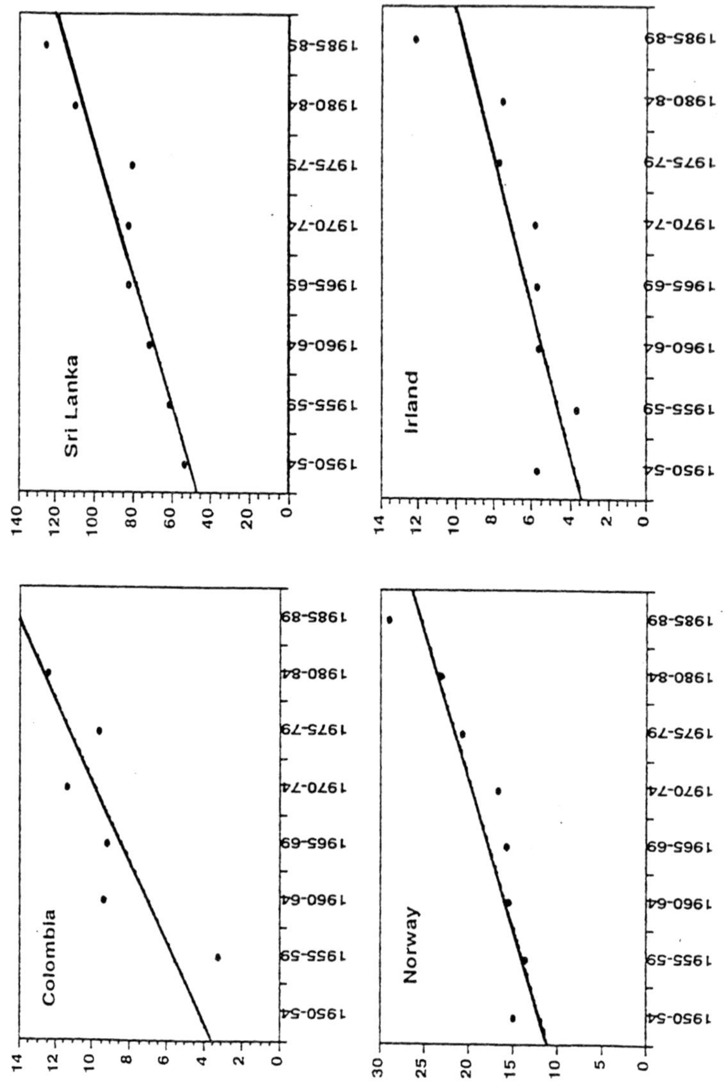

4. Sex Differences in Old Age Suicide

It is well-known that suicide in males is considerably more frequent than in women (see Figure 1). However, it is less well established whether such gender differences are similar for countries within and between continents, and whether such patterns are constant over longer periods of time. Figure 10 shows the medians of male/female ratios of old age suicide rates (per 100,000 population) in four continents during two time intervals which cover 30 years. It is striking to observe that

- the median male/female ratios vary considerably among continents, from 1.8 in Asia to 11.5 in the Americas;

- the male/female ratios are not stable over time, on the contrary: in the Americas the ratio jumped from 7.5 in 1955—59 to 11.5 in 1985—89, while it declined in Asia, Europe and Australia. In Asia it fell to 58% of its earlier value, in Europe to 88% and in Australia to 86%.

Out of the seven countries in the world with highest gender differences in old age suicide, four are in Latin America (Chile, Venezuela, Mexico and Uruguay), one in North America (USA), one in Europe (Finland) and one in Asia (Sri Lanka). Figure 10 shows the corresponding statistics graphically.

The "history" of the gender differences is different in those countries: In Chile and Sri Lanka the male/female ratio increased because the male suicide went up dramatically while female suicide rates remained, more or less, constant. In Mexico and Venezuela the male/female ratio increased because male suicide increased while female suicide, during the same time period, decreased; male increase, however, was very much more pronounced than female decrease. In Finland, both male and female suicide increased over time: but again, male increases were clearly higher than those of old women. Finally, in the USA the gender differences in old age suicide pattern did not change very much during the thirty year interval under consideration.

Figure 10. Medians of male/female ratios of suicide rates in four continents (75^+ years)

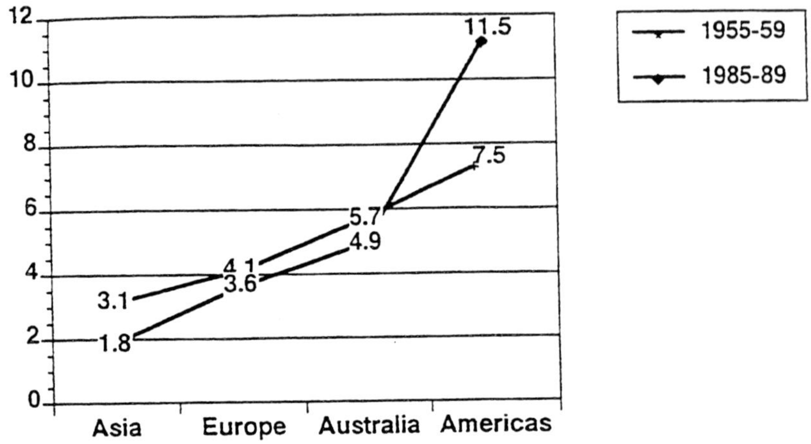

5. Conclusions

Attempts have been made to explain suicidal behavior by means of biological-medical, sociological, psychological and epidemic models. In the biological model, genetic (Szondi, 1948; Lester, 1983), anatomic (Rüegsegger, 1963), biochemical (Mann et al., 1986), or medical factors (Barner-Rasmussen et al., 1986; Hagnell et al., 1981) are seen as determinants of suicidal acts. For example, certain diseases, and in particular psychiatric disorders, are seen as risk factors for suicidal behavior. The sociological model hypothesizes a causal relationship between suicide and social, economic, and cultural factors (Maris, 1975; Platt, 1985). For Durkheim, anomie is the main risk factor for suicide (Durkheim, 1897). The psychological model (Wellhöfer, 1981) includes psychoanalytical explanations (Freud), and explanations based on behaviorism (Watson). Recent research also demonstrates that suicide may have an epidemic component (e.g. cluster suicide, mass suicide, contagion suicide, the Werther effect) (Häfner, 1991). None of these theoretical models seems to be able to fully or only approximately explain the tremendous variation in suicide patterns across countries and time. It may be a rather complex interplay of all or several of the parameters postulated in the various models that are offered to explain suicide behavior.

In spite of all variations, there seems to be a consistent pattern characterizing suicide in old age: it is a phenomenon to be observed in all reporting countries, it is 2 to 12 times higher in males than in females (medians for four continents), it is up to 7 times higher than adolescent suicide (medians for four continents), and the order of magnitude of these indices are constant over time (Figures 11a and 11b).

Figure 11a. Medians of old/young ratios of suicide rates in four continents (male)

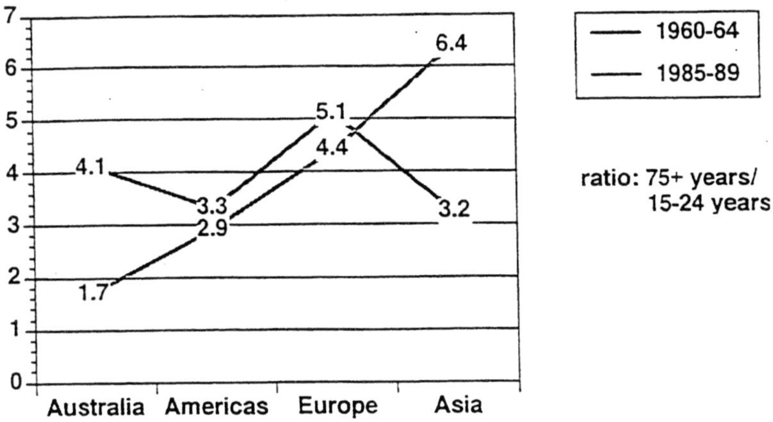

Figure 11b. Medians of old/young ratios of suicide rates in four continents (female)

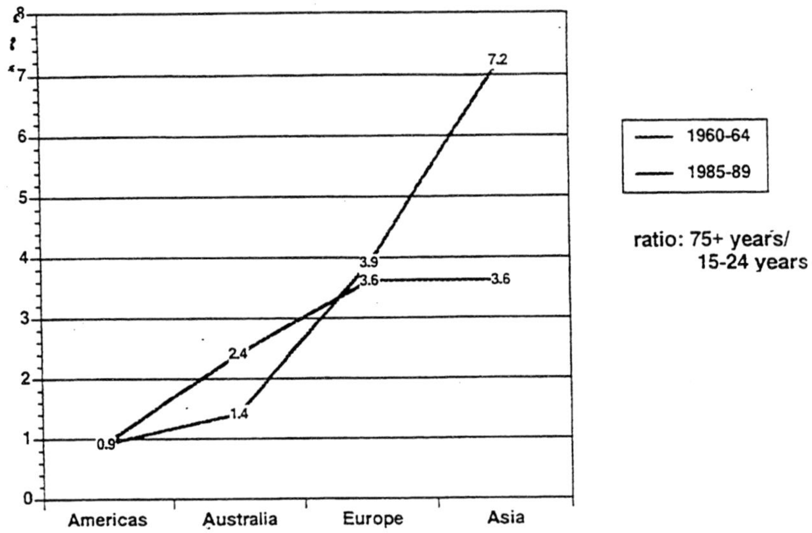

In view of the fact that suicidal acts in patients suffering from affective disorders are up to 40 times higher than for non-psychiatric populations (Black et al., 1985), and that affective disorders are considerably more prevalent in old age than in younger age groups (Sartorius et al., 1983), it may be hypothesized that depression plays a significant role in old age suicideworld-wide.

REFERENCES

Barner-Rasmussen, P., Dupont, A., & Bille, H. (1986). Suicide in psychiatric patients in Denmark, 1987-81. I. Demographic and diagnostic description. *Acta Psychiatrica Scandinavica*. Vol. 73, pp. 441-448.

Black, D.W., Warrack, G., & Winokur, G. (1985). Excess mortality among psychiatric patients. *Journal of the American Medical Association*. Vol. 253, pp. 58-61.

Brugha, T., Walsh, D. (1978). Suicide past and present — the temporal constancy of under—reporting. *British Journal of Psychiatry*. Vol. 132, pp. 36.

Diekstra, R.F.W. (1986). The predictability of suicidal behaviour: The results of a meta—analysis of published studies. Unpublished working paper, Copenhagen: WHO, EURO.

Durkheim, E. (1897). *Le suicide. Etude de sociologie*. Paris: Alcano.

Häfner, H. (1991). Suizid durch Ansteckung? *Therapiewoche*. Vol. 41, pp. 106-114.

Hagnell, O., Lanke, J., Rorsman, B. (1981). Suicide rates in the Lundby study: Mental illness as a risk factor for suicide. *Neuropsychobiology*. Vol. 7, pp. 248-253.

Leenaars, A.A. (1988). Are women's suicides really different from men's? *Women & Health*. Vol. 14, pp. 17-23.

Lester, D. (1983). *Why people kill themselves*. Springfield: Charles C. Thomas.

Mann, J.J., Stanley, M., McBride, P.A. et al. (1986). Increased serotonin and ß-adrenergic receptor binding in the frontal cortices of suicide victims. *Arch. Gen. Psychiatry*. Vol. 43, pp. 954-959.

Maris, R. (1975). Sociology. In Perlin, S. (Ed.), *A handbook for the study of suicide* (pp. 93-112). New York: Oxford University Press.

Monk, M. (1987). Epidemiology of suicide. *Epidemiologic Reviews*. Vol. 9, pp. 51-69.

Platt, S. (1985). Suicide behaviour and unemployment: A literature review. In Westcott, G., Svensson, P.G., Zöllner, H.F.K. (Eds.), *Health policy implications of unemployment* (pp. 87-132). Copenhagen: Health Organization.

Rüegsegger, P. (1963). Selbsmordversuche. *Psychiatrie und Neurologie*. Vol. 146, pp. 81-104.

Sainsbury, P. (1983). Validity and reliability of trends in suicide statistics. *Health Statistics Quarterly*. Vol. 36, pp. 339-348.

Sartorius, N., Davidian, H., Ernberg, G., Fenton, F.R., Fujii, I., Gastpar, M., Gulbinat, W., Jablensky, W., Kielholz, P., Lehmann, H.E., Naraghi, M., Shinfuku, N., & Takahashi, R. (1983). *Depressive disorders in different cultures*. Geneva: World Health Organization.

Schmidtke, A., Häfner, H., Möller, H.J., Wedler, H., & Böhme, K. (1988). Häfigkeiten und Trends von Suizidversuchen in der Bundesrepublik Deutschland — Eine methodische Studie. *Öff. Gesundh.— Wes*. Vol. 50, pp. 272-277.

Szondi, L. (1948). *Schicksalsanalyse*. Basel.

Wellhöfer, P.R. (1981). *Selbstmord und Selbstmordversuch*. Stuttgart: Gustav Fischer Verlag,

WHO (1982). *Changing patterns of suicide behaviour*. Copenhagen: WHO, Regional Office for Europe.

WHO (1977). *International classification of diseases*. Geneva: 9th edition.

WHO (1991). *World Health Statistics Annual 1990*. Geneva: World Health Organiztion.

Guidelines for the Development and Organization of Suicide Prevention Programs

R. J. DYCK

1. Introduction

Of concern to both professional caregivers and the general public is the increasing rate of suicide observed in countries around the world. Not only have the actual suicide rates been increasing, especially among the young (Diekstra and Moritz, 1987; Dyck et al., 1988b), but the prevalence of suicidal behavior in youth has also been escalating (Committee on Adolescence, 1980). In several studies were the prevalence of suicide attempts among normal high school students examined, lifetime rates of 10.5% (Smith and Crawford, 1986) and 8.7% (Friedman et al., 1987) were reported. Such rates are particularly disturbing when compared to the lifetime prevalence rates for suicide attempts in the general population which range from 1.1% to 4.2% (Dyck et al., 1988a; Mintz, 1964; Paykel et al., 1975; Ramsay and Bagley, 1985; Schwab et al., 1972).

In an attempt to significantly reduce these increasing trends in both completed suicides and suicide attempts, many strategies have been proposed and programs implemented. These range from distress lines and crisis centers to suicide awareness education programs, treatment centers and bereavement counselling services. It is unfortunate, however, that many of these programs have been established in isolation from more large-scale, comprehensive approaches to suicide prevention. Program developers and implementators seem to assume that if an isolated suicide awareness education program or distress line is introduced, the prevalence of suicide and suicidal behavior will automatically be substantially reduced.

Eddy and his colleagues (1987), however, have shown that this may not reflect prevailing informed opinion. In an attempt to examine the effectiveness of six major types of interventions proposed to decrease youth suicide (affective education for young persons; identification of high risk groups; school based screening; crisis centers and distress lines; improved suicide prevention training for professionals; and restricted access to methods of committing suicide), suicide prevention experts were asked to estimate the effectiveness of each type of intervention. The investigators found that experts concurred that none of the interventions singly produced a "cure" for youth suicide. Moreover, none of the interventions were perceived to be any more effective than the next.

These statements strongly imply that, in order to have a significant impact on current suicide trends, a suicide prevention program will need to incorporate more than a single type of intervention. Suicide is a multi-dimensional phenomenon (Shneidman, 1985), and any strategy that takes this into account will increase the likelihood that significant reductions in suicidal behavior will occur. The question of how such a comprehensive approach can be realized and what specific content should be contained therein, will be the focus of this chapter.

In addition, two suicide prevention program models will be described, one Canadian and one European.

2. Comprehensive Program for Suicide Prevention: Essential Components

The desire on the part of national and/or regional governments to consider the establishment of suicide prevention programs has often been based upon one or more tragedies of high profile persons or families, and by the increasing awareness that suicide is becoming a major public health problem that requires immediate attention. To ensure that an effective, comprehensive strategy for the prevention of suicide and self-harming behaviors will be developed, two guiding principles need to be given serious consideration:

1. Research, training and information should serve as the foundation upon which the essential services of a comprehensive program are built (*structural support*).

2. A comprehensive program should address, at the very least, the following components:

a. suicide prevention
b. mental health promotion
c. early identification and crisis intervention
d. treatment
e. postvention
(*essential services*)

The structure of such a comprehensive program is presented in figure 1.

A. Structural support

Research

Since knowledge about and understanding of suicidal behavior is extremely limited in comparison to other health-related problems, more research is urgently needed. Epidemiological studies which examine suicide trends as well as identify associated demographic, psychological and sociological parameters should be undertaken. Note, however, that the degree to which such studies improve our understanding of suicidal behavior is dependent upon the accuracy and consistency with which such behavior is classified. Unfortunately, due to the lack of uniform definitions and operational criteria for the classification of suicides and suicide attempts, comparison of statistics between communities, between regions within a country or between countries is difficult, if not impossible. Therefore, efforts must be made to develop a classification system that can be used to determine suicide as the cause of death and to ensure that such criteria are applied throughout the country.

As well, several other types of research need to be given emphasis. Longitudinal and cross-sectional studies examining differences between those who are suicidal and those who are not may provide insights into protective factors that reduce the likelihood of suicidal behavior. Similarly, studies assessing resilient subjects who come from high-risk groups would provide important information with implications for program planning.

One of the major problems in embarking upon the development of a suicide prevention program is that there is so little research which provides answers to the question of what interventions are most effective for whom (Eddy et al., 1987). Thus, evaluative research which examines the outcomes as well as the process of service delivery of different types of interventions would contribute to the overall effectiveness of our suicide prevention efforts.

Figure 1. A comprehensive suicide prevention progam model

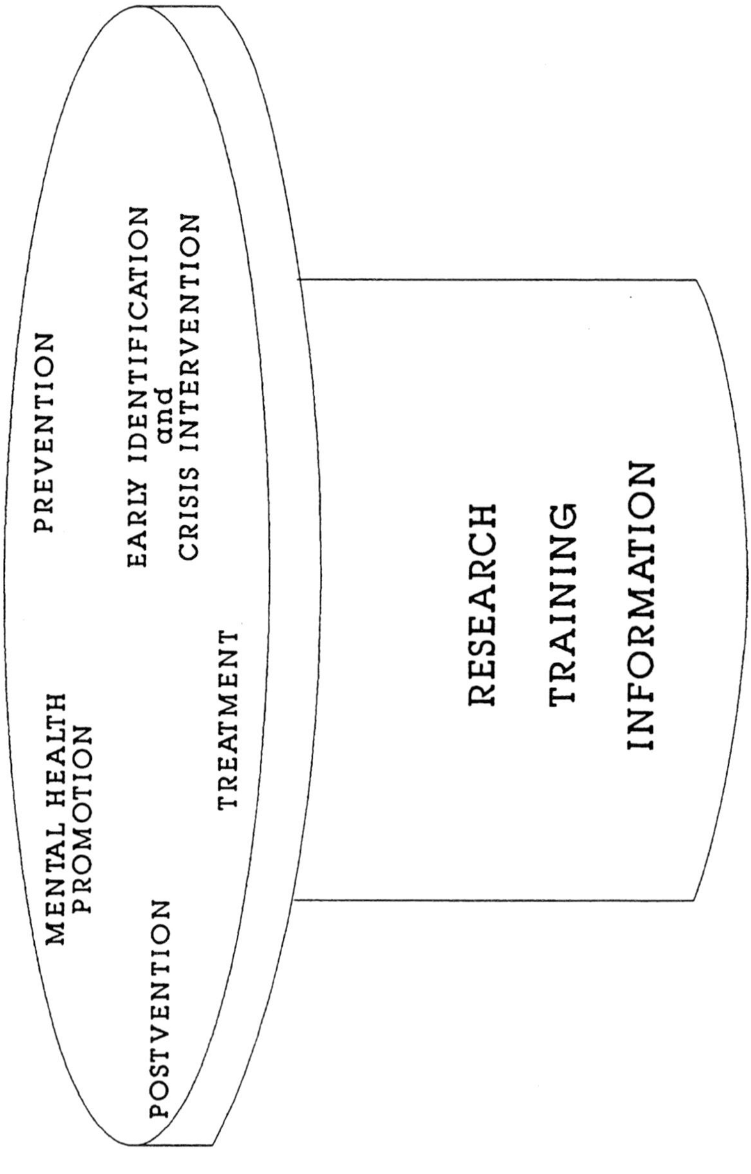

Training

Previous research has indicated that staff in helping agencies have generally received little, if any, training in the various aspects of suicide prevention, intervention and postvention (Boldt, 1976). Apparently afraid of making mistakes, clinical staff preferred to refer suicidal clients elsewhere rather than to treat them themselves. Unfortunately, such referrals were occasionally found returning to the original contact agency after having been transferred from one agency to the next. Therefore, the provision of training to caregivers is essential if the client shuttle from one agency to the next is to decrease, and if suicidal behavior and its impact on family and friends is to be substantially reduced. Regardless of the academic background and qualifications of caregivers, such training should emphasize the following:

a. information about the epidemiology of suicidal behavior;
b. information concerning the risk factors associated with, and the major precipitant of, suicidal behavior;
c. information about the characteristic signs of depression, as well as other clues often associated with suicidal behavior;
d. information on, and training in, the assessment of risk for suicide;
e. training in interpersonal and communication skills necessary to effectively intervene in a suicidal crisis, this should include training in suicide intervention techniques as well;
f. training in the development, identification and utilization of both formal and informal community resources that can provide assistance when required.

It is important to note that in addition to providing such training in in-service education programs, these core training areas also could become incorporated into the academic course work of the various university departments involved in educating caregivers (e.g. medicine, psychology, nursing, education, social work). Emphasis on suicide could also become part of the training received by police, paramedics, clergy, volunteers working on crisis lines or in hospitals, and others who come into contact with potentially suicidal persons.

Additional training in more specialized areas should also be given serious consideration. For example, training in caring for the survivors of suicide, intervening with specific high-risk groups such as youth and elderly, and teaching social and coping skills can assist caregivers to be more effective in their interventions.

Information
Another vital support contributing to overall suicide prevention is having information readily available. For the educator who is coordinating public awareness sessions, for the caregiver who is providing treatment services, for the researcher who is investigating the relationship between specific variables, for the program administrator who is developing a new strategy for service delivery, for the student who is writing term papers, and for the person on the street who is interested in obtaining materials on suicide, easily accessible, relevant information is extremely important. It is from such a knowledge base that constructive and informative planning and decision-making can occur, and that suicide prevention activities can be enhanced.

B. Essential services

Although it is not within the scope of this chapter to develop the rationale for specific elements of a comprehensive suicide prevention program, it is nonetheless important to outline the essential services that should be considered to comprise such a model. Dyck (1988), in describing a model for youth suicide prevention, argued that a comprehensive program should include prevention, crisis intervention, treatment and postvention. However, in light of recent work (Peters, 1988), it may be important to consider mental health promotion as a fifth component.

Prevention
As used in this chapter, prevention consists of a process ensuring that potentially high-risk groups for suicide remain symptom free. In other words, the goal is to prevent from occurring something that does not yet exist within an identified high-risk group by reducing the stressors or other factors that may precipitate such behavior. Thus, not only do the high-risk populations need to be identified in a particular location, but programs that are likely to prevent the onset of a suicidal crisis need to be directed toward these groups.

Mental health promotion
Whereas prevention is usually perceived in terms of a high-risk population remaining symptom free, mental health promotion is aimed at creating a state of well-being where all persons have available to them the personal recourse to realize their aspirations, control and even improve their health, satisfy their needs, and cope with their environment (Peters, 1988). As part

of a comprehensive suicide prevention program, several mental health promotion strategies must be seriously considered. Through government (eg. school health curricula) and/or nongovernment (eg. boys' and girls' clubs, religious organizations) education systems, as well as through the mass media, individuals can be provided with the opportunity to learn and develop the personal resources necessary to cope with the stressors in everyday living. Specifically, they can develop coping, problem solving, decision-making and communication skills which can facilitate a sense of mental well-being. Legislation (e.g. gun control, carbon monoxide emission control in automobiles), as well as the development of community resources in such areas as family life and parent education courses, can also have a significant impact on the general state of well-being. Note that this approach has implications far broader than merely the area of suicide, yet it is very much a part of giving people alternatives to suicide in the face of life crises.

Early identification and crisis intervention
Because the majority of those who commit suicide provide behavioral and/or verbal clues as to their intention, it is important for a whole population, including young people, to be able to identify early a potential suicide and to intervene effectively. Therefore, strategies such as suicide awareness education and suicide prevention training programs directed towards the public, caregivers, and other groups who are involved with high-risk populations (e.g. teachers and parents) would increase not only the number of identifiers, but also the number of persons who can effectively intervene in a crisis. Indeed, the task of suicide prevention is of such magnitude that it requires a coordinated approach in utilizing a network of sensitive and committed lay and professional workers.

In addition to increasing awareness about and enhancing training in suicide prevention, crisis services for the potentially suicidal need to be made available. Such services could include a crisis centre, a 24-hour suicide and crisis "hotline", medical and psychiatric backup (outpatient and inpatient), crisis counselling, mobile outreach, and a short-term stay facility. Moreover, a triage function of referral and transfer of suicidal persons to other regional services for ongoing treatment and follow-up should also be made part of the crisis services.

Treatment
It is not always enough only to identify potential suicides and to intervene immediately. Psychological treatment involving psychotherapy, medicati-

on, and sometimes hospitalization may be required in the long term. Indeed, research has demonstrated that there is a significant relationship between suicidal behavior and diagnosable psychiatric disorders (Dyck et al., 1988; Pfeffer, 1986). Consequently, for mentally ill individuals who are suicidal, treatment of the underlying psychiatric disorder is the most appropriate intervention.

Postvention

The aftermath of suicide can often elicit feelings and behaviors that can destroy families and friendships (Dunne et al., 1987). Not only do families and friends suffer a loss following a suicide, they also experience the pain and shock of a sudden death and they must deal with the stigma associated with suicide including such feelings as guilt, remorse, shame and anger. A very important component of a comprehensive program, therefore, involves helping survivors deal with their grief in a healthy and constructive manner, thereby reducing the risk of suicide among members of this group. A suicide bereavement program which offers assessment, individual and family psychotherapy, and/or a suicide bereavement support group, can be very beneficial to survivors.

3. Comprehensive Program for Suicide Prevention: Developmental Steps

Thus far, the essential components of a comprehensive program have been identified. It is now necessary to delineate the developmental stages involved in achieving the implementation of such a program. Although each region/nation is unique in terms of its culture, politics and protocol, there appear to be at least six necessary steps to developing a program for the prevention of suicide. These are:

a. to gather information
b. to obtain commitments
c. to decide upon an organizational structure
d. to ensure the development of the structural supports
e. to develop an evaluation strategy
f. to anticipate potential obstacles

A. Gather information

Not only is it important to obtain information about the epidemiology of suicide for a particular region, but it is also necessary to ascertain the current status of regional services and programs for suicidal clients. This involves reviewing the literature, communicating with respected scholars and program directors who have delivered services to those in crisis, and assessing information on the effectiveness of different types of programs. Moreover, assessing the level of information about, knowledge of, and training in, suicide prevention among the general public and professional caregivers in the location of interest should be undertaken. Particular attention may be given to such areas as the following: referral practices of agencies dealing with potential suicides; evaluation of programs; standards of care and quality assurance of treatment provided; training of caregivers in suicide risk-assessment and treatment; supervision of caregivers; volunteer resources; extent and type of outreach services; stability of funding for suicide-related programs; systematic development of suicide prevention/mental health promotion pursuits; and, level of support services to high-risk groups and families. On the basis of the research results, recommendations for effective action are expected to evolve.

B. Obtain commitments

In order to initiate the development and implementation of a suicide prevention program, there must be some degree of commitment to the concept by various groups. Mental health related and social service agencies, health care institutions, police, paramedics, schools and the general public need to be supportive of program development and should be prepared to contribute in some way to the overall effort. As well, municipal, regional and national governments need to become partners in a comprehensive program since they not only can provide some level of funding, but they also have a network of government programs that can play a significant role in the ongoing development of the program.

C. Decide upon an organizational structure

Information about the magnitude of the suicide problem, its aetiology, factors related to suicidal behavior, high-risk groups, and availability of and gaps in regional services can serve to focus the planning of a comprehensive suicide prevention program. Indeed, from such findings, a vision for the prevention of suicidal behavior can be established. Following from this vision, explicit goals and objectives which will guide the program to achieve the vision require elaboration. It is through the process of making manifest these goals and objectives that discussion on the organizational structure of the program will also occur. While numerous structures are possible, two will be suggested, together with several potential benefits and disadvantages of each. It should be noted, however, that the specific features of the program need to be worked out within the unique characteristics of each region and their general beliefs and values associated with how services are best delivered.

Community Mental Health Center Model
The Community Mental Health Center has traditionally encompassed a variety of services that can be directly related to the prevention of suicide. Assessment, crisis intervention, referral and transfer to other services within and outside the Center, treatment and consultation are core services offered by most Centers. Furthermore, since such a variety of services are offered, the Centers are often seen by the community as the contact point for obtaining help for those suffering from emotional and behavioral problems, and acquiring information about suicide and the availability of other services in the community.

As the Community Mental Health Center becomes more involved in providing clinical as well as educational and consultation services to the community, it is increasingly able to assume the responsibility for ensuring the development, organization and delivery of the essential services of a comprehensive program. Through its contact with other relevant community services (police, physicians, social services, paramedics, health care institutions), the Center can give leadership to establishing a solid organizational structure within which all parts of the program can be fully developed. Funding, personnel, and effective collaboration and coordination with other relevant services are responsibilities that could be undertaken by the Center. Moreover, the Center could provide leadership and direction in defining the regional suicide needs, identifying both the available and the required resources, and planning and implementing and evaluating all aspects of the program.

Essentially, the Community Mental Health Center would serve as the focal point for contact with all suicide-related services, regardless of whether the services are educational, informational, or clinical.

Potential benefits:

a. As suggested above, the Community Mental Health Center already provides many of the essential services of a comprehensive suicide prevention program. Thus, given the necessary resources, it would not be too difficult to add several responsibilities to the mandate of the Center giving it the full complement of the essential components of a comprehensive suicide prevention program.

b. Since the Community Mental Health Center is already a focal point for dealing with various psychological and behavioral problems, it is an obvious choice for serving a coordinating role in a suicide prevention program.

c. Because the Community Mental Health Center is community based, it is (should be) well-connected with all the services in the community. Thus it is in the position to facilitate collaboration between the services in order to enhance suicide prevention.

Potential disadvantages:

a. Although mental illness is neither a necessary nor a sufficient cause of suicide (Boldt, 1976), locating a suicide prevention program within a mental health center may imply that to be suicidal means to be mentally ill. Not only can this have a stigmatizing effect, but it can also send an implicit message to the community at-large that suggests only mental health professionals can and should deal with suicidal persons.

b. It may be difficult for a community mental health center to become increasingly involved in the essential services of a comprehensive program such as mental health promotion and prevention activities. Traditionally, the mandate for the Community Mental Health Center has been to provide direct clinical services. Consequently, community expectations of the center are that these services will be delivered consistently and without interruption or delay. It may be very difficult to provide time for staff and administrators to become more involved in public education, gatekeeper training, mental health promotion, and social action when the community expects direct client/patient care.

Interagency Suicide Prevention Program Model

Another approach to the organization of a comprehensive program emphasizes community involvement and interagency cooperation. Such a model evolves not only from a belief that the prevention of suicidal and parasuicidal behaviors is a societal and community responsibility, but also from a belief suggesting that the most positive outcomes of a suicide prevention program can be realized through collaborating with others. To be sure, the magnitude of the task is such that it requires a systematic and coordinated approach utilizing a network of agencies and qualified formal and informal caregivers. Following from these beliefs, the model requires two key organizational components, namely, an interagency council and a program coordinator.

In general, the council can be made up of persons representing key community helping agencies (eg., the Mental Health Center, social service/welfare agency, hospital, ambulance, clergy, school, government, recreation center). Their role is to determine the suicide prevention needs of the community, to identify the resources already available, to identify the gaps in service, to specify both short-term and long-term priorities and strategies, to ensure implementation and to evaluate the program. Moreover, since each agency may already be involved in providing suicide prevention services, the council can provide a forum in which agencies can participate together around a common problem for the purpose of coordinating their efforts.

The main purpose of the program coordinator's function is to facilitate the coordination of agencies and the services offered in the fulfilment of the essential components of a comprehensive program. This person works for the council as a whole and serves as its "executive arm".

Potential benefits:

a. This approach models the belief that suicide prevention is a community responsibility and that everyone plays an important role.

b. The interagency model provides access to the different components of the program from many points of entry. An individual in a suicidal crisis, for example, can gain entry relatively quickly into the program through the distress line, police, hospital, school, church, or mental health service. By gaining immediate entry, assistance can be provided during the time that will maximize positive outcomes. Not only will such efficient movement through the system directly benefit the person or institution in crisis, it will also improve the morale and satisfaction of the staff in the agencies involved.

c. This approach can be relatively economical and politically acceptable within a community. No new agency is formed that will require a great deal of additional funding. In fact, each agency in the community is bringing to the suicide prevention program what it already offers or can provide. The interagency model simply provides a framework within which greater cooperation and coordination is facilitated. Indeed, such an approach provides agencies with the opportunity to work out many disagreements, feelings of competitiveness, or feelings of being taken advantage of, which in the long run can only enhance the effectiveness of the program.

Potential disadvantages:

a. Previous conflicts between agencies over such issues as client management, quality of service provided, jurisdiction, and services needed and/or offered, can make working cooperatively difficult.

b. Closely associated with interagency conflicts is the rivalry that can occur within the interagency council over issues of control. It is not uncommon for one agency to try and assume control over program development and implementation or over one of the essential components of the program when in fact such control should be shared. Such a power play can often lead to conflict, apathy, and/or lack of cooperation which will serve to undermine a program in the long run.

c. Because the program coordinator works for the interagency council and not for one specific agency, his/her authority to insist that a particular agency fulfils its role in the program is questionable.

d. Whereas in the Community Mental Health Center model program funding may be built into the budget of the Center, the interagency approach has no appropriate structure to fund the program or even to receive funding from other sources.

D. Development of structural supports

Regardless of the organizational approach chosen, it is extremely important to ensure that a region implementing a suicide prevention program is prepared to deal with the increasing demands for crisis intervention and treatment services. In order to do so, however, both professional and lay caregivers require training in suicide prevention. Thus, a training program needs to be developed and systematically delivered to caregivers throughout the region. Moreover, both information about suicide and on-going research of deliberate self-harming behavior needs to be available. Caregivers require information and research findings in order to increase the likelihood that their particular interventions are effective. Educators, whether involved with children or adults, need the most current information so that their presentations are factual and accurate. The general public often asks for information because of their own personal needs. Therefore, training, information and research need to be in place so that the overall program can be adequately supported.

E. Develop an evaluation strategy

Continual review and evaluation is a necessity for all programs. Procedures and measures need to be established to determine outcomes associated with the program. Clearly, some of the important measures need to evolve from the overall goals and objectives. However, in addition to such purposive outcomes, fortuitous outcomes, (that are by-products of the program not anticipated), also need to be examined. Although it would be desirable if such outcomes were positive, it is possible that some, in fact, may be negative. Moreover, the focus of service delivery itself must be assessed. Therefore, questions such as the following require consideration.

a. Has the program been implemented according to its original design?
b. Is the program delivering services to the originally intended target groups?

c. Are the services being delivered in a cost-effective manner?
d. Are there gaps in the program?

Answers to these general questions can facilitate ongoing, efficient and effective program development. Together with current research findings, program evaluation data, that provide information on outcomes and process, can prevent program stagnation and enhance program effectiveness.

F. Anticipate program obstacles

While there may be great interest in, and motivation to, develop a comprehensive program within a community, region, or nation, planners may nonetheless experience numerous obstacles that can interfere with its implementation. Thus, anticipation of what these obstacles might be, may lead to productive planning which can mitigate their untoward consequences. Rather than an exhaustive list, the following are several of the more common obstacles.

Fear of Emphasizing Suicide
A function of a comprehensive program involves increasing the awareness of, and discussion about, suicide in the general public. It is assumed that through an educational process, potential suicides can be identified earlier and appropriate interventions made more effectively. There are some who argue, however, that increasing the awareness of suicide, especially through the media, can actually increase the frequency of suicidal behavior (Bollen and Phillips, 1982; Phillips and Carstensen, 1986; Gould and Shaffer, 1986). That is, exposing children, adolescents, and adults to movies and news stories about suicide can have a deleterious effect on suicide rates.

Insufficient Research on Suicide Prevention Programs
While much research has focused on the epidemiology of suicide and suicidal behaviors, little attention has focused specifically on what type of intervention program is most effective for which specific target group, (e.g. Eddy et al., 1987). In addition to there being no rational basis for choosing one intervention program over another, Eddy and his colleagues argue that implementing suicide prevention programs can commit resources to ineffective strategies.

Expectations of Immediate Results

Since suicide prevention programs are often established in response to a perceived need in the community, region, or nation, the decision-makers promoting such program development expect results, sooner rather than later. Unfortunately, when it comes to suicide prevention programs, the outcome as reflected by a reduction in the rates may not be realized within a short-time frame. In fact, to have a significant impact on the actual rates, many years, even decades, may be required. This is something that politicians and funders have a difficult time accepting. That a comprehensive program may have numerous outcomes that are important and satisfactory, however, is necessary to acknowledge. To significantly reduce the number of persons engaging in suicidal behavior, to increase the number of informal resources in the community and the number of people who are good listeners and caregivers, to enhance interagency cooperation, and to build a sense of community in which people care for each other, are indeed significant outcomes.

4. Models of Comprehensive Suicide Prevention Programs

Having discussed the essential components and developmental steps of a comprehensive suicide prevention program, it is now important to describe what, to date, has actually been implemented. Two suicide prevention programs, one in Canada and the other in the Netherlands, will be presented. Neither of these programs have initiated all the components that were suggested earlier as comprising a comprehensive program. Nonetheless, both exemplify much of what can be brought to fruition in suicide prevention.

A. The Alberta model for suicide prevention (Canada)

Alberta's model of suicide prevention was originally formulated in a report of a Task Force on Suicide in Alberta (Boldt, 1976), and later refined in 1981 by an advisory committee on suicide prevention established by the Minister of Social Services and Community Health, Government of Alberta (Boldt, 1985). Not only was this committee given the mandate to develop a high-quality, cost-effective program, it was also provided with $800,000.00 per year for the purpose of program development and implementation.

The purpose of the Alberta Model is threefold: to reduce the number of completed suicides; to reduce the number of parasuicides; and to reduce the impact of suicides and parasuicides on individuals, families and communities. Underlying the strategy to achieve these goals are several specific values which include: a belief in the value of human life and that every life is precious; a belief in life-enhancement through healthy living; a belief that the prevention of suicide and parasuicide is a societal and community responsibility, as well as a personal issue; and a belief that through collaboration with others (individuals, groups, agencies), suicide prevention efforts can be made effective. Based upon these beliefs, four specific components were identified to meet the goals of the program. As shown in figure 2, Information, Training, Coordinated Outreach and Research make up the major components of service delivery in the model.

Information

Over the course of gathering information from communities throughout the Province of Alberta, the Suicide Prevention Provincial Advisory Committee (SPPAC) realized that professional caregivers, other gatekeepers and the general public as a whole, had very little knowledge about suicide. As a result, they did not know how to identify and to help a potential suicide, nor were they aware of resources available within a community to assist those who were identified. Consequently, an agency (Canadian Mental Health Association) under a grant from SPPAC, established the Suicide Information and Education Center (SIEC). The purpose of the Center was, and continues to be, to make information on suicide and its prevention available and easily accessible to gatekeepers, the general public, treatment professionals and researchers. Consequently, the Center has developed a computer-assisted resource library containing written and audio visual materials specific to the topic of suicide. Moreover, the Center currently offers back-up support to the community programs by providing research and written resource materials, access to audio visual materials, and brochures and pamphlets. It also publishes a Current Awareness Bulletin, trains people in the different regions to access the Centre, and offers electronic mail service to those on the computer network. Currently, SIEC holds over 12,000 documents and

Figure 2. Alberta suicide prevention program model

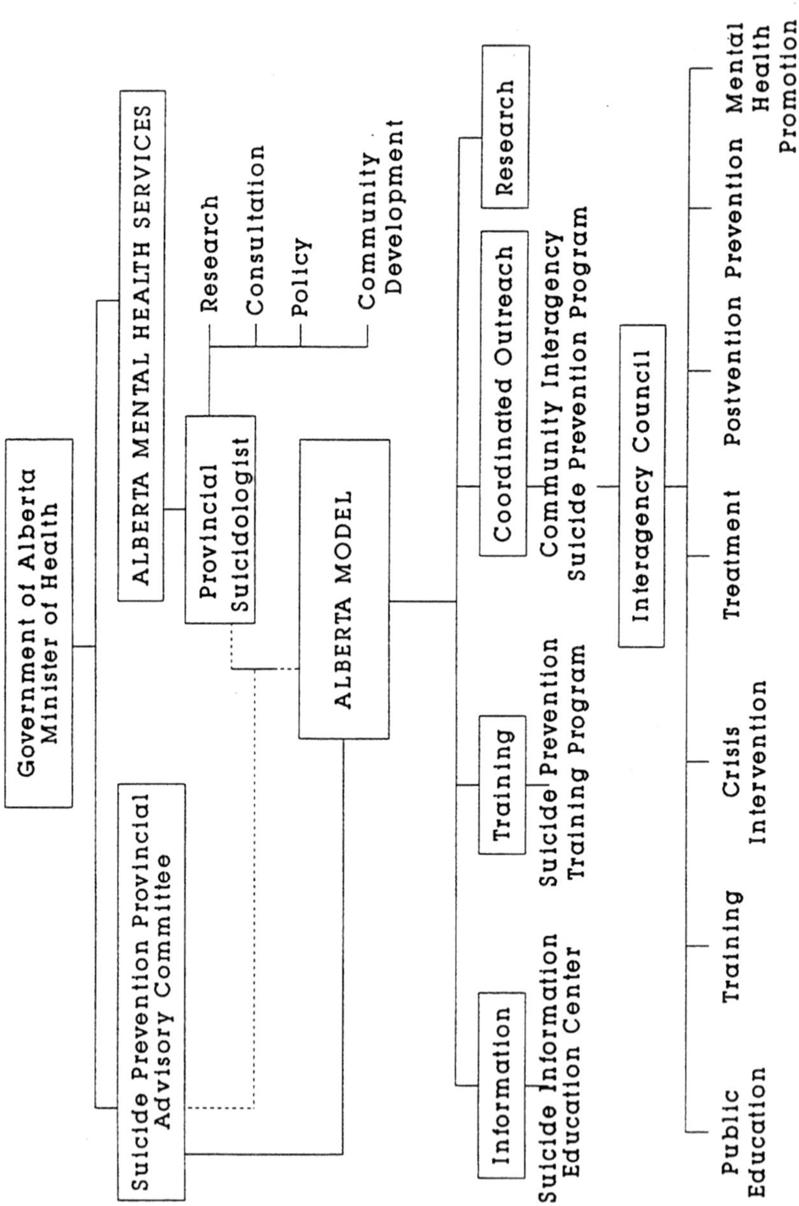

remains accessible to all Albertans through regional computer terminals, mail, and telephone, as well as to people outside of Alberta through various on-line database suppliers.

Training

At the time of this inception, SPPAC found that few universities in Canada offered specific training in suicide prevention, intervention, and postvention. Furthermore, many caregivers in Alberta felt less than adequate in dealing with suicidal individuals. As a consequence, SPPAC provided funding to the same agency, (Canadian Mental Health Association), to develop and deliver a comprehensive training program on suicide prevention. The Foundation Workshop, a two-day program, deals with attitudes and knowledge about suicide, provides a suicide crisis intervention model, and facilitates resource networking. To date, over 6,000 persons in Alberta, and thousands more in other parts of Canada and the United States, have been trained in the program.

Outreach

The high suicide rates of the five smaller urban centers of Alberta, (with populations ranging from 25,000 to 50,000), have made them priority areas for suicide prevention program development. Following community consultation, SPPAC designed a model program which emphasized coordination of existing community agencies for the purpose of providing the essential services of a comprehensive program. Public education, suicide prevention training, 24-hour crisis intervention services complimented by medical psychiatric services, professional treatment, volunteer follow-up, temporary care facility, and suicide bereavement counselling were considered the core services of this Community Interagency Suicide Prevention Program (CISPP) model.

Since value is placed upon the position that suicide prevention is the responsibility of the entire community and not that of a single agency, the organization of the outreach programs in each community involves an interagency coordinating council and a host agency. The council is comprised of representatives from agencies that provide services to suicidal persons or are involved in other suicide prevention activities. Responsibility is given to the interagency council to identify suicide prevention service strengths and weaknesses, to establish local program directions, priorities and goals within the context of the provincial goals and priorities, and to set policies regarding the framework of interagency coordination.

The host agency, which was originally given the role of establishing the infrastructure for the program, currently provides administrative support to the program. Specifically, the host agency in each community prepares the annual program budget, ensures that the funds are properly administered and supports program evaluation activities. Furthermore, because the host agency is represented on the interagency coordinating council, it contributes to the program direction taken by the council.

Each community program receives funding to hire a program coordinator. The coordinator serves as the "Executive Arm" of the council ensuring that the program is developing in accordance with the established goals and objectives. In addition to gathering information about the suicide prevention needs in the community and developing strategies to satisfy those needs, the coordinator is involved in facilitating suicide prevention education, information and training opportunities, and promotes the use of the interagency network of resources. Moreover, the coordinator identifies opportunities for the development of suicide prevention activities in nearby communities. Thus, the coordinator is not just responsible for program development within a single community, but he/she is also responsible for systematically targeting other communities within a specified region for program development.

It is important to point out that there is a strong relationship between the broader, provincial programs that deal with information (SIEC) and training (SPTP) and the local community outreach programs. In particular, the local programs facilitate the utilization of SIEC and SPTP by promoting those services throughout the region, whereas, the provincial programs provide much of the necessary education, information, and training support to the line workers.

Research

In the original design of the Alberta Model, a research center was envisaged which would be located at, or at least affiliated with, a University in the Province. The role of such a center would be to investigate the causal factors relating to suicide, identify types of interventions and treatments that are most effective for specific types of suicidal individuals, and evaluate the ongoing development of specific programs. Unfortunately, to date, this center for research has not been realized. Nonetheless, through the efforts of several individuals, increasing numbers of studies are being conducted which are providing valuable information to the ongoing development of the Alberta program.

The role and function of two key organization components of the model require discussion at this time. First, in 1981 the Suicide Prevention Provincial Advisory Committee was given a very clear mandate to develop a comprehensive suicide prevention program in Alberta. The Committee, which is appointed by the government, continues to have the following mandate:

a. to advise the Minister of Health on the direction and future development of the suicide prevention program in Alberta;
b. to make recommendations for funding programs in the areas of information, training, outreach and research;
c. to review the progress of special projects and programs funded by the government in the area of suicide prevention;
d. to liaise with the Provincial Suicidologist.

The advisory committee fulfils its mandate by helping to articulate and communicate Alberta's vision of suicide prevention, providing provincial coordination and leadership, reviewing suicide prevention program progress reports and budget proposals, meeting with program people, communicating suicide prevention issues and concerns to the Minister of Health, and ensuring that individual programs are systematically evaluated.

Second, the Provincial Suicidologist plays an important role in providing a linkage between government and the various suicide prevention program efforts taking place throughout the province. The Suicidologist is responsible for facilitating the development, implementation, and monitoring of the suicide prevention program in Alberta, conducting research and evaluation studies, as well as encouraging interdepartmental and intradepartmental involvement in suicide prevention. With respect to the latter, the Provincial Suicidologist encourages the various health-related Departments including Education, Social Services, the Solicitor (police, regional jails), Agriculture and Attorney General (responsible for the Office of the Chief Medical Examiner) to become involved in, and contribute to, the suicide prevention program. Within the Department of Health, the Suicidologist ensures the development and implementation of policies related to dealing with those who are suicidal in hospitals, the public health system and mental health clinics. Of course, much of this can be accomplished because the Provincial Suicidologist is an employee of the Department of Health, and is accountable to the Minister through the Division of Mental Health Services.

B. The Netherlands model for suicide prevention

The model of a comprehensive program for suicide prevention in the Netherlands is articulated in a task force report for the Health Council of the Netherlands in 1986 (Diekstra, 1986). This approach is based upon a set of recommendations in the report that reflect four important components, namely, Research, Service Delivery, Information and Training, and Special Risk Groups. Although these particular components are very similar to those found in the Alberta Model and in other task force reports (cf. Diekstra, 1988), the organization appears to be somewhat different.

Research
If effective programs are to be established, information must be gathered through carefully designed research programs. The Netherlands Model suggests that a national research program be established to investigate the cause of, risk factors associated with, and effective methods for preventing suicide and suicidal behavior. Research projects sponsored by the national program would be supervised by national program committees made up of representatives from relevant government ministries, health care agencies and universities.

The national research program is comprised of four essential components. These include:

a. The systematic gathering of valid, national and regional statistics on the prevalence of suicide and suicide attempts and associated demographic, clinical and social characteristics.
b. The funding of multidisciplinary research teams who are committed to investigating the causes of suicide including both potential sociological and biological factors as well as identifying possible risk factors.
c. The carrying out of controlled studies examining different intervention strategies and prevention programs.
d. The carrying out of studies examining different approaches to educating the public about suicide and its prevention, with particular emphasis given to the impact of using the media for such purposes.

Service delivery
It is imperative that services be available to those who are suicidal or have actually engaged in self-destructive behavior. The Netherlands Model sug-

gests that the Community Mental Health Centers in each region of the country may be most appropriate to coordinate the crisis intervention and treatment services for suicidal persons. Indeed, because the Centers are often in the position of being in contact with many different health care agencies and institutions, they have the opportunity to enhance the competence of health care professionals to identify and treat both those with depression and those who are at risk for suicide. Moreover, the Community Mental Health Centers are able to ensure referral and transfer of suicidal persons to other services when necessary as well as to provide consultation services to various health care agencies and workers.

In addition to crisis intervention and outpatient treatment for suicidal persons, medical treatment for attempted suicides in hospital settings requires emphasis. The model asserts that not only must hospital policies be established regarding the assessment, treatment and referral of suicidal persons and their families but short-term stay facilities must be available for prolonged observation.

Training

To reduce the incidence of suicides and suicidal behavior and to mitigate their after effects, the Netherlands Model states that it is essential to provide information and training to health care workers and other gatekeepers (e.g. teachers, school counselors, police, volunteers and staff of emergency telephone services and general public). While each group of caregivers is unique in terms of what specific information and training is required, common areas include the recognition of depression, knowledge of risk factors, crisis intervention and available resources.

Special risk groups

The Netherlands Model identified several high risk groups for whom specific suicide prevention planning is required. Strategies to identify potential suicides among adolescent and young adult populations and to intervene effectively need to be developed and made available both in the secondary school system and in institutions of higher learning (e.g. vocational institutes and universities). Similarly, appropriate policies and procedures for dealing with the elderly require development. Not only is it important to provide information about depressive disorders and its treatment both to caregivers and the elderly themselves, but it is also imperative that proactive outreach services be provided to the elderly living alone and/or the elderly who recently have experienced the death of their partner.

Other high risk groups identified in the Netherlands' Model include incarcerated individuals, chronically mentally ill, alcohol and drug abusers, and survivors of suicide. Regardless of the group, training in identifying and dealing with the potential suicide for the primary workers is suggested as very necessary.

Conclusion

There is nothing in this chapter to suggest that the development and implementation of a comprehensive program is simple or straightforward. Clearly, a review of the literature suggests that while progress is being made, there is still much to be done for the prevention of suicide and suicidal behavior. To explore the underlying causes of suicide, to assess and understand the specific factors contributing to suicidal crisis, to determine the most effective intervention and prevention strategies, and then to develop and implement a comprehensive approach to suicide prevention is what I believe we must all strive towards.

REFERENCES

Boldt, M. (Chairman, 1976). *Report of the Alberta Task Force on Suicide.* Alberta, Canada.

Boldt, M. (1985). Toward the Development of a Systematic Approach to Suicide Prevention: The Alberta Model. *Canada's Mental Health,* 33 (2), 24.

Bollen, D.A. and Phillips, D.P. (1982). Initiative Suicides: A National Study of the Effects of Television News Stories. *American Sociological Review,* 47, 802-809.

Committee on Adolescence of the American Academy of Pediatrics, (1980). Teenage Suicides. *Pediatrics,* 66, 144-146.

Diekstra, R.F.W. (1988). Towards a Comprehensive Strategy for the Prevention of Suicidal Behavior: A Summary of Recommendations of National Task Forces. *Crisis,* 9/2, 119-129.

Diekstra, R.F.W. and Moritz, B. (1987). Suicidal Behavior Among Adolescents. In R.F.W. Diekstra and K. Hawton (Eds). *Suicide in Adolescence.* Nijhoff, Dordrecht.

Diekstra, R.F.W. (Chairman). (December, 1986). *Rapport In zake Suicide (Report on Suicide).* The Hague: Health Council of the Netherlands.

Dunne, E.J., McIntosh, J.L. and Dunne-Maxim, K. (1987). *Suicide and It's Aftermath.* New York, London: W.W. Norton and Company.

Dyck, R.J. (1988). *Suicide in the Young: Implications for Policy and Programming.*

Paper presented at the 20th Annual Behavioral Sciences Conference. Banff, Alberta.

Dyck, R.J., Bland, R.C., New man, S.C. and Orn, H. (1988a). Suicide Attempts and Psychiatric Disorders. *Acta Psychiatrica Scandinavica,* (Supplement, 338). 77, 64-71.

Dyck, R.J., Newman, S.C. and Thompson, A.H. (1988b). Suicide Trends in Canada, 1956-1981. *Acta Psychiatrica Scandinavia,* 77, 411-419.

Eddy, D.M., Wolpert, R.L. and Roserberg, M.L. (1987). Estimating the Effectiveness of Interventions to Prevent Youth Suicides. *Medical Care Supplement,* 25,(12), 57-65.

Friedman, J.M.H., Anis, G.M., Boeck, M. and Difore, J. (1987). Prevalence of Specific Suicidal Behaviors in a High School Sample. *American Journal of Psychiatry,* 144, 1203-1206.

Gould, M.S. and Shaffer, D. (1986). The Impact of Suicide in Television Movies. Evidence of imitation. *New England Journal of Medicine,* 315, 690-694.

Mintz, R.S. (1964). *A Pilot Study of the Prevalence of Persons in the City of Los Angeles Who Have Attempted Suicide.* Paper presented at the 120th Meeting of the American Psychiatric Association. Los Angeles, California.

Paykel, E.S., Prusoff, B.A. and Myers, J.K. (1975). Suicide Attempts and Recent Life Events: A Controlled Comparison. *Archives of General Psychiatry,* 32, 327-333.

Peters, R. (Oct., 1988). *Mental Health Promotion and Community Involvement.* Paper Presented at Alberta Health's Mental Health Symposium. Lethbridge. Alberta.

Phillips, D.P. and Carstensen, L.L. (1986). Clustering of Teenage Suicides After Television News Stories About Suicide. *The New England Journal of Medicine,* 315(11), 685-689.

Pfeffer, C.R. (1986). *The Suicidal Child.* New York: The Grueford Press.

Ramsay, R. and Bagley, C.(1985). The Prevalence of Suicidal Behaviors, Attitudes and Associated Social Experiences in an Urban Population. *Suicide and Life-Threatening Behaviors,* 15(3), 151-167.

Schwab, J.J., Wahrheit, G.J., Holzer, C.E. (1972) Suicidal Ideation in a General Population. *Diseases of the Nervous System,* 33, 745-748.

Shneidman, E.S. (1985). *Definition of Suicide.* New York: Wiley.

Smith, K. and Crawford, S. (1986). Suicidal Behavior Among "Normal" High School Students. *Suicide and Life-Threatening Behaviors,* 16(3), 313-324.

Syer-Solursh, D. (Chairperson, 1987). Suicide In Canada: *Report of the National Task Force on Suicide in Canada to the Minister of National Health and Welfare, the Honourable Jake Epp.* Ottawa, Canada.

The Role of the Community in Assessment, Intervention and Prevention of Suicide and Attempted Suicide

A.R. HORNBLOW

1. Introduction: The Need for an Ecological Approach

The marked increase in suicide and attempted suicide over recent decades justifies their being accorded a place on the list of current major public health concerns. Policy makers and statutory authorities, however, are generally reluctant to see suicide and attempted suicide as public health problems, treating them rather as matters lying within the domain of the psychiatric services. Mental health service providers have tended to accept this without question despite the limited effectiveness of therapeutic interventions directed towards suicide attempters (Dew et al., 1987), and a general recognition of the important if complex causal role of social and economic factors. Epidemiological research has identified for both suicide and attempted suicide a wide range of risk factors, the mix of such factors clearly pointing to the need for a broad-based approach to prevention. For example, recognised risk factors for suicide among adults over 30 include not only such personal and family variables as current major psychiatric disorder, single status, and a family history of suicide, but also lack of social support, and sudden change in social or economic status as occurs during unemployment and undesired retirement (Klerman, 1987). That pervasive social attitudes and values may foster or legitimize self-destructive tendencies is implicit in speculation that rising rates of depression and suicidal behaviour in the Western world are consistent with a hypothesis that we have entered an "age of youthful melancholia" (Klerman, 1988; Joyce et al., in press). The importance of contextual factors in understanding and preventing suicide is further affirmed by evidence that significant risk factors may vary somewhat according to cultural context (Araki and Murata, 1986). Last (1987), commenting on international variations in the frequency of suicide as a certified cause of death, notes that suicide is commonest at times of social and economic distress, decreases in countries at war, and is particularly common among groups whose culture is disintegrating. Thus, the mix of risk factors is a complex web extending beyond the intrapsychic and the familial, to those factors which operate at a community and societal level.

If the determinants of suicide and parasuicide range from the intrapsychic to the societal, then a comprehensive approach to prevention is essential. The need for preventive activity at different levels is as vital in countering suicides as in targeting other public health problems, such as alcohol abuse, where it is recognised that preventive activity directed at a personal level (e.g. early detection of problem drinkers), must be completed by attempts to change community attitudes and behaviour (e.g. through health education), and action at the level of social policy (e.g. controls directed towards the price and availability of alcohol) (Makela et al., 1981). Moreover, as risk factors for suicide and parasuicide sometimes reappear on the lists of determinants of other psychiatric conditions, such as alcohol abuse, preventive programs directed toward suicidal behavior must be integrated with work in related fields.

Despite the complex causality of suicide and attempted suicide a comprehensive approach to prevention is possible, with preventive activity at different levels being directed toward complementary goals. Indeed, such a comprehensive, multi-level approach, involving a wide range of personnel beyond the mental health fraternity, must be the logical response to recent epidemiological findings. Such an approach must include not only the health sector, but other professional groups such as teachers and the police, voluntary agencies and community organizations, and also Government and non-governmental agencies involved in the formulation and implementation of social policy.

The perspective adopted above is in fact that of "The New Public Health" movement which adopts an ecological approach to current major health issues (Acheson, 1986; Last, 1987). The model articulating this approach, and defining levels of activity for preventive and health development programs, is provided in the Ottawa Charter for Health Promotion (WHO et al., 1986).

According to the Charter, health promotion action means: to build healthy public policy, create supportive environments, strengthen community action, develop personal skills and reorient health services. The Charter is, of course, directed at health promotion per se. However, those committed to the prevention of suicide and parasuicide should not draw back at the somewhat blurred boundary between preventive activity and mental health promotion. To do so would be to disregard the fact that addressing the psychological and societal determinants of suicidal behavior will require mobilising of resources, social processes, and forces for health in the community at large. Thus, pressure to build health public policy, create supportive urban environments, and reorient health services away from a dominant institutional model, will be as important as strengthening the community networks and personal coping skills of suicide attempters. Given that the risk factors for suicide and attempted suicide are generally woven together in a pattern of social disadvantage, it is clearly not possible to reduce many of the risk factors for suicide without addressing policies which maintain unemployment, deny equity of access to health services and community supports, and create the physical and psychological hazards of modern urban living.

The creation of socially and emotionally healthy environments, particularly for the young, requires a strong commitment to address issues as wide-ranging as television violence and economic policy. The commitment a century ago which curtailed exploitation of the young, promoted the rights of the disadvantaged, and addressed appalling living conditions in the industrial slums of Europe, led to "The First Public Health Revolution". The challenge of "The New Public Health" is to address the psychological and social forces, the lifestyles, attitudes and behavior, which will erode the health of communities in the closing decades of the 20th century. Those most vulnerable to such processes of psychological and social erosion feature disproportionality in the suicide and parasuicide statistics. To arrest rising rates of suicide and parasuicide will require therefore, not only programs targeted to those at risk, but changes to chose social policies and structures which undermine personal and community well-being.

It may be criticised that such a stance is too general or global. The rejoinder to such criticism is that unless a broad view is adopted, preventive activity will tend to address problems downstream, rather than at their source. The broad perspective does not mean that specific targets and strategies are unnecessary. On the contrary, careful definition of goals and programs is a prerequisite for assessment of progress towards such goals and for rigorous evaluation of the effectiveness of particular programs. In the following sections activities at different levels will be described, around three main themes: first, the need to improve knowledge of suicide prevention services, and their acceptance and use by those at risk; second, the need for more effective intervention strategies; and third, the need to address public policy issues.

2. Improving Knowledge, Acceptance and Use of Crisis Services

The dramatic growth of community-based suicide prevention services over the last three decades reflects widespread acceptance of the crisis intervention philosophy that help must be readily available at the point of need. The development of these services is yet another chapter in the evolution of health care. Historically, new strategies for community support have evolved in response to heightened awareness or changed perception of human need (Hornblow, 1986a). Examples of this may be seen in the development of a network of hospitals in 18th century England, largely as a result of voluntary effort and subscription, and the evolution of mental health care in the United States in response to the enthusiasm and advocacy of reformers such as Dorothea Dix and Clifford Beers. Today's network of crisis intervention services grew out of the recognition, both outside and inside established psychiatric services, of the potential for support through the anonymity and availability of the telephone, and the accessibility of the drop-in center. However, important though telephone counseling and drop-in services are, and will continue to be, as part of the mosaic of mental health supports in the community, their reactive role, and their heavy reliance on caller or client initiative and motivation, had limited their use by those at risk of suicide.

A critical problem encountered by suicide prevention services is that those to whom their efforts are directed frequently do not seek help. A recent review (Shaffer et al., in press) indicates that many of those who attempt suicide are unaware of available services, this being so for the young attempter. Others are too emotionally aroused to take the logical step of seeking help, or are resistant to doing so. It is suggested that the apparent failure of crisis centers to reduce suicide rates may result from the restricted groups that have made use of them. Given that a number of studies indicate hotline and crisis services to be well regarded by potential users, including teenagers, Shaffer et al. conclude that the role of such services could be more effective in preventing suicide if greater use was made of them by those at risk. In other areas of health care, preventive programs, for example immunization of screening, are organized in such a way as to cover whole populations at risk, are procedurally straightforward, and are generally adequately resource and socially acceptable. While programs directed toward infectious diseases and suicidal behaviour may appear to have little in common, to succeed, both must be available, accessible, and acceptable to those in need. For a variety of reasons including complex causation and social stigma, the coverage, acceptability, and utilization of psychiatric preventive programs is far from impressive.

Suicide prevention programs are dependent on the potential attempter, or a friend, family member, or involved professional, identifying the risk and taking appropriate steps to seek help. Thus improved identification and engagement of those at risk requires knowledge and acceptance of suicide prevention services, and effective referral. Strategies of improve knowledge of services may include appropriate advertising, particularly in high incidence areas, perhaps through use of community radio, articles in the press, or notices in telephone books or other sources of community information. That such promotion raises awareness of services is clear from the often reported rise in call rates to telephone counselling services following an advertising campaign. It is critical that such advertising focus on the service provided and not in any way sensationalise suicidal behavior. In addition to improving public knowledge of preventive services, it is important also to improve knowledge among professionals who may be in a position to identify and refer on those at risk. Access to care by those at risk of suicide may be facilitated by improving the assessment and referral skills of a range of professional groups, teachers, police, clergy, occupational health nurses, those in emergency services such as the Fire Department, and those involved in community support of discharged or deinstitutionalized psychiatric patients. They should know where to refer those about whom they are concerned. They should also know that simply giving information about services to a depressed, confused or potentially suicidal individual may be inadequate, and that referrals which are carefully arranged and followed through are more likely to result in appropriate intervention and client compliance. Early identification, support and engagement of high risk individuals is frequently a consequence of sensitive assessment and wise action by professionals in contact with them, particularly as those at highest risk often have impoverished or conflictual personal relationships, and may be unresponsive to please from family or friends. Programs to improve the assessment and referral skills of such professionals therefore have considerable potential from a preventive perspective.

3. Improving Intervention Strategies

Despite the fact that evidence on the effectiveness of crisis intervention services is incomplete and sometimes equivocal, recent reviews accept the important role of such services and highlight areas where intervention strategies might be improved (Dew et al., 1987; Hornblow, 1986b, Shaffer et al., in press).

Increased effectiveness of suicide prevention services will depend on better case identification and referral, better case management and follow-up, better liaison between agencies, and better targeting of training programs to responder skills and client needs. The following sections review developments in different areas of suicide prevention activity and illustrate attempts to improve intervention strategies.

A. Developments in community-based programs

A survey of 50 suicide prevention and crisis services around the world reported by Motto in 1979, provided evidence of a trend toward a broadening range of services, a more active case-finding approach, greater visibility and increased integration into the community care system, and creative leadership by newer and smaller centers as well as the well-established ones. This was being accomplished without relinquishing the traditional respect for anonymity, ever-present availability and a non-judgmental regard for each person's need. Motto noted that innovations in crisis intervention tend to involve either a focus on a new target population, or a new procedure. Examples of the former, emphasizing a more active case-finding approach, will be described in the following sections, with extension of traditional crisis center activity to programs oriented toward the police and schools. Other developments, directed to both new target groups and new procedures will be cited briefly, to illustrate the diversity of community activity in the crisis intervention and suicide prevention field.

Since the establishment of the Samaritans in London in 1953, with suicide prevention as their primary aim, there has been a dramatic expansion of telephone counselling and crisis intervention services, and increasing specialization. There is now a bewildering array of services directed toward the young and the old, victims and perpetrators of assault, the terminally ill and those in grief, the psychologically and physically disabled, those with transmitted and chronic disease, the homeless and the home bound. Most of these services have developed in an ethos of reliance on client-initiated contact and motivation, but are now adapting to the need for a more active case-finding approach, and therapeutic procedures likely to result in a clearer "contract" with clients and greater likelihood of behavior and attitude change. Two services described by Motto are illustrative. The San Francisco Suicide Prevention Centers "Friendship Line" was established specifically for calls to elderly persons who live alone and have very limited contact with others. In such a service it is necessary to have third party callers as a means of identifying the clients initially, but once contact is made there is ready acceptance of the reversal of the usual roles, that is, the Center initiating a call without waiting for an indication of need from the elderly person. In a further illustration of the evaluation of crisis intervention services, Motto found that about half of the 50 suicide prevention services responding to his survey indicated home-visiting outreach services to be a part of their regular activities. Such outreach was far less common two decades or so ago, and the advisability of home outreach was often debated. That this form of outreach is now a regular part of crisis intervention work is a recognition of the basic therapeutic principle that intervention is more likely to be successful if it is oriented closely toward and involves others in the world of the client.

Not only is there a need for interventions to be directed actively toward the context and social support networks of the person expected to benefit from such intervention, but there is a need also for more rigorous identification of the behavioral changes toward which therapeutic interventions are directed and the strategies by which such change might be facilitated. For example, the reactive nature of much telephone counselling tends to preclude the setting of behavior-change goals, and the provision of ongoing support as efforts are made to achieve these goals. An increasing emphasis on "contract" telephone counselling, involving more structured contact between counsellor and caller, may be necessary if telephone services are to break out of the cycle which, for some dependant callers, tends to reinforce helplessness rather than mobilise resources for change. Contract telephone counselling involves regular contact between counsellor and caller, with agreed-on goals for the therapeutic relationship, which may be short or longer term as appropriate. It may be particularly valuable for supporting clients over a period of working through a decision making situation or resolution of interpersonal conflict, or such life-change processes as grieving, retirement or redundancy, or rehabilitation after illness. Contract counselling may also prove a useful way of monitoring and providing limited support to clients with certain ongoing problems or chronic conditions, such as hypertension, alcoholism, diabetes and possibly chronic psychotic disorder (Hornblow, 1986a).

Such extension of traditional roles may require new training models to provide counsellors with appropriate knowledge and skills to facilitate client decision making or attitude and behavior change. Such roles also require appropriate supervision and liaison with other agencies. Shaffer et al. (in press) note that chronically disturbed callers, who have prior suicide attempts and psychiatric treatment, are an especially high risk group for later suicide and generally require more active and aggressive case management than can be offered by a crisis service. Thus it is of critical importance to first assess severity of disturbance, and the possible need for referral elsewhere, before considering with any client the goals and agenda for contract counselling.

B. Law enforcement programs

The relationship between law enforcement and crisis intervention services is an important but often neglected one. Law enforcement officers tend to view mental health services as being of little help to them in dealing with persons they encounter who are experiencing emotional difficulties. Police agencies have traditionally provided the primary 24 hour mobile emergency service in the community. The majority of their activities are not crime related, being concerned rather with family, social or emotional disturbance, and welfare issues. As a consequence, law enforcement officers have a key case-finding role. Cesnik, Pierce and Puls (1977) outline steps taken to develop and maintain a solid working relationship between county law enforcement agencies and a newly established 24 hour crisis intervention program, serving a population of 300,000. The service put professional mental health workers on duty and available to respond anywhere in the county 24 hours a day, on referral from other community helpers. A third of referrals in the first year came from police agencies. In developing the crisis service/law enforcement relationship, discussions with police management personnel revealed the need for specific service objectives to ensure staff responsiveness to the police officers call from a crisis situation. Adequate responsiveness came to be seen as staff (1) being readily and continually available, (2) responding quickly (within 20-30 minutes of the initial call) and in person to the scene of the situation, (3) accepting or sharing responsibility for the disturbed person, (4) formulating and initiating alternative dispositions, and (5) subsequently providing feedback to the officers involved and occasionally letters of commendation where appropriate.

Procedures were designed with full police involvement, including extensive police participation in initial crisis service staff training, and crisis staff "ride-along" with police officers on duty. Police officers were informed, through clear, concise, written and verbal statements of the crisis center's objectives, priorities, limitations and operating procedures. From the outset an important step in the relationship building process was the crisis center's policy of ready and open acceptance of any and all police referrals. Important also was the role of the police Social Service Coordinator who provided liaison between the two services, and handled matters of disagreement or misinterpretation. Further crisis intervention work with law enforcement personnel is described by Danto (1979). His work with police included not only training and back-up in handling suicidal behavior encountered by the police, but also psychological autopsy of suicide by police officers themselves, and assistance in coping with extreme stresses to which police are exposed, such as managing gunman, kidnappers and terrorists.

C. High school and university programs

Suicide and attempted suicide are not uncommon events on a large high school or university campus, and often leave young "suicide survivors" who may themselves be more vulnerable as a result of knowledge of and guilt about their friend's death. While such situations frequently are not well handled, they do provide the opportunity for support to other students contemplating suicide, and the opportunity also to improve preventive programs. U.S. Center for Disease Control statistics indicate that for every completed suicide, 20 teens will attempt suicide, with basic warning signs frequently going unheeded (Cherskov, 1986).

Ross (1980) notes the crucial importance of teachers and those close to students being able to identify "presuicidal behavior" such clues as morbid comments or questions about death, talk about use of firearms, or undue stress relating to family and/or peer relationships. After twelve teenage suicides in a year in a community of approximately 500,000 a preventive program directed toward schools was initiated by Ross and her colleagues at the Suicide Prevention and Crisis Center of San Mateo County (California).

Training programs were run for teachers, and brochures, training kits, bibliographies and guidelines prepared for school personnel. Use was made of the media, a film was produced. Procedures for subsequent consultation and follow-up were set in place. Prior to this project a preliminary survey had been undertaken at several schools. To the question "If you were considering suicide, to whom would you turn for help?" students had overwhelmingly responded "a friend", ahead of parent, other relative, teacher, school counsellor or nurse. For this reason much effort in this project was directed towards students themselves and how they could best help their friends. A brochure was prepared for students, to assist their understanding of pre-suicidal behavior in themselves and their peers. Subsequently peer counselling programs were developed at several schools. Following the project calls for assistance and for back-up support and services increased markedly with, significantly, a shift toward greater consultation with school personnel in their own management of suicidal students rather than after-the-event requests for counselling following suicide or attempted suicide.

Webb (1986) outlines a model preventive outreach program which it is recommended staff should undergo in order to deal with the aftermath of suicide attempts on campus. She recommends also that all colleges should prepare written guidelines for use in the event of suicide on campus. Preparation and distribution of such guidelines would sensitise staff to the possibility of suicide amongst students, and avoid the need for improvization should a suicide crisis occur, by outlining in advance steps to be taken and the person or persons responsible for such action. It is suggested that training sessions should be held annually for residential and support staff. The content of such training should include information about depression and characteristics of pre-suicidal behavior, suicide incidence and risk data, a brief introduction to crisis intervention strategies, and referral procedures. Such training could also include values clarification, given the importance of understanding values behind judgments about suicidal behavior. A further component could be a review of typical grief and mourning processes, given the need for understanding of these processes in working with suicidal survivors. Films, videos, role plays, small group discussions, and lectures form the basis of such a training program, which is structured to include both didactic and experiential components.

The following guidelines are suggested by Ross as the basis of a program to assist colleges in the management of a suicidal crisis:

1. Set up a crisis counselling service.
2. Initiate contact with friends and acquaintances of the suicide victim as soon as possible.
3. Encourage catharsis and expression of feelings among the whole college community.
4. Facilitate "cognitive understanding" about the death.
5. Promote peer contacts among friends of the suicide victim.
6. Encourage commemoration of the death by attendance at the wake, funeral and/or college memorial service.
7. Avoid glamourisation or romanticization of the death.
8. Resume routine activities as soon as possible, while making allowance for the non-participation of students who remain upset.
9. Use outside consultants to meet with counselling staff.
10. Recognize that the aftermath of suicide may last for a long time.

Programs described by Ross and Webb have been outlined in some detail as they illustrate strategies for improving the effectiveness of preventive programs in schools and universities. Some points may be debated, for example, the extent to which catharsis and commemoration of the death should be encouraged must be set against the real risk of reinforcing morbid introspection and "copy cat" behavior. Shaffer et al., (in press) indicate that some school-based programs are not only ineffective but may even be harmful to some vulnerable participants. If so, this would suggest suicide prevention programs in schools should perhaps focus on helping staff identify and refer those students of the problem of youth suicide. Nevertheless, despite these points of current debate, the programs described above represent a planned approach to suicide prevention, tailored to be the specific context of an educational institution, with clear goals and guidelines, the appropriateness of which is open to objective evaluation.

D. Principles for suicide prevention training programs

Increasing the effectiveness of any suicide prevention program —whether in crisis services, law enforcement agencies, schools, or elsewhere— requires explicit attention to training issues. Whether stated explicitly or not in describing the programs outlined above, good training of staff or volunteers is a fundamental ingredient in all good preventive programs. A number of key principles in setting up training programs for those involved in suicide prevention are outlined below. These principles are applicable to brief training programs, of only a few sessions, and also to longer ones with more ambitious goals.

First, those involved in a suicide prevention program should know the justification for it, in terms of community need, and the target groups likely to benefit from their efforts. A suicide prevention program will be ineffective, and indeed may do harm, unless it has the acceptance of those who are expected to implement it, inter-disciplinary backup and support networks are known and in place, and there is also a clear expectation that organizational and procedural matters will be attended to conscientiously. The nature of ongoing support and follow-up offered to clients should also be known.

Second, the knowledge, skills and attitudes to be acquired or fostered through a training program should be clearly identified, as too should the learning strategies and components of the program through which its educational objectives are to be achieved. Necessary knowledge may be acquired through reading, lectures, films, videos, etc. but must be presented in such a way that its relevance is apparent, the level appropriate, and "knowledge overload" does not squeeze out skill learning and opportunities to examine attitudes and values. A simple before-and-after test, constructed in such a way as to be acceptable to the group, can establish prior knowledge, and gains as a result of the program.

Third, skills to be learned should be stated in behavioral terms, demonstrated, practiced, and opportunity given for feedback on performance. Basic skills to be acquired may be those of listening to and reflecting back feelings, gently probing for depressive or suicidal thoughts, and facilitating referral where appropriate. A variety of strategies may be employed to facilitate skill learning.

Appropriately structured role-plays can be particularly effective, as too can the use of video. Ratings made on simple assessment tools such as the visual analogue scale (Davies et al., 1975; Hornblow and Kidson, 1976; Goldney, 1979), shown in Appendix A, can form a basis for comparing and discussing group members' judgments of depression, anxiety or suicidal intent of "clients" seen on video or observed in role-plays. Skills in understanding personal selfconcepts and life-themes, reflected in past patterns of action and statements individuals make about themselves, can be explored through case presentations or exercises such as that shown in Appendix B. Referral skills can be practiced through a role-played telephone conversation between a "referring agent" and an outside "counsellor" to whom a potentially suicidal student is being referred. Role-played telephone conversation can be more effective if chairs are back-to-back to avoid non verbal cues and the "client" is present to be fully involved in the referral process.

Fourth, attitudes and values relating to suicidal behavior should be explored and discussed, but in such a way as to avoid personal judgment of contrary viewpoints, and recognizing also that such discussion may expose personal vulnerabilities and elicit feelings of anxiety or defensiveness. Vignettes of real life situations may be used to facilitate discussion of values and attitudes. Exercises such as that in Appendix C may also be useful, if necessary adapted to suit the group and context.

Psychological inventories such as Diekstra and Kerkhof's (1988) Suicide Attitude Questionnaire may assist exploration of attitudes values but if used in a training context require a high level of trust within the group, time to discuss personal perspectives without pressure and a skilled group facilitator.

4. Tackling Public Policy Issues

This chapter began by advocating an ecological approach to suicide prevention. Work with professional and community groups beyond the mental health services, as outlined in preceding sections, is part of such an approach. Also part of an ecological view of suicide prevention is the need for community action to counter processes, conditions and social structures which foster self-destructive behavior. This may require initiating programs directed toward community education, changing of public attitudes, and the fostering of informed debate on matters of social and economic policy.

Since Durkheim the sociology of suicide has focussed on the causal significance of social conditions. The association between suicide rates and social disadvantage, levels of unemployment and such societal ills as substance abuse, suggests the preventive programs will be of limited effectiveness without attention also to community attitudes and social policy.

A policy issue of direct interest to suicidologists on both sides of the Atlantic has been that of controlling access to the means often used to commit suicide. Detoxification of gas in Europe and stricter gun control laws in the United States have been seen as reducing method-specific suicide rates. However, it appears likely that reduced availability of one method may possibly be associated with increased use of others (Lester and Murrell, 1982). Research on this issue is as yet unclear, and trends difficult to establish because of the many confounding factors. However, should further analysis indicate that stricter gun control laws are likely to reduce suicide rates, then this issue may need to be accorded higher priority on the agenda for social debate. While control of the methods of suicide and parasuicide appeals as a strategy to reduce suicide rates, many methods now used (such as vehicle exhaust gas, hanging, wrist cutting) are not open to control in the same way as was possible through the phasing out of domestic gas, or reduced prescribing of potentially lethal drugs. Thus it would appear unlikely that attempts through legislative means to control the methods used to commit suicide will affect rates in any substantial way.

Another approach at a public policy level has been to focus the attention of policy makers, and the public at large, on social determinants of mental illness and mental disorder. Policy makers commonly seek advice on mental health issues from experts within the State funded health sector, however given the low priority often accorded to mental health matters, such advice, if sought at all, may have little impact on social and economic policy. In New Zealand, The Mental Health Foundation, an independent trust with significant funds from a National telethon, has consistently pursued a policy of drawing public attention to determinants of mental illness and suicide (Abbott, 1982; Hornblow, 1985). Social and economic costs associated with increased rates of suicide and attempted suicide, rising unemployment and substance abuse, and reduced social support have become matters for Government and public debate, through extensive use of surveys, special reports, media releases, television programs, seminars and other activities. A range of strategies has been directed toward television and domestic violence.

Television production and programming guidelines may be cited as an example of one area where important public policy issues can be addressed. It may be argued that, in our media-dominated world, there is a need for the development and implementation of clearer guidelines to reduce adverse psychological effects of televised destructive or disturbed behavior. High levels of violence and dysfunctional family relationships may sell television programs, but may also undermine norms for caring, tolerance, and acceptable conduct, and social taboos against violent behavior including suicide. Sections within the television industry are likely to defend their right to screen economically profitable programs whether or not these may be considered to have potential for psychological damage to the vulnerable. Such defence may be on the grounds that the causes of psychological damage are complex or unproven, that individual or corporate rights are being infringed, or that the television industry will suffer economic loss and unemployment. Such arguments have been used by the tobacco industry for decades in order to maintain high profile promotion strategies and sales levels, and to counter the anti-smoking movement, and have only recently been challenged successfully in a number of countries. For those concerned to promote health, a major challenge is to establish the conditions under which the media may undermine or strengthen psychological or social well-being, and facilitate informed debate over the role of the media in creating psychologically and socially supportive environments. If such matters are to be put on the public agenda for debate, with a view to changing social attitudes and policy, a carefully prepared and coordinated approach is vital, with expertise drawn from a range of disciplines and sectors within society.

A range of activities directed toward changing public attitudes or policy are of course undertaken by mental health advocacy groups in many countries. Such advocacy is often controversial and its impact on social process and Government policy difficult to establish. Nevertheless, even the multifactorial causation of suicide, parasuicide and other forms of psychological disturbances, and the common substratum of social and environmental determinants of such conditions, coordinated effort involving a wide variety of community groups is required to mobilize public concern and facilitate policy change if preventive efforts are to succeed.

Summary

An array of causal factors, ranging from the intrapsychic to the societal, contribute to suicidal behavior. The approach to the prevention of suicide and parasuicide must be an ecological one, with preventive activity using a range of strategies and occurring at different levels. Such an approach must involve not only the health sector, but other professional groups, community organizations, and government and non-governmental agencies involved in the formulation and implementation of social policy.

Critical problems encountered at present by suicide prevention services are that those to whom their efforts are directed frequently do not seek help, and the efficacy of current preventive strategies is still being established. Access to care by those at risk of suicide may be facilitated by improving knowledge and acceptance of crisis services, and the assessment and referral skills of a range of professional groups, in particular the police, and teachers. To increase effectiveness, suicide prevention services have broadened and refined their activities in recent years, developing a range of procedures and programs more carefully targeted to client needs and circumstances. Fundamental to the increased effectiveness of crisis services is a strengthening of training programs. At a societal level, addressing the social and economic determinants of suicidal behavior requires coordinated activity directed toward changing of public attitudes and the fostering of informed debate on matters of social and economic policy.

REFERENCES

Abbott, M. (ed.), (1982). *Mental Health Foundation of New Zealand/NZ Psychological Society symposium on Unemployment: Papers and Reports.* Auckland, N.Z.: Mental Health Foundation.

Acheson, R.M. (1986). An ecological approach to preventive medicine. *Journal of The Royal Society Medicine,* 79, 636-638.

Araki, S. and Murata, K. (1986). Social life factors affecting suicide in Japanese men and women. *Suicide and Life Threatening Behavior,* 16 (4), 458-468.

Cesnik, B.I., Pierce, N., and Puls, M. (1977). Law enforcement and crisis intervention services: a critical relationship. *Suicide and Life Threatening Behaviour,* 7 (4), 211-215.

Cherskov, M. (1986). Hospitals join the battle to stop teen suicides. *Hospitals,* 60 (11), 98-100.

Danto, B.L. (1979). New frontiers in the relationship between suicidology and law enforcement. *Suicide and Life Threatening Behavior,* 9 (4), 195-204.

Davies, B., Burrows, G., and Poynton, C. (1975). A comparative study of four depression rating scales. *Australian and New Zealand Journal of Psychiatry,* 9(1), 21-24.

Dew, M.A., Bromet, E.J. and Brent, D. (1987). A quantitative literature review of the effectiveness of suicide prevention centers. *Journal of Consulting and Clinical Psychology,* 55(2), 239-244.

Diekstra, R.F.W. and Kerkhof, A.J.F.M. (1988). Attitudes toward suicide: development of a Suicide Attitude Questionnaire (SUIATT). In Möller, H. Schmidtke, A., Wells, R. (Eds) *Current Issues in Suicidology.* New York: Springer, 462-476.

Goldney, R.D. (1979). Assessment of suicidal intent by a visual analogue scale. *Australian and New Zealand Journal of Psychiatry,* 13, 153-155.

Hornblow, A.R. (1985). Preventive and promotional goals of community mental health services. *In Psychiatry-The State of the Art: Vol. 7; Epidemiology and Community Psychology.* Pichot, P., Berner, P., Wolf, R. and Thau, K. (eds.). New York: Plenum, 331-336.

Hornblow, A.R. (1986a). The evolution and effectiveness of telephone counselling services. *Hospital and Community Psychiatry,* 37(7), 731-3.

Hornblow, A.R. (1986b). Does telephone counselling have preventive value? *Australian and New Zealand Journal Of Psychiatry,* 20, 23-28.

Hornblow, A.R. and Kidson, M.A. (1976). The Visual Analogue Scale for Anxiety: A Validation Study. *Australian and New Zealand Journal of Psychiatry,* 10, 339-341.

Joyce, P.R., Oakley-Browne, M.A., Wells, J.E., Bushnell, J.A., Hornblow, A.R. Birth-cohort trends in major depression: increasing rates and earlier onset in New Zealand. *J. Affective Disorders,* in press.

Klerman, G.L. (1987). Clinical epidemiology of suicide. *Journal of Clinical Psychiatry,* 48, 12 (Suppl.), 33-38.

Klerman, G.L. (1988). The current age of youthful melancholia. *British Journal of Psychiatry,* 152, 4-14.

Last, J.M. (1987). *Public Health and Human Ecology,* East Norwalk (Conn.): Appleton and Lange.

Lester, D. and Murrell, M.E. (1982). The preventive effect of strict gun control laws on suicide and homicide. *Suicide and Life Threatening Behavior,* 12(3), 131-140.

Makela, K., Room, R., Single, E., Sulkunen, P., Walsh, B. (1981). *Alcohol, Society and the State. Vol 1: A Comparative Study of Alcohol Control.* Toronto: Addiction Research Foundation.

Motto, J.A. (1979). New approaches to crisis intervention. *Suicide and Life-Threatening Behavior,* 9(3), 173-184.

Ross, C.P. (1980). Mobilizing schools for suicide prevention. *Suicide and Life-Threatening Behavior,* 10(4), 239-243.

Shaffer, D., Garland, A., Fisher, P., Beacon, K., Vieland, V. (in press). Suicide crisis centers: a critical reappraisal with special reference to the prevention of youth suicide. In Goldston, F.E., Heinickie, C.M., Pynoos, R.S. and Yager, T. (Eds.), *Prevention of Mental Health Disturbance in Childhood.* New York: American Psychiatric Association.

Webb, N.B. (1986). Before and after suicide: a preventive outreach programme for colleges. *Suicide and Life Threatening Behavior,* 16(4), 469-480.

World Health Organization, Health and Welfare Canada, Canadian Public Health Association. (Nov. 1986). *Ottawa Charter for Health Promotion.* International Conference on Health Promotion, Ottawa, Canada.

Appendix A: *The visual analogue scale-depression*

Please put a cross on the line shown below to indicate *how the person felt* during the videotaped segment of the interviewer. A mark at the extreme *left* end would indicate that she/he was feeling *not at all depressed.*

A mark at the extreme *right* end would indicate that she/he was feeling the *most depressed* you could ever imagine. A mark near the center would indicate that she/he felt *moderately depressed.*

Please indicate on the line below her/his greatest depression during the interview.

Not at all depressed ------------------------------------ Very depressed

Appendix B: *Exploring selfconcepts and life themes*

In the course of development, through an ongoing process of self-observation, we build up some sort of picture of who we are as unique individuals. We achieve some awareness of our goals and motives, but discover also that these are often complex and unclear. We perceive consistency and change in our thoughts, feelings and behavior. We evaluate our attitudes and actions in terms of social standards and our own values.

The purpose of this exercise is to explore some of our own individual self concepts and life themes, by making important statements about ourselves and tracing these back over time.

On the back of this sheet you will see six boxes, and six lines to the right of the boxes. In each of the six boxes make one *important* statement about yourself as a person. Two of the statements should be about how you *relate to others*. Another two statements should be about yourself in *relation to work/achievement/success.* The remaining two statements should *not* be about the relating you, or the working you, but about the *solitary you*, the you that you are glad, or sad to be with when you are alone. You will gain more from the experience if your comments are self evaluative ("I believe I am a good teacher"), rather than simply factual ("I am a teacher"). Your comments do not have to be all positive—this is an exercise in self-understanding, not self-congratulation!

Once you have entered your six statements in their respective boxes turn your attention to the lines to the right of the boxes. These are time lines, or life lines, the left extreme of each line representing the point at which you were born and the right end the present point in time. On the line for each statement indicate:

a) the approximate point/period when you were first able to make that statement about yourself, and

b) any events, circumstances, or people which/who have had an influence on your making or remaking of that statement about yourself.

Figure 1:

Now
TIME LINES
Birth
SOME STATEMENTS ABOUT ME
ME AND OTHERS
ME AND WORK
ME AND MYSELF

Appendix C: *Destructiveness in relationships*

Violent and destructive behavior is a part of life. It may be directed towards others, or oneself, and be frighteningly obvious, as in war or suicide, or quietly corrosive, like rust, undermining confidence and coping skills. Sometimes such behavior is considered necessary, justified, and morally right, and sometimes unnecessary, unjustified, and wrong. At the bottom of the page is a list of events which vary in their destructiveness (destructiveness which may be actual or potential), and vary also in the justification for the action taken. Plot on the graph, if you can, each of the events on the list, according to what you see as the level of destructiveness of the event and the justification for it.

HIGHLY
DESTRUCTIVE

NOT AT ALL
DESTRUCTIVE

NOT AT ALL JUSTIFIED — HIGHLY JUSTIFIED

Events:
1. Sexual abuse of a child.
2. Smacking a child's hand near a hot element.
3. Drug overdose by a teenager after a minor family argument.
4. Letting an aggressive 10 year old boy watch violent TV programs.
5. Attempted suicide by an unemployed family man.
6. Suicide by an elderly person with cancer who lives alone.

How to Evaluate and Deal with Acute Suicide Risk

Guidelines for Health Care Workers

A. J. F. M. KERKHOF AND R. F. W. DIEKSTRA

1. Introduction

Purpose of this chapter is to provide different categories of health care workers in different settings with the core knowledge for detection, evaluation and treatment of acute suicide risk. This chapter is meant to be highly practical in nature. It provides guidelines, instruments and questions that can be used by trained mental health care workers as well as by general (primary) health care workers with no specific training in behavioral sciences or psychiatry. The chapter is based on the most widespread clinical wisdom that is considered to be helpful in the assessment of and interventions with persons having an elevated suicide risk, and on the most persistent findings in empirical research.

One of the guidelines for the authors is the need to provide practical recommendations also for health care workers who are working in countries where no tradition of suicide prevention programs exists. Since most of the work in this area has been done in European and North American countries, one necessarily has to draw heavily on experiences from these parts of the world. It might well be therefore that some of the recommendations may not be applicable to other parts of the world. Specific lines of questioning may be considered intrusive or unacceptable in certain countries, and therefore should be adapted in a culturally sensitive way in order to be compatible with the own national and cultural context.

This chapter is divided into three parts. In the first part a brief overview is presented of the most important risk factors that are known to be associated with elevated suicide risk. The second section is devoted to the assessment of suicide risk including the use of standardized risk scales. In the last part interventions with persons having an elevated suicide risk are summarized.

2. Risk Factors

Suicidal behavior always is determined by a multitude of factors. A psychiatric disorder may lead to suicidal feelings not only in itself, but also because it may cause the person to elicit negative reactions from his environment, which in turn increase his loneliness, which aggravates his symptoms and dependency on caregivers, etc. Emotional turmoil or crisis may or may not lead to suicidal behavior depending on many factors, like the availability of social relationships or other resources for support, the use of alcohol, impulsiveness, and some mere coincidental factors, or last-minute events, that may play a decisive role in the outburst of suicidal behavior. All this makes it clear that the occurrence of suicidal behavior in the last instance cannot be predicted with absolute certainty.

It is mostly not possible to single out one factor, or one event that exclusively caused a suicidal act. Following the death of a spouse, there are additional reasons why this particular person committed suicide, while so many others in comparable circumstances did not. Therefore it is important to look at several risk factors at the same time or in combination in order to calculate a rough estimation of the likelihood that a particular person will carry out suicidal behavior. Only then is it possible to identify a fairly high risk group, e.g. older male depressed alcoholics who recently suffered loss from a spouse or close relative (Murphy, 1986). It is even possible to quantify the risk for suicidal behavior in this group by stating that approximately one out of every five will carry out suicidal behavior under these conditions. But we cannot predict which one out of these five depressed alcoholics will eventually commit suicide. This is too heavily dependent on coincidental factors, such as the availability of a recent suicidal model.

In the following section the most important risk factors for suicidal behavior are briefly reviewed. In table 1 an overview of important risk factors is presented, together with rough estimates of suicide risk for persons influenced by these factors, whether working alone as isolated factors or in combination with other risk factors.

Table 1: Risk of a person attempting or committing suicide this year, related to risk factors working either as a single factor or in combination with other risk factors.

Risk factors	Working alone as a single risk factor	Together with several other risk factors
PSYCHOLOGICAL CONDITIONS		
1. depression	elevated	high
2. alcohol/drug dependence	elevated	high
3. other psychiatric disorder	low	elevated
4. effects of traumatic life events	low	elevated
PHYSICAL CONDITIONS		
5. physical disease	low	elevated
6. age and sex (male over 50 years)	low	elevated
BEHAVIORAL CONDITIONS		
7. marital status (without partner)	low	elevated
8. social isolation	low	elevated
9. deviance	low	elevated
10. suicidal ideation and preparation	low	high
11. suicidal communication	elevated	high
12. previous parasuicide	elevated	high
CIRCUMSTANCES		
13. recent loss	low	high
14. loss of status and finances	low	elevated
15. suicidal model	low	elevated

low risk = less than 1 out of 1,000
elevated = more than 1 out of 1,000
high risk = more than 1 out of 100

This table might be helpful in conducting a thorough personal anamnestic interview. It should not however substitute such an interview. This table should be used together with other assessment procedures and suicide risk scales. No statistical prediction can be used on this display of risk factors, nor can this table alone justify any interventions. It is only meant as a means for further exploration.

1. Depression

Eventually some 15 % of severely depressed patients (major affective, bipolar disorder) will commit suicide (Sainsbury, 1986). Most persons who attempted or completed suicide were depressed shortly before their act, although not necessarily in a severe form. Important facets of the suicide risk in depressives must be attributed to feelings of inferiority and hopelessness that take away any positive outlook on the future (Beck et al, 1989). Sometimes depressed patients carry out suicidal behavior when they are recovering from their depression. When assessing depressed persons it is important to inquire after possible self destructive tendencies or habits in depressed states.

2. Alcohol and drug dependence

Some 20 to 25 % of all suicides are alcohol dependent. Eventually some 15% or more of all alcoholics will commit suicide (Roy, 1985). As such it is one of the easiest recognizable risk factors for suicide. It concerns mainly men (five out of six completed alcoholic suicides) who usually had a long history of drinking, often for over 10 years or more. Especially interpersonal loss, such as a divorce, can trigger impulsive and aggressive suicidal behavior in alcoholics. Nearly all alcoholics who commit suicide have been drinking shortly before the act (Murphy, 1986).

What is valid for alcohol dependence also holds for other substance abuse. Although not documented as thoroughly as is the case with alcohol dependence, substance abuse is considered a serious risk for developing suicidal tendencies and eventual suicidal behavior (Roy, 1985). It concerns the misuse of hard drugs like heroine, cocaine, opiates, and other mind changing substances, the misuse of medicines like barbiturates and sedatives/ analgetics, and the sniffing of glue and other chemicals to alter states of consciousness.

Some deaths through overdose are in fact suicides. Those who are addicted to more than one substance are at highest risk. The left-alone children in the mega-cities who smoke crack, sniff glue or engage in other addictive activities, not only risk serious brain damage but also may have an increased risk for developing suicidal careers.

3. Other psychiatric disorders

A considerable percentage of all suicides is carried out by persons admitted to a psychiatric hospital (in some countries more than 10 %), or having a definite psychiatric disorder while not being admitted. As mentioned before, severely depressed patients (major depression, bipolar disorder) have a high risk of suicidal behavior, especially when they consider themselves to be untreatable. Those that seem to be resistant to therapy are at high risk. Patients suffering from psychosis may be suicidal especially when having delusions, hallucinations and/or hearing voices which order them to commit suicide. Also persons with severe ideas of persecution may be at risk. Patients with the diagnosis of schizophrenia have a suicide mortality ratio of at least 5 %, may be even 10 % (Miles, 1977; Roy, 1986). Patients with borderline and anti-social personality disorders are known to have an elevated risk for suicidal behavior. Psychiatric (in)patients may be vulnerable to changes in living conditions, as is a changing of ward or pavilion. Note that it may not be the psychiatric disturbance as such that predisposes to suicidal behavior. Sometimes the consequences of a psychiatric disorder may be suicidogeneous, e.g. in not having any family ties, not being able to share feelings with confidants, and sometimes substandard living conditions.

4. Traumatic life events

It is becoming increasingly clear that many suicidal persons have suffered traumatic life events. Many female suicide attempters, especially those that repeat over and over again, have been the victim of sexual abuse or incest in their childhood (Van Egmond and Jonker, 1988). As a result they suffer from basic mistrust in human relations, have difficulties finding a life companion, have serious and longlasting sexual problems and suffer intense feelings of inferiority and inadequacy. Also some women who attempt suicide have been seriously beaten by their husbands shortly before their attempt. And in some cases the battering continues even after the attempt. Rape and assault not seldomly have been observed in suicide attempters' histories. This also holds for men, although such cases are seldomly reported. Prisoners may be victim of (homosexual) rape. It is only recently that science has acknowledged the long lasting and devastating effects of sexual abuse.

All kinds of traumatic events, such as war, forced migration, torture, being a refugee, or being a victim of other natural or man made disasters, can have disruptive effects over prolonged periods of time. Traumatic effects may follow the loss of a child, stillbirth or abortion. Serious car accidents may lead to long lasting emotional problems. Most people one way or the other succeed in coping with traumatic life events. Some do not and become suicidal, probably because of the accumulation of still other risk factors.

5. Physical disease

Suicide can be the result of an extremely painful and/or completely invalidating physical disease, which penetrates all aspects of life unendingly and which is felt to be intolerable and unbearable. Such an impairment of life can make people want to stop living. Especially when there are no relatives to comfort or alleviate the suffering, suicidal tendencies may be expected. In some diseases suicidal tendencies can be expected, as in the case of multiple sclerosis, Huntington's disease, HIV-disease (AIDS), and sometimes in cancer. The prevalence of physical illness in suicides is at least 25% and in at least 10% it appears to be an important contributing cause (Whitlock, 1986). Being informed of a highly threatening diagnosis such as cancer or HIV-infection or AIDS, may trigger suicidal behavior (Kerkhof, 1991). Vital exhaustion, whether or not concomitant to depression, may also elicit suicidal feelings.

6. Age and sex

In the European countries and in the United States men commit suicide more often than women (about 1.5 to 2 times as many). Suicide figures in these countries are higher for older age groups. Suicide is most prominent in old age where irreversible impairment and social isolation prevail. Suicide attempts (or parasuicides) are more carried out by women (about 1.5 to 2 times as often) than by men. Most attempters are relatively young. More than half are under 35 years of age. Many suicide attempters are living with parents or with a partner, indicating that in many cases interpersonal motives are predominant. Persons attempting and persons completing suicide in the U.S. and in European countries are considered to be two different populations, which only partially overlap. Repetition can shift a person from the population of suicide attempters to the population of suicides, this being more likely for those suicide attempters that look like suicides in many aspects (e.g. in sex, age, treatment history, etc.).

7. Marital status

In the so called western world, persons without a partner (divorced, separated, widowed and never married) have a higher risk for committing suicide than those with a life companion, especially the recently divorced and widowed.

In other parts of the world, notably in India and China, the socio-demographic picture is somewhat different. In India many suicides are found among young females. The explanation for this must be found in the system of arranged marriages, problems with dowry and difficulties with the family-in-law. Young married women often have difficulties with mothers-in-law on matters of independence, authority, and prescribed behavior. They are frequently held responsible for quarrels about finances with the bride's parents (Venkoba Rao, 1975; Kerkhof and Nathawat, 1989). In China too, it is reported that many young women commit suicide, especially in rural areas. More than half of these suicides are believed to be caused by family disputes and marital problems. Young women seem to be inflicted by strict rules of conduct within family life, stemming from time honoured traditions, and at the same time suffering from transitions to more modern life in the big cities, where lengthy separations from the extended family can be imposed.

8. Social isolation

Suicidal ideation may flourish when persons are socially isolated. This may be the case after the death of a spouse, or after a divorce. But also this may be the case for people who never got married, or people who have difficulties in making contact with others. Social withdrawal is commonly observed shortly before suicidal behavior. A diversity of circumstances may lead to or reflect isolation and feelings of loneliness and despair. Note that most isolated people will never commit suicide. Only when this isolation leads to disintegration of the personality, as e.g. is the case with depressed people, this may be a decisive contributing factor.

9. Deviance

Social isolation and feelings of inferiority can be influenced by objective or subjective deviancy. All characteristics which set somebody apart from his environment, or which elicit discrimination, can contribute to suicidal ideation. Homosexuality is such a factor. It may hinder adolescents in being accepted by peers and in developing self identity, this being also heavily dependent on the cultural context. Religion, ethnic background, political conviction, physical abnormalities and social class, among others, can lead to a mismatch of the person with his environment. Even without any visible mismatch, a person can feel misplaced and abnormal in his environment. This can be observed among children who are neglected by their parents or who are regularly beaten up or sexually abused. Delinquency generally estranges a person from society, his environment and eventually from his close relatives. Suicidal behavior is quite common in jails and prisons, generally in the beginning of incarceration. Even in jails and prisons some people are more deviating than others. Foreigners and those sentenced to long terms of imprisonment may be at high risk for suicidal behavior (Kerkhof and Bernasco, 1990).

10. Suicidal ideation and preparation

Most persons with high suicide risk are observed to suffer from a narrowing of their mental functioning towards the end of their suicidal development, the so called "tunnel vision". The person is captured in a downward spiral of self defeating thoughts and obsessive images, totally concentrated on the only outcome that is considered possible: suicide (Ringel, 1953).

The person is clearly regressed in his thinking, cannot correct himself anymore, and comes into a state of confusion. He cannot concentrate anymore on arguments or thoughts about consequences of his behavior on relatives. The person may erroneously come to the conviction that his existence only is a burden to others and that suicide would mean a great relief for his relatives. The most concrete risk factor for suicide, this narrowing of mind, however is not easily observed on the outside. In order to assess this risk factor, health care workers should probe some questions specifically focussed on this suicidal preoccupation.

11. Suicidal communication

Many persons prior to their suicidal behavior send some direct or indirect signals to their environment, communicating their state of despair. Unfortunately, these signals are not always understood. People may say things as "I wish I was dead", or "I don't care having an accident now" or "I will not longer be a burden to you". Sometimes there is a strong suicidal tendency hidden in such a statement, which, ambivalently, is not always conveyed very clearly. Others very explicitly say to their relatives and health care professionals that they are going to commit suicide. Even then many times they are not believed. Yet, those talking about suicide or threatening to commit suicide are at high risk. The popular notion that people who talk about suicide or threaten to do so will not commit suicide, is not true.

12. Previous suicide attempts and self destructive behavior

More than half of all persons attempting or completing suicide have made one or more previous non-fatal attempts. Follow up studies of cohorts of suicide attempters show that up to 40 % will repeat their attempt. Within the first two months after a previous attempt the risk of repetition is about 15 to 20 % (WHO, 1982; Kerkhof, 1985), but risk for repetition is far greater for repeaters than for first-evers. Many suicidal persons have carried out self destructive behaviors in the past, which may not always have been noticed as such. Disfigured parts of the body because of cuts with glass or razor blades may be early signals of a suicidal development.

13. Recent loss

A major loss, such as the death of a spouse or the death of somebody else who is very near and dear, or the loss of a spouse because of a divorce, can trigger depressive feelings including suicidal tendencies. In the process of normal as well as in the process of complicated bereavement, suicidal preoccupation can occur as part of the transition of values and the reflection on the meaning of life which has to be redirected to new circumstances. When the person's live is seriously impaired by this loss so that social isolation results, suicidal risk can be quite serious. Also the loss of other highly valued conditions or capacities (work, status, intellectual functioning) can elicit suicidal feelings.

14. Loss of status and financial loss

Loss of work or retirement sometimes lead to social disruption as a consequence of a breakdown of social roles in which the person had invested an important part of his identity. Financial bankruptcy may have deleterious impact on the self esteem. Joblessness may strengthen feelings of hopelessness already existent. Note that the effects of loss of work and status may be greater for those without a close supportive network.

15. Suicidal model in family or in direct environment

Having had a father or mother or other close relative who committed suicide may brand somebody as a person who runs a risk of doing the same. Excessive fear for this possibility can function like a self fulfilling prophecy. In some families in which there runs a hereditary disease, as in the case of Huntington's disease, a series of family members may have committed suicide. Note that suicidal behavior cannot be transferred through hereditary mechanisms. What can be transferred are some forms of depression, schizofrenia and physical hereditary diseases. The transfer of suicidal behavior can only be accomplished through modelling or vicarious learning. The imitation effect of news and fictional stories about suicide in journals and television emissions is demonstrated (Schmidtke and Häffner, 1988). Clustering of suicide attempts and suicides in groups of interconnected people (schools, friends, families) is often reported. In most cases the mere presence of a suicidal model cannot be considered a serious risk factor for suicidal behavior. In combination with other risk factors, however, it can become important.

3. Assessment of Suicide Risk

Suicide risk is not always obvious. Only seldom does a client present himself as a suicidal patient. Sometimes a client is brought into the health care worker's office by relatives who feel worried about depressive symptoms or behavior that they consider peculiar, or who feel threatened by suicidal communication. Most often however clients do not explicitly convey their suicidal ideation. It therefore becomes crucial in what way the health care worker can elicit from the patient or explore with the patient whether he indeed entertains suicidal thoughts and help to express them or make them clear in the consultation.

In trying to do so, the health care worker should be aware that patients do not always spontaneously provide the answers that are needed for a thorough evaluation. In many cases reluctance or shame to express thoughts and feelings is manifest, perhaps motivated by the wish not to appear weak or silly. Sometimes patients do not want to bother others with this kind of "moaning". It may be that people do not dare convey thoughts on suicide because of an anticipation of punishment or out of fear of being put away in a mental institution.

It is therefore important that the health care worker behaves diplomatically and refrains from any normative or judgmental statement about having death wishes or suicidal ideation. The health care worker should take his time to gently and tactfully, but determinedly, ask the necessary questions to obtain the information needed. From the way he puts his questions the patient can infer the attitudes of the health care worker. A restrictive or condemning attitude towards suicide on the part of the health care worker will undoubtedly be noticed by the patient. This may lead to further reticence. The most important information can usually only be obtained by questioning. The health care worker should not be satisfied with vague answers, but determinedly repeat his questions over and over again in order to ensure that the patient is explicit in stating e.g. yes or no having made one or more previous suicide attempts, yes or no at this moment having recurring fantasies of throwing himself in front of a train, etc. It is stressed here that a tactful and determined line of questioning will help the patient to come out of his mental isolation. In many cases the health care worker will be the only one to whom a suicidal patient can express himself. When a patient is suicidal, his thoughts are constantly dwindling around death and dying and related topics. A genuine interest in this mental preoccupation in many cases will be gladly welcomed by the patient.

The health care worker cannot be apprehensive in each and every case that comes to his attention. He or she has to be selective on the basis of the aforementioned risk factors. Whenever one or more risk factors are present the health care worker may become suspicious of suicidal ideation, however ambiguous this might be. Whenever the symptoms of depression are present, the health care worker should investigate death wishes. This also holds for alcohol and substance abuse. This alertness for suicide risk could be guided by some systematic procedures for the evaluation of potential suicide risk, such as suicide prediction scales, assessment procedures for depression and hopelessness, scales for the evaluation of suicidal ideation and for the suicide intent of persons who recently attempted suicide. These systematic procedures are discussed briefly below.

A. The use of suicide risk scales

Suicide risk scales are lists of variables that usually cover the area of the aforementioned risk factors. Individual risk scores are obtained by weighing and totalling the scores on all items. These scales are supposed to provide an evaluation within a few minutes based on a limited number of questions. As such they can give an indication which needs further elaboration in the personal interview. In an overview of suicide risk scales Burk et al. (1985) concluded that most well-constructed scales are capable of identifying persons with a high probability of future suicide, although some false positive predictions are inevitable.

The following classes of suicide risk scales can be used: risk scales for suicide attempters (e.g., Buglass and Horton, 1974; Van de Loo and Diekstra, 1970; Pallis et al. 1982, 1984), risk scales for patients in a depressed or suicidal state (e.g., Motto and Heilbron, 1976), risk scales for unselected psychiatric patients (e.g., Farberow and MacKinnon, 1974), and risk scales for clients of a suicide prevention center (e.g., Lettieri, 1974). Prediction scales however, are meant to be applied with cases where suicide potential already has been suspected or where suicide risk is known in the group of patients where this particular patient comes from. In order to administer or apply such scales therefore, there needs to be a global assessment that enables the health care worker to decide whether this particular patient fits one of the known high risk groups, or has a chance of becoming a high risk person in the near future. In appendix A and B two risk scales that are widely used for estimating subsequent suicidal behavior in suicide attempters are presented (Pallis et al. 1982, Van de Loo and Diekstra, 1970). The risk of repetition is higher for those who attempted suicide with a strong suicide intent (Beck et al., 1974ab, see appendix C) and a high risk-rescue-rating (Weissman and Worden, 1972).

B. The assessment of depression and hopelessness

In order to accurately evaluate the potential suicide risk, the health care worker should be able to diagnose depression and to assess the severity of this condition. It is recommended to use DSM-III-R diagnostic criteria (American Psychiatric Association, 1987). A summary of criteria for Bipolar and Depressive disorders is given in Appendix D. If a definite depressive or manic episode is diagnosed, a further investigation of the suicidal potential is always needed.

If the health care worker is not, or does not feel qualified to make the diagnosis of depression, the use of Beck's Depression Inventory (BDI, Beck et al. 1961) can contribute to the assessment of the severity of the depression and to an evaluation of suicide risk. One of the items of the BDI explicitly asks for suicidal ideation. This 21 item scale can be given to the patient to fill in, or can be administered orally by the health care worker. Usually within 10 to 15 minutes a total score can be obtained, which gives an estimation of the severity of the depression. Note that this BDI score does not replace a psychiatric diagnosis. It only serves as a quick tool that helps the health care worker in his assessment procedure. Other depression self- or observer rating scales can be used as well, such as the Self-rating Depression Scale (SDS, Zung, 1965), the Hamilton Rating Scale for Depression (HRS, Hamilton, 1967) and the Montgomery-Åsberg Depression Rating Scale (MADRS, Montgommery and Åsberg, 1979) which are used in many places. The BDI however has the advantage that it facilitates the communication of depressed thoughts and suicidal ideation in the interview.

One of the most relevant aspects of depression is the so called hopelessness, or pessimism about the possibilities to overcome this depression and the problems that caused it. According to Beck, hopelessness is a chore characteristic of depression and serves as the link between depression and suicide. A series of studies investigating the relationships between hopelessness, depression and suicidal behavior supported the importance of this construct and the use of the Beck Hopelessness Scale (BHS) as a useful tool in the assessment of suicide risk a.o. in hospitalized depressed patients (Beck et al. 1985; 1989).

4. The Assessment of Suicidal Ideation

Whenever someone says he is going to commit suicide or whenever he threatens to commit suicide, or whenever other people or the health care worker feel worried or threatened by a suicidal communication, the person involved should be considered at high risk. All suicidal communication should be taken seriously. Even in case someone repeatedly threatens to commit suicide, may be over a period of many years, these threats should not be discarded, but treated as desperate cries for help. Many people who committed suicide have vainly tried over and over again to attract attention this way. There is mostly an appeal to others in these repeated communications, a cry for help. The health care worker should not be mislead by these motives alone, because next to this there are also more death-oriented motives. It is the delicate balance of death orientations and orientations towards others/life that should be the focus of attention. Both orientations ambiguously exist at the same time. The orientation towards others/life disappears only at the latest moment, when there is the aforementioned narrowing of mind, or tunnel vision.

The health care worker can evaluate the acuteness of the suicide risk by asking the person questions like:

- How often do you think about killing yourself ?
- Did you make preparations or plans how to kill yourself ?
- How urgently is it that you end your life ?
- Can you go on for another day or must you stop immediately ?
- How many pills do you have, what kinds of pills ?
- Do you have a gun at your place or hidden elsewhere ?
- Do you hear voices ordering you to end your life ?
- Did you write farewell letters ?
- Did you make up your last will ?
- Did you say goodbye to certain persons ? Who are they ?
- Did you give away some of your belongings ?
- What is the main reason you want to end your life ?
- Did you ever before take too many pills or harm yourself ?
- Have you been drinking the last four hours ?
- Did you get some sleep last night and the night before ?

Questions like these are the best way of obtaining the relevant information needed for a thorough evaluation. It is not true that this line of questioning will elicit suicidal behavior. These questions are meant to monitor the way of thinking of the patient. The health care worker will notice that these questions may promote communication with the patient. A seriously suicidal patient cannot discuss many other things anyway.

The answers to these questions will enable the evaluation of suicide risk. When the patient says he is in a big hurry, that he cannot stand another five minutes of living, that he has definite plans, made a last will, said goodbye to certain people, that he has pills which turn out to be potentially dangerous and has these in sufficient quantity, or that he has studied the time table of the trains running through his city, and that he decided which train to jump in front of etc., then this person has an acute risk of committing suicide. When however the person has not yet gathered pills or has not yet decided on a specific method, and has not chosen a specific time or a time limit before which he has to end his life, etc., then the acuteness of the suicide risk is somewhat less.

In his estimation of the suicidal ideation of a patient the health care worker can use the Scale for Suicide Ideation (SSI, Beck et al. 1979) designed to quantify the intensity of current conscious suicidal intent by scaling various dimensions of self-destructive thoughts or wishes. The SSI is completed by the health care worker based on the patient's answers in a semi-structured interview (See appendix E). If the person seems to be confused, with some delusional thinking, or when the patient cannot communicate with the health care worker to a minimal extent, the risk of suicide can be quite considerable. The health care worker should look for signs of the suicidal narrowing of mind in which the person can only concentrate on one outcome, namely suicide, and is not able anymore to concentrate on relatives or on solutions other than suicide. Characteristic is the inability to listen to arguments, so the health care worker should not expect too much understanding for counterarguments.

Suicide risk may be more present because of heavy drinking in the last few hours (and the days before), because of the use of hard drugs or a mix of medicines, because of sleeplessness during the last few nights, or because of anxiety attacks. The health care worker should carefully monitor the present psychological state and look for signs of emotional crisis. The level of depression of the last few days should be carefully assessed. Nonverbal cues, like avoidance of eye contact and signs of self negligence, may help to complete the clinical picture. The suicide risk is more acute when there are more suicide risk factors in the past or in the present. The health care worker should vigorously strive to obtain the information on any of the aforementioned risk factors, perhaps by gathering this through relatives or friends. So if this information learns that the person has attempted suicide many times before, that he recently made many statements of killing himself, that he is considered an alcoholic and that his wife recently left him, then there is no doubt this person has a high risk of committing suicide. If this information learns that this person has been admitted several times to a psychiatric hospital, that he has recurrent manic episodes, has been treated many times without success, and recently has been moved to another ward, then too there may be a serious suicide risk. When the patient is still open to communication with others, is listening fairly reasonably, is responding with eye contact, etc., the suicide risk is somewhat less, but it can become worse in the next few days if no help is provided. The evaluation of suicide risk is never completed without a thorough inquiry into the reasons someone has to commit suicide. In fact these reasons and circumstances are far more important to be discussed than all topics concerning the suicide risk. For it is only in coping with these reasons that any change in suicidal intentions can be expected. Furthermore when the topic of the conversation is limited to the suicide risk only, this part of the problem is emphasized too much. In the ideal case, the health care worker, after having assessed thoroughly the acuteness of the suicide risk, diplomatically changes the accent of the conversation into the problems and circumstances which led to the suicide risk.

5. How to Deal with Acute Suicide Risk

The risk of suicide is of course most acute when someone has ingested pills or otherwise made a suicide attempt and has not yet deceased. Immediate medical, life saving action is called for, whenever the patient is unconscious or drowsy. But also when the patient has ingested unknown quantities of medicines or whenever it is unknown what kind of pills the patient has taken, medical surveillance is recommended. Some seemingly unharmful pills like aspirin or paracetamol may have deleterious effects.

In between the moment when the intoxicated or injured person is found and the moment the person arrives at the hospital, a number of life saving activities can take place: remove ropes or objects which the person used to strangle himself, provide for oxygen, stop arterial bleeding, and so forth. As quick as possible find a doctor, get an ambulance, or bring the person to a hospital. Try to remove medicines by having the person vomit, but don't do this whenever the person is unconscious, or when he ingested acid or strychnine. In order to facilitate medical treatment, try to find as much information as possible about the brand of medicines, the quantities ingested, try to find wrappings, medicine instructions, etc. See that this information is transferred to the physician who is treating the patient in the hospital.

When confronted with acute suicidal risk where no pills have been taken yet, or where no other acts are initiated yet, the health care worker may wish to reduce this risk by utilizing one or more of the following strategies:

a. offering close personal contact, communication and understanding;
b. removal of pills, guns, ropes and other means that might be used;
c. influencing the psychological state of the person in crisis;
d. influencing the reasons why this person wants to commit suicide;
e. influencing relationships with relatives and others;
f. admission to a psychiatric hospital, involuntary if necessary.

A. Offering personal contact

The most powerful preventive strategy for acute suicide risk is to offer a close personal contact with an understanding and caring person who is willing to stay and to be available to share the emotional turmoil and despair. Someone who is able to promise not to leave the suicidal person alone, for as long as the crisis lasts. The first principle for this kind of crisis intervention is never to leave the person alone. The health care worker doesn't need to exert this close personal supervision himself. There may be family members, partners, friends, or neighbors who could be instructed to stay in the presence of the person concerned, that means to eat, sleep, walk, etc., with this person without losing eye-contact. May be there are others that could be asked to do this close supervision, like volunteers from church-organizations, from a local Samaritan branch, from a crisis center or S.O.S. line, etc., according to local circumstances. The person concerned could be asked to stay at one of his family members' residence, or at a friend's place. The health care worker should prevent the suicidal person to go back home when there is no one there to exert some kind of personal guidance. The health care worker should arrange things in such a way that he, or another professional, is always accessible, preferably by telephone, in order to give advice to the persons involved. In some cases this might mean a 24 hours around the clock accessibility. In doing so the health care worker can establish a personal relationship with the suicidal person. This personal relationship might be the ultimate life saving condition for some suicidal persons.

B. Removal of means

A second strategy concerns the removal of potentially deadly means to kill oneself. The health care worker could try to ask the suicidal person to hand over pills that may have been collected, a gun that is hidden, a piece of rope that may have been prepared, etc. All strategies directed towards the prevention of the act to be carried out, can be considered. Removal of alcoholic beverages may be very effective because many people take alcohol prior to suicidal behavior in order to loosen impulse control. This removal strategy could best be discussed openly with the suicidal person. The health care worker can explain to the person concerned that it is important to hand over these means so that he can keep them temporarily until the crisis is over. This protects against impulsive acting which might be regretted by the person himself when he or she could have had the time to think it over. Try to convince the person not to make final decisions in this state of crisis.

C. Influencing psychological state

A third strategy can be directed to the changing of the psychological condition of the suicidal person. A powerful strategy is to have the suicidal person express all of his feelings. The expression of emotions is in itself a way to make contact with others, or to break through an emotional state of isolation. Particularly the expression of rage, anger, aggression and feelings of resentment and revenge might help the person to feel better, especially when there is someone who can understand these feelings. The expression of feelings of inferiority and remorse may facilitate communication of the reasons for wanting to die. The feeling of sadness becomes less hopeless when expressed towards others.

Important aspects of the psychological condition that need to be covered are feelings of tension, fatigue and anxiety, that may result from weeks and months of emotional crisis. It might be advisable to use medication when a suicidal person did not sleep for a prolonged period of time. The dose however should be scheduled on a day to day basis. In some cases benzodiazepines might be given to relax the patient somewhat, but here too close supervision and day to day doses are necessary. Medication however should not be used as a substitute for crisis intervention, it can only be part of a more comprehensive strategy.

D. Influencing reasons for wanting to die

Expression of feelings facilitates the fourth aspect of a suicide intervention strategy, the discussion of reasons why this person wants to end his life. A genuinely expressed interest on the part of the health care worker into the suicidal person's problem history promotes a mutual understanding of the dynamics of the death wish. Included here are feelings of ambivalence, of hope, and of helplessness. A thorough investigation of all problem-solving strategies tried in vain by the suicidal person is important here. This might lead to the identification of problem solving strategies that may not have been tried yet by the suicidal person, or to maladaptive coping strategies that might be amenable to treatment, or such an investigation might lead to the identification of basic values and norms that might have been threatened and that play an important role in the suicidal dynamics.

A fundamental constant factor in these psychodynamics is the theme of ambivalence. Suicidal persons are known to suffer from approach- avoidance conflicts, or better stated, the wish to die and the wish to live that go together at the same time. This means that suicidal persons do show an openness to suggestions even when they think they have finally decided to kill themselves. The health care worker therefore has the opportunity to challenge the suicidal person's reasoning and decisions. In the decision to end his life the feelings of depression and hopelessness play an important role. The health care worker could use his knowledge of depression to try to convince the suicidal person that his depression will probably get better in due time, that this condition is treatable and that he should try another treatment before making definite decisions.

E. Influencing relationships

One of the reasons why people become suicidal is to be found in social isolation due to disturbed relationships with partners, friends or family members, or the lack of relationships with significant others. A fifth facet of reducing the acute suicide risk is to involve the next of kin, or the most near and dear to the person, in the crisis intervention process. If the person in question allows so, the health care worker could ask parents, partners or others to come over and to help the suicidal patient to come through this crisis. Discussing the reasons for the death wish with the next of kin might promote mutual understanding and open up some outlooks for the future.

When however the suicidal person has no relationships at all, the task of the health care worker becomes much more difficult. It is important to investigate in that case why this person has no friends or relatives. That might promote understanding of his death wish.

F. Admission to a psychiatric hospital

A final strategy in reducing acute suicide risk is to have the person admitted to a psychiatric hospital in order to be guarded against himself. This strategy is likely to be followed whenever there is evidence that the person is clearly confused in his thinking, is having delusions or other psychotic manifestations, especially when the person is hearing voices ordering him to commit suicide. In these cases the possibilities to have suicidal persons taken into intramural care are definitely life saving. Whenever there is no psychiatric hospital or crisiscenter in the vicinity, it might be wise to limit the movement for this person temporarily, but the person should never be left alone. To lock a suicidal patient up in a room without company might turn out to be very counterproductive. Even in these cases the presence of another human who cares and tries to understand is much more powerful as a prevention tool than is isolated confinement. It has to be emphasized here that in many cases there is no need for a psychiatric hospital admission. The first five strategies mentioned above will be sufficiently effective to refrain from this last possibility. At the other hand there is no need for too strict a reluctance to have people admitted to a psychiatric hospital. In some cases it is the only suitable strategy.

Conclusion

Acute suicide risk can be reduced, according to experienced health care workers. Scientific evidence for this statement however, is difficult to obtain. There is no experiment that could prove the effectiveness of preventive strategies beyond any doubt. Clinical wisdom that accumulated over the years converged into some recommendations that are briefly summarized in this chapter. One attitudinal factor that could enhance the health care worker's skills to deal with acute suicide risk is the conception of suicide as a rational behavior that people may choose when their living conditions are sufficiently unbearable. It might help to ask suicidal persons to dispute whether there is really no other way of solving this unbearability of life. In such a dispute, it might turn out that the suicidal person has considered all facets and made a rather comprehensive overview of his living conditions and the options for improvement. More often however, such a discussion reflects despair and ambivalence. The more a health care worker is willing to view suicide as a normal topic of discussion, the more opportunities he creates for the expression of ambivalence, which in turn might facilitate further help seeking behavior.

REFERENCES

American Psychiatric Association (1987). *Diagnostic and Statistical Manual of Mental Disorders, Third Edition, Revised.* Washington, DC, American Psychiatric Association.

Beck, A.T., Brown, G., & Steer, R.A. (1989). Prediction of Eventual Suicide in Psychiatric Inpatients by Clinical Ratings of Hopelessness. *Journal of Consulting and Clinical Psychology, 57,* 309-310.

Beck, A.T., Kovacs, M., & Weissman, A.(1979). Assessment of Suicidal Intention: The Scale for Suicide Ideation. *Journal of Consulting and Clinical Psychology, 47,* 343-352.

Beck, R.W., Morris, J.B., & Beck, A.T. (1974a). Crossvalidation of the Suicidal Intent Scale. *Psychological Reports, 34,* 445-446.

Beck, A.T., Schuyler, D., & Herman, I.H. (1974b). Development of Suicidal Intent Scales. In: A.T. Beck, H.L.P. Resnik, & D.J. Lettieri (Eds.). *The Prediction of Suicide.* Bowie, Maryland, The Charles Press.

Beck, A.T., Steer, R.A., Kovacs, M., & Garrison, B. (1985). Hopelessness and Eventual Suicide: A 10-Year Prospective Study of Patients Hospitalized With Suicidal Ideation. *American Journal of Psychiatry, 142,* 559-563.

Beck, A.T., Steer, R.A., & Ranieri, W.F. (1988). Scale for Suicide Ideation: Psychometric Properties of a Self-Report Version. *Journal of Clinical Psychology, 44,* 499-505.

Beck, A.T., Ward, C.H., Mendelson, M., Mock, J.E., & Erbaugh, J. (1961). An Inventory for Measuring Depression. *Archives of General Psychiatry 4,* 561-571.

Beck, A.T., Weissman, A., Lester, D., & Trexler, L. (1974c). The Measurement of pessimism: The Hopelessness Scale. *Journal of Consulting and Clinical Psychology, 42,* 861-865.

Buglass, D., & Horton, J. (1974). A Scale for predicting subsequent suicidal behavior. *British Journal of Psychiatry, 124,* 573-578.

Burk, F., Kurz, A., & Möller, H.J. (1985). Suicide Risk Scales: Do They Help to Predict Suicidal Behavior? *European Archives of Psychiatry and Neurological Sciences, 235,* 153-157.

Egmond, M. van, & Diekstra, R.F.W. (1989). The Predictability of Suicidal Behavior: The Results of a Meta-analysis of Published Studies. In: R.F.W. Diekstra, R. Maris, S. Platt, A. Schmidtke, & G. Sonneck (Eds) *Suicide and its prevention.* Leiden, Brill (pp 37-61).

Egmond, M. van, & Jonker, D. (1988). Seksueel misbruik en lichamelijke mishandeling: risicofactoren voor (recidiverend) suicidaal gedrag bij vrouwen? *Tijdschrift voor Psychiatrie, 30,* 21-38.

Farberow, N.L., & MacKinnon, D. (1974). A Suicide Prediction Schedule for Neuropsychiatric Hospital Patients. *Journal of Nervous and Mental Disease, 158,* 408-419.

Hamilton, M. (1967). Development of a rating scale for primary depressive illness. *Brit. Journ. of Social and Clinical Psychology, 6,* 278-296.

Kerkhof, A.J.F.M. (1985). *Suicide en de Geestelijke Gezondheidszorg.* Amsterdam, Swets & Zeitlinger.

Kerkhof, A.J.F.M. (1991). *Suicidal Behavior Among People With HIV And Aids.* (Report on a WHO consultation). Copenhagen, World Health Organization, Regional Office for Europe.

Kerkhof, A.J.F.M., & Bernasco, W. (1990). Suicidal Behavior in Jails and Prisons in The Netherlands. *Suicide and Life Threatening Behavior, 20,* 123-137.

Kerkhof, A.J.F.M., & Nathawat, S.S. (1989). Suicidal behavior and attitudes towards suicide among students in India and the Netherlands. In: R.F.W. Diekstra, R. Maris, S. Platt, A. Schmidtke, & G. Sonneck (eds). *Suicide and its prevention.* Leiden, Brill (pp 144-159).

Kreitman, N. (1986). The Clinical Assessment and Management of the Suicidal Patient. In: A. Roy (Ed.). *Suicide.* Baltimore, Williams & Wilkins.

Lettieri, D.J. (1974). Suicidal Prediction Scales. In: A.T. Beck, H.L.P. Resnik, & D.J. Lettieri (eds.). *The Prediction of Suicide.* Bowie, Maryland, The Charles Press.

Loo, K.J. van de, & Diekstra, R.F.W. (1970). The Construction of a Questionnaire for Prediction of Subsequent Suicidal Attempts: A Preliminary Study. *Nederlands Tijdschrift voor de Psychologie en haar Grensgebieden, 25,* 95-100.

Miles, P. (1977). Conditions predisposing to suicide: a review. *Journal of Nervous and Mental Disorders, 164,* 24 231-246.

Montgomery, S.A., & Åsberg, M. (1979). A new depression scale designed to be sensitive to change. *British Journal of Psychiatry, 134,* 382-389.

Motto, J.A., & Heilbron, D.C. (1976). Development and Validation of Scales for Estimation of Suicidal Risk. In: E.S. Shneidman (Ed.). *Suicidology: Contemporary Developments.* New York, Grune and Stratton.

Murphy, G.E. (1986). Suicide in alcoholism. In: A. Roy (ed.). *Suicide.* Baltimore, Williams & Wilkins (pp 89-96).

Pallis, D.J., Barraclough, B.M., Levey, A.B., Jenkins, J.S., & Sainsbury, P. (1982). Estimating Suicide Risk among Attempted Suicides. I. The Development of New Clinical Scales. *British Journal of Psychiatry, 141,* 37-44.

Pallis, D.J., Gibbons, J.S., & Pierce, D.W. (1984). Estimating Suicide Risk Among Attempted Suicides. II. Efficiency of Predictive Scales after the Attempt. *British Journal of Psychiatry, 144,* 139-148.

Ringel, E. (1953). Der Selbstmord. Maudrich, Vienna.

Roy, A. (1985). Suicide and Psychiatric Patients. *Psychiatric Clinics ofNorth America, 8,* 2, 227-241.

Roy, A. (1986). Suicide in Schizophrenia. In: Roy, A. (ed.). *Suicide.* Baltimore, Williams & Wilkins (pp 97-112).

Sainsbury, P. (1986). Depression, Suicide, and Suicide prevention. In: Roy, A.(eds.). *Suicide.* Baltimore, Williams & Wilkins (pp 73-88).

Schmidtke, A.S., & Häffner (1988). Public attitudes towards and effects of the mass media on suicidal and deliberate self-harm behavior. In: R.F.W. Diekstra, R. Maris, S. Platt, A. Schmidtke & G. Sonneck (eds.). *Suicide and its prevention.* Leiden, Brill (pp 313-330).

Venkoba Rao, A. (1975). Suicide in India. in: N.L. Farberow (eds). *Suicide in Different Cultures.* Baltimore: University Park Press.

Weissman, A.D., & Worden, J.W. (1972). Risk-Rescue-Rating in suicide assessment. *Archives of General Psychiatry, 26,* 553-560.

Whitlock, F.A. (1986). Suicide and Physical Illness. In: Roy, A. (ed.). *Suicide.* Baltimore, Williams & Wilkins (pp 151- 170).

World Health Organization (WHO) (1982). *Changing Patterns in Suicide Behavior.* Euro-reports and studies. Copenhagen. Zung, W.W.K. (1965). A Self-rating Depression Scale. *Archives of General Psychiatry, 12,* 63-70.

Zung, W. (1965). A Selfrating Depression Scale. *Archives of General Psychiatry,* 12, 63-70.

Appendices

Appendix A	:	Pallis long scale for estimating suicide risk and attempted suicide (Pallis et al. 1982)
Appendix B	:	Questionnaire for the Prediction of Subsequent Suicidal Attempts (Van de Loo and Diekstra, 1970)
Appendix C	:	Suicide Intent Scale (SIS, Beck et al. 1974ab)
Appendix D	:	DSM-III-R criteria Depressive Disorders (APA, 1987)
Appendix E	:	Scale for Suicide Ideation (SSI, Beck et al. 1979)

Appendix A : *Pallis et al. 1982 Scale for Estimating Suicide Risk among Attempted Suicides.* (long scale)

	categories	: weight	categories	: weight
1. Sex	male	: 7.25	female	: 5.00
2. Age	over 45	: 5.00	under 45	: 0.67
3. Number of marriages	once/never	: 5.00	twice or more	: 3.58
4. Current employment	unemployed	: 3.50	employed	: 2.50
status	social sec	: 5.0	retired	: 0.42
5. Living conditions	alone	: 6.50	not alone	: 5.00
6. Social class	high(I-II)	: 8.58	low (III-IV)	: 5.00
7. Drinking in parents	no	: 5.00	yes	: 3.25
8. Family history of psychiatric treatment	yes	: 6.75	no	: 5.00
9. Admitted to psychiatric hospital last year	no	: 5.00	yes	: 3.17
10. Reduction in income last year	yes	: 7.08	no	: 5.00
11. Breaking off from spouse or lover last year	no	: 5.00	yes	: 4.00
12. Suicidal communication last year	yes	: 8.00	no	: 5.00
13. Hypnotics for more than one year	yes	: 6.25	no	: 5.00
14. "Row"in last 48 hours	no	: 5.00	yes	: 3.75
15. Retardation last month	yes	: 9.17	no	: 5.00
16. Energy/fatigue last month	no	: 5.00	yes	: 1.75
17. Irritability last month	no	: 5.00	yes	: 0.83
18. Duration of current illness more than one year	yes	: 7.67	no	: 5.00

Range = 66.42 to 112.2 cut-off point = 86.50. Higher scores mean "high risk for subsequent suicide".

Appendix B: *Questionnaire for the Prediction of Subsequent Suicidal Attempts.* (Van de Loo and Diekstra, 1970).

1.	Is this person male?	yes = 1
2.	Is this person white?	yes = 1
3.	Is this person 45 years of age or older?	yes = 1
4.	Is this person separated, divorced or widowed?	yes = 1
5.	Is this person unemployed or retired?	yes = 1
6.	Has this person been treated for an acute or chronical physical disease? (within 6 months before suicidal act)	yes = 1
7.	Does this person live alone?	yes = 1
8.	Does this person suffer from a nervous or mental illness, mood or behavioral symptoms, alcohol abuse, drug addiction or delinquency?	yes = 1
9.	Has this person sustained (within the last 6 months) a loss, financial or with regard to status, or a bereavement of a beloved person?	yes = 1
10.	Did this person attempt suicide by hanging, fire-arms, drowning, jumping from high places, or throwing himself for a vehicle?	yes = 1
11.	Was this person unconscious or unable to answer questions because of the attempt?	yes = 1
12.	Did this person attempt suicide before or threaten to do so?	yes = 1
13.	Was this person admitted to a psychiatric hospital after his attempt?	yes = 1
14.	Did this person take preparations such as writing (a) letter(s) concerning his suicide attempt?	yes = 1

For every yes-answer one point is counted. A total score of 5 or more suggests high risk for subsequent suicidal behavior.

Appendix C: *Suicide Intent Scale.* (SIS, Beck et al. 1974ab).

To be scored by interviewer: circle 0, 1, or 2 for each question.
Questions 1 through 8 inquire after a rating by the interviewer.
Questions 9 through 15 according to patient's statement.

I. OBJECTIVE CIRCUMSTANCES RELATED TO SUICIDE ATTEMPT

1. *Isolation*
   0. Somebody present
   1. Somebody nearby or in visual or vocal contact
   2. No one nearby or in visual or vocal contact

2. *Timing*
   0. Intervention is probable
   1. Intervention is not likely
   2. Intervention is highly unlikely

3. *Precautions against discovery / intervention*
   0. No precautions
   1. Passive precautions (as avoiding others but doing nothing to prevent their intervention; alone in room with unlocked door)
   2. Active precautions (as locked door)

4. *Acting to get help during/after attempt*
   0. Notified potential helper regarding attempt
   1. Contacted but did not specifically notify potential helper regarding attempt
   2. Did not contact or notify potential helper

5. *Final acts in anticipation of death (e.g., will, gifts, insurance)*
   0. None
   1. Thought about or made some arrangements
   2. Made definite plans or completed arrangements

6. *Active preparation for attempt*
   0. None
   1. Minimal to moderate
   2. Extensive

7. *Suicide note*
   0. Absence of note
   1. Note written, but torn up; note thought about
   2. Presence of note

8. *Overt communication of intent before the attempt*
   0. None
   1. Equivocal communication
   2. Unequivocal communication

II. SELF REPORT

9. *Alleged purpose of attempt*
   0. To manipulate environment, get attention, revenge
   1. Components of 0 and 2
   2. To escape, surcease, solve problems

10. *Expectations of fatality*
    0. Thought that death was unlikely
    1. Thought that death was possible but not probable
    2. Thought that death was probable or certain

11. *Conception of method's lethality*
    0. Did less to self than he thought would be lethal
    1. Wasn't sure if what he did would be lethal
    2. Equaled or exceeded what he thought would be lethal

12. *Seriousness of attempt*
    0. Did not seriously attempt to end life
    1. Uncertain about seriousness attempt to end life
    2. Seriously attempted to end life

13. *Attitude toward living/dying*
    0. Did not want to die
    1. Components of 0 and 2
    2. Wanted to die

14. *Conception of medical rescueability*
    0. Thought that death would be unlikely if he received medical attention
    1. Was uncertain whether death could be averted by medical attention
    2. Was certain of death even if he received medical attention

15. *Degree of premeditation*
    0. None; impulsive
    1. Suicide contemplated for three hours or less prior to attempt
    2. Suicide contemplated for more than three hours prior to attempt

---

A score of 13 or more is indicative for a strong suicide intent and a high risk for subsequent suicidal behavior.

Appendix D: *Summary criteria Bipolar and Depressive disorders according to DSM-III-R.* (American Psychiatric Association, 1987).

Bipolar Disorders:

Essential features of bipolar disorders are manic or hypomanic episodes, usually interspersed with depressive episodes. The criteria for a Manic Episode are (DSM-III-R, p 217):

A. A distinct period of abnormally and persistently elevated, expansive, or irritable mood.
B. During the period of mood disturbance, at least three of the following symptoms have persisted (four if the mood is only irritable) and have been present to a significant degree:

1. inflated self-esteem or grandiosity
2. decreased need for sleep, e.g. feels rested after three hours sleep
3. more talkative than usual or pressure to keep talking
4. flight of ideas or subjective experience that thoughts are racing
5. distractability, attention too easily drawn to unimportant or irrelevant external stimuli
6. increase in goal-directed activity (either socially, at work or school, or sexually) or psychomotor agitation
7. excessive involvement in pleasurable activities which have a high potential for painful consequences, e.g., the person engages in unrestrained buying sprees, sexual indiscretions, or foolish business investments.

C. Mood disturbance sufficiently severe to cause marked impairment in occupational functioning or in usual social activities or relationships with others, or to necessitate hospitalization to prevent harm to self or others.

If criteria A and B are present, but not C, a "Hypomanic Syndrome" is present. In case of (suspicion of) a manic or hypomanic syndrome, a thorough psychiatric evaluation is needed (for comprehensive criteria, see DSM-III-R-Manual). Suicidal tendencies may come forward rather suddenly and impulsively, mainly towards the end of depressive episodes that alternate with manic episodes (Kreitman, 1986).

Depressive Disorders:

There are two depressive disorders: Major Depression and Dysthymia (or Depressive Neurosis). Some of the criteria for Major Depression (DSM-III-R, p.; for full diagnostic criteria see DSM-III-R-Manual) are:
At least five of the following symptoms have been present during the same two-week period and represent a change from previous functioning; at least one of the symptoms is either depressed mood (1) or loss of interest or pleasure (2).

1. depressed mood most of the day, nearly every day, as indicated either by subjective account or observation by others
2. markedly diminished interest or pleasure in all, or almost all, activities most of the day, nearly every day
3. significant weight loss or weight gain when not dieting (more than 5 % in a month), or decrease or increase in appetite nearly every day
4. insomnia or hypersomnia nearly every day
5. psychomotor agitation or retardation nearly every day
6. fatigue or loss of energy nearly every day
7. feelings of worthlessness or excessive or inappropriate guilt

8. diminished ability to think or concentrate, or indecisiveness
9. recurrent thoughts of death (not just fear of dying), recurrent suicidal ideation without a specific plan, or a suicide attempt or a specific plan for committing suicide.

In its severe forms Major Depressive Episodes may show psychotic features, such as delusions and hallucinations of inadequacy, guilt, disease, death, nihilism, or deserved punishment, or mood-incongruent delusions of persecution, thought insertion, thought broadcasting, or control. Suicide risk can be quite serious here. Suicide risk is also present if the Major Depressive Disorder is of the Melancholic Type, when at least five of the following are present (DSM-III-R, p 224):

1. loss of interest or pleasure in all, or almost all, activities
2. lack of reactivity to usually pleasurable stimuli
3. depression regularly worse in the morning
4. early morning awakening (at least two hours before usual time)
5. psychomotor retardation or agitation
6. significant anorexia or weight loss (e.g., more than 5 % in one month)
7. no significant personality disturbance before first Maj. Depr. Episode
8. one or more previous Major Depressive Episodes followed by complete or nearly complete recovery
9. previous good response to specific and adequate somatic antidepressant therapy, e.g., tricyclics, ECT, MAO-inhibitors, lithium.

The essential feature for Dysthymia or Depressive Neurosis is a chronic disturbance of mood involving depressed mood (or possibly an irritable mood in children and adolescents), for most of the day, more days than not, for at least two years (one year for children and adolescents). In addition, during these periods of depressed mood there are at least two of the following present (DSM-III-R, p 232):

1. poor appetite or overeating
2. insomnia or hypersomnia
3. low energy or fatigue
4. low self-esteem
5. poor concentration or difficulty making decisions
6. feelings of hopelessness

Appendix E : *The Scale for Suicide Ideation.* (SSI, Beck et al. 1979).

I. CHARACTERISTICS OF ATTITUDE TOWARD LIVING/DYING

1. Wish to live
    0. Moderate to strong
    1. Weak
    2. None

2. Wish to die
    0. None
    1. Weak
    2. Moderate to strong

3. Reasons for living/dying
    0. For living outweigh for dying
    1. About equal
    2. For dying outweigh for living

4. Desire to make active suicide attempt
    0. None
    1. Weak
    2. Moderate to strong

5. Passive suicidal attempt
    0. Would take precautions to save life
    1. Would leave life/death to chance (e.g., carelessly crossing a busy street)
    2. Would avoid steps necessary to save or maintain life (e.g., diabetic ceasing to take insulin)

II. CHARACTERISTICS OF SUICIDE IDEATION/WISH

6. Time dimension: Duration
    0. Brief, fleeting periods
    1. Longer periods
    2. Continuous (chronic), or almost continuous

7. Time dimension: Frequency
    0. Rare, occasional
    1. Intermittent
    2. Persistent or continuous

8. Attitude toward ideation/wish
    0. Rejecting
    1. Ambivalent; indifferent
    2. Accepting

9. Control over suicidal action/acting-out wish
    0. Has sense of control
    1. Unsure of control
    2. Has no sense of control

10. Deterrents to active attempt (e.g., family, religion; possibility of serious injury; irreversibility)
    0. Would not attempt suicide because of a deterrent
    1. Some concern about deterrents
    2. Minimal or no concern about deterrents

11. Reason for contemplated attempt
    0. To manipulate the environment; get attention, revenge
    1. Combination of 0 and 2
    2. Escape, surcease, solve problems

III. CHARACTERISTICS OF CONTEMPLATED ATTEMPT

12. Method: Specificity/planning
    0. Not considered
    1. Considered, but details not worked out
    2. Details worked out/well formulated

13. Method: Availability/opportunity
    0. Method not available; no opportunity
    1. Method would take time/effort; opportunity not readily available
    2a. Method and opportunity available
    2b. Future opportunity or availability of method anticipated

14. Sense of "capability" to carry out attempt
    0. No courage, too weak, afraid, incompetent
    1. Unsure of courage, competence
    2. Sure of competence, courage

15. Expectancy/anticipation of actual attempt
    0. No
    1. Uncertain, not sure
    2. Yes

IV. ACTUALIZATION OF CONTEMPLATED ATTEMPT

16. Actual preparation
    0. None
    1. Partial (e.g., starting to collect pills)
    2. Complete (e.g., had pills, razor, loaded gun)

17. Suicide note
    0. None
    1. Started but not completed; only thought about
    2. Completed

18. Final acts in anticipation of death (e.g., insurance, will, gifts)
    0. None
    1. Thought about or made some arrangements
    2. Made definite plans or completed arrangements

19. Deception/concealment of contemplated attempt (refers to communication of ideation to interviewing clinician)
    0. Revealed ideas openly
    1. Held back on revealing
    2. Attempted to deceive, conceal, lie

A sample of 90 patients who were hospitalized for self-destructive ruminations obtained a mean total score of 9.43 (Sd=8.44), according to Beck et al. (1979), while a sample of 50 outpatients who sought psychiatric treatment for their depression, obtained a mean total score of 4.42 (Sd=5.77). In a sample of 207 suicidal inpatients (Beck et al. 1985), no differences were found between completers and noncompleters during a follow up period of 5-10 years (means are 11.7 resp. 12.8).

Guidelines for the Training of Lay-Workers in Suicide Prevention

N. WHITING

1. Introduction; The Role of the Non-Professional

Where does suicide begin? The urge towards self-destruction may be felt long before a person comes into professional care. Indeed many, whatever their needs, never reach the professional, and some are able, often with other support, to come to terms with their situations, to control the suicidal urge and to retain a hold on life.

The necessary support is often called for at the moment of crisis, or it may be needed over a period of time. The professional may not be available at the crisis moment, neither is he always able to provide the type of back-up required; indeed the professional-client relationship is not necessarily appropriate for this purpose.

Non-professional befriending, with its minimal power differential, may be the more effective mode, one that may be invoked where professional intervention is not indicated, or as a complementary service to that of the professional.

The voluntary or complementary worker often acts as a safety net and a first contact to the potentially suicidal. The effectiveness of this role depends upon the qualities of the carer but also upon the way in which these have been developed and realised through training. Because suicide is a sensitive and emotional subject not easily discussed, it is not enough to depend solely upon the awareness and goodwill of people for the support of the suicidal. Better education in human relationships and feelings is called for in society as a whole; and, for those who are not professionals in the field of suicide prevention but who are in a position to offer non-professional help to the suicidal, training in awareness of and response to suicide risk is essential.

These lay-workers in suicide prevention, sometimes referred to as "human services personnel", comprise the following groups:

a) Staff in organizational roles which sometimes bring them into potentially supportive contact with people in crisis: e.g. teachers, social workers, prison officers.

b) Those whose work may bring them into contact with people in crisis, not infrequently, but usually in circumstances which do not allow for continuing supportive relationships: e.g. police and other emergency services, and people such as bar-tenders, lawyers, bank managers, hair-dressers, receptionists, who enter the lives and sometimes the homes of others and who may therefore be a human contact at a moment of crisis.

c) People in volunteer organizations whose work not infrequently brings them into contact with suicidal people: e.g. agencies specializing in support and services to those with specific disabilities or medical conditions, etc.

d) Self-help groups, working in similar fields to those in c), but generally in less structured ways and often at a local scale.

e) Those in volunteer organizations concerned specifically or predominantly with caring for the suicidal. People in groups a) and b) may be able to give valuable support to those in crisis, though constraints of time and of role conflict may inhibit the development of a continuing or entirely open relationship.

Those in groups c) and d) may be able to develop continuing support, though the needs of the suicidal are not the main focus of the service they offer. It is people in group e) who are able to, and who should, focus upon suicidal feelings and behavior rather than upon other needs of their callers. But people in all of these groups have to be sensitive to signs of suicide risk and able to respond appropriately if they are to be effective as lay-helpers in suicide prevention.

This chapter is concerned with the development of the attitudes, skills and knowledge that enable lay-people to recognize and support those at risk of suicide. It discusses particularly the selection and training of volunteers in suicide prevention agencies (i.e., those in group e), and in so doing, it includes material that could be adapted for use in the training of the other groups identified above; so readers interested in those groups may wish to be selective in their use of this chapter.

A. Availability of lay-helpers in suicide prevention

Many people in crisis want desperately to talk to someone who will really listen, who will simply accept them as they are at that moment, and who will refrain from making judgments or proposing solutions. The student may turn to a teacher, the offender to his probation officer, the old person to a day care worker, because they are there on the spot at the time; or they may turn to strangers in a suicide prevention agency because, as strangers, they have no other obligations or relationships to get in the way. In either case, the helper is physically there, but becomes really and fully available only if the caller feels accepted and supported. Hence the need for the sort of preparation discussed in this chapter, whether this is as training for voluntary work in an agency or incorporated in training for an occupation with a probability of some contact with people in crisis.

In the case of suicide prevention agencies, their publicity is vital if they are to be truly available. Only through adequate public information will they attract people as callers and as volunteers. They must inform the public about modes of contact, whether this be by telephone, by personal visit, or by letter, and confidentiality must be assured. Ideally, the service should be available for 24 hours a day; suicidal feelings are not subject to office hours. Where this ideal is unattainable, a back-up service should be offered if possible—for instance, the telephone number of another center.

Availability also means acceptability to the caller. To be truly available the carer must be open and welcoming, and must be willing to listen attentively through presenting problems or testing approaches before the more sensitive issues can merge. Availability is more than just a physical presence.

B. The Caller-Carer relationship

The relationship between caller and carer is characterised by its informality and by the absence of the symbols and ritual of authority which are inherent in the client-professional relationship. Yet it is not the same as ordinary friendship. Neither party chooses the other, and the caller retains the right to break off the relationship at any time; and the aim of befriending is to make itself unnecessary. The purpose of the relationship is simply "giving the warmth of human presence to those out in the cold" (John Eldrid, in The Samaritans, 1978).

Neither is befriending the same as counselling. The difference between the two is a broad frontier zone rather than a sharply defined boundary line, and consists in the extent to which contracts are agreed between parties, to which intended outcomes are specified, to which a program of contacts is agreed; counselling tends to strengthen these definitions, befriending leaves them open. But many skills are common to both. Of course, some callers are in need of something beyond befriending; medical, psychological or other types of professional help may be indicated. A befriender may help a caller to obtain such guidance, but he may make a referral only with the caller's freely given agreement. It is not the befriender's role to offer advice; this could be hazardous for all parties and should always be avoided.

2. Recruitment and Selection of Volunteers

Volunteers preparation starts even before the individual applies for membership, in that he knows something about the agency through its reputation and publicity, and he is already shaping his attitude towards it. Therefore the agency's publicity and recruitment policy must be appealing, informative and accurate, and its standards and reputation must be carefully preserved.

Not everyone is able to undertake the type of service offered by a befriending agency. Certain qualities are necessary and certain inclinations would be inappropriate. It is therefore helpful if the agency ensures that potential applicants can find out how it works and what it expects of its volunteers. Information meetings for this purpose, held prior to the selection procedure itself, and even before formal application, are recommended. On the basis of full information, most of those unsuited to the work will make their own decision not to proceed with an application.

An organization devoted to caring for deeply troubled people makes heavy demands upon its members. The emotional load can be considerable at times, and it is exacerbated by the requirement of confidentiality, which forbids volunteers to discuss their callers with anyone outside the agency. It is therefore important that the family and friends of a potential volunteer understand that they may be called upon for support at times of pressures whose causes they cannot share.

Selection must therefore be thorough. But this is a task which volunteers in a supportive agency may find particularly difficult. They are trained to accept people as they find them and to refrain from making judgments; yet as selectors, they must probe and make decisions about people. Training for this work is therefore essential, especially in interview skills.

People are motivated in many ways to volunteer for such service. Spare time and altruism are necessary but not sufficient reasons. A desire to fill time may indicate a need to fill emotional space; and altruism must be expressed in acceptance, not prescription. A sample selection procedure is outlined in Appendix A.

3. Training of Lay-Helpers: Some General Considerations

The role of the non-professional lay-helper in suicide prevention is to accept and support the caller through befriending, as described above.

Are befrienders born or taught? Is an inborn capacity for non-judgmental caring in some people, or can it be learned by anyone? This is not the place for a discussion of the nature/nurture debate, and the position taken here is that the qualities and potential for this type of service, while present in many people, need to be developed. The process is largely a matter of gaining sufficient confidence to acknowledge ones vulnerability yet to retain that measure of control which the caller needs and expects in the befriender.

"Training" is often thought to be an inappropriate word for a process of self-development and self-realization. However, for want of a generally accepted alternative, the term will be used throughout this chapter.

We are concerned here with adults learning. Some will have no experience of formal learning since leaving school; others may have undergone all kinds of further education. The trainer may have to help with some basic learning skills such as participation in group discussion. Yet all will share a motivation towards this form of service, and there may indeed be no advantage in possessing formal qualifications. There may be tasks of un-learning to be faced, since preparing for non-judgmental non-directive befriending is mainly a matter of developing attitudes and values and handling emotions—the very areas of human experiences so often sadly under-developed in formal education systems.

The adult learner is in fact the greatest resource available to the trainer. He has abilities and experience that simply have to be adapted to the context of befriending suicidal people. He has, of course, a lot to learn, but there is relatively little that the trainer has to teach.

Therefore an element of "negotiated learning" is appropriate; a process in which the teacher and learner agree on what is to be learned. People learn more effectively when they see the relevance of what they are learning, and when they have helped in defining the objectives. A sense of "ownership" arising from sharing in the definitions of learning needs will help in overcoming the anxieties that many adults feel when they return to learning, perhaps after many years.

The concept of negotiated learning does not deny the responsibility of the trainer. Negotiation is not abdication; and with his deeper understanding of the requirements of the service, the trainer must play a major role in identifying learning needs. But his very experience, or perhaps in some cases his lack of experience, may lead him into inflexibility and questionable assumptions, which the process of negotiation can help to correct.

4. The Pre-Service Preparation Course

A. Aims and scope of pre-service training

Pre-service training is necessary in the interests of the caller, the volunteer himself, and the reputation of the agency. It not only trains the volunteer for his work but it gives him time to feel his way towards membership, thus serving as a form of "rite de passage" and building the supportive climate which is essential in such an organization.

Yet pre-service training cannot do the whole job. It should aim to produce a volunteer who has not only the competence to be let loose on the public in the agency's name, but the desire to go on learning. A commitment to in-serve training should be required of every volunteer.

Pre-service training should ensure:

a. that the volunteer knows the principles to which the agency works and has begun to make them his own. This is a matter of attitudes and values;

b. that the volunteer has acquired adequate skills in the befriending media which the agency uses (telephone, face-to-face, letter writing);

c. that the volunteer has the necessary knowledge of people in the types of situation that may lead to suicidal behavior; and of the procedures of the agency.

These requirements involve attitudes, skills and knowledge distinguishable for purposes of description, but merging in the practice of befriending, which may be defined as expressing certain values through the application of skills and knowledge.

These issues are developed in this section, and suggestions for the content of a training course are given in Appendices B and C.

B. Length of pre-service course

A pre-service training course should be only long enough to achieve its aims, and no longer. Its purpose is not only to cover every possible eventuality that could occur, and the understandable temptation on the part of a conscientious trainer to do that should be resisted.

Local circumstances may effect the decision on the actual length of the course, but it is suggested that about 18 to 24 hours is probably about right. In addition, there must be individual tutorial help and at least two reunion meetings of the class during the period of probationary service.

C. Structuring the course

How should the course be structured? Should there be short meetings at weekly intervals or should longer periods (a full day or a week-end) be incorporated?

A weekly meeting of 2.1/2 hours over a period of several weeks has the advantage that input at each meeting is necessarily limited, and there is time for reflection and "learning in sleep" between each meeting. On the other hand, the course is more fragmented and particular care has to be taken to ensure progression. Also, it may take several meetings before the participants come to work as a group.

A class which meets for a full day or over a week-end develops as a group more readily. Members do not have to "get into gear" so often, and as a consequence this structure leads more easily to productive work on the sensitive subjects that necessarily form much of the content of the course. But a week-end, or even a full day, can prove intellectually and emotionally exhausting for people unaccustomed to this type of work.

A course consisting of two or three full days with a number of short meetings between is likely to offer the benefits of both approaches.

D. Size of class and type of accommodation

A class of five or six can develop well as a group. Below this number the limited range of interaction reduces the effectiveness of the group. With ten or more there must be facilities for dividing the class for group work. A room large enough for the whole class with smaller rooms for group work is ideal.

This arrangement also facilitates the use of telephone practice where equipment is available (see below). If only one room is available, it should be large enough for groups to work separately with minimal interference with each other.

Furniture arrangements should be informal, and if trainers have to use a table, they should make sure that it does not become a barrier behind which they take refuge. Chairs should be comfortable, but not sleep-inducing, and generally a circular arrangement is preferable to rows, since most of the work will be interactive (See Section 6).

E. Equipment

Elaborate equipment is not substitute for good teaching. Used well, suitable equipment can enhance learning, but good teaching can be achieved with the simplest of resources.

People learn through all the senses, not only by being talked at. For example, visual reinforcement is powerful (See Appendix D on visual presentation), and the feel of a telephone in the hand enhances the effectiveness of a practice role play.

The following list of equipment would allow for the use of all the teaching methods outlined in Appendix D; but each training team must make its decisions according to preference and practicality.

- Paper and pencils for each member
- A paper flip chart and marker pens
- Chalkboard and/or overhead projector are useful for larger groups
- Telephone training set: two interconnected telephones, with loudspeaker and tape-recorder
- Audio-tape cassette player/recorder
- Video-tape recorder with monitor(s)
- Video-tape camera, for use in face-to-face training
- For training team: access to duplicating and photocopying facilities.

F. The training team

Even in a small class, it is desirable to have two trainers, and with larger classes other experienced volunteers can be brought in to help with role demonstrations and role play. The training team should meet before each class to decide on strategies and on allocation of tasks, and after each class for an immediate evaluation of the session.

The training team should consist mainly of members of considerable experience, both in the field of befriending and, if possible, in some teaching context, to ensure familiarity with the basic concepts and skills of learning and teaching—though trainers should beware of importing the more formal methods of instruction into this field, where such methods are inappropriate. The inclusion of one or two more recently recruited members in a training team can help to maintain vitality; and while continuity is important, it should be remembered that a long-standing training team can become a major power base in an organization, and periodic changes in membership and style are desirable. The training team should liaise closely with those responsible for selection of new volunteers and for supervising trained volunteers; trainers will receive evaluative feed-back from the latter, and may be able to offer constructive comment to the former (See Section 7 on evaluation).

The training function in an agency consists of two rather different tasks: pre-service training of new volunteers and in-service training of all serving volunteers. It may be preferable to appoint separate teams for these tasks, though they should cooperate closely, perhaps through the mediacy of a single training officer.

The trainer is a teacher, and as a teacher, must be a learner constantly learning about the subject, but also about the task of facilitating the learning of others. The teacher learns from colleagues and from trainees, but also from sources beyond these local boundaries. Without refreshment from outside, teaching is likely to become repetitious and eventually stagnant.

The subject matter of training courses concerned with suicide necessarily includes reference to specialized subjects in which the training teams are themselves not qualified or expert. Visiting specialized speakers can be invited, but generally to in-service sessions rather than to the pre-service course.

In the in-service program, a visiting speaker may deepen the understanding of the experienced volunteer, who is able to relate this knowledge to his role as a befriender. In a pre-service course, the inclusion of specialist speakers carries the implied message to the new and inexperienced volunteer that the role for which he is training is the identification and perhaps the solution of the problems discussed by the specialists. Unassimilated information can tempt the volunteer into the dangerous luxury of unskilled diagnosis and divert him from his proper role, simple though daunting enough, as a befriended.

G. Designing a pre-service course

Three general principles are helpful in the general design and detailed planning of a course:

a. The course is about caring for the suicidal, and this should be the focus of every session. Many subjects will be considered during the course-medical and psychological problems, social deprivation, bereavement and loss, and many others; but always the question must be asked and satisfactorily answered: "What is the bearing of this upon caring for the suicidal?"

b. The experience of the training course should lead to development of the individual and the group. Individual development should be seen in each member's growing ability to utilize appropriate skills and

knowledge, and in a deepening understanding of and empathy with people. Trainers should monitor each trainee's development in order to help the trainee to assess progress.
Monitoring is also a progressive indicator of the trainee's suitability for this kind of work, though the evidence it provides may have to be used only when a trainee proves unsuitable. Monitoring should be in the form of qualitative notes on the trainee's reactions to group situations, sensitivity in role play, quality of contribution in discussion and understanding of issues; quantitative assessment (marks, grades) are inappropriate in a field in which the learning is almost entirely in the affective realm.
Group development should be expressed in a growing corporate identity which will form a basis of the support necessary in the stressful work that volunteers will undertake.

c. The teaching approaches and the plan of each meeting and of the course as a whole should take account of the learner's situation and should be appropriate to the aims and subject matter of the course.

Further discussion of teaching methods will be found in Section 6.

Constant reference to these three principles during the planning of a course will serve to integrate and give shape to the course and to reduce the danger of fragmentation. A course consisting of a series of sections on separate subjects (e.g. psychological problems, sexual problems, problems of youth, etc.) is not only fragmented, but also suggests to the learner that he is being trained to identify and categorise problems, and by implication, to solve them. Some of the subjects listed in Appendix B require special attention, but much of the knowledge that is necessary can be planned to arise in the context of case studies, in which the principles outlined above are given expression.

Variety method is necessary in each meeting, to retain interest (see Section 6). It is also desirable to plan each meeting to include:

- Some recapitulation of main teaching points from the previous meeting. This can be done by question and answer, or by a short case study or role play to bring out these points. Such recapitulation is both a reinforcement of learning and a check for the trainer on any gaps or misunderstandings.

(The equivalent element in the first meeting of a course could be the use of material from members own experience: e.g. "Think of a difficult time in your own life. How were you helped through it?").

- Some new ideas and/or skills. These should be explained or demonstrated, as appropriate, and opportunity given for discussion or practice.

- Some revision of ideas and skills from earlier sessions. These will often be in role play, case study, or in "machine gun" exercises (see Appendix D), and should often contain some element or complexity to stimulate further thought on the subject.

- Time for question and answer and for further discussion, as members find necessary. It is nearly always found that more time is needed than is planned.

H. Probationary phase

Following the preparation course there should be a probationary period before the new volunteer is accepted into full membership. This period is a bridge between the pre-service and in-service phases of training and it accustoms the new volunteer to the practice of continued training throughout his service. But it also serves to illuminate his pre-service learning through experience, particularly if a number of "reunion meetings" of the pre-service class are held during this period.

Reunion meetings serve the following purposes:

a. Pre-service learning is further developed in the light of experience.
b. Further material not deemed essential at the initial stage may be introduced.
c. Some disillusionment may set in during the early stages of service, when the high expectations of new volunteers are not always met. Reunion meetings can allow the expression and resolution of these difficulties.
d. These meetings can provide evaluative feedback for the training team.

Throughout the probationary period the new volunteer should work closely with an experienced volunteer (preferably not a member of the training team), whose task is essentially one of support and guidance through this crucial phase. The quality of this support may be a factor not only in the new volunteer's development but even in his decision about continuing membership.

5. In-Service Training

A. Organizing in-service training

We should not have to remind ourselves that in caring for suicidal people we are sometimes close to the boundary between life and death. The skills, insights and sensitivity must be developed continually. The person who continues to offer himself as a befriender for a long period on the basis of his pre-service training alone could be putting callers at risk. It is therefore essential that an agency in this field provides good in-service training, and that every volunteer avails himself of it.

Provision of in-service training is in some respects a more difficult undertaking than pre-service training. The constituency is diffuse; instead of a regular small class all at initial level, we have perhaps 100 or more volunteers of widely differing experience, who can prove themselves to be critical students!

So we should turn their very experience to advantage, and utilize them as our main resource. Wherever possible, much of the in-service training in an agency should involve the members in participatory learning, and the workshop format is well-suited to this. (See Appendix D). An in-service training team will design and organize the program, but the workshop format allows many other volunteers to be involved, for example, as discussion group leaders and in role demonstrations.

The form of in-service training meetings will be determined by circumstances. Occasional meetings of the whole membership strengthen corporate identity as well as providing a vehicle for statements of policy or notifications of procedural changes. From time to time a visiting speaker may be invited, perhaps as a specialist in a related field. The contents of such talks should be relevant to the role of the agency, and ample time should be allowed for participatory activity to ensure that the relevance is established.

It may be possible for much in-service training to be carried out in smaller groups, meeting in the agency's premises or in members' homes. The programs for these meetings are drawn up by the in-service training team, and group leaders are chosen and briefed carefully.

In-service training is not only a matter of programs of meetings. Members are developing continuously through informal discussion of their work (which should never degenerate into mere gossip, for this demeans both caller and volunteer). Creative discussion of this type is both an indicator and a generator of high morale and motivation in the agency. Further, the supporting and supervisory system, which is vital in this type of service, has also an educational role; the supervisor or leader, in discussing cases with the volunteers, is necessarily though informally acting as a tutor, and is an important link with the in-service training team for the communication of identified training needs.

B. Other necessary areas of training

Any group of people co-operating to offer a service have to agree upon aims and objectives, and upon guidelines for attaining these; they develop to some degree a division of labour; they have to acquire resources and devise ways of making decisions about their use. In a word, they become an organization.

Organizational skills (e.g. management of people, of finance, of resources) are therefore necessary, and while it is likely that people with some of these skills will be found in a group of volunteers, there may be many others with little experience in these fields. Some basic training in such matters as leadership, committee procedures and roles, financial management and public relations may be necessary. This is not the place to develop these topics, but their necessity must be noted. Without effective management, the service offered by the agency will inevitably suffer.

6. Teaching Methods

A. Range of methods

In a voluntary agency, people may be asked, on the basis of a good "track-record" as befrienders, to take on a training role. If they have no previous experience of teaching or training, this may be daunting, and the temptation is to take refuge in "defensive teaching"—that is, any technique (usually lecturing) which fills the time and minimises opportunities for challenge to the teacher's authority. "Defensive teaching" is a sure recipe for boredom and poor learning on the part of the trainee, and for frustration of the trainer.

Appendix D gives a number of teaching methods which are readily available and which are appropriate to different situations. In fact, they are not all separate and mutually exclusive methods; for instance, "case study" may be the basis of discussion or role-play, and "brainstorming" may be used in the course of a talk. Some are matters of class organization rather than teaching method (e.g. pairs, triads, groups); the whole list should be thought of as "ways of facilitating learning".

Two of the headings in that list are widely used in training for work with people, and require more explanation than can be given in the Appendix. These, group work and role-play, are discussed below.

B. Group work

Working in groups offers the opportunity for people to express themselves more readily than is possible in a large class. It should therefore play a large part in training classes, and the purpose and organization of the group should be thought out carefully.

In training courses, groups serve four main (and overlapping) functions:

Function	Use	Examples
Discussion	promoting and examining ideas	detailed study of a question, or a topic, or of case study material
Support	to help individuals cope with their feelings	the supportive climate of a group can help to resolve emotive situations
Committee	to make decisions	a group may have to formulate a solution to a task; or to agree a group report; or to decide questions of its own logistics
Social	to enhance group feeling, to help people enjoy the group in a "safe" setting.	this function predominates as the group assembles and departs, and at natural breaks; it also operates incidentally at other times (e.g. in "aside" comments and through humour).

In pre-service classes, the group leader is likely to be a member of the training team, or an experienced volunteer brought in for this purpose. The leader's role varies with the purpose which the group is serving at any moment. At times of social purpose, the leader's task must be unobtrusively to see that no-one is excluded; in "committee", his role is more formal, to ensure that the objective is attained. In discussion phases, the role will depend partly upon the task in hand and partly upon the climate of the group; to ensure real discussion, he will facilitate and not dominate, and will gently encourage the reticent and restrain the effusive. At all times he will have a supportive role, and must be particularly vigilant for signs of distress.

The optimum size of a group is said to be about eight, though it is often not possible to achieve this, and groups somewhat smaller or larger than this can work well. The seating arrangement influences the effectiveness of a group. Chairs arranged formally in rows allow members to see a lecturer and his visual materials, but do not allow easy interaction between members of the group. Circular or semi-circular seating arrangements encourage easier communication between all members.

C. Role-play

Role-play is a learning approach in which members of a class put themselves in the place of people in an imagined situation. Most commonly, in the present context, the roles are those of a caller and a lay befriender, though others, such as a supervisor or leader, may be brought into the situation, which may be either a telephone or a face-to-face contact.

Instructional teaching is of limited value in the areas of attitudes, values and feelings with which we are largely concerned, and it is in these areas, as well as in the practice of skills, that role-play can be a powerful medium, for it involves the participant, sometimes more deeply than he expects, in the emotion of the situation. The "...as if..." comes close to reality. For this reason, the situations simulated should not knowingly be close to those within the participant's own experience (for we are engaged in training, not therapy). If the role play context should happen to cause distress to a participant, support must be given by the trainer and the whole group. Even if strong emotion is not apparent, time must be given after every role-play for the participants to come out of role and back to reality. One trainer should be uninvolved in the role-play in order that everyone may recognize him as a link with the reality outside the exercise.

Role-play is not the same as acting. Acting is playing a role in order to affect other people in some desired way; role-play is a mode of personal exploration and experience, a vehicle for one's own learning. In a training class the role player is not playing to an audience, but is trying himself out in handling emotions and using skills. He is practicing, in a safe setting in which mistakes do no harm, the work for which he has volunteered.

The person in the role of caller is given a brief synopsis of the situation, perhaps with some special instructions if the purpose is to test out his partner in some way. For example:

> "Woman, 60, seems to want friendly chat, and keeps to safe subjects at first (e.g. prices in the shops, young people's behavior, etc.). Finds the house difficult to manage since husband died. One married daughter, who does not come very often."
>
> Give the following information *only if asked:*
>
> "To-day is second anniversary of husband's death, and the feeling of loss is getting worse. Now feels life not worth living. Saved up sleeping tablets, intends to take them tonight."

The befriender is being tested out on his ability to develop trust in the caller and to give her opportunity to say what she really wants to say; she needs to be "given permission" to talk about her suicidal thoughts.

It may take a little time for trainees to relax into role-play. At first, situations presented to them should be simple and the duration short. For example, a first experience of role-play could consist of no more than the first three of four exchanges between caller and befriender, simply to give the flavour of responding to a distressed person. Also these early exercises should be done in pairs, so that members are in effect working privately. Conscientious trainers may have to curb their desire to listen in and to correct every fault; learners need time and space to develop their confidence.

Every meeting of the course should include some role-play in order to give regular practice in listening skills and in assessing suicide risk. The situations can be made progressively more demanding and the duration may be extended gradually. "Triads" may sometimes be used, the third person acting as silent observer whose comments in the subsequent "debriefing" may be particularly helpful.

In the early stages, the learner should generally play the role of befriender; but later he should sometimes be the caller, for it is only through taking this role that he comes near the experience of being befriended. However, when asked to do this he should be given a brief to build upon, as a safeguard against any temptation to base a story upon a distressing episode in his own life.

Where possible, a telephone training circuit should be set up. This gives the role-play a greater sense of reality, and loud speaker and tape recorder facilities enable a role-play to be heard by the class or recorded for subsequent study as required. If such a system is not available, trainees find it helpful to hold a "dead" telephone in the hand to stimulate the real situation. In practicing telephone befriending, role players should be placed in positions that prevent eye contact and the messages of body language.

For trainees who have to be prepared for personal contact with people in crisis, face-to-face role-play must be provided, and these role-plays should incorporate all the details of such contacts, including greeting the caller, seating arrangements, and ending the contact.

At certain times in a training course, trainers may wish to teach by use of role demonstrations. The purpose is entirely different from that of role-play as described above. In role demonstration the "players" are performing to an audience, not to develop their own learning, but to demonstrate a particular point. Use of role demonstration include:

- illustration of characteristics of depression (more effective than merely describing them), and the response to them;
- demonstrating ways of asking about suicidal thoughts;
- demonstrating ways of handling a silent call;
- demonstrating ways of ending a call.

The danger in such demonstration is that trainees may be tempted to see these as exact models to be imitated. To avoid this, they should be required to practice these skills through their own participation in role-play.

D. Choice teaching method

A teaching method should be appropriate to the subject matter, the learning objectives and the class situation.

People can receive information in a lecture; but they cannot learn a skill by being told. People may learn about characteristic situations through case-study; but they need time for discussion and reflection if they are to understand the general principles behind specific instances.

We need variety in teaching, and the list of methods and modes of class organization in Appendix D notes the types of teaching contexts for each. The choice of method is important in maintaining interest during a session. For example:

- variety can be introduced into a talk by incorporating "buzz groups" and by the use of visual methods;
- after a long sedentary session, an activity movement will stimulate the class;
- after the class has been fragmented by working in pairs or small groups, they should be brought together again as one unit.

In planning a training program or a single training session, the training team should not only consider the content but should also ask themselves how best to arrange things so that, at each point, people are likely to learn effectively.

7. Evaluation

Evaluation is an essential element in training. Trainers must ask the question "How are we doing?", and they should take account of the answers in planning the next phase—in which may be long-term planning or the next meeting of the training course.

Evaluation is a continuous process carried out during as well as at the end of a course, and long afterwards as well—though there are points at which it is given formal expression. It is engaged in by everyone involved in the training process: the trainers, the trainees, and those in supervisory or leadership roles. The final arbiter is, of course, the caller, whose judgement on us we may never know.

The purpose of evaluation is to improve things; so the process may be seen as a cycle, with each phase of evaluation feeding ideas back into the system. This cycle is illustrated in Figure 1 as it applies to the pre-service.

8. Issues in the Role and Training of Non-Professionals

A. Volunteers and professionals

The non-professional must always beware of stepping beyond the proper limits of his competence and role. He does not make diagnoses nor offer advice; his role is bounded by the limits of befriending. He must watch that he is not tempted by the expectations of a caller to go beyond these limits. Neither should he anticipate outcomes such as may be agreed or expected in the more formal relationships of therapy or counselling. His competence lies in his ability to accept and listen without making judgments or offering solutions to what he imagines to be the others problem. His role is much like that of a friend, except that this friendship requires no reciprocity and is set up with the intention that it will terminate when no longer necessary.

Neither the professional nor the non-professional should underestimate the significance of this role nor the skills required for its performance. In suicidal crisis it can save a life.

B. Accountability

Trainees, and indeed experienced volunteers, are rightly concerned over questions of accountability and responsibility. In pre-service courses and in in-service training when appropriate, the subject should be opened up for discussion.

A voluntary agency set up to befriend the suicidal should not purport to recommend courses of action for its callers. The caller makes his own decisions about his life, and is responsible for them. The volunteer is accountable to the caller and to the agency for the proper discharge of his role according to the declared principles of the agency, but he is not responsible for the decisions and actions of another person.

The distress of a caller, and sometimes his desire to off-load the responsibility for decision-making, brings pressure to bear on a concerned volunteer. Trainers and supervisors have to be alert for indications of volunteers' anxieties, and time and opportunity must be given for their resolution.

Figure 1: The evaluation cycle

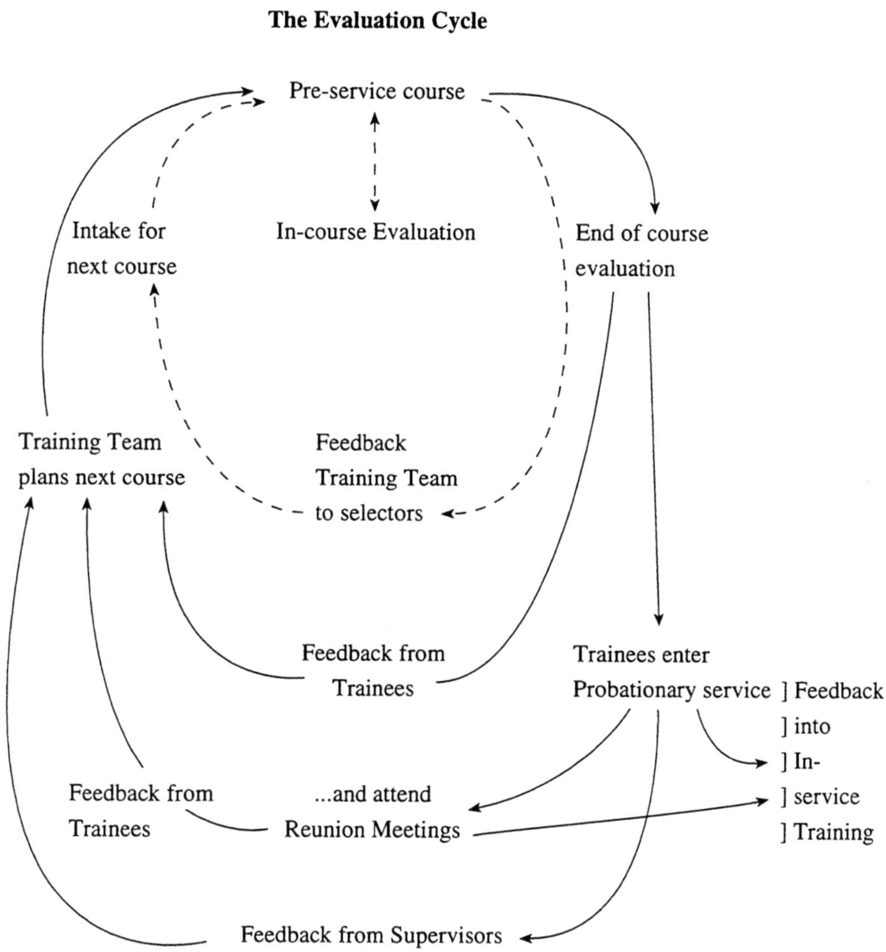

C. Confidentiality

People seeking support in their distress must be assured of confidentiality.

An agency's policy and practice in respect of confidentiality must be clearly defined and needs to be understood by all volunteers, and it is therefore a subject for continued attention in pre-service and in-service training. It is not enough to quote the words of a policy to trainees; they need to work through case-studies in which confidentiality is an issue in order that they may see the policy in action.

As with other emotionally demanding subjects in a training program, such as suicide, sexual matters or aggression, it is generally advisable to introduce the principle at issue in a low-key context. Having accepted the idea, trainees are more able to consider more demanding circumstances in which their ability to hold to the principle will be challenged.

Two examples will illustrate this graded approach:

a. A woman contacts the agency. Some time later, a man claiming to be her husband makes contact and demands to know whether she has been in touch. The confidentiality requirement is clear and there is no difficult moral issue here (though even this relatively undemanding type of case needs to be worked upon in role play).

b. A man contacts the agency, and in the course of the contact he states that he has committed a serious crime. Here, the volunteers' ability to maintain confidentially is tested more seriously, and the issues in such a case must be the subject of role-play and discussion in training programs.

Even more demanding are cases involving children, and it is here that the volunteer may be under most pressure to break confidentiality. In all cases the support of the supervisor or leader must be sought. Volunteers must be assured that they are expected to use the agency's internal support system; far from expressing weakness on the volunteer's part, it is a further safeguarding of the quality of support for the caller. Volunteers must not be expected to carry alone the burdens that are often placed upon them. For this reason, it is vital that callers and volunteers understand that anything that is said may if necessary be shared with the leadership of the agency; confidentiality is between the caller and the agency, not the individual volunteer.

Not infrequently a person under professional treatment may also seek befriending support from a voluntary agency. The confidentiality principle must still apply, though of course the caller's freely given consent could allow liaison between the agencies.

The confidentiality issue is discussed further in Appendix E.

REFERENCES

The bibliography is arranged in two parts: Section A lists books on suicide and related subjects that are authoritative but appropriate to the needs of the non-professional. Section B lists books on or relevant to training of non-professionals.

Section A

Eldrid, J. (1988): *Caring for the Suicidal.* London, Constable. Contains, as well as valuable insights into suicidal behavior, much practical guidance on immediate and long-term support and on interaction between volunteer and professional.

Hoff, L.A. (1978): *People in Crisis.* Addison Wesley Publishing Co. A major study of crisis (not only suicidal). Chapters 5 and 6 relate to suicidal behavior.

Jacobsson, L., Gustavsson, L., & Salander-Renberg, E. (1988): *Om Sjalvmord (on Suicide).* Raben and Sjogren, Kristianstad. A simple but authoritative book addressing a non-professional readership with information and insight on suicide and on how the lay person can help in its prevention. (In Swedish).

Keir, N. (1988): *I Can't Face Tomorrow.* London, Thorsons, 2nd. Edn. A wide ranging study of suicide, containing guidance on warning signs and the help that can be given by non-professional people.

Samaritans, The. (1978): *Answers to Suicide.* London, Constable. A collection of twenty papers answering questions on aspects of suicide posed by Chad Varah.

Samaritans, The. (1987): *Suicide Prevention - Information for Teachers and Counselors in New York City.* The Samaritans of New York City, P.O.Box 1259, Madison Square Station, New York, NY 10159.

A booklet available in English or Spanish which sets out very clearly what a lay person involved in suicide prevention needs to know. Permission is given for the booklet to be copied.

Shneidman, E.S. (1985): *Definition of Suicide.* New York, Wiley. Basic reading for anyone working with the suicidal.

Varah, Ch. (1988): *The Samaritans; Befriending the Suicidal.* London, Constable, Revised Edn. A collection of papers edited (and several written) by the Founder of the Samaritans, covering most of the subjects listed in Appendix B.

Section B

Berne, E. (1987): *Games People Play.* Penguin. While it is about neither suicide nor training, it offers stimulating reading on human behavior.

Evans, N. (1985): *Post-Education Society; Recognising Adults as Learners.* London, Croom Helm. Chapter 2 is particularly useful, and includes guidance on planning a program of adult learning.

Feek, W. (1988): *Working Effectively.* London, Bedford Square Press. A guide to evaluation methods, written for non-professional organizations.

Heather, B. (1984): *Sharing: A Handbook for those involved in Training in Personal Relationships and Sexuality.* London, FPA Education Unit. Guidance on experiental methods, with details of practical activities.

Holloway, C. & Otto, S. (1985): *Getting Organized: A Handbook for Non-Statutory Organizations.* London, Bedford Square Press. Particularly useful on planning, team work and evaluation.

Hoggarth, L. & Grisbook, D. (1985): *Planning your Training Programme.* Leicester, National Council for Voluntary Youth Services. A short guide to training activities, applicable to any voluntary organization.

Lake, T. & Acheson, F. (1988): *Room to listen, Room to Talk.* London, Bedford Square Press. Although directed towards counselling and therapy, it offers useful introductory reading.

Lauffer, A. & Gorodesky, A. (1977): *Volunteers: Volume 5 in Sage Human Services Guides.* Beverly Hills, Sage Publications. An overview of the volunteer role: recruitment, screening, training and evaluating.

Milroy, E. (1982): *Role play: A Practical Guide.* Aberdeen University Press. Useful material that can be adapted to the trainer's own context.

Van Ments, M. (1988): *The Effective Use of Role Play.* Kogan Page, 2nd. Edn. Practical applications as well as a thorough theoretical base.

Appendix A: *A sample selection procedure for a volunteer agency*

1. Information

Interested people are invited to bring family or close friends whose lives will be affected should the applicant be accepted.

The meeting should include:

- a short introductory talk on the work of the agency and the need for this work in the community;
- some pointers to the agency's methods and principles. This could be by film or video if available or by a short role demonstration;

- questions of fact and discussion on issues on the minds of those present. These must be responded to honestly, but detail on procedures should be avoided - it is not a training class!

Publicity information should be available, and it is suggested that application forms be made available at the end of the meeting, to be returned after due thought rather than in a moment of philanthropic zeal.

2. Selection day

Applicants are invited to a selection day, which should include:

- Further opportunity for questions about the agency;
- An interview for each applicant (personal and sometimes sensitive aspects of the applicant's life may have to be explored, so it is necessary that a substantial part of interview time is on a one-to-one basis—a format more likely to allow the applicant to "open up");
- Discussions in small groups, staffed by experienced members as leaders and observers. These discussions should be:

a) on topics of general concern in the community, e.g. a current controversial question—the purpose being not to reach a conclusion on the topic but to allow the selectors to observe the behavior of applicants as they become involved in the process and thus come to behave more naturally than in the formality of interview;
b) on questions arising from a role demonstration, by members of the selection team, involving conflict hiding deeper issues (e.g. a parent complaining of teenage child's behavior, but complaints hiding deeper distress about failing marriage). The purpose is to observe applicants as they discuss the episode, noting those who are able to listen through to the deeper level and those whose concern is to propose solutions to the presenting problem.

Each applicant will have been seen in a number of different situations by several selectors, who then meet to make their decisions.

Criteria for acceptance:

The applicant should have shown evidence of:

- ability to listen and accept without making judgments on people;
- ability to respond sensitively and intelligently to human situations;
- self-knowledge, but not undue introspection;

- openness to continued learning;
- ability to work individually and in a team, and to accept the disciple of the organization.

Criteria for rejection:

The applicant will have shown evidence of:

- membership being sought as a support for own emotional needs, or as an opportunity for proselytizing;
- a desire to rehearse own wisdom and experience;
- a tendency to make rapid judgments;
- a desire to offer advice and to define and solve the problems of others;
- inability to listen and to empathise.

After the meeting, the selectors decide on each applicant, and letters are sent. Letters of rejection need to be particularly sensitive to the applicants' feelings.

The above procedure gives time for consideration by both parties, whose decisions are made in a context of maximum information.

It also allows for:

- feedback to publicity team on applicants knowledge of and assumptions about the agency;

- feed forward to training team on any special characteristics or attitudes noted during selection day.

Appendix B: *Content of pre-service course*

The following list proposes the subjects that should be included in a pre-service course. The items do not necessarily have to be taught as separate units; many will arise in the course of role-plays and case studies (see Section 6 and Appendix D for teaching methods).

1. Suicide:

   - coming to terms with our own feelings
   - suicidal and parasuicidal behavior
   - indicators of suicide risk (See Appendix C)

2. Befriending:

    - acceptance and empathy
    - helping caller to talk about suicidal feelings
    - assessing and responding to suicide risk (See Appendix C)
    - avoidance of problem-solving and advice-giving
    - recognising and managing manipulation

3. The agency's procedures:

    - for dealing with emergencies
    - for consultation and support
    - for responding to particular types of call (eg third party, information, silent calls, calls from other agencies)

4. Telephone skills:

    - the initial response; developing and ending a call
    - characteristics of telephone befriending

5. Face-to-face skills:

    - welcoming the caller; developing and ending a call
    - seating arrangements; body language

6. Subjects for special study:

    - bereavement and other loss
    - depression
    - the sexual element in calls: sexual gratification or call for help?
    - young callers: characteristic approaches; anxiety of volunteers
    - "addicted" callers: response to the over-dependent
    - unhelpable callers: recognition and response

7. Administration:

    - office layout and procedures.

Appendix C: *A guide to assessment of suicide risk*

The following is used by The Samaritans in training volunteers in assessing suicide risk and responding in an appropriate way. The Guide is referred to in the course of role-plays and case study discussions.

A. Has the caller a *suicide plan*?

- Is his death imminent?
- Has he planned his death in detail (sudden or slow method?)
- Has he planned a suicide gamble or gesture (rather than a certainty?)
- Has he definite suicidal thoughts, but no plan?
- Has he vague thoughts about suicide?
- Has he no suicidal thoughts?

These plans imply (from top to bottom) *imminent danger, high risk,* through *moderate risk to low risk.*

B. The risk may be increased if *other factors* are present:

• Previous suicidal acts	Increases risk greatly
• Loss of hope	
• Recent broken relationship	Any one of these
• Isolation	increases risk
• Rejection	considerably
• Depressive illness	
• Possession of means of suicide	Any one of these
• Putting affairs in order	increases risk
• Dependence on alcohol / drugs	significantly
• Elderly/ill/chronic pain	Any one of these increases risk slightly

C. *Response* to suicide risk

Risk level (assessed from suicide plan response and other factors)

Suicide attempt now	-	Arrange treatment if caller allows
Imminent danger	-	Stay with caller
High risk	-	Fix another meeting very soon
Moderate risk	-	Hear out and let go (unless there are other reasons for further meeting).

Appendix D: *Teaching methods and organization*

The following list describes the main methods of teaching and class organization suitable for use in training non-professionals. Use of various methods is discussed in Section 6.

METHOD	USED	COMMENTS
Lecture or talk	Economic way of presenting factual material, of explaining concepts and of giving information.	Unless the lecturer is unusually good, the talk should be short. Better to make only a few major points and to provide material for subsequent discussion. Where possible use other methods in conjunction with talk: eg, visual presentation question/answer, brainstorming, buzz groups. Discussion to draw upon resources of class members • to encourage participation • to ascertain level of learning and identify gaps. Discussion group leadership skills are necessary. See section 6.
Pairs	Useful for discussion and practice of listening skills.	A non-threatening setting in which people are most likely to express themselves freely. See also buzzgroups and the discussion of role play.
Triads	As for pairs.	Groups of three trainees may be used much as pairs. See discussion of role-play.
Brain-storming	Useful for stimulation thought and ideas. A lively way of starting a session of reviving the pace.	Trainer asks members to call out their first thoughts (single words) about the subject: he writes these on a board as they arise - so they are in no particular order. As ideas become exhausted, class invited to derive order and meaning from the random words: What do these words tell us about our response to the subject?
Buzz-groups	Useful and for checking understanding of an idea; or for generating further ideas.	Class is asked to discuss, in pairs of threes, an idea of proposition. Each buzz-group may then report back its response in order that the whole class share outcomes.

METHOD	USED	COMMENTS
Written material, hand-outs	Before a class, as preparation; during a class, as material to be worked upon. After a class, as consolidation or further reading.	Hand-outs should be brief (for longer passages, refer class to books, articles). Notes or tabulations are useful. Distribute at start of a class only if the handout is to be used during the class - otherwise attention will be on hand-out rather than the class!
Case Study	To introduce trainee to the type of situation he will meet. To make more specific the general principles presented in a class.	Details of a specific case (usually fictional or heavily disguised, because of confidentiality) are given for discussion or as a basis for role-play; the former is less demanding, but it may lead to emphasis on problems rather than on the feelings of those involved.
Role-play	To bring learner as close as possible to real situations. Particularly valuable in learning about practical expression.	For discussion of role-play, see Section 6.
Simulation	Learning procedures through activity in a save setting.	Learning and reinforcement through activity with an element of competition and fun. Role-play is a simulation of reality; but here the term refers to a larger exercise in which many aspects of the agency's work may be involved. A whole episode may be played through in extended role-plays: caller contact, consultation with supervisors, further contact with caller, administrative follow-up etc. It may be possible to set up a practice telephone circuit that can present trainees with "real" situations such as engaged lines.

METHOD	USED	COMMENTS
Games	Learning and reinforcement through activity with an element of competition and fun.	A "game element" may be introduced into many activities - can be useful in lightening a heavy session. eg - "Thumbs game" role demonstration of a call, with every member of class giving "thumbs up/down" to each of the befrienders's responses, according to their judgments of its suitability. Any "thumbs down" or disagreement is taken up and discussed. Artificial, but can be very lively and stimulating.
"Machine gun"	To check that trainees know the rules and can keep to them under pressure. Useful for revision of basic ideas.	Very short caller role-plays, each pressurizing the befriender to "break the rules" in some way (eg to break confidentiality, to take sides, to offer quick solution or advice, etc.). Pace must be maintained. The story is not followed through, attention being entirely upon the response to the issue presented.
"Goldfish bowl"	To promote discussion on attitudes and group processes. Useful in training a training team.	Two task groups, sitting in an inner and outer circle. Inner group discusses an issue (eg the way a situation should be handled), while outer group observes and then comments on attitudes and group processes. For training trainers, inner circle may role-play a training team discussing different approaches during a meeting on policy and methods.
Visual presentation	To clarify and reinforce what is heard. To stimulate interest. To provide variety.	Writing must be large enough to be read easily. Building up summary of talk on chalkboard, etc: key words or headings are written up as the talk proceedings, giving, by the end, a visual reminder of the talk. Tables or figures should contain only minimal information; complex data displayed for a short time confuse the learner. Generally, statistics presented in diagram form are more effective. (Detailed data, if necessary, are better given in handouts for later study).

METHODS	USED	COMMENTS
Visual presentation (continued)		Pictures (eg cartoons, pin-man drawings) can be very effective. Media: Chalkboard: immediate, ephemeral, and cheap. Flip-chart: writing in space is limited, so use in small groups. Overhead projector: either for immediate, ephemeral presentation; or for previously prepared material. Overly technique is effective. Slides: could be useful for displaying prepared material. Video tape: a) prepared video tapes: should be followed by discussion etc. to avoid passive acceptance b) video-camera - either in closed circuit TV or by subsequent play-back: very useful in learning about face-to-face work and in the training of trainers. Film: as in video (a). Preferable if audience is large, but generally less easy to use than video tape.
Audio tapes	a) To make available good and authoritative speakers. b) To promote participation. c) To learn about one's own voice. d) To provide music.	a) As with talks, concentration soon drops; but playback is available if a point needs to be debated or emphasized. b) This applies to the "stop tape" prepared as a participatory exercise, to be stopped at key points for class discussion. c) Each trainee's voice is recorded (especially over telephone), and played back for comment. d) From time to time, music can be an effective aid to learning, eg as a mood-inducer, or through a song with a relevant message.
Workshops	To enhance learning by co-operating on a group project.	The essence of the workshop approach is participation. The presenter's task is to prepare linked activities centered on the workshop theme in which every member can participate. In the course of the workshop, a number of the above approaches will be used.

Appendix E: *A further note on confidentiality*
(See Section 8.)

People troubled by intimate, deeply personal and perhaps even incriminating worries are likely to speak of these matters only with the assurance of confidentiality; and where suicide is a possible outcome of their distress, talking to another person may save a life. The listener must recognise this trust and understand the possible consequences of breaking it.

A helping agency should define its position on confidentiality as clearly as possible and ensure that its workers understand and abide by this position. As an example, the fourth of the "Seven Principles" of the Samaritans is quoted:

> "The fact that a person has asked the help of the Samaritans, together with everything he has said, is completely confidential within the organization unless permission is freely given by the caller for all or part of such information to be communicated to someone outside the organization. A Samaritan volunteer is not permitted to accept confidences if a condition is made that not even the Director should be informed of them."

The interests of both caller and befriender are safeguarded by confidentiality being "within the organization" and not vested in the individual befriender.

In the United Kingdom (with certain exceptions in Northern Ireland at present) there is no legal obligation to give information to anyone on anything except acts of treason or terrorism, though in a court of law, of course, a witness must answer questions. Each country has its own laws and procedures, in the light of which an agency's policy on confidentiality should be drawn up, and legal advice should be sought.

Preventing Suicide by Restricting Access to Methods for Suicide

D. LESTER

1. Introduction

The major thrust of suicide prevention in the 1960s and 1970s was in creating suicide prevention centers whose major service was to counsel suicidal clients. Research has also explored which methods of counseling clients prove more effective in reducing the risk of suicidal behaviour and which antidepressants proved most effective and least likely to result in suicidal overdoses (Lester, 1987a).

However, a growing hypothesis during the last decade is that suicide might be prevented by restricting access to lethal methods for committing suicide (Clarke and Lester, 1989). Initially, this suggestion came from Australia, where it was found that reducing the size of prescriptions and wrapping the tablets in plastic blisters appeared to cut their use in completed and attempted suicide. Then the detoxification of domestic gas in Great Britain not only virtually eliminated the use of domestic gas for suicide, also but appeared to lead to a reduction in the overall suicide rate.

Thus, it appears that restricting access to methods for suicide may be an effective method for preventing suicide. However, the critical question that follows upon this suggestion is whether people would switch to an alternative method for suicide if their preferred method was unavailable.

David Lester and his colleagues conducted a series of studies during the 1980s on this problem, and this chapter will present the major results of their research.

2. Firearms

A. The effect of strict handgun control laws

The USA consists of 50 states (48 continental plus Alaska and Hawaii), each of which is permitted to pass its own laws on the control of firearms. Bakal (1968) examined the handgun control laws of each state and coded them for the presence of various characteristics, such as whether a licence is required to sell handguns at retail stores, whether sales are reported to the police, and whether a permit is required to purchase a handgun.

Lester and Murrell (1980) created a Guttman scale of strictness for the 48 continental states of the USA from these codings and found that states with the strictest handgun control laws had the lowest firearm suicide rates and the lowest overall suicide rates in 1960 and 1970. Those states with the stricter handgun control laws and the lower firearm suicide rates did not have higher suicide rates by poisons or hanging/strangulation, though the suicide rate by "other" methods was higher. Thus, Lester and Murrell concluded that switching to an alternative method for suicide did not occur in states in which the handgun control laws were stricter.

Further analysis of the data (Lester, 1984) showed that the restrictions on the selling and purchasing of handguns were the most critical characteristics of the laws in the association with lower firearm suicide rates. Restrictions on carrying were unrelated to firearm suicide rates. Finally, controls for social variables (such as percent of blacks and percent of males in each state) did not eliminate these associations. Lester (1987b) examined the power of the strictness of handgun control laws and the moral attitude toward suicide as predictors in explaining the suicide rates of the continental states. The strictness of the handgun control laws and the percentage of citizens attending church (the operational measure of moral attitudes toward suicide) were both highly correlated with the states' suicide rates, giving a multiple correlation of 0.68, thereby accounting for 46 percent of the variation in the states' suicide rates.

B. Attempting to measure the extent of firearm ownership in the states

There are no measures of firearm ownership for each state of the USA. However, several indirect measures are available. Lester (1987c) examined the relationship between the accidental death rate from firearms in each state and the percent of homicides committed with firearms with the suicide rate.

The accident death rate using firearms was positively associated with the firearm suicide rate, but not with the overall suicide rate. Similar associations were found for the percent of homicides committed with firearms. (The strictness of handgun control laws was negatively associated with overall suicide rate.)

Lester (1989) has also explored the use of per capita subscriptions to three firearm magazines in the states of the USA as measures of firearm ownership. Per capita subscription rates to the three magazines were positively correlated to the firearm suicide rate and to the overall suicide rate.

C. Actual firearm ownership

Measures of actual firearm ownership are available for the nine major regions of the continental USA (though not for the 48 individual states). Lester (1988a) found that this measure was positively associated with the firearm suicide rate, but not to the overall suicide rate. Lester (1988b) compared these results for the USA with results from an analysis of data from Australian states. In Australia too the per capita ownership of firearms in the states was positively related to the firearm suicide rate but not to the overall suicide rate.

D. A time-series analysis of firearm ownership in the USA

The previous studies were regional studies over the states and major regions of the USA and Australia. Clarke and Jones (1989) obtained data on the household ownership of firearms in the USA as a whole from 1959 to 1984 using data from national polls. Their time-series analysis identified that the ownership of handguns was associated with the firearm suicide rate and with the overall suicide rate.

3. Car Exhaust

A. Detoxifying car exhaust in the USA

In 1968, the USA began to impose emission control for motor vehicles in order to clean up the environment. The result was that the carbon monoxide content in car exhaust dropped from 8.5% to 0.05% by 1980. This has made suicide more difficult to commit using car exhaust. Poisoning from carbon monoxide takes much longer, increasing the risk of intervention by others and changes of mind in the suicidal person. Death from simple suffocation (elimination of oxygen) also takes much longer than poisoning by carbon monoxide.

Clarke and Lester (1987) explored the effects of the reduced toxicity of car exhaust on the use of car exhaust for suicide in the USA, and they compared this trend with the same period in England and Wales where emission controls have not been imposed on motor vehicles.

Clarke and Lester found that the use of car exhaust for suicide in the USA has leveled off and perhaps slightly declined in the USA since 1968. (It must remembered that older, more toxic cars are still in use and that the emission control system can be disconnected to permit gas richer in carbon monoxide to fill the car or garage.) In contrast, in England and Wales, the use of car exhaust for suicide has risen dramatically since 1970.

Clarke and Lester saw their results as indicating the usefulness of reducing the lethality of a method for suicide in reducing the suicide rate or preventing dramatic increases in the rate.

B. A regional study of car ownership and suicide

Lester and Frank (1989) have explored the relation between a simple measure of overall car ownership in the states of the USA (regardless of the year in which the car was made) and the use of car exhaust for suicide.

Lester found that per capita ownership of cars was related to the suicide rate using car exhaust, but not to the overall suicide rate. Thus, the more cars are available in a state, the more they are used for suicide.

4. Domestic Gas

The effects of detoxification of domestic gas in England & Wales, Scotland and The Netherlands

Clarke and Mayhew (1988) have documented accurately the gradual detoxification of domestic gas in England and Wales and the declining suicide rate using domestic gas and overall. They showed that the two curves follow each other extremely closely. In 1958, there were 2637 suicides using domestic gas out of 5298 suicides comprising 49.8 percent of the total number of suicides. By 1977, there were eight suicides using domestic gas out of 3944, comprising only 0.2 percent of the suicides.

Clarke and Mayhew (1989) then explored why Scotland and the Netherlands did not experience an overall decline in their suicide rate as domestic gas was detoxified. They presented evidence to show that the suicide rates were rising in those two nations when domestic gas was detoxified, and they argued that this rising suicide masked the effect of the detoxification of domestic gas on the overall suicide rate. More recently, Lester (1990) has shown that the detoxification of domestic gas in the USA resulted in a decrease in the use of domestic gas for suicide but did not appear to have any impact on the total suicide rate.

However, in this context, the data presented by Clarke and Lester (1987) become relevant. Their data show that the use of car exhaust is rising dramatically in England and Wales in recent years. It may be that those who might have used domestic gas if it were still toxic are now turning to car exhaust. Thus, perhaps people will switch to a similar method to their preferred method if their preferred method is unavailable. In the USA, Lester (1990) noted that, during the period when domestic gas was becoming less popular for suicide as it became less lethal, car ownership was growing and became more common as a method for suicide.

5. Studies in Japan

Recently, Lester and Abe (1989a, 1989b, 1989c) conducted a series of studies in Japan on this strategy for preventing suicide. They found that, as domestic gas was detoxified, its use for suicide decreased without any sign of evidence that people displaced to other methods for suicide. Similarly, restrictions on prescriptions for sedatives and hypnotics resulted in a decline in their use for suicide without any evidence that people increased their use of other methods for suicide. Finally, the increasing ownership of cars in Japan was accompanied by an increase in the use of car exhaust for suicide without any evidence that people switched from other methods for suicide.

Thus, these studies from Japan confirm the potential usefulness of this strategy for preventing suicide.

Implications for a theory of suicide

It is common to think of suicide as a desperate measure, chosen by seriously dysfunctional people who are at their wits' end. It seems unlikely that such people would be deterred by the effort needed to overcome the restrictions placed upon obtaining a lethal amount of their preferred method for suicide.

However, the present viewpoint suggests that suicide may be a logical decision made by people based upon rational issues such as the availability of different methods for suicide (Yeh and Lester, 1987). Many people when asked say that they would consider one and only one method for suicide. If access to this method was restricted, then suicide may well be averted in these people. The necessity of switching to a less preferred method may introduce costs that were not originally present. For example, those who fear the pain of a bullet and the disfigurement of the wound would in all probability not switch to firearms were medication no longer available.

6. Will People Switch Methods for Suicide

Although this is the critical question for this method of preventing suicide, very few studies are relevant to the issue. It remains a matter of opinion. However, one suggestion can be made.

Rich et al. (1990) documented that the imposition of strict gun control laws in Toronto resulted in a decrease in the use of guns for suicide and a corresponding increase in the use of jumping (primarily in front of subway trains). Thus, apparently, people switched methods for suicide. However, if the new method is less lethal than the former method, then there is a greater likelihood that suicidal attempters will survive and, therefore, completed suicide will have been prevented.

However, Lester (1988c) has argued that a failure to make lethal methods and venues for suicide less available may render people legally liable for civil damages. For example, all houseowners in the USA must fence in swimming pools in their back yards or face civil liability should some stranger drown in their pool. Lester argued that the municipal government in the Bay Area in California might be held similarly liable by those whose relatives jump from the Golden Gate Bridge, a popular suicide venue which is not fenced in.

Lester argued that suicide prevention organizations should therefore agitate for stronger firearm control laws, the fencing in of suicide venues, smaller prescriptions of less lethal medications, prescriptions of suppositories rather than oral tablets, and related measures to reduce the availability of methods for suicide. A list of possible measures is shown in Appendix A.

Conclusions

The present chapter has reviewed a series of regional and time series studies on the effects of reducing the availability of firearms, toxic car exhaust and toxic domestic gas on suicide. Though the data do not provide data for a definitive conclusion, the results do indicate that reducing the availability of a method for suicide reduces its use for suicide and may also reduce then overall suicide rate if the method restricted is commonly used and a lethal method. In the latter case, people who switch methods for suicide are forced to switch to a less lethal method for which survival is more likely.

It is likely that more research on this important topic will appear in the next few years, hopefully permitting us to evaluate this method of suicide prevention more precisely.

REFERENCES

Bakal, C. *No right to bear arms.* New York: Paperback Library, 1968.

Clarke, R. V. & Jones, P. R. Suicide and increased availability of handguns in the United States. *Social Science & Medicine,* 1989, 28, 805-809.

Clarke, R. V. & Lester, D. Toxicity of car exhausts and opportunity for suicide. *Journal of Epidemiology & Community Health,* 1987, 41, 114-120.

Clarke, R. V. & Lester, D. *Suicide: closing the exits.* New York: Springer Verlag, 1989.

Clarke, R. V. & Mayhew, P. The British gas suicide story and its criminological implications. *Crime & Justice,* 1988, 10, 79-116.

Clarke, R. V. & Mayhew, P. Crime as opportunity. *British Journal of Criminology,* 1989, 29, 35-46.

Lester, D. *Gun control.* Springfield: Thomas, 1984.

Lester, D. Preventing suicide. In J. Morgan (Ed.) *Suicide.* London, Ont.: King's College, 1987a, 69-78.

Lester, D. An availability-acceptability theory of suicide. *Activitas Nervosa Superior,* 1987b, 19, 164-166.

Lester, D. Availability of guns and the likelihood of suicide. *Sociology & Social Research,* 1987c, 71, 287-288.

Lester, D. Gun control, gun ownership and suicide prevention. *Suicide & Life-Threatening Behavior,* 1988a, 18, 176-180.

Lester, D. Restricting the availability of guns as a strategy for suicide prevention. *Biology & Society,* 1988b, 5, 127-129.

Lester, D. The AAS and political activism. *AAS Newslink,* 1988c, 14(2), 8.

Lester, D. Gun ownership and suicide in the United States. *Psychological Medicine,* 1989, 19, 519-521.

Lester, D. The effects of detoxification of domestic gas on suicide in the United States. *American Journal of Public Health,* 1990, 80, 80-81.

Lester, D. & Abe, K. The effect of restricting access to lethal methods for suicide. *Acta Psychiatrica Scandinavica,* 1989a, 80, 180-182.

Lester, D. & Abe, K. The effect of controls on sedatives and hypnotics and their use for suicide. *Clinical Toxicology,* 1989b, 27, 299-303.

Lester, D. & Abe, K. Car availability, exhaust toxicity, and suicide. *Annals of Clinical Psychiatry,* 1989c, 1, 247-250.

Lester, D. & Frank, M. L. The use of motor vehicle exhaust for suicide and the availability of cars. *Acta Psychiatrica Scandinavica,* 1989, 79, 238-240.

Lester, D. & Murrell, M. E. The influence of gun control laws on suicidal behavior. *American Journal of Psychiatry,* 1980, 137, 121-122.

Rich, C. L. & Young, J. G., Fowler, R. C., Wagner, J., & Black, N. A. Guns and suicide. *American Journal of Psychiatry,* 1990, 147, 342-346.

Yeh, B. Y. & Lester, D. An economic model for suicide. In D. Lester; *Suicide as a learned behavior.* Springfield: Thomas, 1987, 51-57.

Appendix A: *Ways To Limit Access To Lethal Methods For Suicide*

Cars:
- emission controls (to reduce carbon monoxide content)
- change shape of tail pipe to end in a narrow slit (to make attachment of hose difficult)
- have automatic ignition turn-off once engine has idled for five minutes

Domestic Gas:
- switch to less toxic natural gas
- automatic gas turn-off if gas not lit within 30 seconds
- make oven doors hinged at base (to make it difficult to put one's head in)

Jumping:
- fence in bridges
- fence in tops of high buildings
- restrict access to the tops of buildings
- fence in parking garages

Poisons:
- put the common household poisons in child-proof containers

Firearms:
- pass and enforce strict gun control laws
- require members of gun clubs to store guns at the club in secure rooms

Medications:
- limit size of prescriptions
- eliminate automatic refills of prescriptions
- do not prescribe without seeing and evaluating patient
- enclose pills in plastic blisters
- prescribe as suppositories rather than as oral tablets
- set up monitoring system to catch multiple prescribing of patient by several doctors/pharmacists
- prescribe less toxic medications (eg. Mianserin rather than Amitriptyline)
- set up systems to prevent forging/changing prescriptions by patients (eg by having physicians directly input prescriptions into pharmacies by computer)

Attempted Suicides:
- collect lethal agents/implements before releasing attempters to their homes

Suicide in Western Samoa
An Example of a Suicide Prevention Program in a Developing Country

J.R. BOWLES

1. Introduction

In 1981 the YMCA of Western Samoa initiated the formation of a suicide study group with the aim to help understand and if possible devise prevention strategies in what appeared then as an epidemic calamity in exponential growth. Other groups represented were the Health Department, Justice Department, Fellowship of Churches and at times people co-opted from the Police, Education Department, Agricultural Department, media representatives and anyone else who could possibly make a useful contribution. The author of this chapter was invited to represent the Health Department having been recently appointed as a psychiatrist there at that time.

The Suicide Prevention project was not a well planned and controlled experimental study because members of the study group were otherwise fully occupied, and their work on the project was done voluntarily. There was no specific funding allocation beyond the clerical costs of the meetings which were held at approximately monthly intervals at the YMCA. Data collection was at best simplistic and although highly motivated the members were distracted by the awful imperatives of the escalating death rate in otherwise essentially healthy people.

The account that follows gives a description of a Suicide Prevention Program in which special attention is paid to the method chosen by the victim. The data will be presented mainly in the form of tables and graphs and should be read rather like a picture book with an essentially simple message.

2. Background

The study of suicide and related phenomena is a complex field with few easy answers. For the individual involved there are usually many antecedent factors which lead to the circumstance of self harm. From those who survive to talk about these things we learn that the wish to die is not always paramount. Their apparent uncertainty of intention is an indication of ambivalence or perhaps a reluctance to talk in retrospect about the decision to live or die.

For a social group the patterns of suicide and/or attempted suicide are likewise complex and are often interpreted as an indication of social process. Stable patterns are compared with those elsewhere, while changes over time within a socio-cultural group attract attempts of explanation, especially if the changes are rapid and significant in size.

With a generally recognised recent increase in suicide rates in many places and especially a relative increase in younger people, prevention of suicide or deliberate non-lethal self harm remains a major concern. The complexity of the subject and the multi-dimensional nature of the aetiology has however meant that simple and effective strategies are not easily apparent. Some of the studies of outcome of attempts to prevent or reduce suicide in population groups have indicated disappointing results given the amount of effort expended. Clearly then there is more to be learned and each bit of information needs to be assessed for relevance and value.

One area of potential study is directed at the method chosen for self harm, i.e. poison, firearm, hanging etc. This is especially pertinent if in a particular population a chosen method has become so predominant and its notoriety is such that the people begin to automatically equate suicide/self harm with that method. In such a circumstance prevention strategies have potentially more effect if the intervention can significantly reduce the modal method without a compensatory rise in other methods. Useful gains are then possible.

This idea appeals to common sense, and in the crisis situation of a potentially suicidal person with intent and a method available there is agreement that getting rid of the method is sensible. Acute intervention gives the potential victim a chance to reappraise the situation and perhaps divert from an impulsive, emotionally overloaded act of self harm. The counter argument states that restrictions on potential methods are often impractical and essentially naive. Suicidal people denied one method will find or choose another and the only true course of action is to study and understand the psychosocial roots of the problem in order to devise a properly based intervention strategy. There is no doubt that understanding the psycho-social and biological dimensions of suicide is a fundamental objective, what is in question however is the prospect of interventions aimed at reducing the impact of particular methods in some circumstances.

Kreitman (1976) reported a significant fall in suicide in the U.K. following a reduction in the inherent toxicity of the domestic gas supply there. Suicide by gas poisoning had become a predominant method and the fall of deaths by this means was not replaced by a compensatory rise in another. A similar beneficial outcome has been attributed to the reduction in the widespread prescription and hence availability of barbiturates although the frequency of overdosing with other drugs perhaps less toxic has continued. Lester (1990) and others have also proposed that attention to the method(s) of common choice is a pertinent area of study.

3. Western Samoa

During the interval between 1956 to 1988 the number of suicides in Western Samoa varied as shown in Figure 1 (Appendix A), which also shows the population census data obtained each five years 1956, 1961,..1986. Clearly the increased suicide frequency was not due to simple population growth and indicates an alarming increase of rate in this small, geographically isolated group of people. In 1981 with a population of 156,349 there were a total of 49 suicides giving a base rate of 31.3 per 100,000 compared with 6.1 in 1971. In clinical terms this meant that (in 1981) there was on average about one death per week and as will be shown below a similar number of survivors.

A proper starting point for the study was to obtain statistical data which were both reliable and valid. Figures for suicide and non-lethal self harm were collected retrospectively from the records available from the Police, Health Department and Coroner and where possible combined for cross-validation. Archival records from old newspapers were also consulted to supplement the other sources. As well as these retrospective data a prospective study was initiated in 1981 which aimed at concerted cooperative effort between these departments and with the hospital staff using a dedicated questionnaire (Appendix E). Thus while all such data will possibly underestimate true frequencies and especially so in the case of non-lethal parasuicide, the 1981-83 figures were rigorously cross checked. It should also be noted that the population was small enough to allow a total survey and the country sufficiently compact to preclude population groups being isolated and beyond scrutiny.

Suicide is known in Samoan history, as indicated by mention in their old legends and more recently since European contact as recorded by Pratt (1862). Freeman (1983) gives information about twenty-two cases of suicide (sixteen males and six females) that he collected from various sources for the interval 1925-1966 which is consistent with the low incidence end of the graph in Figure 1. In their Bibliography on Culture and Mental Health in the Pacific Islands, Rubinstein and White (1983) list 100 references to suicide in that region, many of these refer to a similar escalation of suicide in Micronesia, (predominantly young men who hang themselves). Only eight refer to Western Samoa, six of which refer to publications since 1980 which describe the events here discussed. Older people of the present population agreed that suicides occurred in the past, but at most infrequently, and nothing like this more recent unprecedented increase.

Another common source of uncertainty in suicide/parasuicide data is the problem of deciding between deliberate intent and accidental self harm. This issue is discussed for example by Adam (1985) and in two W.H.O. publications (1974, 1982) where the differences between suicide and attempted suicide are emphasised. In these Samoan cases most were well substantiated by information from relatives or close associates and any doubtful cases excluded. As will be discussed below many of those people who died had the clinical and epidemiological features more commonly associated with parasuicide and a nonfatal outcome irrespective of the actual intent at the time. Most were young and otherwise healthy, pre-existing mental illness was not generally recognised before the event and their associates later attributed their behaviour to causes other than illness, eg. intoxication, being chastised or doing something that could expose themselves or their family to ridicule or punishment. The predominant associated affective states were of anger, resentment, jealousy, shame or humiliation and a sense of rejection rather than devitalised persistent depression. The events were in many cases impulsive rather than well planned and arose in circumstances of acute or chronic interpersonal conflict and tension. Young women were represented more frequently than is usually the case in suicide data and the males were often alcohol affected at the time of the event. The difference in these Samoan cases was that instead of "overdosing" with some relatively innocuous substance they frequently used the highly toxic herbicide **paraquat.** An unusual consequence of this was that some drank enough of the concentrate to die quickly, others took a small amount and suffered a painful and anxious recovery while many in an intermediate category took several days to die. In these cases there were usually some signs of recovery, then a period of uncertainty, and eventual progressive respiratory failure (see notes on paraquat, see p. 187). Thus with these people it was possible to interview them and to assess in retrospect their mental state prior to the crisis event and subsequently over the interval to their eventual death.

4. The Data

If figure 1 is re-drawn to show the paraquat related suicides as in figure 2 (Appendix A), the significance of this factor becomes obvious. The background non-paraquat suicides show an increase through the 1970's and 80's, perhaps roughly in keeping with suicide rates for young people elsewhere, but the rise and fall and later lesser rise was mainly attributable to the variation in the paraquat statistic. From a public health point of view we sought to explain the rise to 1981, with due regard for the paraquat factor, and attempted to reverse the process by means of a publicised campaign to be described below.

Table 1 (Appendix B), shows the suicide data for 1981 according to age group, gender and method and table 2 comparable data for those who survived. Note that for this year over 80% of both deaths and survivors were associated with paraquat.

By the end of 1983 the rates had fallen and we were able to see where the changes had occurred. Equivalent data for 1983 are shown in tables 3 and 4, while tables 5 and 6 show the calculated differences between 1981 and 1983 in each of the tabulated categories, (Appendix B). The 27 less deaths shown in table 5 can be largely attributed to the 26 less paraquat deaths, 19 of which were in the 20-34 age group. Note also that there was not a compensatory rise in other methods although the extra four male hangings suggested possible examples of alternative choice. Similarly the overall reduction in attempted suicide shown in table 6 was apparently due to the 16 less paraquat poisonings against a minor drift to less toxic other poisons.

The tables also show that other poisons were generally not lethal and that hanging and firearms were almost exclusively male choices.

5. Age Analysis and Population Profile

The population distribution over five year cohort groups from the 1981 census is shown in figure 3 (next page) and is further elaborated in condensed form in the first part of table 7 (Appendix C). It is clear from these figures that the population is heavily weighted in the younger age groups, with almost 60% of the population below 20 years of age. Note also the marked reduction in the numbers of both males and females over the age range 15-30 in the population distribution.

Examination of table 7 (Appendix C) shows:

(1) Suicides by age group and gender for 1981, 1982 and 1983.
(2) Attempted suicide as above.
(3) Rates per 100,000 for the age groups and total population for males and females in both categories.

Figures 4, 5, and 6 (see next pages) show the rate information in graphic form which highlights the similarities and differences for male-female and suicide-parasuicide categories. The main differences between the deaths and survivors appeared in the older, (beyond 30) group and more so in males. This might suggest that there was a covert bimodal distribution in the male rates with a minor subgroup of males who were more conventionally suicidal (in the sense of suicide statistics seen in other countries), while the others represented a convergence of suicide/parasuicide brought about by the lethality and predominant use of paraquat.

By using the wider age groupings of table 8 (Appendix D) and calculating rates it was possible to compare these Samoan rate data with the 1980 W.H.O. statistics that I had available at that time. I chose for comparison the profiles of Norway, Switzerland, USA, and Hungary because they showed different rate variation over age groups and I presumed that they would be reasonably compiled and reliable. The graphs shown in figures 7 and 8 (see next pages) restate the emphasis on youth vulnerability in Western Samoa and the opposite of the usual increase of suicide rates seen with age elsewhere. It should be noted however that the rate calculations are labile because of the small numbers in each cell, for this reason also I have used a three year average to calculate the rates in table 7.

Figure 3. Population profile – Western Samoa – 1981 census

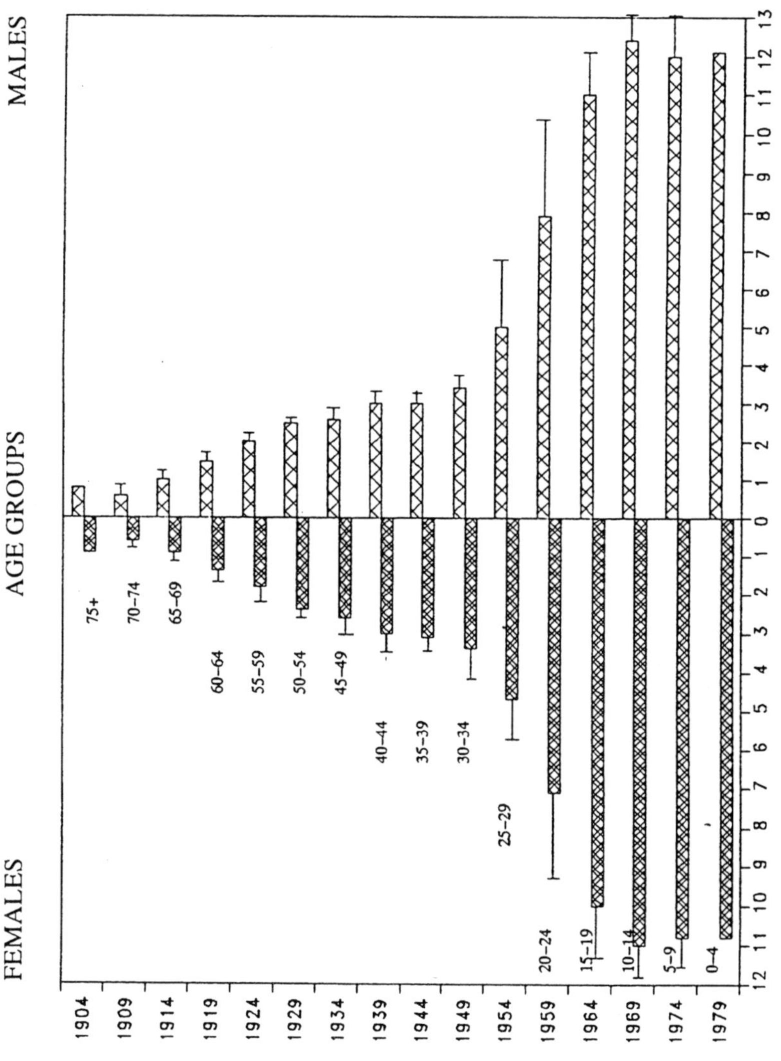

Figure 4. Suicide and attempted suicide (average rates 1981-1985), males and females

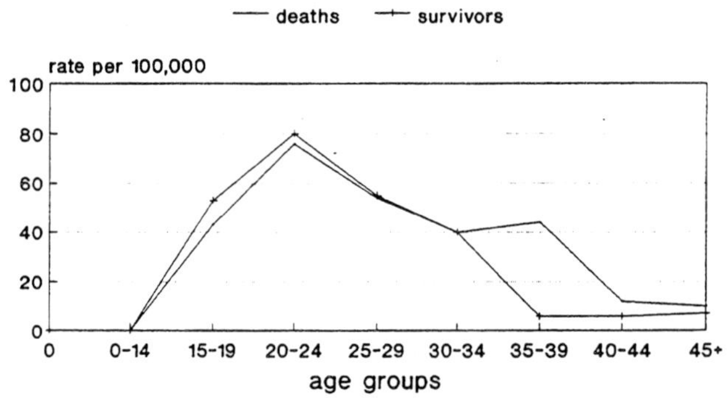

Figure 5. Suicide and attempted suicide (average rates 1981-1985), males only

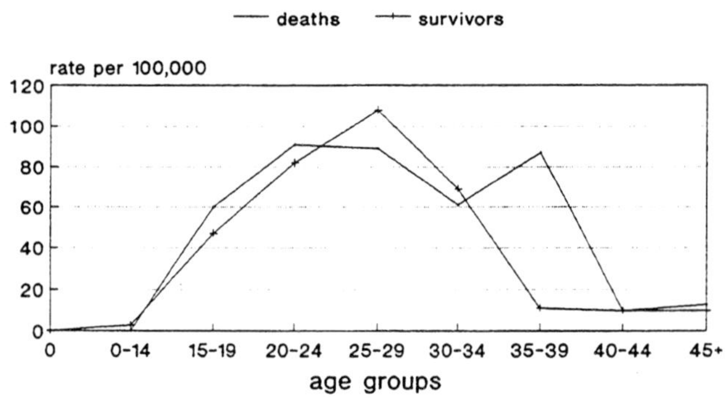

Figure 6. Suicide and attempted suicide (average rates 1981-1985), females only

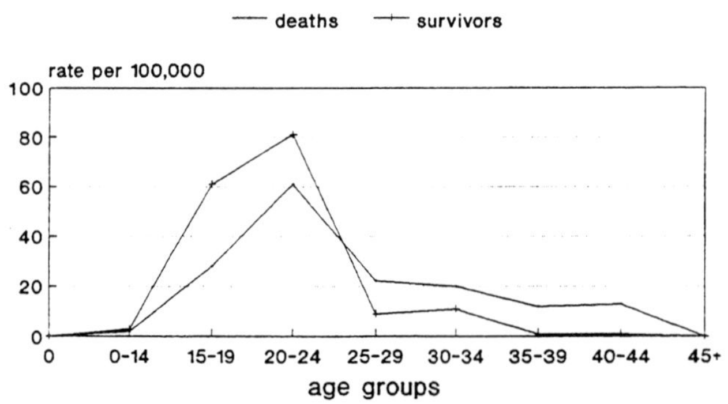

Figure 7. Male suicide, W-Samoa compared with other countries

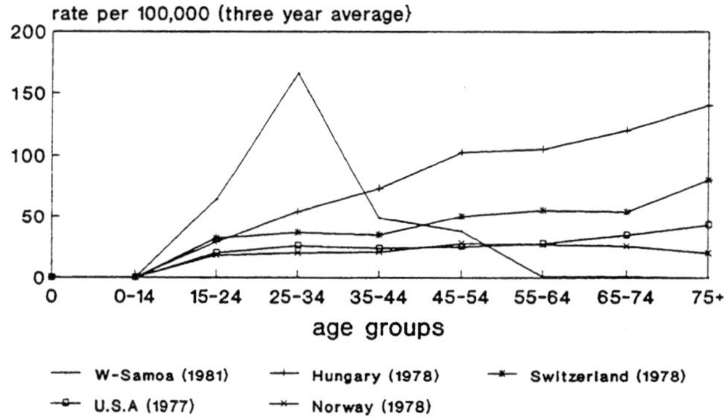

Figure 8. Female suicide, W-Samoa compared with other countries

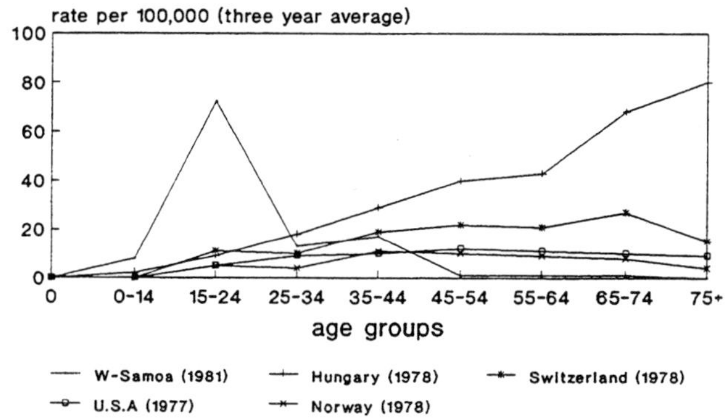

The comparisons above which show the numbers of suicides and parasuicides being approximately equal is another unusual finding. In most surveys parasuicide is much more frequent. This suggests that in the above data some cases of parasuicide may have been missed, or as implied earlier that parasuicide became suicide on account of the lethality of the poison. Because of the special interest in gathering data at that time it can be reasonably asserted that cases presenting to the Health Department would have been recorded and a more likely explanation is that some trivial self harm events were kept secret.

When cases of suspected self harm came to one or other of the Government hospitals an attempt was made to record the relevant information on a single sheet questionnaire (see Appendix E). On the back of this sheet were recorded other facts or opinions of psycho-social importance, a sort of psychiatric history and primitive psychological autopsy. This enquiry was conducted by myself but with the help of young Samoan nurses with training in psychiatric interviewing skills. Even though English is an obligatory language in Western Samoa, with the complexity of the interpersonal interactions that preceded many of the self harm events an interpreter sensitive to the cultural nuances of the story was essential. A copy of the actual sheet is shown and perusal of the questions will give an indication of some of the concerns that we wanted to learn more about. The following are some further explanatory notes about elements of the questionnaire.

A. *Day of the week*

We had the idea that presentations to hospital because of deliberate self harm were more likely on weekends (partly because of increased alcohol consumption). The results for 1978-1982 were as shown for combined suicide/parasuicide in table 9.

Comparing totals for Monday, Tuesday and Wednesday with those for Friday, Saturday and Sunday there emerges a significant difference (*) which is even more apparent in later data which separated males from females and furthermore male completed suicide. That analysis is not further enlarged here since it does not show anything new or unexpected. Samoan males like males elsewhere increase their suicide potential significantly when alcohol affected, and this was further substantiated in the clinical histories obtained.
(*) Calculating Student's $t=3.43$ and $t(0.005,28)=2.76$

Table 9: Suicide and parasuicide 1978-82 days of the week

	M	T	W	Th	F	Sa	Su	U/K	Total
1978	8	11	10	7	14	15	15	3	83
1979	9	8	6	16	18	12	8	3	80
1980	7	9	5	6	16	12	11	2	68
1981	12	15	11	9	11	10	15	11	94
1982	10	7	8	13	9	11	10	0	68
Totals	46	50	40	51	68	60	59	19	393

B. Poison enquiry

Paraquat was imported as a liquid concentrate which is diluted for spraying as a contact herbicide. It is known to be toxic on dermal absorption and the supplier advocates the use of protective clothing, a caution not always carefully heeded in tropical Samoa. Accidents of spill, spray or ingestion were usually differentiated from those events of intended self-harm although some who initially claimed accidental ingestion later admitted to such intent.

A practical problem of storage of the unused residues arose and in many houses there was some paraquat about, often in a used beer bottle (the universal container). Because traditional Samoan houses lacked external walls, lockable cupboards were scarce and the paraquat was often readily accessible. Accessible to a person in a state of emotional crisis or despair, with potentially dire consequences. When the significance of the paraquat factor became evident we made the facts known through a public information campaign by means of the local radio. This was however only a part of a more extensive campaign which will be discussed below. It was hoped that if people knew that in the event of a poisoning they would be asked who was responsible for the safe storage then the general level of care in this matter would improve.

The suppliers of the paraquat (Imperial Chemical Industries) were duly concerned about what was happening and through a toxicologist (Dr. R. E. Davies) provided information and more particularly, first aid kits for all of the district hospitals. In this regard Dr. Davies was especially helpful and it is probable that many Samoans owe their lives to his work. First aid was directed at preventing or at least minimising enteric absorption. This was done by giving the patient fine particulate matter to which the paraquat would preferentially adsorb and be deactivated. Fuller's Earth was used as the adsorbent and this was followed by a purgative. Paraquat ingestion was confirmed by the presence of the typical ulceration of the mouth and/or detecting paraquat in the blood or urine.

As a doctor of the Health Department so involved with these cases I assembled as much information as I could about paraquat toxicology and treatment, and beyond that I also set up a general poisons information center in the National Hospital which proved useful in other poisoning cases.

In a further attempt to reduce the paraquat morbidity and mortality an emetic was added to the concentrate for sale (hence the question about spontaneous vomiting). We also considered adding a stanching agent but decided after due consideration that the legitimate users would reasonably complain.

In the years 1981-83 there were 77 paraquat fatalities, however there were also 72 cases of paraquat poisoning who survived, so it was evident that the prompt first aid treatment was useful although the efficacy of the emetic remained unproven from this study.

C. About having a title

Self determination and autonomy is not automatically acquired with age in Western Samoa. Executive power over others in the extended family or village is given to some, usually older person(s), who is then called a "Matai". Matai titles are conferred usually only after serious deliberation and debate because the Matai has the responsibility of looking after the others, of apportioning material goods and making decisions about what the others may or may not do. Matais only can be elected to become a member of Parliament and until the recent elections of 1991 only Matais could vote.

We of the suicide study group formed the opinion that among other things, the suicide/parasuicide phenomena were psycho-social statements about powerlessness, frustration and emerging hopelessness in the young and non-titled. Generally a Samoan would not expect to have such a title conferred before about forty years of age if at all. As expected very few Matais appeared in our data.

D. Religion

The national motto is "Samoa is Founded on God". In 1830 John Williams of the London Missionary Society made first contact with the Samoans and Christianity in various denominations has flourished more or less since that time. In the 1981 census data only 0.2% declared no religious affiliation and 0.3% made no statement, thus 99.5% proclaimed their attachment to a religious faith where Congregational 47.3%, Catholic 21.7%, Methodist 16.2% and Mormon 8.3% were the main denominations. We looked for any disproportionate distribution of suicide/parasuicide among them and found no significant evidence to support such an argument. While the Samoan people have a highly demanding attachment to traditional Christianity they also hold a robust belief in other forms of the supernatural. The spirits of dead relatives hold powerful relevance in contemporary domestic affairs, sometimes in the form of spirit possession of or influence over a distressed family member. More generally there are district spirits or "Aitu" to plague the unwary, vain, evil and mendacious. When I considered the history of some of these young people, who saw themselves trapped in a relatively powerless personal situation, it seemed possible that death and transition to a higher status was an attractive option. The idea however remains untested in this study.

E. Known psychiatric illness

As mentioned above the usual association between suicide and mental illness and in particular major mood disorder was not seen in the majority of these cases. On retrospective evaluation of their mental status before the self harm event, the predominant pattern was one of dysphoria associated with frustrated drives and a sense of trapped helplessness. The precipitating event was typically some breach of the code of acceptable behavior followed by an angry and critical response from a parent or other similar person in an authoritative position. Some of the histories showed that this criticism was at times poorly received and had an accumulative effect such that on some particular occasion the "victim", perhaps alcohol affected or otherwise sensitised, sought to escape.

There was one clear case of a pre-existing psychotic illness in a girl who had the delusional belief that her father had been taken away. She set fire to herself and subsequently died of the extensive burns.

Chronic alcoholism was a contributing factor in some cases but acute intoxication with disturbed judgement and disinhibition was far more significant in many male cases as was implied above in the day of the week analysis.

F. Living away from Samoa

It is evident from the population pyramid in figure 3 that there is a significant net loss of the population in the age groups 15 to 30 which can only be attributed to out migration. For example considering the cohort born in 1959 +/- 2 years and using the 1976 census data we see that the 10398 males in the 15-19 age group fell by 2530 to 7868 in the 20-24 age group recorded in the 1981 census five years later. This represents a fall of 27.7% of the cohort over that time interval. From 1981 to 1986 there was a further loss of 1828 or 26.3%. Similar losses apply to females and over other cohorts.

Out migration is a potent sociologic factor in shaping this population profile and is also a strong ambition for most young Samoan people. Going away is the path to better life opportunity, education, experience, enjoyment and employment prospects. Young people thus employed in New Zealand will earn esteem in the family by sending money back while a less favoured sibling will struggle with the economic privation at home. He or she will be expected to work hard with perhaps less praise and recognition and very little money, if any, to buy personal things like those owned by the young people they read about or see in the movies or as visiting tourists. Furthermore being at home means that you are around when things go wrong and family tensions erupt as they inevitably do in this or any other close-knit society. This is a potent arena to generate envy, dissatisfaction and dysphoria if so many others seem to be able to get away and you are blocked, perhaps for ever. The age groups most involved in out migration were precisely those for whom the suicide/parasuicide data were most alarming. We had learned from New Zealand, Australia and the USA (where Samoans often go as immigrants), that the Samoan people once there did not have suicidal behavior of this magnitude. For example the New Zealand National Health Statistics Centre data for Samoans in New Zealand (in 1986 there were 62,553), showed that from 1978-81 there were only four Samoan suicides (3 male, 1 female) and one of these was born in New Zealand. The Australian Bureau of Statistics informed me that there were no Samoan suicides in Australia in the period 1968-1981. It appeared then that this was a local problem and required local, culturally relevant analysis. Over recent years there has been an increasing drive to migrate at least temporarily and as noted many do achieve this goal which raises the expectation of the population in general. Against this trend however, there has been an increasing limitation of acceptance into some of the traditional host countries. New Zealand and the US in particular have set restrictive quotas. Thus for some people the hope of being able to go to these other places has become an unlikely prospect. It is my impression that this was one of several complex interactive factors which led to the recent emergent vulnerability of the young who are obliged to remain at home in contemporary Western Samoa.

6. Paraquat

Paraquat is a bipyridylium herbicide which kills plants when sprayed onto the green foliage in the presence of sunlight. It is deactivated if washed off the plant by rain too soon after application and is said to be strongly bound to soil particles at normal pH values and not have residual biotoxicity. It is widely used in tropical agriculture. Animal toxic effects are complex and apart from direct tissue corrosion there is a later effect in the lungs where the paraquat cation is concentrated and causes a transformation of molecular oxygen to a superoxide radical which causes cellular damage and, as mentioned earlier, progressive respiratory failure.

Paraquat was first introduced into Western Samoa in 1972 by a private company and the first fatal poisonings occurred in 1973. Subsequent increased government importation went to the Agriculture Store for redistribution and sales to the public. The import figures, sales to the public, numbers of paraquat poisoning and associated deaths are shown in table 10 (Appendix F) and were compiled from combined data made available to me from the Agriculture Store and I.C.I. together with our assembled study information.

The graphs of these data are shown in figure 9 and suggest a plausible association between the supply and subsequent availability and the recorded poisonings. (There appears to be about a one year "pipeline" delay factor). From 1980 to 1983 import figures went down, (I was told because of problems with finance), then there was an increase to 1986-1987 and although I do not have data for sales to the public there is now available evidence to show another rise in paraquat poisoning from 1984 through 1987.

Thus although it was not prospectively contrived to show a point this co-variation has almost gone through an A-B-A experimental sequence. The interesting question is whether the fall in paraquat poisoning and associated suicide over the years 1981 to 1984 can in any way be attributed to the lesser general availability of the substance in the community. An alternative contending proposition is that our suicide information and prevention campaign had an effect in the desired direction or the effects were simply additive or independent.

Figure 9. Availability of poison and the recorded poisonings

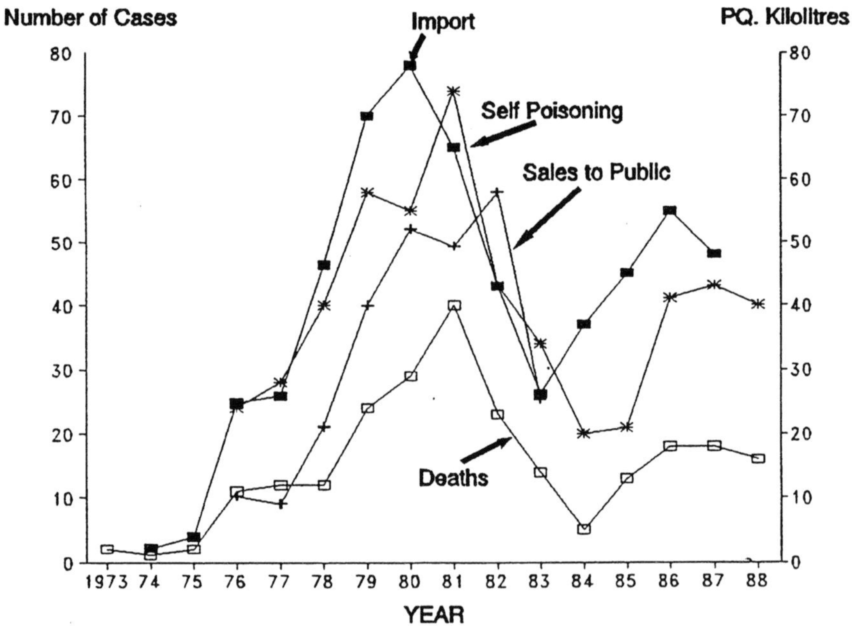

7. Suicide Prevention Campaign

By May of 1982 we had assembled enough information about the progression of events and the obvious significance of paraquat poisoning to plan and conduct a campaign to put this to the public. This was done by means of a radio address, newspaper articles (in both Samoan and English) and subsequently a public meeting where people were invited to come and express their points of view. We knew that it was important to be sensitive to the cultural issues and although I and the other members of the study group composed the text for the radio address it was carefully scrutinised by our Samoan colleagues and advisors for suitability of language and the proper etiquette of formal presentation. Perhaps it should be mentioned here that Samoan culture places great value on the correctness of address in formal meetings where specially appointed orators will earn considerable esteem by showing their linguistic skills and knowledge of traditional oratory. To have not followed such guidelines would have condemned our message to obscurity and relative ignore irrespective of the intrinsic importance of the content. We were also aware of the public sensitivity about what was happening and generally known by means of ordinary information spread in the community. The Samoan people are very proud of their long tradition of extended family cohesion, social structure, management of inter-personal and inter-group disputes. Being told by an outsider such as myself and other non-Samoans of the study group that their social order was going bad in such a dramatic fashion was seen by many as a humiliating condemnation. Reactions to this were predictable and took the form of denial, displacement and indignation. For this reason too I had to be absolutely sure that "our" suicide/parasuicide data was as correct as could be possibly obtained and certainly not a sensationalist over statement of the true state of affairs. The information given was to be reliable objective data fed into the "system" to generate debate about possible causes and remedies in the villages, churches and other public forums. We thought that we had to convey the idea that this was a local Samoan problem that needed local consideration and solutions. I knew there was a similar "epidemic" of suicide in Micronesia, also with a predominance of young males, from the writing of Fr. Fran Hezel (1977). There were also similar sociologic issues in the apparent causes of suicide in these two places but for our purposes then it was important to have the Samoan people concentrate on the local issues. The original draft of the radio address is reproduced here to give an idea of the tone and content and to reiterate some of the above information. (Some extra comments will be added in *italics* to explain the rationale of some of the points).

"Good evening. I am Rev. Sapolu of the Fellowship of Churches and I have been asked to speak to you about a serious problem we have here in Western Samoa."

He was chosen as our "orator" because he was well known and respected and would be accepted as a trustworthy local person.

"This is the problem of suicide and attempted suicide among our people. It is a problem which is causing concern and appears to be getting worse over recent years. This address to you now is an attempt to give available up to date information for all the people of Western Samoa and it is the first part of a national campaign to give reliable information and start people thinking about two important questions."

1. Why is this happening?
2. What can we do about it to help prevent further cases in the future?

"It is not my intention tonight to offer final answers to these questions. The answers and probably more questions will possibly emerge in the days ahead when people recognise the problem and begin to think and talk about it in detail. Some may not be aware of the magnitude of the problem nor of the characteristics of those most at risk. Others who know some of the details have not been able to find easy answers. The answers must come after we accept the problem and give it proper serious thought and debate.

Since last year a group of people have been meeting to gather information and study the problem as it is here in Western Samoa. Those people are representatives from the Fellowship of Churches, the YMCA, the Health and Justice Departments. Others have also helped in giving information and suggestions. Some also who had attempted suicide have given information about themselves and the reasons why they wished to die. The study has provided some information which I want to share with you although the important questions remain unanswered."

The information then is as follows:

(1) Death by suicide has increased significantly since the early 1970s.

(2) Attempted suicide has also increased and many die as a result.

(3) In the early 1970s and especially since about 1976 the rise in death rates has been most apparent in young men aged about 15-35. Men beyond the age of 45 have by comparison a much lesser risk.

(4) More recently there has been a similar increase in deaths among young women. Older women are also less at risk.

(5) Thus we see that here in Western Samoa it is the young people who for whatever reasons are most likely to die from suicide. This is not so in most other parts of the world where death by suicide is more common in older people.

(6) Suicide here is the greatest cause of death among the young and otherwise healthy people.

(7) The present death rate by suicide in young people here in Western Samoa is the highest in the world when compared with figures available from other countries as recorded by the WHO statistics.

(8) Death by drinking the weedkiller paraquat has accounted for most of the rising death rate over these recent years. Death from other methods has remained relatively unchanged.

(9) Paraquat is used effectively as a weedkiller in many countries for its agricultural importance but nowhere else is the problem of deliberate or accidental poisoning as serious as it is here.

There was at that time a contentious debate about actually banning paraquat entirely. We knew however that there were powerful and influential people who had a vested interest in continuing the importation and we did not want to be aligned with a lobby group likely to fail.

(10) Accidental death through drinking paraquat has also been reported, sometimes even in infants. Some people who have deliberately

poisoned themselves with paraquat and survived for some time, say they did so because they were upset and they knew where they could get it at home.

(11) Death by paraquat can be slow and painful. Many people regret their action soon after taking the poison but only very prompt treatment can give hope for survival once it is swallowed.

(12) Suicide is not equally distributed among all the villages as about 2/3 of them have no recently recorded cases, however despite this the problem should be of concern to all the people.

Suicide in a family or village brought with it not only the inevitable grief but also recriminations and shame. Some families suffered humiliation and actual punishment because one of their young suicided and thereby transgressed in the judgement of their religious or moral principles. We of the study group did not want to get diverted into inter village rivalries although we did keep a confidential record on a map locating each of the reported cases.

"And what are the reasons? Individual cases are all different but there are some general similarities. There is often a situation of conflict in the family and a failure of adequate communication between the people concerned, but there is no single explanation for all the cases seen. The matter is complex and involves the interaction of many factors. Answers which are too simple miss the important underlying factors and too often seek to blame one group or another. Such answers are not helpful and cause resentment and denial and are likely to inhibit further meaningful debate. Debate and discussion are however only the first part of a useful response to the problem. If and when possible solutions are proposed there must be a practical response and something is done to reduce this tragic rise in suicidal death. One possible simple thing would be to ensure that poisons are not left easily available to someone so distressed by personal feelings that they are able to quickly give in to an impulse of self harm. Without an easily available means, especially one so publicised as paraquat some of these people may find another way to deal with their distress and live. If you have ideas about how the problem can be reduced you are invited to come to a public meeting at the YMCA at Savalalo. Thank you for your attention."

8. Outcome

Following this address and the subsequent public meeting where questions and answers were exchanged with the members of the study group, the campaign shifted to debate in schools and comments in sermons in the churches and no doubt other forms of discussion in the villages. We waited and observed the subsequent emerging figures. These are shown in table 11 which is a record of suicides in monthly intervals of each of the years 1981, 1982 and 1983.

Comparing the four month totals over the three years we see 14, 19, 16, 14, 6*, 15 and 10, 9, ** 3. Where it would appear that if the campaign did have an effect it did not last very long, and the main effect was to reduce the male rate for a few months. Ironically the national fervour and excitement associated with the games of 1983, ** on this table, appeared to have a greater effect than our campaign. Using the 1981 and 1982 figures and a x^2-test the apparent reduction fails to reach significance at the level of 0.05, x^2= 6.71, df=5, for the combined data but taking males only with the serial figures 7, 14, 12, 11, 2, 12 then x^2= 10.1 and significant at 0.10. The result should however be read in the context of those 14 less deaths from 1981 to 1982.

Table 11: Suicides by months of the year 1981-1983

	J	F	M	A	M	J	Jy	A	S	O	N	D	Total	
Males	3	2	2	0	4	3	5	2	2	3	5	2	33	
Females	2	4	1	0	1	2	2	0	0	1	2	1	16	
Totals	5	6	3	0	5	5	7	2	2	4	7	3	49	1981
Males	3	1	4	3	0*	0	2	0	5	4	2	1	25	
Females	0	1	1	1	2	0	1	1	1	0	0	2	10	
Totals	3	2	5	4	2	0	3	1	6	4	2	3	35	1982
Males	3	1	3	3	1	5	1	0**	0	0	0	1	18	
Females	0	0	0	0	2	0	0	0	1	0	1	0	4	
Totals	3	1	3	3	3	5	1	0	1	0	1	1	22	1983

* = Campaign of May 1982 (The 2 female deaths of that month occurred early in May before the campaign).

** = South Pacific Games held in Western Samoa in August 1983.

9. Discussion

It was only in the years since leaving Samoa and getting back in touch with "Western" information about suicide that I learned that similar recent escalation was also happening in Europe, Australia, the US and other countries such as China and Africa. At that time however, in Samoa, the urgency was to try to turn the tide against the suicide rise as was apparent there and then. We had planned a follow up campaign for 1983 but the South Pacific Games loomed on the calendar and the national concerns were almost entirely diverted to that endeavour. Looking at the suicide data from that time now we can perhaps appreciate the effect of the social cohesion brought about by such a shared enterprise. Similar falls in national suicide rates have been noted during the wars in Europe in this century. The data I have presented make then following suggestions.

1. The availability of the paraquat and the public acceptance of its misuse as a vehicle of self-harm was a relevant factor in the rise and fall of the suicide/parasuicide figures as shown.

2. The usual distinctions between suicide and parasuicide and furthermore the male : female ratio can be distorted by the choice of a method by both sexes which has a high intrinsic lethality.

3. There is some prospect of actual reduction of suicide number or rates where a frequently chosen method is made less accessible, whether it is coal gas in the UK or paraquat in Western Samoa. The frequent use of firearms in the US or the emerging use of motor vehicle exhaust gas in Europe may be similar cases for consideration.

4. Social events can intrude on group suicide data, here the campaign had a possible if temporary reduction effect and the games likewise an association in time even if the cause and effect relationship remains speculative. In the final analysis we could not know which of the two factors referred to (reduction of import and sale or the exhortation of the campaign) was the more significant in explaining the observed reduction of paraquat misuse.

Some final opinions

Where an intervention is planned which provides fact and/or opinion for the public or some special target group, careful attention must be paid to the particular characteristics of that group. What might be a good idea in one place could fail, or worse be counter productive in another without appropriate adaptation. Even with our attempt to make the data presentation to the public non-provocative there were some adverse reactions and hostile comments. It was partly because of this sensitivity and my lack of awareness about the possible significance of these findings beyond Western Samoa that I have been hesitant to present them for more general publication. On this point I would like therefore to thank the Director General of Health in Western Samoa for permission to publish the data as obtained in that department.

Summary

From 1975 an apparent dramatic escalation of suicide rates for young people in Western Samoa caused sufficient concern that a suicide studygroup was initiated to verify the available data and attempt to devise a prevention strategy. Deliberate self poisoning with the herbicide paraquat was the modal means of suicide and this became the focus of attempted prevention. Data is presented to suggest that reducing the impact of a predominant means can reduce the total rate without a corresponding increase in other methods.

The data also showed a lack of the usual distinction between suicide and parasuicide, a predominance of suicide among the young and similar rates for males and females. Comparisons are shown with data from other countries and some socio-cultural factors are considered in attempting to explain the observations described.

REFERENCES

Adam K. S. (1985). Attempted Suicide. Symposium on Self-Destructive Behaviour. *The Psychiatric Clinics of North America 8.* (2) 183-202.

Freeman D. (1983). *Margaret Mead and Samoa.* Australian National University Press, Canberra. 220-222.

Hezel F. X. (1977). Suicide Epidemic among Micronesian Youth. *South Pacific Bulletin 27,* (2) 5-10.

Kreitman N. (1976). The Coal-Gas Story: UK suicide rates 1960-1971. *Br. Journal Prevention Soc. Medicine 30,* 86.
Lester D. (1990). Restricting access to Methods for Suicide in Japan. Presented at the 3rd. European Symposium: *Suicidal Behaviour and Risk Factors,* Bologna.
Pratt G. (1862). *Pratt's Grammar and Dictionary of the Samoan Language.* Apia: The Malua Press.
Rubinstein D., White G. (1983). Bibliography on Culture and Mental Health in the Pacific Islands, *19,* (1-2).
Shaffer D., Garland A., Gould M., Fisher P. & Trautman P. (1988). Preventing Teenage Suicide: A Critical Review. *J. Am. Acad. Child Adolesc. Psychiatry 27,*(6) 675-687.
WHO (1974). Suicide and Attempted Suicide. *Public Health Papers 58,* Geneva.
WHO. Euro. (1982). Changing patterns in suicide behaviour. *Reports and Studies 74,* Report on a WHO Working Group. Copenhagen.

The author, Bowles, would like to thank the Computer Services Unit, The Prince Charles Hospital for their assistance in preparing this document.

Appendix A: *Population and suicidal deaths: Western Samoa*

Figure 1

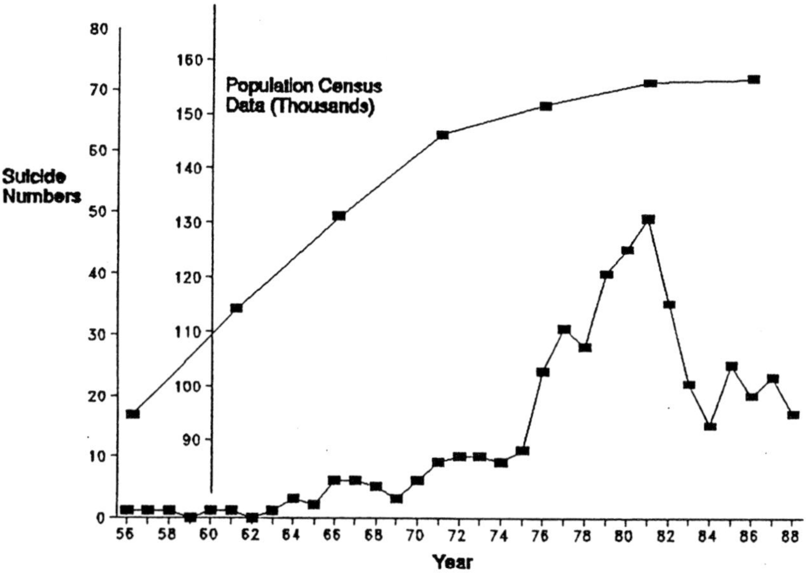

Census Year	1956	1961	1966	1971	1976	1981	1986
Total Population	94846	114427	131377	146627	151983	156349	157158

Year	56 57 58 59	60 61 62 63 64	65 66 67 68 69	70 71 72 73 74	75 76 77 78 79	80 81 82 83 84	85 86 87 88
No. Suicides	1 1 1 0	1 1 0 1 3	2 6 6 5 3	6 9 10 10 9	11 24 31 28 40	44 49 35 22 15	25 20 23 17

Figure 2

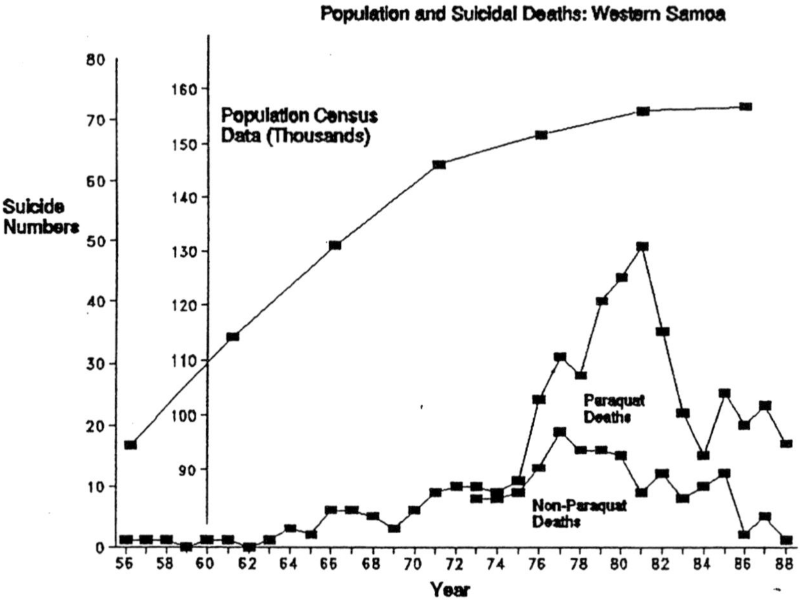

Year	73	74	75	76	77	78	79	80	81	82	83	84	85	86	87	88
Paraquat Deaths	2	1	2	11	12	12	24	29	40	23	14	5	13	18	18	16

Appendix B: *Suicide and attempted suicide: Analysis by age group and method.*

Table 1. DEATHS 1981

Method	Sex	Age Groups 0-14	15-19	20-24	25-29	30-34	35-39	40-44	45+	Totals	
Paraquat	M	1	4	5	6	5	3		2	26	
	F	1	2	9	1			1		14	40
Other Poison	M									0	
	F	1	1							2	2
Hanging	M			1		1				2	
	F									0	2
Firearm	M	1	1	1					1	4	
	F									0	4
Other Method	M				1					1	
	F									0	1
Totals	M	2	5	7	7	6	3	0	3	33	
	F	2	3	9	1	0	0	1	0	16	
		4	8	16	8	6	3	1	3	49	

Table 2. SURVIVORS 1981

Paraquat	M	4	3	4	6	3		1	2	23	
	F	1	2	7	1					11	34
Other Poison	M		1	2		1				4	
	F	1	1	1						3	7
Hanging	M		1							1	
	F									0	1
Firearm	M	1			1					2	
	F			1						1	3
Other Method	M									0	
	F									0	0
Totals	M	5	5	6	7	4	0	1	2	30	
	F	2	3	9	1	0	0	0	0	15	
		7	8	15	8	4	0	1	2	45	

Table 3. DEATHS 1983

Method	Sex	Age Groups 0-14	15-19	20-24	25-29	30-34	35-39	40-44	45+	Totals	
Paraquat	M		3	4	2		1		1	11	
	F		1			1	1			3	14
Other Poison	M									0	
	F									0	0
Hanging	M		2	1			1		1	5	
	F			1						1	6
Firearm	M								1	1	
	F									0	1
Other Method	M				1					1	
	F									0	1
Totals	M	0	5	5	3	0	2	0	3	18	
	F	0	1	1	0	1	1	0	0	4	
		0	6	6	3	1	3	0	3	22	

Table 4. SURVIVORS 1983

Method	Sex	0-14	15-19	20-24	25-29	30-34	35-39	40-44	45+	Totals	
Paraquat	M	1	2	4	5					12	
	F		3	3						6	18
Other Poison	M		1	3	2					6	
	F		4	1						5	11
Hanging	M									0	
	F									0	0
Firearm	M									0	
	F									0	0
Other Method	M			1						1	
	F									0	1
Totals	M	1	3	8	7	0	0	0	0	19	
	F	0	7	4	0	0	0	0	0	11	
		1	10	12	7	0	0	0	0	30	

Table 5. DEATHS DIFFERENCES 1981-1983

Method	Sex	0-14	15-19	20-24	25-29	30-34	35-39	40-44	45+	Totals	
		Age Groups									
Paraquat	M	-1	-1	-1	-4	-5	-2		-1	-15	
	F	-1	-1	-9	-1	+1	+1	-1		-11	-26
Other Poison	M										
	F	-1	-1							- 2	- 2
Hanging	M		+2			-1	+1		+1	+ 3	
	F			+1						+ 1	4
Firearm	M	-1	-1	-1						- 3	
	F									0	- 3
Other Method	M									0	
	F									0	0
Totals	M	-2	0	-2	-4	-6	-1	0	0	-15	
	F	-2	-2	-8	-1	+1	+1	-1	0	-12	
		-4	-2	-10	-5	-5	0	-1	0	-27	

Table 6. SURVIVORS DIFFERENCES 1981-1983

Method	Sex	0-14	15-19	20-24	25-29	30-34	35-39	40-44	45+	Totals	
Paraquat	M	-3	-1		-1	-3		-1	-2	-11	
	F	-1	+1	-4	-1					- 5	-16
Other Poison	M			+1	+2	-1				+ 2	
	F	-1	+3							+ 2	4
Hanging	M		-1							- 1	
	F									0	- 1
Firearm	M	-1				-1				- 2	
	F			-1						- 1	- 3
Other Method	M			+1						+ 1	
	F									0	1
Totals	M	-4	-2	+2	+1	-5	0	-1	-2	-11	
	F	-2	+4	-5	-1	0	0	0	0	- 4	
		-6	+2	-3	0	-5	0	-1	-2	-15	

Appendix C: *Suicide and attempted suicide: Western Samoa 1981-1983*

Table 7

AGE ANALYSES AND RATES

Age Group	0–14	15–19	20–24	25–29	30–34	35–39	40–44	45+	Age Unknown	Totals
Males	36524	10919	7868	4968	3212	3043	2986	10813	494	81027
Females	32715	9977	7132	4705	3450	3122	3014	10811	396	75322
Total	69239	20896	15000	9673	6862	6165	6000	21624	890	156349
% of Population	44.4	13.4	9.6	6.2	4.4	3.9	3.8	13.8	0.5	100
Cumulative %	44.4	57.8	67.4	73.6	78	81.9	85.7	99.5	100	

Population Data 1981 Census

Deaths

Year	81 82 83	81 82 83	81 82 83	81 82 83	81 82 83	81 82 83	81 82 83	81 82 83	81 82 83	81 82 83	**Deaths**
Males	1 0 0	5 9 5	7 9 5	8 2 3	6 0 0	3 2 2	0 1 0	3 1 1	0 1 2	33 25 18	76 Male
Females	2 0 0	3 4 1	9 3 1	1 2 0	0 1 1	0 0 1	1 0 0	0 0 0	0 0 0	16 10 4	30 Female
Total	3 0 0	8 13 6	16 12 6	9 4 3	6 1 1	3 2 3	1 1 0	3 1 1	0 1 2	49 35 22	106 Total
3 Year Total	3	27	34	16	8	8	2	5	3	106	

Rates per 100000										
Average 3 yrs Total	1.4	43.1	75.6	55.1	38.9	43.3	11.1	7.7		22.6
Male	0.9	58	89	87.2	58.6	76.7	11.2	15.4	N.A.	31.3
Female	2.0	26.7	60.8	21.3	19.3	10.7	11.1	0		13.3

Table 7 continued

Survivors

Year	81 82 83	81 82 83	81 82 83	81 82 83	81 82 83	81 82 83	81 82 83	81 82 83	81 82 83	81 82 83	Survivors
Males	4 0 1	6 6 3	6 5 8	6 3 7	5 2 0	0 1 0	1 0 0	2 2 0	0 0 0	30 19 19	68 Male
Females	2 1 0	3 8 7	9 4 4	1 0 0	0 1 0	0 0 0	0 0 0	0 0 0	0 0 0	15 14 11	40 Female
Total	6 1 1	9 14 10	15 9 12	7 3 7	5 3 0	0 1 0	1 0 0	2 2 0	0 0 0	45 33 30	108 Total
3 Year Total	8	33	36	17	8	1	1	4	0	108	

Rates per 100000										
Average 3 year Total	3.9	52.6	80	58.6	38.9	5.4	5.6	6.2		23
Male	4.6	45.8	80.5	107.4	68.4	11	11.2	12.3	N.A.	28
Female	3.1	60.1	79.5	7.1	9.7	0	0	0		17.7

Appendix D: *Suicide rates by age and gender (1981)*

Table 8. 1981 SUICIDE RATES BY AGE GROUP AND GENDER.

Age Group	0-14	15-24	25-34	35-44	45-54	55-64	65-74	75+
Males Suicides	1	12	14	3	2	0	0	0
Population	36524	18787	8380	6029	5040	3546	1549	678
Rate	2.7	63.9	167	49.8	39.7	0	0	0
Females Suicides	2	12	1	1	0	0	0	0
Population	32715	17109	8155	6136	5013	3289	1569	940
Rate	6.1	70.1	12.3	16.3	0	0	0	0

Appendix E.: *(Copy of questionnaire)*

SELF INFLICTED INJURY 0R SUICIDE (attempted, completed or suspected)

Tick boxes as required. Write further details overleaf.

NAME .... Sex M ❑ F ❑ Age (or d.o.b.)........
ADDRESS .... Upolu ❑ Savaii ❑ Other❑..............
Date of incident .... Date of Admission.......... Hosp. Rec. No......

Day of week of incident. M❑ T❑ W❑ Th❑ F❑ Sa❑ Su❑

Condition on arrival at hospital: Alive ❑ Dead ❑
Outcome: Alive ❑ Dead ❑ Not Admitted ❑ Ward Location ❑
Method of Injury: Paraquat ❑ Other Poison ❑ Gun Shot ❑ Hanging ❑
Other method ❑

Specify, If Poison.. Where was it obtained ? ....

What was the container ? ....

Who was responsible for safe storage ? ....

Where was it stored ? ....

Approximately how much was consumed ? ....

Was it diluted ? ....

Was the incident considered: accidental ❑ Deliberate ❑ ?
Was first aid given before arrival? No ❑ Yes ❑
Specify....... Did the person vomit? No ❑ Yes ❑ Spontaneously ❑

Forced ❑ Other..............................

Personal details: Married ❑ Single ❑ Separated ❑ Divorced ❑

Who does the person live with? .... Number of children.......

Employment............. Does this person have a title? Yes ❑ No ❑
For women: Pregnant? Yes ❑ No ❑ Possible ❑ Unknown ❑

Has there been a previous attempt? No ❑ Yes ❑
• Details......... Known previous medical illness ....
• Known previous psychiatric illness ....
Had the person been drinking alcohol? No ❑ Yes ❑ Detail ....

Educational level........... Previous police record ? No ❑ Yes ❑
Has this person lived away from Western Samoa? No ❑ Yes ❑

Religion................................

Circumstances: Record overleaf any relevant details about the incident.

E.g. Were there known precipitating factors?
Has there been recent or chronic conflict with other people?
Was the persons behaviour abnormal in the preceding hours or days?
Did the person warn anyone about the impending incident, was a suicide note written?

Record if possible the person's own account of the incident.

Name of informant.......................... Relation to patient ....

Contact address ....

Who else could give information? ....

Appendix F.: *Paraquat import, sales and poisoning*

Table 10. PARAQUAT IMPORT, SALES AND POISONING

Year	73	74	75	76	77	78	79	80	81	82	83	84	85	86	87	88
PQ.Import Kilo l*		2	4	25	26	46	70	78	65	43	26	37	45	55	48	N/A
PQ. Sales*				10	9	21	40	52	49	58	25	not available				
Self Poison				24	28	40	58	55	74	43	34	20	21	41	43	40
PQ. Suicide	2	1	2	11	12	12	24	29	40	23	14	5	13	18	18	16

* Figures rounded to nearest integer.

The Prevention of Suicidal Behaviour:
a Review of Effectiveness

A.J.F.M. KERKHOF and R.F.W. DIEKSTRA

Introduction

Suicidal behaviour constitutes a serious social and health problem. It puts a considerable drain on resources in both primary and secondary health care. Suicide is in many countries of the world among the eight leading causes of death for the general population, and among the three leading causes of death for young people aged 15 to 24 (WHO, 1989). Suicide concerns 1 to 3% of all deaths in countries reporting to the World Health Organization. The number of suicide attempts treated in medical settings has increased considerably in the last decades (Diekstra, 1989; Platt et al., 1992). Any large innner city hospital in the Western world is likely to treat hundreds of suicide attempters a year, especially in emergency wards. The mean suicide attempt rate in 14 European centers was found to be 167 per 100,000 males and 222 per 100,000 females aged 15 years and over (Platt et al., 1992). The economic resources that are involved in health care are clearly enormous.

One would expect that the development of programs for intervention and prevention of suicidal behaviour would have been assigned an important public health priority. This, however, is not the case. There is probably only one country in the world with a national suicide prevention program: Finland. There are only few countries in which there is an active interest in suicide prevention on the part of governments. However there is variety of programs on regional and local community levels in many countries. Traditionally these activities rely heavily on volunteer organizations, cooperating with health professionals and human services personnel (teachers, police). Some of those programs date back the beginning of this century when social concern for the "victims of the industrial society" was growing. It took some sixty years before federal and national governments hesitantly came to take an interest in the suicide problem and started to provide funds for preventive activities.

Consequently, although there is a rich and scholarly literature on sociological, psychological and biological aspects of suicide, there is a scarcity of studies on the development and evaluation of programs for treatment and prevention. As will become clear from the remainder of this chapter, from a scientific point of view the prevention of suicidal behaviour is still in its infancy.

Prevention, intervention and aftercare

Prevention of suicide at the primary level is aimed at persons who are currently not feeling or manifesting any suicidal tendency, with a view to decrease the risk that such a tendency will afflict them in the future. This could be accomplished by eliminating or alleviating circumstances that may promote distress and suicidal behaviour, such as mental disorder, unemployment, prejudice, and isolation. Prevention at this level is slow to render effect because it demands societal changes, or changes in behaviour of large social groups, a notoriously gradual occurrence at best. As far as we know there is not one single study in the literature describing and evaluating a primary prevention program that deals specifically with suicidal behaviour. The only possible exception can be made for so-called school-based suicide prevention programs. Some of these programs address the whole school community, but others are exclusively geared towards the detection and management of students with severe emotional problems or suicidal crises. We will describe and discuss school-based programs as a separate category.

Most preventive efforts have been aimed at the secondary or intervention level, after suicidal tendencies or conditions that carry a high risk for such tendencies have become apparent. One often employed method is the crisis intervention center or suicide prevention center telephone service or 24-hour "lifelines" or "hotlines" for those who are suicidal or in despair. Once suicidal tendencies have become manifest as ideation, depressive symptomatology or a non-fatal suicide attempt, medical, psychological and social interventions may be employed followed by some form of therapy to alleviate the circumstances and problems leading to the suicidal crisis. Over the last 30 years a considerable number of studies have been published in which such interventions and their effects on subsequent suicidal behaviour are described.

Another type of preventive measure includes the restriction of easy access to lethal methods for suicide, such as the switch from coal gas to natural gas, gun control, and restriction of dosage and type of medication. Most of these measures however have occurred for reasons other than preventing suicide.

Aftercare or "after the fact" prevention refers to efforts to aid those who remain following a suicide of a family member, partner or friend and who are often deeply affected by the death. Preventive measures at this level have only recently received attention and no systematic studies evaluating such measures are available.

School-based programs

A new approach to suicide prevention that has received a great deal of attention involves curriculum-based prevention or education programs. The number of such programs introduced into schools in the USA after 1984 continues to grow (Garland et al., 1989). Outside the USA there are only few other countries where such programs have been developed, such as The Netherlands (Mulder et al., 1989) and Canada (Dyck, 1995, this volume). These programs have been described in detail elsewhere (Garland & Shaffer, 1990; Ross, 1980; Shaffer et al., 1988). The main goals are: to raise awareness of the problem of adolescent suicide; to train participants to identify adolescents at risk for suicide; to educate participants about community mental health resources and referral techniques; and to prevent suicidal behaviour later in the life span. The programs are presented by mental health professionals or educators and are most commonly aimed at secondary school students, their parents, and educators.

The contents of a typical suicide prevention program for students include a review of statistics of adolescent suicide; a list of "warning signs" of suicide, usually emphasizing symptoms of depression; a list of community mental health resources and how to access them; and a discussion of skills for referring a student or peer to counselling, stressing concerns about confidentiality. A minority of programs also include a component on problem-solving skills training or stress reduction.

While specific methods and contents vary across programs, the theoretical model guiding them is consistent. Virtually all of the suicide prevention programs employ a stress model of suicide, as opposed to a mental illness model (Garland et al., 1989). Suicide is presented as a reaction to extreme psychosocial or interpersonal stress and the link to mental illness is strongly denied, or at least underemphasized. The curricula often explicitly state that people who commit suicide are not mentally ill and that everyone is vulnerable to suicidal behaviour. The rationale behind this approach is that the destigmatization of suicide will encourage students who are feeling suicidal to identify themselves and to seek help.

In reviewing over 300 prevention programs of various types, Price et al. (1989) concluded that the most effective programs are based on a sound foundation of empirical knowledge. That knowledge should include a clear understanding of the risks and problems confronting the target population. Another essential element is the collection of data to inform planners how well the program achieves its goals or how it can be modified to do so. Unfortunately, most suicide prevention programs have fallen short on one or both of these requirements.

Some curriculum-based programs are not founded on current empirical knowledge of the risk factors of adolescent suicide. By de-emphasizing or denying the fact that many adolescents who commit suicide are mentally ill, these programs misrepresent the facts. A considerable number of youth suicides have diagnosable psychiatric illnesses (Brent and Kolko, 1990; Shaffer et al., 1988; Shafii et al., 1988; Pardes and Blumenthal, 1990). Shafii et al. found that 95% of a group of 23 youth suicides had a serious diagnosable psychiatric disorder. Shaffer et al. found symptoms of major depressive disorder in one quarter, drug and alcohol abuse in about one third of the sample, and a history of aggressive and antisocial behaviour in almost one half of the victims.

In their attempt to "destigmatize" suicide some school-based suicide prevention programs may be, in fact, normalizing the behaviour and reducing potentially protective taboos. Suicide is sometimes portrayed as a reaction to common stresses of adolescence, namely problems with parents and teachers, problems with relationships, performance anxiety, and peer pressure. The link between stressful experiences and suicide may be the one message retained by the adolescent attending a suicide prevention program, regardless of the well-intentioned messages about seeking help.

The incidence of adolescent suicide is sometimes exaggerated in suicide prevention programs since one of the programs' goals is to increase awareness and concern about the problem. This exaggeration seems unnecessary in that surveys of teenagers indicate that they are certainly aware of the problem (The Gallup Organization, Inc., 1991; Kalafat and Elias, 1992). The danger of exaggeration is that students may perceive suicide as a more common, and therefore more acceptable act. They may also become unnecessarily anxious about the possibility of suicide in their immediate peer group.

Another problem is the common use of print or visual media to present case histories of adolescents who have attempted or committed suicide. The purpose is to teach students how to identify friends who may be at-risk for suicidal behaviour. However, the method may have a paradoxical effect in that students may closely identify with the problems portrayed by the case examples and may come to see suicide as the logical solution to their own problems. A documentary on the suicide of an adolescent broadcasted in Germany on television that was meant to prevent suicides turned out to inspire more suicides after and because of this documentary (Schmidtke and Häffner, 1988). The model behaviour, jumping in front of a train, was imitated in excess of what might be expected on the basis of control periods, in the period following the broadcasting. The modelling effect was greater for young viewers than for old viewers. This study, the best empirical evidence regarding the imitation effect, shows the importance of restraint in using fictional models.

Finally, at the practical level, suicide prevention programs may never reach their target population, i.e., adolescents most at-risk for suicide. Incarcerated and runaway youths have extremely high rates of suicide as do drug abusers (Memory, 1989; Stiffman, 1989) and they will not be in the audience. And even if they were, it would not be surprising if awareness programs alone did not affect them positively. Many reports suggest that suicide victims are likely to have been absent from school prior to their suicidal act (Hawton, 1986). Therefore students who are regularly attending school are not the highest risk group. Program developers might argue that the programs are not primarily intended to address the suicidal child, but rather to encourage peers to identify and seek help for someone who may need it. Nevertheless, a program aimed at a general audience of adolescents who are not at highest risk may be inefficient. Future suicide prevention efforts should also be based on the valuable empirical data that can help to identify children who are at-risk for suicide so that they can be referred to more therapeutic interventions.

As to effectiveness, although many curriculum-based suicide prevention programs have been operating since 1981 (Garland et al., 1989), there are only a few published evaluation studies using a control group (Nelson,

1987; Ross, 1980). Spirito and colleagues' (1988) evaluation of a suicide awareness program for ninth graders is one of the exceptions. Approximately 300 students who attended the program were compared with about 200 students in a geographically matched control group. All students completed a battery of exercises covering suicide, hopelessness, helping behaviours, and coping skills prior to, and ten weeks after the implementation of a six-week curriculum in their health classes. The results indicated that the program was minimally effective in imparting knowledge, and was ineffective in changing attitudes. Slight increases in knowledge among girls were associated with program attendance. In another similar study by the same research group (Overholser et al., 1989) boys changed in the undesirable direction, i.e., increased hopelessness and maladaptive coping responses.

In another large, well-controlled study in New Jersey, Shaffer et al. (1991) found few positive effects of three suicide prevention curriculum programs and some possible negative effects. The programs lasted approximately three hours and were implemented collaboratively by mental health professionals and educators. The sample included approximately 1,000 teenagers who attended the programs, and 1,000 students in a demographically matched control group. Pre- and post-program assessments were made about knowledge and attitudes towards suicide and help-seeking from adults, knowledge about mental health resources, and self-reported suicidal behaviour.

Most students rated the programs as helpful, but only 41% found them interesting; females and minority students were most likely to rate the programs favourably. The majority of students who attended the programs were fairly knowledgeable about suicide prior to program participation, and most held favourable attitudes toward help seeking. In particular, students listed an average of more than three warning signs of suicide. Approximately 80% believed that suicidal threats should be taken seriously, and said that they would refer a friend to a counsellor if they believed the friend to be at-risk for suicide. Program attendance did not affect these knowledge or attitude variables. A minority of students before and after expressed unfavourable attitudes such as the belief that suicide can be a good solution to problems, or that suicidal confidences from friends should never be disclosed. Program attendance did not effect a significant change in these students' attitudes either. Program attendance was associated with a small, but significant increase in the number of students who responded that suicide could be a possible solution to problems. Most importantly, however, there was no significant increase or reduction in self-reported suicidal ideation or suicide attempts following program implementation. However, there were data suggesting that the students most at-risk for suicide (those who said they had made a previous attempt) found the programs upsetting (Shaffer et al., 1990). While this does not necessarily indicate a negative effect, it is concerning.

Program evaluation research is underdeveloped and final conclusions about the effectiveness of school-based suicide prevention programs cannot be drawn on the basis of these few studies. The programs were of short duration and the evaluations only included self-report measures of knowledge, attitudes, and behaviour. However, there is little evidence that the programs have the desired effect on knowledge and attitude variables, and there is some suggestive evidence that the programs may have a deleterious effect on some students. Further evaluation is clearly needed, with an emphasis on the assessment of behavioural variables including suicidal behaviour and help-seeking behaviour.

Another way of preventing suicide and parasuicide lies in intervention with suicidal adolescents. To our knowledge, there are no well-controlled efficacy studies in this field. Kienhorst et al. (1992) derived some intervention strategies for dealing with suicidal adolescents, indicating that they should focus on three main targets: 1) improving the suicidal adolescent's stressful life situation, which may include family therapy. Attention should be given to the treatment of possible traumatic experiences such as sexual abuse, unwanted pregnancies and induced abortions; 2) changing a 'negative' cognitive style with a special focus on hopelessness; 3) changing the behavioural problem solving and/or coping strategies with special attention on replacing the withdrawal reaction by more adequate strategies.

Suicide prevention centers

Virtually all metropolitan areas as well as many urban areas in European countries, the United States and Canada now have at least one crisis intervention or suicide prevention center. These centers typically provide a 24-hours hotline plus referrals to other mental health or social work agencies. In some cases they have a walk-in center and trained volunteers who can act as "befrienders" or confidants to persons in crisis. There are also innumerable telephone emergency or crisis lines in operation that deal with problems of living in general and are therefore not specifically geared to suicidal individuals.

Shneidman and Farberow (1957, 1965) originally outlined the rationale for suicide crisis centers as follows: suicidal behaviour is often associated with a crisis situation, and the victim often experiences ambivalence about living and dying. People have a basic need for interpersonal communication which will often be expressed in a last minute "cry for help". Although crisis or suicide prevention centers may employ mental health consultants, such as trained psychiatrists, psychologists and psychotherapists as external consultants or as staff members, the actual work is usually carried out by lay persons with varying degrees of training and expertise. Traditionally the clergy has played an important role in the foundation and operation of crisis centers and this is still the case in many centers.

Although crisis or suicide hotlines were already present in several large European and Northern American cities before World War II, the spread of such services really began in the early sixties, stimulated by the establishment of The Samaritans in London and the first Suicide Prevention Center in Los Angeles.

Suicide prevention centers are essentially equipped for secondary prevention, that is to say for early intervention with persons who carry an elevated risk for suicidal behaviour. Generally such centers do not have an active outreach; they do not systematically seek out and try to establish contact with groups in the community who can be considered high risk. It is essentially the suicidal person who has to contact the center.
It is for that reason that studies on the efficacy of such centers have addressed two major facets of their functioning: whether centers attract persons with an elevated risk for suicidal behaviour; and whether they prevent these individuals' suicide or suicide attempt (Lester, 1974; Bridge et al., 1977; Dew et al., 1987).

These facets are closely entangled, for if centers do not attract high-risk individuals, it goes without saying that they will not exert any major reducing influence on suicide rates.

In a review of studies addressing these two questions, and the only one thus far using meta-analysis as the method of reviewing, Dew and her colleagues (1987) draw the following general conclusions. First of all, centers indeed seem to attract a high-risk population: center clients were more likely to commit suicide than were members of the general population (7 studies analysed). The average client-suicide rate ranges from 2 times higher to almost 109 times higher than the general population rate. Individuals who committed suicide were more likely to have been clients of a suicide prevention center than were members of the general population (6 studies analysed). The average annual client rate among suicides ranges from 2.5 times higher to almost 10 times higher than the client rate in the general population.

Next, the verdict on the question whether the suicide rate decreases more in communities with a suicide prevention center than in communities without such a center, has to remain "undetermined". Of the five studies analysed three show an effect in favour of center effectiveness, whereas the other two do not. Combined, however, there was virtually no effect, suggesting that the center establishment has neither a positive nor a negative overall effect on community suicide rates.

Given the fact that centers are at least somewhat successful in attracting the population they are designed to help, the question arises whether center effectiveness should not be established within specific cohorts rather than simply across the entire population of a community. Miller et al. (1984) reported data on specific cohorts. They compared 28 center communities with 48 control communities over the period 1968-1973 and found no significant difference in the overall suicide rate change between those two groups of communities. However, the suicide rate for white women and girls under age 25 showed a large and significant decrease in communities with a center as compared to control communities. This finding is especially important because in the United States as well as in many other countries young white women are the most frequent users of prevention centers and telephone emergency services.

Since this group is also characterized by a relatively very high rate of attempted suicide, the question arises whether prevention center evaluations should focus on outcomes other than suicide, such as attempted suicide. Unfortunately, there are no studies available yet that have examined other kinds of outcome in a scientifically sound way.

In addition, suicide rates are influenced by a multitude of factors and their interactions (such as unemployment rate, divorce rate, drug/alcohol (ab)use, prevalence of mental disorders, changes in age and sex composition of populations) that can obscure an effect of a suicide prevention center in a community. None of the studies carried out thus far on the effectiveness of centers has been able to control adequately for the possible influences of those factors, one of the reasons being that it is extremely difficult, if not impossible, to obtain the necessary data on them. Furthermore there are always other agencies in the community that contribute to suicide prevention, such as psychiatric outpatient departments, privately operating psychiatrists and psychologists. This makes it difficult to filter out the effects of only one of them.

In sum, it is not possible to conclude that suicide prevention centers do prevent suicide, while at the same time it is safe to conclude that these centers indeed deal with persons who are at greater risk for suicidal behaviour. Even though the actual percentage of clients who commit suicide annually remains a small percentage of all clients seen, the corresponding suicide rates indicate that the potential for prevention of suicidal deaths by these centers is substantial.

The literature on client characteristics and effects of prevention centers is exclusively anglosaxon, the only exception being the Danish study by Nielsen and Videbech (1973). It therefore remains to be seen whether the potential role with regard to suicide prevention applies to other parts of the world as well.

Finally, it is important to mention the strong conviction among the organizations that suicide prevention centers do prevent suicides. Volunteers and staff may think that they prevented someone from committing suicide. Also there are statements from individuals who say they are being prevented from suicide solely by the efforts of the center. That does not, however, count as empirical evidence for the efficacy of these centers on the community level.

Aftercare programs for hospital treated suicide attempters

In the past 30 years the numbers of people treated in hospitals following a suicide attempt or parasuicidal act have increased dramatically in most countries (Diekstra, 1989). In recent times, attempted suicide and parasuicide are being defined as follows: "an act with nonfatal outcome, in which an individual deliberately initiates a non-habitual behaviour that, without intervention from others, will cause self-harm, or deliberately ingests a substance in excess of the prescribed or generally recognized therapeutic dosage, and which is aimed at realizing changes which the subject desired via the actual or expected physical consequences" (Platt et al., 1992, p 99).

A considerable percentage of those treated in hospital after a suicidal act are "repeaters", i.e. have received hospital treatment before for the same reason. Estimates of the percentage of attempters that have made earlier attempts vary between 20 - 60%. Follow-up studies show that the risk of repetition is particularly high in the first few months after discharge from treatment or hospital: approximately 10% makes another attempt within the first three months. This percentage rises to 15% after one year and to 30 - 40% after 10 to 15 years (Kerkhof et al., 1982; Kerkhof, 1985).

As to the outcome of subsequent attempts, there is a remarkable difference between studies published before and after 1982. From the first group of studies it emerges that approximately 1% of suicide attempters dies from the consequences of a subsequent attempt within one year after discharge. After 2 years this percentage rises to 2%, after 3 years to 3% and so forth, until it reaches approximately 10% after 10 years. Thereafter the percentage remains stable at this level.

Since 1982 a growing number of studies has been published indicating that the percentage of repeaters dying from a suicide attempt can be as high as 8 to 10% within two years after a previous attempt followed by treatment or admission in hospital (Kerkhof et al., 1988). It remains to be seen whether this is an "acceleration" phenomenon or a reflection of a true increase in risk for suicide among suicide attempters, or an artefact caused by the use of better research methods.

Anyway, suicide attempters constitute a group with a very high risk for suicide - a rate 50 to 100 times the overall population rate - and therewith a pool from which many of the future suicides will be drawn. This raises the issue as to the possibilities for prevention of suicide by interventions specifically geared towards reducing the risk of subsequent attempts among suicide attempters in contact with medical services.

Screening of the literature reveals 18 publications reporting a systematic evaluation of the effects of special aftercare programs for suicide attempters.

In terms of design these studies can be divided into two categories: those using a retrospective and those using a prospective design. Studies in the first category retrospectively collected data on the treatment history of suicide attempters after an index attempt and related those data to incidence of further attempts, either with a fatal or non-fatal outcome.

Greer and Bagley (1971) followed patients presenting at a casualty department with deliberate self-poisoning or self-injury. 204 out of 211 patients were traced after 18 months. They found that subsequent suicide attempts occurred significantly more among patients untreated than among patients treated by a psychiatrist, prolonged treatment being associated with the best prognosis. Unfortunately, the patients were not randomly allocated to the treatment or no treatment conditions, so that this finding is not truly validated. Kennedy (1972) likewise compared three aftercare groups (admitted to the Edinburgh Regional Poisoning Treatment Center, referred to psychiatrists elsewhere, or not referred at all). He found significant differences in further suicidal behaviour: those that were treated in the RPTC had the lowest number of subsequent attempted suicides in a follow up period of one year (12% versus 38% and 37% in the referral and no-referral groups). But, as Kennedy himself noted, the only way of properly evaluating the effectiveness of the RPTC would be a controlled experiment with patients randomly allocated to treatment conditions, an experiment which he and many researchers after him, considered ethically unjustified.

While retrospective studies report a relationship between more specialized psychiatric or more intensive psychosocial treatment on the one hand and lower incidence of suicidal acts on the other hand, suggesting a reducing effect of such treatments (Greer & Bagley, 1971; Kennedy, 1972), such results have to be taken with great caution due to poor matching of comparison groups with regard to factors like motivation for treatment and reasons for offering treatment.

The design used in most prospective studies can be described as follows. When a patient has been admitted or treated in a hospital for the physical consequences of a suicide attempt, he or she is seen as soon as possible by a psychiatrist, a psychologist or another member of the treatment or research team in order to assess the social and mental health status as well as the suicide risk. Consequently the patient is more or less randomly assigned to one of several treatment conditions or to a control group (Chowdhury et al., 1973; Welu and Pickard, 1974; Ettlinger, 1975; Termansen and Bywater, 1975; Oast and Zitrin, 1975; Litman and Wold, 1976; Motto, 1976; Gardner et al., 1977; Welu, 1977; Wullemier et al., 1978; Gibbons et al., 1979; Liberman and Eckman, 1981; Hawton et al., 1981; Hawton et al., 1987; Möller, 1989; and Allard et al., 1992). Sometimes the control group consists of all suicide attempters seen in the year previous to the start of the experimental treatment (cf. Ettlinger, 1975; Wullemier et al., 1978).

Experimental conditions in most studies are either the usual minimum procedure (one or a few interviews with a psychiatrist, psychologist or social worker during admission and referral to family physician or other health care professional after discharge) or a treatment program specially designed for suicide attempters (including regular individual or group sessions, usually on a once a week basis during a period of 3 to 6 months). The individual or group sessions focus mainly on helping the patients in alleviating or solving social and practical problems in their everyday lives.

After termination of the treatment there are one or several follow up meetings, in which changes in social conditions, psychological wellbeing and behaviour problems are assessed, including subsequent suicidal acts.
A typical problem in this kind of study is presented by Oast and Zitrin

(1975). They selected 495 patients admitted to a psychiatric ward due to suicide attempts or gestures, and randomly allocated 265 persons to the experimental treatment condition. The treatment consisted of extra aftercare check-ups, intensified personal guidance, and possibly even out-reach contacts in the patients' homes. It turned out that at the start, nearly half of the experimental group (48%) could not be contacted for participation in the study (15% were institutionalized at the time of the first reaching out contacts, 6% were traced to the point that they left the New York City, 14% were untraceable (no address, no address of friends or relatives), in 11% of the cases it seemed appropriate to respect the patient's resistance and to discontinue active follow up). Furthermore, of those persons that could be contacted, only 69 (= 26% of the selected patients) were willing to start the experimental condition (refused prolonged treatment, did not show up at appointments, no continuing problem, hospitalization was a mistake, etc.). In an appreciable number of cases the major obstacle was the patient's crisis orientation to medical attention: they contacted the services only at times of crisis, and when the crisis subsided they broke off contact and resisted referral for continuing help (Oast and Zitrin, 1975, p. 145). It goes without saying that such a state of affairs is not beneficial for reaching scientifically based conclusions.

These kinds of problems do show up regularly, even in the better designed studies that claim positive results. Welu and Picard, for instance, state that "nearly half of the suicide attempters in the comparison group were not contacted by the end of the four month follow-up period and presumably were lost because of inadequate follow-up mechanism" (Welu and Picard, 1974, p. 450). The claim that the experimental group showed less further suicidal behavior that the (remaining) controls is therefore not substantiated.

Almost all studies report on projects that were in operation for a limited number of years after which they were terminated often due to lack of further funding. Unfortunately, most of the prospective studies have not used a proper controlled design in which patients have been randomly assigned to either a treatment or non-treatment group, also because of practical considerations (Streiner and Adam; 1987).

Not surprisingly, the overall picture with regard to efficacy of special aftercare programs that emerges from the studies reviewed contains a number of contradictions. Only four studies report a reduction in suicidal behaviour in the special aftercare condition, compared to fourteen studies where no differences were found. (Liberman and Eckman, 1981; Wulliemier et al., 1978;

Termansen and Bywater, 1975; Welu, 1977). When scrutinized carefully, on the methodological points mentioned above, the results of these four studies may be questioned.

No effect was found for a program offering antidepressant medication (Montgomery et al., 1983). In one study (Litman and Wold, 1976) that focused exclusively on chronic suicidal persons with a high risk for repetition, no effect was found of a special aftercare program with regard to suicides and suicide attempts in comparison with a control condition.

The most recent study in this series, using a methodologically well-structured design, found - convincingly - no effect at all (Allard et al., 1992). 224 subjects were offered participation in a study; 150 actually enrolled (others did not meet inclusion criteria, were already under treatment elsewhere, were incapable of consenting, language barriers, would not be able to keep appointments). 76 patients were randomized to the experimental group, 74 to the comparison group (no differences regarding sex and age). The intensive intervention program consisted of: "an explicit treatment plan for each patient, a schedule of visits, at least one home visit, written or telephone reminders, or home visits in case of missed appointments, referral to usual psychiatric resources after the experimental treatment, if applicable. The treatment plan could include any combination of support or psychoanalytically oriented psychotherapy, psychosocial, drug, or behavioral therapy, according to the needs of the patient and the training of the therapist. Free use was made of outside resources such as Alcoholics Anonymous, when needed" (Allard et al., 1992, p. 306).

A positive characteristic of this study is that only 24 subjects dropped out of the study in the follow up period, equally distributed between the experimental and the control group (13 versus 11). Results showed that 22 subjects (35%) in the experimental group and 19 subjects (30%) in the comparison group made at least one suicide attempt in the two years following randomization (not significant). Three completed suicides occurred among experimental subjects and one among the comparison subjects. Clearly the intensive intervention did not have the intended effect.

In sum, the identification of effective methods for the prevention of further episodes of suicidal behaviour continues to be a problem. It is noteworthy, however, that some of the studies reviewed have found that the special or intense forms of treatment have a positive effect on other outcomes such as psychological and social functioning of patients. For our understanding of such findings, some explanations may be offered. Most of the special treatment programs focus on the alleviation of the immediate emotional and social problems of the patient. Consequently it is not at all certain whether the patient indeed learns different ways of coping with identical or similar problems whenever they recur.

In the majority of the studies no data have been collected on the sequential relationship between psychiatric diagnosis and risk of repetition. It might well be that new episodes of acute psychiatric disturbance are an important factor of suicidal recidivism. Most special aftercare programs do not seem to be particularly tailored to deal with such conditions.

No studies control for the effect of treatment history on subsequent suicide attempts. Many suicidal patients have previously been in contact with helping agencies and health care professionals. Their experiences in this respect may rather be negative and may give rise to negative expectations of further help after the index attempt and therewith to rather low compliance (Möller, 1989).

Finally, selecting patients for a specific treatment method on the basis of the fact that they have attempted suicide might in itself be a questionable procedure. Suicidal behaviour can be reached via different roads and it might be more appropriate to select treatment modalities on the basis of "how the patient got there", i.e. using the underlying social and psychological problems as criterion, instead of on the basis of one particular symptomatic behaviour. The available literature testifies to the fact that selecting a specific treatment for a specific subgroup of suicidal persons, such as suicidal persons suffering from a depressive disorder, might be preferable.

Therapies for affective disorders

The evidence for a close relationship between mental illness and suicidal behaviour is convincing. Although the percentages may differ, most studies on the topic concur in the conclusion that the majority of persons dying through their own hand suffer from an ascertainable mental disorder at the time of their death. Of the suicides suffering from a mental illness, most are diagnosed as having depressive disorders. About 15% of patients suffering from major depression finally die by their own hand, while 50 to 60% of persons committing or attempting suicide suffer from depressive disturbances (Sainsbury, 1986). It is therefore necessary to investigate the question whether effective methods for the treatment and/or prevention of depressive disorders will also have an effect on the prevention of suicidal behaviour.

Within contemporary psychiatry three modalities for the treatment of depressive disorders are psychotherapy (ranging from classical psychoanalysis via interpersonal approaches to behaviour therapy), antidepressant drug therapy and electroconvulsive therapy (ECT). Literature reviews indicate that all three modalities are effective in diminishing, reducing and preventing depressive disorders and that the differences in efficacy between them are relatively small for unipolar depressive disturbances, while drug treatment and ECT seem to be considerably more effective in bipolar depression (Tanney, 1986).

If all three modalities are effective in depressive disorders where suicidal behaviour is a recognized complication, the question arises as to the available evidence for their efficacy in diminishing, reducing and preventing suicidal behaviour.

With regard to psychotherapeutic treatment modalities, the conclusion is that psychotherapy deserves its place among the therapies for depression and has a symptom reducing effect, including reduction of suicidal ideation, but it is not possible to state anything definite with regard to its effect on the incidence of suicidal behaviour. The reason for this is that among the controlled studies in this area studies that use subsequent suicidal behaviour as an outcome criterion are virtually non-existent.

With regard to antidepressant drug therapy the situation is not much different. Several studies (Montgomery et al., 1983) indicate that antidepressant medication, if prescribed and used appropriately, may have an effect on suicidal ideation and possibly on suicidal behaviour, but at the same time such medication might also be a risk factor since many suicidal patients overdose with their antidepressant medication.

Remarkably, we know most about the effectiveness of ECT in preventing suicidal behaviour. In his review Tanney (1986) used several methods to evaluate the impact of ECT on the frequency of suicidal behaviours in affective disorders. On the one hand one can compare the number of suicidal deaths in different treatment periods (pre-ECT versus ECT and post-ECT). Although Tanney suggests that the available studies warrant the conclusion that introduction of ECT had a reducing effect, careful examination of their designs indicate that these are all retrospective and do not accurately specify the distribution of the patients included in the studies over the diagnostic categories. Therefore, any definite conclusion with regard to the effects of ECT on suicidal behaviour on the basis of this set of studies is premature.

However, when we on the other hand look at the set of published controlled studies on the role of ECT in reducing suicidal behaviour in depressed patients, the picture that emerges is somewhat clearer. Five out of six studies (Tanney, 1986) show a preventive effect of ECT. The one exception (Babigian & Guttmacher, 1984) found no advantage to ECT in preventing suicide within five years of the first psychiatric hospitalization for depression. Since the number of patients in this latter study is larger than the total sum of patients included in the other five studies, a meta-analytic review would probably conclude that the verdict on the preventive effect of ECT is still "undetermined". However, the control group used in Babigian and Guttmacher's study presumably included many patients who received antidepressant and other psychotropic drug therapy as well as continuation and maintenance therapies.

This raises the question as to the differential effects of ECT versus drug therapy and other treatment modalities in reducing suicidal behaviour in patients suffering from affective disorders. Again there is a scarcity of information. The only controlled study that reported on differential outcome of ECT versus antidepressant drug therapy (Avery & Winokur, 1978) suggests an advantage to ECT when suicide attempts, not suicides, are used as outcome criterion. Several other studies using retrospective designs failed to show such a difference between ECT and antidepressant drug therapy (Tanney, 1986). Our conclusion is a cautious one: the available evidence for a preventive effect of ECT is at most suggestive, but certainly not convincing.

Restriction of easy access to lethal methods

The oldest method of preventing suicide is the removal or obstruction of means to commit suicide. Admitting patients to a closed ward with intensive supervision and removal of knives, razorblades, ropes and locking away medication inevitibly reduces the possibility of giving in to a suicidal impulse. Locating such a closed ward on the ground floor, and using non-flammable materials may add to the feelings of security of patients and staff. The effectiveness of such measures seems to be undisputed, at least in the short run. Of course in this way many suicides have been prevented, or at least postponed. There is however no way of measuring the effectiveness of such methods because there is no experimental design that could be applied ethically. The application of such restrictions to suicidal behaviour may have suicide-promoting effects as well. The concentration of highly suicidal patients in one place may have unwanted effects such as stigmatization and imitation. It appears that making a closed ward completely "suicide-proof", if that would be possible at all, would obstruct ordinary daily living, would complicate treatment and would in the end violate basic human rights. There is no empirical evidence whatsoever that the policy of (involuntary) admission to a psychiatric hospital would prevent suicides on a national or regional level. In fact many suicides take place within the boundaries of psychiatric hospitals. But that is to be expected with such a high density of suicidal patients. The question remains how many of these patients would have committed suicide when they would not, or could not have been admitted. This is a question that cannot be answered. There is empirical evidence however that quite a number of recently discharged patients commit suicide, especially among those patients that were admitted because of suicide risk (Kerkhof, 1985). All this only testifies that many highly suicidal patients are identified as having such a risk, that they are being concentrated in places where specialized treatment is available, and that the transfer from the psychiatric hospital to the outside world is a rather critical period.

A similar situation can be found in prisons and police lock-ups. Strict measures to prevent suicide temporarily reduce the risk of actual suicidal behaviour. Yet the incidence of suicide is ten times higher in jails and prisons than in the population (Kerkhof and Bernasco, 1990). What this means for the assessment of the effectiveness of these preventive measures is unclear. Given the characteristics of incarcerated persons one might even claim that these suicide rates in jails and prisons are extremely low.

Because many suicides are made impulsively, some people claim that the removal of means that are easily accessible would reduce the number of impulsive acts (Lester, 1988, 1992). One might think of preventing people from reaching the roofs of high buildings, restrict the possiblity of opening windows, etc. Barbiturates are notably dangerous in overdoses. The shift from barbiturates to other medication (such as benzodiazepines) during the seventies, however, has not been accompanied by a substantial decrease in suicides. Gun control legislation, especially gun ownership, seems to be related to differences in regional suicide rates, as well as homicide rates (Lester, 1988). Whether this finding opens possibilities for suicide prevention is questionable. The switch from coal gas to natural gas in the United Kingdom in the sixties showed a marked decline in suicide due to domestic gas, while suicide due to non-gas methods increased at the same time, but not in all age-sex subgroups (Kreitman, 1976). Whether this reflected a causal relationship is still questionable (Crombie, 1990). Note that this switch was economically driven, and not with a view of suicide prevention

(Lester, 1992). Car emission control may have an incidental impact on suicide (Lester, 1992). But all of these methods do not seem to offer possibilities for purposeful suicide prevention on a large scale.

Discussion and conclusions

From this review of the literature on suicide prevention programs or methods it can be concluded that there is no empirical evidence whatsoever that any of the measures designed to reduce suicides has a substantial effect. This is not to say that no suicides and attempted suicides are being prevented by the approaches and methods that are currently in operation. What it does mean is that no data, sufficiently hard and replicated, are available that testify to such an effect.

There are methodological shortcomings in many effectiveness studies, there are ethical objections against experimental designs, and there are doubts about the representativity of the populations being studied. But there are more substantial shortcomings in many of the programs being studied, in the sense that there may often be a problem in the match between treatment and problem, between program goals and participants' lack of resources. Essentially there is a complexity of causation of suicidal behaviour.

There are societal, psychological and biological variables involved in each and every case of suicide and attempted suicide. It might well be that we have not yet sufficiently defined distinct subgroups of suicidal persons. The tendencies to self-destruction are not yet fully understood. Even the definitions of attempted suicide, deliberate selfharm and self-injurious behaviour are not yet fixed: we might in fact be studying different forms of behaviour with different psychodynamics under a rather vague concept such as attempted suicide. Suicide and attempted suicide - in all its diversity - are behaviours that can be reached via several pathways. And every pathway has numerous outcomes other than suicide. Maybe we should concentrate more on these pathways. For example, there is evidence that sexual and physical abuse in childhood increases the likelihood that suicidal tendencies will appear later in life (Van Egmond and Jonker, 1988; Van Egmond et al., 1993). One suicide prevention strategy would be to "work for the reduction in the incidence of sexual and physical abuse of children and to provide good psychotherapy for those so abused" (Lester, 1992, p. 46). Similarly, the improvement of psychotropic medication might not only improve the mental health of people, but might also prevent suicide. The prevention of loneliness and depression in the elderly might also have some effect on suicidal behaviour. All of these pathways to suicide deserve attention and should be incorporated into national suicide prevention programs. Whether the effects of such programs on incidence rates of suicide and attempted suicide will ever be detectable, remains to be demonstrated.

REFERENCES

Allard, R., Marshall, M. & Plante, M.C. (1992). Intensive follow-up does not decrease the risk of repeated suicide attempts. *Suicide and Life Threatening Behavior*, **22**, 303-314.

Avery, D. & Winokur, G. (1978). Suicide, attempted suicide, and relapse rates in depression. *Archives of General Psychiatry*, **35**, 749-753.

Babigian, H.M. & Guttmacher, L.B. (1984). Epidemiologic considerations in electroconvulsive therapy. *Archives of General Psychiatry*, **41**, 246-253.

Brent, D.A., & Kolko, D.J. (1990). The Assessment and Treatment of Children and Adolescents at Risk for Suicide. In: S.J. Blumenthal, & D.J. Kupfer (Eds.). *Suicide over the Life Circle.* Washington, American Psychiatric Press.

Bridge, T.P., Potkin, S.G., Zung, W.W.K., & Soldo, B.J. (1977). Suicide Prevention Centers: Ecological Study of Effectiveness. *The Journal of Nervous and Mental Disease*, **164**, 1, 18-24.

Chowdhury, N., Hicks, R.C. & Kreitman, N. (1973). Evaluation of an after-care service for parasuicide (attempted suicide) patients. *Social Psychiatry*, **8**, 67-81.

Cohen-Sandler, R., Berman, A. & King, R. (1982). Life stress and symptomatology: Determinants of suicidal behavior in children. *Journal of the American Academy of Child Psychiatry*, **21**, 178-186.

Crombie, I.K. (1990). Suicide in England and Wales and in Scotland: An examination of divergent trends. *British Journal of Psychiatry*, **157**, 529-532.

Dew, M.A., Bromet, E.J., Brent, D. & Greenhouse, J.B. (1987). A quantitative literature review of the effectiveness of suicide prevention centers. *Journal of Consulting and Clinical Psychology*, **55**, 239-244.

Diekstra, R.F.W. (1989). Suicide and attempted suicide: An international perspective. *Acta Psychiatrica Scandinavica* (suppl. 354), **80**, 1-24.

Egmond, M. van & Jonker, D. (1988). Seksueel misbruik en lichamelijke mishandeling: risicofactoren voor (recidiverend) suicidaal gedrag bij vrouwen? *Tijdschrift voor Psychiatrie*, **30**, 21-38.

Egmond, M. van, Garnefski, N., Jonker, D. & Kerkhof, A. (1993). The Relationship between Sexual Abuse and Female Suicidal Behavior. *Crisis, The Journal of Crisis Intervention and Suicide Prevention*, **3**, 129-139.

Ettlinger, R.W. (1975). Evaluation of suicide prevention after attempted suicide. *Acta Psychiatrica Scandinavica (suppl.)*, **260**, 1-135.

Gallup Organization, Inc. (1991). *Teenage Suicide study: Executive Summary.* (Available from the Gallup Organization, Inc.).

Gardner, R., Hanka, R., O'Brien, V.C., Page, A.J.F. & Rees, R. (1977). Psychological and social evaluation in cases of deliberate self-poisoning admitted to a general hospital. *British Medical Journal*, **2**, 1567-1570.

Garland, A. & Shaffer, D. (1990). School-based adolescent suicide prevention programs. In M.J. Rotheram, J. Bradley & N. Obolensky (Eds). *Planning to live: Evaluating and treating suicidal teens in community settings*. Tulsa: University of Oklahoma Press.

Garland, A., Shaffer, D. & Whittle, B. (1989). A national survey of adolescent suicide prevention programs. *Journal of the American Academy of Child and Adolescent Psychiatry*, **28**, 931-934.

Gibbons, J.S., Butler, J., Urwin, P. & Gibbons, J.L. (1979). Evaluation of a social work service for self-poisoning patients. *British Journal of Psychiatry*, **133**, 111-118.

Greer, S. & Bagley, C. (1971). Effect of psychiatric intervention in attempted suicide. A controlled study. *British Medical Journal*, **1**, 310-312.

Hawton, K. (1986). *Suicide and attempted suicide among children and adolescents*. Beverly Hills, CA: Sage.

Hawton, K., Brancroft, J., Catalan, J., Kingston, B., Stedeford, A. & Welch, N. (1981). Domiciliary and out-patient treatment of self-poisoning patients by medical and non-medical staff. *Psychological Medicine*, **11**, 169-177.

Hawton, K., Mc.Keown, S., Day, A., Martin, P., O'Connor, M. & Yule, J. (1987). Evaluation of out-patient counselling compared with general practitioner care following overdoses. *Psychological Medicine*, **17**, 751-761.

Hoberman, H.M. & Garfinkel, B.D. (1988). Completed suicide in children and adolescents. *Journal of the American Academy of Child and Adolescent Psychiatry*, **27**, 689-695.

Holding, T.A. (1974). The BBC "Befrienders" series and its effects. *British Journal of Psychiatry*, **124**, 470-472.

Kalafat, J., & Elias, M. (1992). Adolescents' Experience with and response to Suicidal Peers. *Suicide and Life Threatening Behavior*, **22**, 3, 315-321.

Kennedy, P. (1972). Efficacy of a regional poisoning treatment center in preventing further suicidal behaviour. *British Medical Journal*, **4**, 255-257.

Kerkhof, A.J.F.M. (1985). *Suicide en de Geestelijke Gezondheidszorg*. Lisse: Swets & Zeitlinger.

Kerkhof, A.J.F.M. & Bernasco, W. (1990). Suicidal behavior in jails and prisons in The Netherlands. *Suicide and Life Threatening Behavior*, **20**, 123-137.

Kerkhof, A.J.F.M., Diekstra, R.F.W. & Koster, A.M. (1982). *Over de effectiviteit van nazorgprogramma's voor suicidepogers; een literatuuroverzicht*. Rijksuniversiteit Leiden, Vakgroep Klinische Psychologie.

Kerkhof, A.J.F.M., Wal, J. van der & Hengeveld, M.W. (1988). A typology of persons who attempted suicide with predictive value for repetition: a prospective cohort study. In H.J. Möller, A. Schmidtke & R. Welz (Eds). *Current issues of suicidology* (pp. 193-203). Berlin/Heidelberg: Springer Verlag.

Kienhorst, C. W. M., De Wilde, E. J., Diekstra, R. F. W. & Wolters, W. H. G. (1992). Differences between adolescent suicide attempters and depressed adolescents. *Acta Psychiatrica Scandinavica*, **85**, 222-228.

Kreitman, N. (1976). The coal gas story: United Kingdom suicide rates 1960-1971. *British Journal of Preventive Social Medicine*, **30**, 86-93.

Lester, D. (1974). Effect of suicide prevention centers on suicide rates in the United States. *Health Services Reports*, **89**, 37-39.

Lester, D. (1988). Gun control, gun ownership and suicide prevention. *Suicide and Life Threatening Behavior*, **18**, 176-180.

Lester, D. (1992). Is there a need for suicide prevention? *Crisis, The Journal of Crisis Intervention and Suicide Prevention*, **2**, 94.

Liberman, R.P. & Eckman, T. (1981). Behavior therapy vs. insight-oriented therapy for repeated suicide attempters. *Archives of General Psychiatry*, **38**, 1126-1130.

Miller, H.L., Coombs, D.W. & Leeper, J.D. (1984). An analysis of the effects of suicide prevention facilities on suicide rates in the United States. *American Journal of Public Health*, 74, 340-343.

Möller, H.J. (1989). Efficacy of different strategies of aftercare for patients who have attempted suicide. *Journal of the Royal Society of Medicine*, **82**, 643-647.

Montgomery, S.A., Roy, D. & Montgomery, D.B. (1983). The prevention of recurrent suicidal acts. *British Journal of Clinical Pharmacology (suppl.)*. **15**, 183-188.

Mulder, A., Methorst, G. & Diekstra, R. (1989). Prevention of suicidal behavior in adolescents: the role and training of teachers. *Crisis*, **10**, 36-51.

Memory, J.M. (1989). Juvenile suicides in secure detention facilities: Correction of published rates. *Death Studies*, **13**, 455-463.

Motto, J.A. (1976). Suicide prevention for high risk persons who refuse treatment. *Suicide and Life Threatening Behavior*, **6**, 223-230.

Nelson, F.L. (1987). Evaluaton of a youth suicide prevention school program. *Adolescence*, **38**, 813-825.

Nielsen, J. & Videbech, T. (1973). Suicide frequency before and after introduction of community psychiatry in a Danish island. *British Journal of Psychiatry*, **123**, 35-39.

Oast, S.P. & Zitrin, A. (1975). A public health approach to suicide prevention. *American Journal of Public Health*, **65**, 144-147.

Overholser, J., Hemstreet, A.H., Spirito, A. & Vyse, S. (1989). Suicide awareness programs in the schools: Effects of gender and personal experience. *Journal of the American Academy of Child and Adolescent Psychiatry*, **28**, 925-930.

Pardes, H., & Blumenthal, S.J. (1990). Youth Suicide: Public Policy and Research Issues. In: S.J. Blumenthal & D.J. Kupfer (Eds.). *Suicide over the Life Circle*. Washington, American Psychiatric Press.

Platt, S., Bille Brahe, U., Kerkhof, A.J.F.M., Schmidtke, A. (1992). Parasuicide in Europe: the WHO/EURO multicenter study on parasuicide. I. Introduction and preliminary analysis for 1989. *Acta Psychiatrica Scandinavica*, **85**, 97-104.

Price, R.H., Cowen, E.L., Lorion, R.P., Ramos-McKay, J. (1989). The search for effective prevention programs: What we learned along the way. *American Journal of Orthopsychiatry*, **59**, 49-58.

Ross, C.P. (1980). Mobilizing schools for suicide prevention. *Suicide and Life Threatening Behavior*, **10**, 239-243.

Sainsbury, P. (1986). Depression, suicide and suicide prevention. In A. Roy (Ed.). *Suicide*. Baltimore: Williams and Wilkins.

Schmidtke, A., & Häffner, H. (1988). The Werther effect after television films: new evidence for an old hypothesis. *Psychological Medicine*, **18**, 665-676.

Shafii, M., Steltz-Lenarsky, J., McCue Derrick, A. (1988). Comorbidity of mental disorders in the post-mortem diagnosis of completed suicide in children and adolescents. *Journal of Affective Disorders*, **15**, 227-233.

Shneidman, E.S. & Farberow, N.L. (1957). *Clues to suicide*. New York: McGraw-Hill.

Shneidman, E.S. & Farberow, N.L. (1965). The Los Angeles suicide prevention center: A demonstration of public health feasibilities. *American Journal of Public Health*, **55**, 21-26.

Shaffer, D., Garland, A., Gould, M., Fisher, P. & Trautman, P. (1988). Preventing teenage suicide: A critical review. *Journal of the American Academy of Child and Adolescent Psychiatry*, **27**, 675-687.

Shaffer, D., Garland, A., Vieland, V., Underwood, M. & Busner, C. (1991). The impact of curriculum based suicide prevention programs for teenagers. *Journal of the American Academy of Child and Adolescent Psychiatry*, **30**, 588-596.

Shaffer, D., Vieland, V., Garland, A., Rojas, M., Underwood, M. & Busner, C. (1990). Adolescent suicide attempters: Response to suicide prevention programs. *Journal of the American Medical Association*, **264**, 3151-3155.

Spirito, A., Overholser, J., Ashworth, S., Morgan, J. & Benedict, D. C. (1988). Evaluation of a suicide awareness curriculum for high school students. *Journal of the American Academy of Child and Adolescent Psychiatry*, **27**, 705-711.

Spirito, A., Brown, C., Overholser, J. & Fritz, G. (1989a). Attempted suicide in adolescence: a review and critique of the literature. *Clinical Psychology Review*, **9**, 335-363.

Spirito, Overholser, J. & Stark, L. (1989b). Common problems and coping strategies II: Findings with adolescent suicide attempters. *Journal of Abnormal Child Psychology*, **17**, 213-221.

Stiffman, A.R. (1989). Suicide attempts in runaway youths. *Suicide and Life Threatening Behavior*, **19**, 147-159.

Streiner, D.L. & Adam, K.S. (1987). Evaluation of the effectiveness of suicide prevention programs: a methodological perspective. *Suicide and Life Threatening Behavior*, **17**, 93-106.

Tanney, B.L. (1986). Electroconvulsive therapy and suicide. In R. Maris (Ed). *Biology of suicide*. New York: The Guilford Press, pp. 116-140.

Termansen, P.E. & Bywater, C. (1975). S.A.F.E.R.: A follow-up service for attempted suicide in Vancouver. *Canadian Psychiatric Association Journal, 20, 29-34.*

Welu, Th.C. & Pickard, K.M. (1974). Evaluating the effectiveness of a special follow-up program for suicide attempters: A two year study. In: N. Speijer & R.F.W. Diekstra (Eds.). *Proceedings 7th International Congress on Suicide Prevention*. Amsterdam/Lisse, Swets and Zeitlinger.

Welu, T.C. (1977). A follow-up program for suicide attempters: Evaluation of effectiveness. *Suicide and Life Treatening Behavior*, **7**, 17-30.

World Health Organization (1989). *World Health Statistics Annual*. Geneva, World Health Organization.

Wullemier, F., Kremer, P. & Bovet, J. (1978). Comparative study of two intervention modes on suicide attempters hospitalized in the general hospital. In *Proceedings 9th IASP Congress*, Helsinki 1977, Oy-Länsi-Savo: Mikkeli.

Suicide and the Media Research and Policy Implications

D.P. PHILLIPS AND K. LESYNA

We gratefully acknowledge the assistance of Jose van Dijk, who translated Dutch articles for us. As always, we very much appreciate the helpfulness and technical support of Michael O'Hagan and Michael Corrigan of the University of California, San Diego Social Science Computer Center.

1. Introduction

Most people contemplating suicide are at some point ambivalent in the face of such a fateful and irreversible decision (Weisman and Worden, 1972; Shneidman, 1985). This ambivalence leads naturally to a question that has seldom been asked in the literature: What are the factors which lead an indecisive person to suicide rather than to some alternative solution to distress? Why do some alcoholics choose suicide, while others join Alcoholics Anonymous? Why do some lonely people reaffiliate, while others kill themselves? Why do some depressed people seek treatment, while others seek death? In short, what are the factors which make some people choose constructive solutions to their problems, while others choose a destructive alternative like suicide?

This question falls naturally into two parts: First, what leads some people to destructive rather than to constructive solutions? Second, if a destructive solution has been chosen, why do some individuals opt for suicide rather

The preparation of this chapter was assisted by a generous grant from an Anonymous Foundation, for unrestricted research by the senior author.

than less extreme forms of destructive behavior? A full-scale answer to these questions is not known, but much research suggests that one of the factors leading a distressed individual to suicide is the publicizing of model "suicides" in the mass media. These publicized suicide stories seem to function as "natural advertisements" for the idea of suicide.

It may be possible to reduce the effectiveness of these advertisements by drawing on findings in various fields, including decision-making and advertising. These fields also suggest some ways for constructing effective "anti-suicide stories-advertisements" for alternatives to suicide. Thus, although studies on suicide stories appear at first sight to have rather gloomy implications, they also suggest some positive conclusions as well: modeling processes can lead ambivalent individuals towards suicide or towards more constructive alternatives.

In this chapter we will try to accomplish four tasks. First, we will review the literature on the impact of publicized suicide stories. Second, we will review findings in other literatures, in order to discover ways to decrease the effectiveness of "pro-suicide" stories and increase the effectiveness of "anti-suicide" stories. Third, we will suggest a list of research topics which remain to be addressed, and some ways in which this research can be facilitated by public-health services, mental-health professionals, and the mass media. Finally, we will summarize the main points of the chapter.

2. Review of the Literature on the Imitation of Publicized Suicides

A. Studies on the effect of non-fictional suicide stories

Effect of newspaper stories

In the first modern study of the topic, Motto (1967) approached the problem indirectly by assuming that during a newspaper strike there would be a reduction in the publicity accorded to suicide stories. In a study of seven U.S. cities, he compared the suicide rate during a newspaper strike to the mean rate for the previous five years, controlling for population increase, other population characteristics, seasonal variation, and yearly trends. He found no evidence to support his hypothesis that suicides would decline during strikes.

In a later study Motto (1970) compared the suicide rate during a 268-day newspaper strike in Detroit with the mean rates for the same calendar period of the previous four years and the subsequent year. He found a significant reduction in the number of suicides by females, especially those under age 35, in the period of the newspaper strike.

Blumenthal and Bergner (1973) replicated Motto's Detroit study using New York City data. Unlike Motto, they found that the suicide rate during the strike period was not significantly lower than the mean rate of the previous three years for any age- or sex-specific group. They noted that the different findings may result from the fact that New York City's strike, unlike Detroit's, affected only half of the city's newspapers.

The studies by Motto and by Blumenthal and Bergner are affected by several methodological problems. First, they do not take into account the effect of radio or television news during the newspaper strikes, or the effect of newspapers brought in from out-of-town. These alternative news sources might well have publicized any noteworthy suicides that occurred during the newspaper strike. Second, there may not in fact have been any noteworthy, publishable suicides during the newspaper strike; if so, the newspapers failure to publicize these non-existent stories could not be expected to affect the suicide rate. Third, a newspaper strike introduces many changes in a city; some of these changes (like the cessation of suicide stories) may decrease the suicide rate, some may increase it, and some may make no difference. Until these methodological problems can be resolved, Motto's study design is inherently inconclusive: one cannot easily determine whether the behavior of suicides during newspaper strikes supports or undermines the hypothesis that suicide stories function as natural advertisements.

Phillips (1974) used a different study design to provide a more direct estimate of the impact of suicide stories. This research approach will be described in some detail because it has been the prototype for nearly all subsequent studies of newspaper suicide stories. Using Facts on File (1946-1968) and the New York Times Index (1946-1968) Phillips generated a list of suicide stories appearing on page one of the New York Times. Phillips examined official U.S. monthly suicide statistics to estimate the effect of front-page suicide stories, 1947-1967 (after correction for the effects of trends and seasons on suicides). U.S. suicides rose significantly just after front-page suicide stories. Phillips named this post-story rise in suicide "the Werther effect", after Goethe's fictional hero whose suicide was thought by contemporary observers to have triggered imitative acts.

To increase confidence in the hypothesis that publicized suicide stories elicit a rise in U.S. suicides, Phillips tested additional predictions that should hold if suicide stories trigger imitative behavior; he also assessed competing explanations of the findings. If the Werther effect occurs because of imitation, then: 1) Suicides should peak after the publicized story, but not before. 2) The more publicity given to a story, the larger the suicide peak should be. 3) Suicides should peak mainly in the geographic area where the suicide story is publicized. The data were consistent with all of these predictions.

Phillips then assessed six competing explanations (of which the four most plausible will be summarized here). 1) The "coroner explanation" asserts that the publicized suicide prompts the coroner to shift ambiguous deaths into the category of suicide from the competing categories of accident, homicide, and undetermined death. Given this explanation, deaths in competing categories should decrease after a suicide story. Because no such decrease is seen, the "coroner explanation" is not plausible. 2) The "precipitation explanation" asserts that publicized suicides merely hasten suicides that would have occurred anyway, even in the absence of a suicide story. Given this explanation, the post-story peak in suicides should be followed by an equally large drop in suicides, caused by suicides "moving up" their death-dates. Because no such drop is seen, the "precipitation explanation" is implausible. 3) The "prior conditions explanation" asserts that a prior change in social conditions—for example, a worsening of economic conditions—produces a rise in both publicized and unpublicized suicides. Given this explanation, the rise in suicides after a suicide story should not correlate with the amount of publicity devoted to that story. Because such a correlation is in fact observed, the "prior conditions" explanation is implausible. 4) The "bereavement explanation" asserts that suicide stories elicit grief, rather than imitation, and this grief prompts additional suicides. Given this explanation, celebrity deaths should trigger additional suicides, even if these deaths are not by suicide. This prediction is not consistent with the data, and thus the "bereavement explanation" remains implausible. After assessing these and other alternative explanations, Phillips concluded that the best available explanation of the Werther effect is that it is caused by processes related to imitation or suggestion. The detailed psychological processes involved could not be precisely identified with the mortality statistics he was studying.

In a sequel, Phillips (1977; 1979) sought to estimate the influence of publicized suicide stories on motor vehicle fatalities (MVF) in California, 1966-1973. Many researchers have suspected that some motor vehicle crashes may have a suicidal component. If this is so, MVF, like overt suicides, should peak after publicized suicides. Controlling for weekday and monthly fluctuations in MVF, holiday weekends, and yearly linear trends, he found that: 1) MVF rise significantly after (but not before) publicized suicides, with a 31% peak in MVF on the third day following the story. 2) The more publicity given to the story, the greater the rise in MVF. 3) This rise occurs mainly in the area where the suicide story was publicized. 4) Single-vehicle crashes increase more than other types just after the publicized story. 5) Drivers dying just after a suicide story are similar to the person described in that story. 6) However, passengers dying just after a suicide story are not similar to the person described in the story. 7) Stories about murder-suicides tend to be followed by multiple-vehicle crashes involving passenger deaths, while stories about suicide alone tend to be followed by single-vehicle crashes involving driver deaths. Phillips assessed alternative explanations for the findings and concluded that the best available explanation is that publicized suicides elicit a rise in suicides, some of which are disguised as motor vehicle fatalities.

Bollen and Phillips (1981) replicated the principal California findings, using data for Detroit, 1973-1976. To test whether Phillips's findings were an artifact of his quasi-experimental method, they analyzed the Detroit data with both the quasi-experimental method and linear regression techniques. Both analytic procedures revealed a statistically significant peak in MVF three days after a publicized suicide. They estimated a 35%-40% increase in MVF on the third day, as compared to the 31% increase found for California.

The study of California MVF indicated that murder-suicide stories and "pure" suicide stories have different effects. Prompted by this observation, Phillips (1978; 1980) examined the impact of U.S. murder-suicide stories on U.S. non-commercial airplane crashes. Anecdotal evidence suggests that some of these crashes have a purposive component; if so, non-commercial airplane crashes should also peak after murder-suicide stories, just as auto crashes do. Phillips found that: 1) After publicized murder-suicides there is a peak in non-commercial plane crashes. 2) This peak persists for about nine days, and then the crash level returns to normal. 3) The greater the publicity given to a murder-suicide, the greater the peak in non-commercial plane crashes. 4) The peak occurs mainly in U.S. states where the murder-suicide receives the most publicity. After assessing alternative explanations for these findings, Phillips concluded that publicized murder-suicide stories elicit imitative murder-suicides, some of which are disguised as airplane accidents.

Wasserman (1984) reexamined Phillips's findings (1974), extending the time period from 1946-1968 to 1946-1977. Using multivariate time-series to control for seasonal effects, economic cycles, and war, Wasserman found a significant rise in the U.S. suicide rate after stories about celebrity suicides, but no such rise after non-celebrity suicide stories.

Stack (1984) added more than ten publicized stories which Wasserman had inadvertently overlooked. When these stories were included, Stack found a significant effect both for celebrity and for non-celebrity stories. Phillips and Carstensen (1988) uncovered similar findings with a different data set.

Stack (1987) tried to estimate whether some types of celebrity suicide stories had an unusually large effect on U.S. monthly suicide rates, 1948-1983. Controlling for unemployment, war, and seasonal effects, he found that the U.S. suicide rate rose significantly after suicide stories about U.S. political and entertainment celebrities. Stories about other types of celebrities (e.g. foreigners) were not followed by a rise in suicide. The more publicity given to the suicides of entertainment and political celebrities, the greater the rise in the suicide rate. The evidence also suggested that peoples age, sex, and race affect their identification with celebrity suicides.

Thus far, we have confined discussion to U.S. studies, which make up most of the literature. These studies typically report that: 1. Overt and covert suicides rise significantly after publicized suicides. 2. The more publicity given to a story, the greater the rise in suicides thereafter. 3. The rise is greatest where the story is most heavily publicized. To date, the only explanation which fits these and related U.S. findings is that suicide stories trigger imitative behavior.

The evidence from European studies, however, is more equivocal. This may stem partly from methodological differences in the U.S. and European research traditions. For example, an English study (Barraclough, Shepherd and Jennings, 1977) sought to determine whether Portsmouth suicides were preceded by an unusually large number of news reports on suicide inquests. In contrast to the U.S. approach, the English researchers started from a tabulation of suicide statistics and looked backward for news reports of suicide. In addition, the English study examined reports of suicide inquests rather than suicide stories. Finally, and most importantly, the English study did not confine attention to front-page reports of suicide. Indeed, nearly all the inquest stories were carried on inside pages of the newspaper. This study found a significant association between inquest stories and the suicide rate of men under 45. However, this association was not found for three other age/sex groups. Failure to find an association is not surprising, because earlier work on U.S. data found no evidence linking suicide rates with inside-page reports of suicide.

A Canadian study by Littman (1985) used a similar approach and sought to discover whether a subway-suicide epidemic in Toronto was preceded by an unusually large number of newspaper reports on suicide. Littman examined a wide range of newspaper items (articles, editorials, features) and did not restrict attention to front-page stories. He found no evidence linking a surge in subway suicides with a prior surge in newspaper items about suicide.

A team of Dutch researchers conducted two careful studies which replicated the U.S. research methodology in many respects. Most notably, they restricted attention to front-page stories. The first of these studies (Ganzeboom and de Haan, 1982) reported that "Our results are inconclusive. For suicide and traffic accidents, mortality rates tend to rise 3-8% on a monthly basis (about the same amount as Phillips revealed), but this is not significant at conventional significance levels (though very near so)."

Though Dutch and U.S. researchers use similar methodology, they study suicide stories which differ in some important and interesting ways. U.S. newspapers almost always 1) explicitly convey the idea of suicide in the headline, and 2) report the name of the suicidal victim. In contrast, Dutch newspapers are much more circumspect: Kopping, Ganzeboom, and Swanborn (unpublished paper) found that only half of the Dutch reports explicitly referred to suicide in the headlines, and only 45% of the reports revealed the name of the suicidal victim. Newspaper readers often scan a headline and do not read the rest of the story. Hence, many people may not think of suicide unless the idea is explicitly conveyed in the headline. Even when one does read the suicide story, one may be relatively unmoved by the narrative if the suicidal victim is presented as an anonymous individual. 3) About 50% of the Dutch suicide stories involved multiple victims—these were typically stories about murder followed by suicide (Kopping, Ganzeboom and Swanborn, undated). In contrast, this percentage was much smaller in the typical U.S. study.

Ganzeboom and de Haan (1982) did not distinguish between explicit-headline versus ambiguous-headline suicide stories, but the later Dutch study found that monthly Dutch suicides (1955-1984) increased significantly more after explicit-headline stories than after ambiguous-headline stories. In addition, the length of the suicide story was significantly related to the increase in Dutch suicides thereafter.

Despite the statistical significance of these findings, Kopping, Ganzeboom, and Swanborn considered their data provided inconclusive support for the hypothesis of imitative suicide. First, their monthly analysis revealed no association between other characteristics of the suicide story and the rise in suicides thereafter. For example, well-known suicides did not appear to have an unusually large impact on the fluctuation of suicides. In addition, the presence of a photograph had no apparent impact on the suicide rate after the story. Second, an analysis of a subset of daily suicides (1974-1984) failed to provide evidence of imitative suicide.

These negative findings need not reduce confidence in the hypothesis of imitative suicide. Nearly all the Dutch findings (both positive and negative) are consistent with earlier reports in the literature. This replication of the Dutch results suggests that they are real and not chance fluctuations in the data. For example, both the U.S. and the Dutch studies reported: 1) a failure to find a link between the celebrity status of the victim and the subsequent rise in suicides (Phillips and Carstensen, 1988; Stack, 1987); 2) a failure to find a link between the presence of a photograph of the victim and the subsequent rise in suicides (Phillips and Carstensen, 1988). Similarly, the positive Dutch finding linking the length of the newspaper story with the subsequent rise in suicides is consistent with much earlier U.S. work (Phillips 1974, 1978, 1979, 1980; Stack 1987) which also showed a dose-response relationship. Finally, the Dutch daily analysis may have been inconclusive because it failed to focus on explicit-headline suicide stories and failed to correct for the marked effect of holidays on suicides (a regular feature of the U.S. studies). Until this effect is corrected for, one cannot get a valid estimate of the effect of suicide stories.

These considerations suggest that conclusions based on U.S. studies need to be modified in the light of the European findings: 1) Suicides peak after front-page suicide stories in which the idea of suicide is explicitly conveyed in the headline. 2) The more publicity given to the suicide story, the greater the peak in suicides thereafter. 3) The rise in suicides is particularly large in the areas where the suicide story is most heavily publicized. The next section indicates that studies of televised suicide stories also support the hypothesis of imitative suicide.

Effect of television stories

TV suicide stories have been studied less often than suicide stories in the newspaper. The first investigations of the topic (Phillips 1978; 1980) examined the impact of both TV and newspaper stories on U.S. airplane accidents. Phillips (1980) found that "the correlation between newspaper coverage and crashes (r = .734) is almost as high as the multiple correlation between newspaper-television coverage and crashes (R = .737). Evidently, newspaper coverage alone predicts crashes almost as well as newspaper and television coverage combined."

Bollen and Phillips (1982) sought to replicate the findings from Phillips's 1974 research using TV rather than newspaper stories. They restricted attention to heavily publicized stories—those appearing on two or more TV network evening news programs. Applying regression techniques to daily rather than monthly suicide statistics they found a significant rise in the number of U.S. suicides after (but not before) publicized TV news reports about suicides. Their findings indicated that the effect of a given suicide story lasts at most ten days. Thus, the duration of the story-effect seems to be about the same for suicides, auto accidents, and airplane accidents.

Baron and Reiss (1985) claimed that the results of Bollen and Phillips (1982) could be an artifact of hetroscedasticity (which was not corrected for in Bollen and Phillips's original paper). In response, Phillips and Bollen (1985) showed that their original findings remained statistically significant after hetroscedasticity was corrected for. Baron and Reiss (1985) also suggested that Bollen and Phillips (1982) had only partially corrected for the confounding effects of holidays on suicides. In response, Phillips and Bollen (1985) noted that their results remained statistically significant after they omitted suicide stories which occurred near the holidays.

Phillips and Carstensen (1986) studied the daily suicide rate of U.S. teens (1973-1979) after 38 U.S. TV news or feature stories about suicide. Teen suicides rose significantly in the week after a suicide story appeared on TV; the adult rate also rose, but not significantly. The more publicity given the suicide story, the more the teen suicide rate went up. Suicides rose just as much after feature stories about suicide as after news reports about a specific suicide. Phillips and Carstensen assessed six alternative explanations for their findings (including the explanations assessed by Phillips (1974)). At present, the only explanation that fits the data is that TV news stories about suicide trigger an increase in teen suicides.

In a sequel, Phillips and Carstensen (1988) expanded their work on network TV news stories by almost tripling the time period under analysis (from 1973-1979 to 1968-1985) and by analyzing the effect of suicide stories on various demographic groups. Like Bollen and Phillips (1982), they restricted attention to heavily publicized suicide stories—those appearing on at least two TV news programs. They selected stories in this fashion because their earlier findings (1986) indicated that the suicide rate increased only after suicide stories that were carried on two or more TV programs:

After multi-program suicide stories, teen suicides increased by an average of 5.29 per story (t= 4.32, p= .0003, one-sample two-tailed test, n= 22). After single-program stories, teen suicides fell by an average of -0.36 per story (t= 0.32, p= .75, one-sample two-tailed test, n= 16). There was a significant difference between the effect of single-program versus multi-program stories (t= 3.42, p= .0015, two-sample test with approximately 35.8 d.f.).

Applying a time-series regression model to California data, they found that both male and female suicides increased significantly 0-7 days after multi-program suicide stories. Nearly every demographic group displayed a rise in suicides after publicized suicides, but the Werther effect was strong only for teens. Phillips and Carstensen suggested that since teens behaved quite differently from the next highest age group, 20-29 year-olds, future studies of "youth" suicides should not combine the two groups, as in many past studies. Phillips and Carstensen's findings indicate that the Werther effect is not stronger for those groups that are already predisposed to suicide, i.e., males, whites, the non-married, and people of retirement age. For nearly every demographic group, suicide stories have a large effect in comparison with other temporal variables (e.g., day of the week, month, etc.). However, the effect of a story is not large when compared with demographic variables (e.g., race, age, and sex). They point out, however, that the suicide story is more amenable to social control than the other temporal and demographic variables they discussed. Thus, e.g., it is easier to reduce the suicide rate by reducing the publicity accorded to a suicide story than by attempting to manipulate variables like sex, race, and age.

In a study sponsored by the National Broadcasting Corporation, Kessler et al. (1988) examined the fluctuation of U.S. suicides after TV suicide stories, 1973-1984. The NBC study and that by Phillips and Carstensen (1988) differed in several important ways: First, and most important, the NBC study did not restrict attention to multi-program suicide stories, despite the evidence that only these stories are known to affect suicides. Secondly, the NBC study examined a shorter time period (1973-1984 versus 1968-1985). Thirdly, in contrast to all recent studies on the topic, the NBC investigation failed to test for the effects of autocorrelation and heteroscedasticity, which are known to bias significance tests. The NBC study replicated Phillips and Carstensen's earlier finding (1986) of a statistically significant increase in teen suicides after TV stories (1973-1979). Most of these were multi-program stories. However, after adding many stories for 1980-1984 (most of which were single-program) the NBC study found a non-significant rise in suicides after suicide stories (1973-1984).

In a thorough, thoughtful critique of the NBC study, Clark (1989) notes a finding that is tabulated by the NBC authors, but not discussed in the text of their study: "celebrity suicides were significantly associated with subsequent teen suicides over the period 1973-1984." Clark conjectured that "by expanding the number of suicides included in their analysis with one-time broadcasts on programs like the Today Show, CBS Morning News, or 60 Minutes, the likelihood is that Kessler and colleagues inadvertently diluted their sample with non-celebrity cases and feature stories, and thus diluted the observed association between news broadcasts and teen suicide rates." After making several methodological criticisms in addition to those mentioned above, Clark raised "a question of how neutral a major force in network news broadcasting can remain when responding (scientifically or otherwise) to evidence that certain kinds of news reports may have a damaging impact. There is an appearance that the network is refuting studies which criticize its news policies."

Sonneck et al. (1991) conducted what appears to be the only field experiment on this topic. On the basis of the mass media research reviewed in this chapter, the Austrian Association for Suicide Prevention, Crisis Intervention, and Conflict Resolution persuaded the two largest Austrian newspapers to reduce drastically the amount and type of publicity they accorded to Viennese subway suicides. Beginning in June, 1987, these stories were omitted entirely or buried in the back pages of the newspaper, with few details provided. Figure 1 shows the fluctuation in Viennese subway suicide before and after the change in publication policy. It is evident that subway suicides were increasing markedly up to June 1987; after this date there was a marked drop in the incidence of subway suicides, which have remained infrequent ever since. In contrast, Viennese suicides from other causes did not display this abrupt reversal of trend around June, 1987.

In sum, studies of non-fictional TV suicide stories consistently support the following conclusions: 1) Multi-program suicide stories are followed by a statistically significant peak in suicides. 2) The peak is particularly strong for teens. 3) Because the peak appears only after multi-program stories, this suggests that a suicide story is most likely to have an effect if it is heavily publicized. Thus, studies of newspaper and TV stories indicate a dose-response relationship between the publicity given to a suicide story and the rise in suicides thereafter.

Figure 1. Number of Viennese subway suicides (in six-month periods) before and after the two largest Austrian newspapers curtailed their coverage of subway-suicides. The arrow indicates the date at which the newspapers changed their publication policies. (After Sonneck et al., 1991)

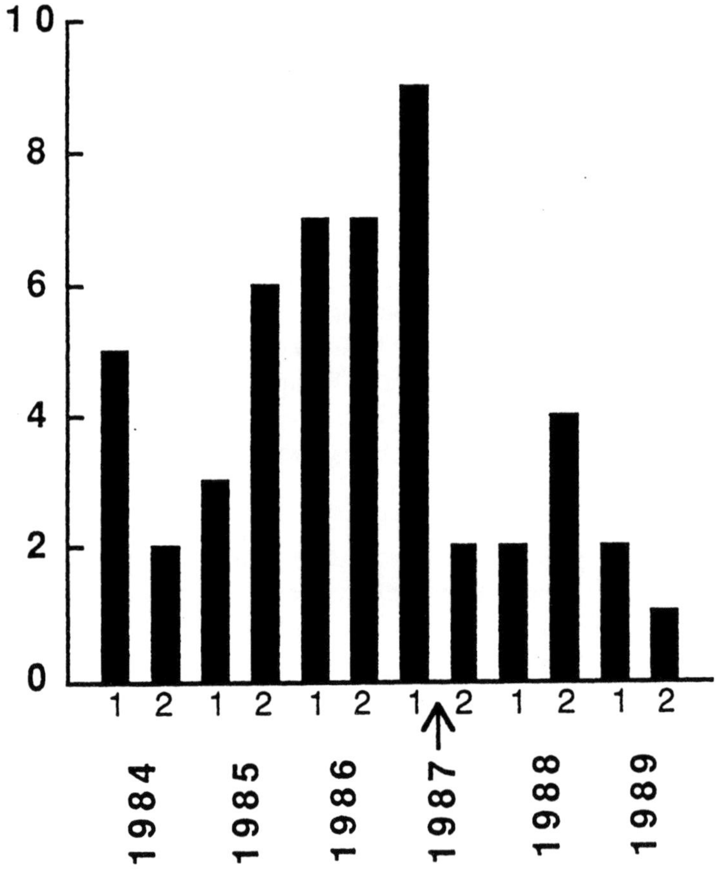

B. Studies on the effect of fictional suicide stories

As we have seen, studies of highly publicized non-fictional suicide stories generally report a post-story rise in suicides. When we turn to fictional suicide stories, evidence for a story effect is much less clear.

Holding (1974) conducted the first empirical study on the effects of fictional suicide stories. This, like all subsequent investigations to date, dealt with stories appearing on TV. Holding investigated the effect of a 1972 11-episode weekly series ("The Befrienders") on the parasuicide rate in Edinburgh. The series dramatized the role of the Samaritans, a suicide prevention service. Each episode dealt with a suicidal situation, and one episode ended in a death.

The TV series may have been simultaneously advertising two very different solutions to life problems: 1) suicide, and 2) getting help from a suicide prevention agency. Thus, the fluctuation of suicidal behavior after "The Befrienders" throws an uncertain light on the question of imitative suicide. Although Holding found a rise in the number of people visiting the suicide prevention center during the series and the four weeks thereafter, he found no significant decrease in the number of people admitted for attempted suicide to Regional Poisoning Treatment Center. Holding (1975) also looked at the effect of the same weekly series on completed suicides and undetermined deaths in Edinburgh. He found no significant change in the number of suicides and undetermined deaths in the ten weeks of the series or the ten weeks afterward.

After identifying suicide stories from weekly newspaper summaries of soap opera plot, Phillips (1982) found a significant peak in suicides, motor vehicle deaths and nonfatal accidents after soap opera suicide and parasuicide stories were broadcast in the U.S. in 1977. The peaks were larger for females than for males, as would be expected from the predominantly female audience of soap operas.

Using superior data provided by the TV industry, Kessler and Stipp (1984) noted that the newspaper summaries used by Phillips (1982) provided inaccurate dates for some of the suicide stories. Using the corrected dates of broadcast, they found a non-significant rise in suicides and motor vehicle fatalities after soap opera suicide stories.

Following the broadcast on February 1986 of an overdose suicide attempt by a soap-opera character on British TV, several British hospitals reported increased attendance for overdoses at their accident and emergency departments (Ellis and Walsh, 1986; Fowler 1986). Platt (1987) examined data from 63 British hospitals on the number of cases the hospitals treated for deliberate overdose in the week after the broadcast and in a control period of the week preceding it. Controlling for trends and seasonal fluctuations, he found that the incidence of parasuicides by overdose peaked significantly for persons aged 45 and over. Platt was puzzled by this peak in an older age group and suggested that it was an unreliable finding, despite its statistical significance. He noted that the TV program primarily appealed to young people, and that identification with the parasuicidal character would be presumably be greater for people in her age group (30-44). He felt that a conservative but fair conclusion must be "Case not proven. Though the portrayal by or reporting of suicide in the mass media has been shown to increase suicidal behavior in the general population, clear evidence that the presentation of a fictional parasuicide has a similar effect is lacking."

Williams et al. (1987; undated) drew similarly cautious conclusions. They took a closer look at two of the hospitals that had reported increases in overdoses after the February, 1986 broadcast of the parasuicide on British TV. Although Williams et al. found increases in overdoses at both hospitals following the broadcast, the increases were part of a trend that had begun in December for one hospital and in January at the other. In both hospitals the trend continued for several weeks after the observation period. Williams et al. also examined the case notes for most of the patients who had come to the hospitals for overdoses during the observation period and compared them to those for people who came during a control period. Patients in the control group were significantly more likely to have taken a prior overdose than those in the experimental group, but the researchers noted that since the total number of people who came to the hospitals was not significantly higher after the broadcast, this finding should be interpreted "with caution". They were similarly cautious in interpreting a second finding: patients who attended the hospital during the observation period were more likely to have taken analgetics (as the TV character did) than were the patients from the control period.

Ostroff et al. (1985, 1987) provided stronger evidence for imitation of a fictional suicide. From October 1984 through February 1985, four fictional movies dealing with the topic of suicide were broadcast on TV in the United States. Ostroff et al. (1985) reported an increase in the number of adolescents admitted to a Connecticut hospital for attempted suicide after the February broadcast of the fourth TV movie, which was about the effect of a teen couple's suicide on their parents. In the remainder of the month after the broadcast, the hospital admitted 14 adolescents with overdoses; two of the

14 had taken overdoses in a suicide pact similar to that portrayed in the movie. The monthly number of adolescent overdoses was much smaller (less than 5) in control periods consisting of the two previous months and February of the previous year.

In a subsequent study of the same Connecticut hospital, Ostroff and Boyd (1987) looked at data for the entire year and found that the mean number of suicides per month was 1.9, except for February, when the fictional suicides occurred. In February, there were 16 attempts, 14 of them in the period after the fictional suicide. All of these attempts involved overdoses. Ostroff and Boyd found that all of the adolescents involved had watched the movie. One boy and girl planned their suicide attempt immediately after watching the movie together.

Gould and Shaffer (1986) studied the effects of all four TV movies on the number of teen attempted suicides in the greater New York area. They also examined the effects of three of the four movies on suicides by the same group. Both attempted and completed suicides rose significantly after the broadcasts. After assessing several alternative explanations for their findings, they concluded that the broadcasts probably triggered some suicidal behavior.

Phillips and Paight (1987) replicated Gould and Shaffer's work on completed suicide. Using data on all teen suicides in California and Pennsylvania, and applying the statistical methods of Gould and Shaffer, they found no evidence that teen suicides peaked after the three movie broadcasts previously examined by Gould and Shaffer. This result held even after Gould and Shaffer's New York data were combined with the California and Pennsylvania data.

Berman (1988) also replicated part of Gould and Shaffer's study (1986). He added a later movie and excluded two of Gould and Shaffer's movies because they occurred so close together that their separate effects could not be easily assessed. He examined a nationwide sample of more than 6000 suicides and found no significant increase in the total number of suicides after the three broadcasts. However, he did find some evidence suggesting that suicides were prompted to use the specific methods portrayed on the TV programs.

Gould et al. (1988) expanded their earlier study by analyzing the effects of the three movies on teen suicides in four urban areas: New York, Cleveland, Dallas, and Los Angeles. There was a significant post-movie peak in teen suicides in the New York and Cleveland areas, but no such peak in Dallas or Los Angeles. They suggested that this discrepancy may have occurred because the educational programs accompanying the movies were more or less intensive in the different areas.

To date, the strongest evidence for imitation of a fictional suicide comes from an ingenious German study by Schmidtke and Häfner (1988). In 1981 and in 1982 West German TV broadcast a six-episode fictional movie about a 19-year-old male student who killed himself by jumping in front of a train. Using nationwide data, Schmidtke and Häfner found a significant rise in the number of railway suicides after the broadcasts. The rise was strongest in young males, who were most similar to the suicidal model. Schmidtke and Häfner assessed the possibility that only the method of suicide had shifted to that of the model while the overall number of suicides had not increased, and found that the evidence was not consistent with this alternative explanation of the findings. Their data suggested that the imitation effect probably lasts much longer than the period indicated by Phillips's studies.

The study by Schmidtke and Häfner is unique in focussing on multi-program fictional stories: Each of the episodes in the German TV series repeated a segment showing the train-suicide of the teenage boy. It is noteworthy that the strongest evidence of imitation of fictional suicide stories comes from a study of multi-program stories. Thus, studies of both fictional and non-fictional TV suicide stories support the view that multi-program stories elicit imitative behavior, whereas single-program stories do not.

"Scholars dispute, but the case is still before the court", said Horace two thousand years ago. Few literatures in social science are free from controversy, and the literature on imitative suicide is no exception. However, although some of the investigations reviewed above report no imitative effects, these are almost always studies which did not limit their attention to heavily publicized stories. When attention is focused on explicit suicide stories which are clearly labeled and heavily publicized, studies repeatedly support the following conclusions:

1. Overt and covert suicides increase significantly after clearly labeled nonfiction suicide stories which are heavily publicized on TV and in newspapers.
2. The more publicity given to a suicide story, the greater the increase in suicides thereafter.
3. The increase is largest in the geographic areas where the story is most heavily publicized.
4. The increase is proportionally largest for teens, but also evident in other demographic groups.

5. The evidence strongly suggests that non-fictional suicide stories elicit imitative suicides. But when we turn to the impact of fictional suicide stories, evidence of imitation is less strong, though still suggestive.

3. Implications from other Fields for the Coverage of Suicide Stories and "Anti-Suicide" Stories

The studies we have examined are in the epidemiological tradition, which assesses the effect of environmental factors on mortality. Many epidemiological studies are concerned with the effects of physical factors, like polluted water or polluted air. In contrast, the studies we are examining are concerned with cultural factors, particularly, the mass media. Relatively few moral questions are raised when governmental agencies seek to purify the air or the water, but the situation is quite different with regard to the cultural environment. How can one reduce the impact of suicide stories without at the same time infringing on freedom of speech or freedom of the press?

Although censorship would be unacceptable to almost everyone, it may be possible to use the weight of the evidence on imitative suicides to persuade members of the news media to limit voluntarily the publicity they accord to suicide stories. Indeed there is already some evidence of voluntary restraint on the part of the news media and others involved with suicide stories. Some public-health investigators will no longer talk to reporters about incipient suicide clusters because of a fear of imitation (Centers for Disease Control, 1988), and some media representatives have voluntarily decided not to cover certain suicide stories. Pell and Watters (1982) found that 10 out of 36 editors of the largest Canadian newspapers said that the fear of imitative suicides had influenced the publicity they accorded to a story.

As news editors learn about the detrimental effects of publicity, some may choose to reduce the coverage they give to suicide stories; others may choose to change the way in which these stories are presented. In this section, we will discover from advertising and related fields some approaches which might help to minimize the effects of suicide stories and maximize the effects of "anti-suicide" stories (these are stories and advertisements that report or promote alternatives to suicide).

Suicide and anti-suicide stories can vary on at least four dimensions:

1. the nature of the message
2. the frequency, timing and length of the message
3. the nature of the messenger
4. the placement of the message in the media.

By varying a story's position on each of these dimensions, it may be possible to affect its impact. We will begin by looking at suicide stories and then examine anti-suicide stories and advertisements.

A. Lessons from advertising and related fields for coverage of suicide stories

Nature of the message

Nearly all advertisements (ads) convey a homogeneous, focused message. Thus, e.g., a cigarette company or a food conglomerate will typically promote only one of its products in each message. The rationale for this procedure is obvious: informing the consumer of several alternatives will reduce the probability that he or she will select any one of them. This suggests that the effect of a suicide story can be reduced if the story "advertises" several alternatives to suicide (like counseling or a suicide prevention service).

Many print ads display the equivalent of a newspaper headline, which catches the attention of the reader and compactly summarizes the fundamental message of the ad. These headlines are typically focused, clear, and unqualified, because experience has shown that headlines of this type are maximally likely to affect behavior. This suggests that newspaper headlines about suicide should have the opposite qualities: if possible, they should be vague, circumspect, and unexplicit, and fail to summarize the main point of the suicide story. Indeed we have already seen from Dutch data that headlines having some of these qualities (e.g., failure to mention suicide explicitly) fail to trigger imitative suicide.

Tversky and Kahneman (1981) found that people lose their enthusiasm for an option when the option is linked with negative outcomes. At present, most suicide stories do not stress (or even report) the suffering and disfigurement experienced by many suicides. Nor do suicide stories typically report the extreme pain suffered by relatives and friends of a suicide. If these negative consequences were emphasized, or at least reported, in the suicide story, this might affect a suicidal persons decision to commit suicide. In this connection, it is interesting to note that an epidemic of female suicides in ancient Sparta was reportedly ended by an official proclamation that henceforth all female suicides would be displayed naked in the marketplace. 2500 years before Tversky and Kahneman, the Spartan government apparently changed the preference for the suicide option by linking it to an additional negative outcome.

Commercial messages frequently link the advertised product to attractive qualities like sex, freedom, or patriotism. The product is presented in a romantic, rather than instrumental or natural light. Thus, e.g., the Virgina Slims cigarette is linked with women's emancipation and is not presented as a tobacco-filled paper tube capable of inducing chemical and psychological reactions. Similarly, U.S. advertisements link Chevrolet with archetypical U.S. traditions like apple pie and baseball, and do not merely present the car as an efficient, convenient machine for transportation. In a parallel fashion, news stories about teen suicides sometimes present them in a romantic and idealized light: a youth, who is portrayed as an exemplar of tragic, doomed romantic love, commits suicide like Romeo, rather than face an empty future. One TV story about a teen suicide pact focused in on a yellow rose as the last scene in the story. Romantic treatment of this sort enhances the effect of advertisements and seems likely to enhance the effect of suicide stories, as well.

Frequency, timing and length of the message

Many advertising studies (reviewed in Comstock et al., 1978) indicate that the repetition of an ad increases its effect. These findings are consistent with the literature on imitative suicide, which indicates that suicide stories have the largest effect if they are repeated on several days (Phillips, 1974), in several newspapers (Phillips, 1979), or on several TV programs (Phillips and Carstensen, 1988). Thus, studies in advertising and elsewhere suggest that the impact of a suicide story can be reduced if the story is not repeated, either from day to day, or from network to network.

Advertising studies (Comstock et al., 1978) indicate that longer advertisements on TV result in greater recall of the messages. Newspaper research (Comstock et al., 1978; Kopping et al., unpublished paper) suggests that longer stories attract more readers. These findings suggest that suicide stories, "natural advertisements" for suicide, should be short whenever possible.

Nature of the messenger

Advertisements commonly use several types of spokespersons, including the trustworthy expert, and the "person who is just like you or me". If at all possible, TV suicide stories should not be conveyed by either type of person (Bogart, 1984). Dabbs (1964) found that "non-copers" are more affected by people like themselves than they are by strong, assertive people who actively change their life circumstances. It is a truism that suicides cannot cope with their environment, and Dabbs's finding suggests that "non-copers" should be used as spokespersons in suicide stories. More generally, the effect of the suicide story might be reduced if reporters do not allow sympathetic, ordinary people to convey the reasonableness of suicide.

Placement of the message.

Front-page stories in newspapers are read more often than those on any other page (Comstock et al., 1978). This suggests that suicide stories should be confined to the inside pages of the newspaper. Indeed, as noted above, inside-page stories have no detectable effect on the suicide rate.

A print ad is commonly presented in a single, compact rectangle; presumably advertisers prefer this format because it is maximally effective. In contrast, some newspaper stories are continued from page to page, so that some effort is required to follow up the story, disentangle it from other accounts, and read it in its entirety. The effect of a suicide story will probably be reduced if it is presented in a straggling rather than a compact format.

Advertisers are reluctant to place their messages close to advertisements for competing products. Thus, one very rarely sees a commercial for Toyota immediately adjacent to one for Volkswagen. The competing messages presumably distract the consumer, and remind him or her of the value of alternative options. This suggests that the effectiveness of a suicide story could be reduced by placing it next to a story about an alternative to suicide (e.g., Alcoholics Anonymous, religious services, a Suicide Prevention Center, psychological counseling, or a support group).

Conversely, some types of placement may actually magnify the effect of the suicide story. Asch's classic work (1955) showed that a person was unlikely to engage in a deviant act if he perceived that he was the sole deviant in a sea of conformists. He became more likely to behave defiantly if one other person modeled the deviant act, and yet more likely to behave defiantly if two model deviants were presented to him. These considerations suggest that the effect of the suicide story will be enhanced if it is placed adjacent in time or space to another suicide story. In addition, the suicide story is likely to have an amplified effect if it alludes to a "suicide epidemic" or to other, unrelated suicides. If at all possible, then, a suicide story should not be presented as if it were just another example in a general category of "epidemic suicides".

In sum, editors may wish to consult the following guidelines when deciding on the presentation of suicide stories. The use of these guidelines seems likely to reduce the impact of suicide stories.

- the story should mention several alternatives to suicide (like counseling or a Suicide Prevention Center)
- the story should not mention other, unrelated suicides or a suicide epidemic
- the story headline should be vague and not mention suicide explicitly
- the story should link suicide with negative outcomes like pain for the suicide and for his or her survivors
- the story should not be presented in a romantic or idealized manner
- the story should not be repeated
- the story should be short
- if a long story is unavoidable, it should not be presented in a single compact block, but should be allowed to straggle over several pages
- the story should be presented on an inside page of the newspaper
- the story should be placed adjacent to "competing" stories or advertisements which describe alternatives to suicide
- editors should avoid presenting authorities or sympathetic, ordinary people as spokesperson for the reasonableness of suicide.

B. Lessons from advertising and related fields for coverage of anti-suicide stories

Because guidelines for anti-suicide stories can be inferred in most cases from the above discussion, only a brief treatment of the topic will be needed, and this will generally be confined to suggestions which are not immediately obvious from our earlier considerations of the issues.

Nature of the message

In view of Asch's findings, anti-suicide stories and ads should stress the fact that suicide is actually a very rare coping mechanism (accounting for only 1% - 2% of all deaths) and that alternatives to suicide (like counseling or calling a Suicide Hotline) are much more common than suicide is.

Frequency, timing and length of message

Anti-suicide ads should be more frequent during time periods with a high suicide rate, e.g., immediately after some holidays (Phillips and Wills, 1987). Selective scheduling of this sort could be effective against adult suicides, but is likely to be less so against teen suicides, since these do not appear to vary significantly around holidays or by season (Phillips, 1984).

For both adults and teens it is desirable to schedule anti-suicide stories when a suicide story has appeared. Because the effect of non-fictional suicide stories seems to persist for about ten days, anti-suicide stories could profitably be scheduled for the day of a suicide story and for the nine days thereafter. The more the anti-suicide ads are repeated, the better the recall of the message is likely to be.

Nature of the messenger

Since some research on imitation of publicized suicides suggests that demographic characteristics like sex, race, and age mediate imitation of the suicide model (Smidtke and Häfner, 1988; Phillips, 1977, 1979; Stack, 1987), the people conveying anti-suicide messages should be similar to the members of the targeted audience whenever possible. Messages aimed at teens, for example, might feature teen celebrities who were once suicidal talking about how suicide is not the answer, about how they got help, and about how glad they are to be alive today. Because Dabbs's (1964) research indicates that "non-copers" are most influenced by other "non-copers", the teen celebrities might be most effective if they stressed their own non-coping pasts.

In view of Asch's findings, a single spokesperson against suicide might be relatively ineffective (especially if suicidal members of the audience believe that suicide is widespread). A more effective approach might involve several spokespersons who each say that suicide is rare and that constructive solutions to distress are very much to be preferred.

Placement of the message

Although teens are highly susceptible to the influence of suicide stories, they generally watch less TV (Comstock et al., 1978) and read fewer newspapers then other age groups (Bogart, 1984) so anti-suicide ads aimed need to be carefully placed. Weekly dance and music video shows are targeted specifically at teens, and anti-suicide ads broadcast on these programs would probably be advisable. Similarly, effective anti-suicide stories or ads could be placed on radio stations and magazines which are targeted at teenagers.

Anti-suicide stories should be placed on the front page if possible, but they may also have an impact if they appear in other sections of the newspaper. For example, women are more likely to read personal-advice columns in newspapers than any other newspaper content (Bogart, 1984), so anti-suicide messages targeted at them might be very effective if published as letters to the advice columnist or as advice from the columnist. Anti-suicide stories should not be restricted to conventional newspapers but should also be placed in "scandal" newspapers, like The National Enquirer; these newspapers have many more readers than any conventional newspaper.

In sum, it may be useful to display anti-suicide stories according to the following guidelines. Some of these recommendations may be more appropriate for news stories, and others for advertisements. For convenience, both types are referred to below as "stories".

- the story should convey that the overwhelming majority of troubled people choose something other than suicide in seeking to solve their problems
- if possible, the story should not mention suicide as a legitimate alternative to other problem-solving techniques
- the story should indicate that alternatives to suicide often have positive outcomes for the troubled person and for his or her family
- the story should not be presented in a cold, neutral manner
- the headline to the story should be arresting and explicit, and provide an accurate summary of the contents of the story
- the story should be repeated
- the story should be scheduled during periods of high suicide rates, e.g., just after some holidays
- if possible, the story should be long
- the story should appear on the day and for a number of days afterward a suicide story is publicized
- if possible, the story should use many spokespersons who have one or more of the following characteristics: sympathetic, prestigious, or authoritative
- in addition, spokespersons in the story should stress their "non-coping" pasts
- if possible, the story should appear on the front page or in other media settings which are maximally likely to reach troubled groups, e.g., the advice columns of the newspaper
- the story should be placed adjacent to similar stories about constructive coping techniques, and to dissimilar stories about suicide. This procedure is likely to enhance the effect of the anti-suicide story and diminish the effect of the suicide story.

4. Research Topics which Remain to be Addressed, and some Ways in which this Research can be Facilitated

Although much has been learned about effects of the media on suicide, many questions remain unanswered. In this section we will first discuss seven areas in which research is needed. Then we will indicate some ways in which this research can be facilitated by media organizations, mental-health professionals, and governmental agencies.

A. Recommendations for future research

Replications and generalizations

The studies reviewed in section II have been conducted in only five countries—the United States, Great Britain, Holland, West Germany, Canada and Austria. More areas need to be studied so that we can learn which media effects are particular to a cultural group and which are more universal in nature.

The studies we have reviewed almost always concern stories publicized in traditional newspapers and on national TV programs. We also need to learn about the effects of stories publicized in other media—in tabloids, on the radio, on local TV programs, in movies, in newsmagazines, perhaps even in books. In some school districts, specific books are required reading for all students in certain grades, for example, Romeo and Juliet, Anna Karenina, or The Sorrows of the Young Werther. In all of these books, the hero or heroine commits suicide. It would be valuable to determine whether these books elicit a different type of behavior than is true for books on other themes.

Studies on the effects of different types of suicide stories

Most studies on the topic have dealt with nonfictional rather than fictional suicide stories. Future work should seek to redress this imbalance. Research in the area is likely to be most useful if it is restricted to repeated stories. This is because suicide stories seem to function as natural advertisements, and, as with all advertisements, the effect is generally enhanced by repetition.

Nearly all studies on imitative suicide examine the impact of stories about a completed suicide. It is important to determine whether other types of stories also provoke imitative suicides. For example, do suicides increase after the media publicize an unsuccessful attempt at suicide? Car crashes are known to increase after stories about suicide; do car crashes also increase after stories about car crashes?

The U.S. Centers for Disease Control (1988) have suggested that the precise method used by a publicized suicide should not be released to the media. When the details are included in the suicide story—e.g., the name and dosage of the poison used—does the story have an unusually large effect? Conversely, when the suicide story focuses primarily on the grief-stricken survivors of the suicide, does this diminish the effect of the story on imitation? In general, is the effect of a story reduced when the suicide story contains negative comments about suicide?

Studies identifying behaviors affected by suicide stories

The vast majority of studies have examined the effects of suicide stories on completed suicides. Future studies should also examine the effects of publicized suicides on types of quasi-suicidal behavior, e.g., unsuccessful suicide attempts, calls to suicide prevention centers, and visits to therapists.

Some studies indicate that fatal car crashes increase after suicide stories. Do non-fatal car crashes also increase? Is this increase larger for serious than for minor car crashes? Is there also a post-story increase in other types of accidents and in various types of undetermined deaths?

Studies on readers, listeners and viewers

Very little is known about the reading, listening, and viewing habits of suicidal people. Knowledge of these habits would help to enhance the impact of anti-suicide stories and, perhaps, reduce the effect of suicide stories.

Studies on media owners and managers

Pell and Watters (1982) found that most Canadian editors in their sample had formal policies on the coverage of suicide stories. Is this true in other countries? What features of a suicide story determine whether it is considered worth placing on the front page? In general, we need to learn more about the extent to which editors change their policies about suicide stories after they have been educated on the impact of suicide stories.

Studies on anti-suicide stories and ads

We need research on whether suicide and parasuicide rates do in fact drop after stories and ads about suicide-prevention centers. When should these ads run? Are they most effectively placed on TV, billboards, the radio, in magazines, or in pamphlets distributed at schools?

Some types of stories are not explicitly aimed at reducing the general suicide rate but may nonetheless have this effect. For example, syndicated advice columns are extremely popular. What happens to the suicide rate after a survivor of a suicide attempt writes to an advice columnist saying that she is happy she did not die? What happens after a grieving family member writes to describe the pain he has felt after his son committed suicide? Does the suicide rate decline after the advice columnist lists alternatives to suicide and provides telephone numbers for suicide prevention centers?

So far, we have limited discussion to alternatives to suicide (like counseling) which are provided by mental health professionals. Other implicit alternatives to suicide are provided by religious leaders. What happens to the suicide rate when an evangelist like Billy Graham brings a religious crusade to town?

Studies on psychological mechanisms producing the Werther effect

The evidence linking suicide stories with imitative suicides is persuasive, and there is no obvious alternative explanation which accounts for the cumulative findings reported here, especially the finding that the rise in suicides after the suicide story is correlated with the amount of publicity devoted to the story. Nonetheless, all the studies we have reviewed suffer from two obvious underlying problems which need to be addressed in future research: 1) No one has yet demonstrated that the "excess" people who killed themselves after (say) Marilyn Monroe's death in fact had heard of her suicide (although this certainly seems likely). 2) The detailed psychological mechanisms connecting the suicide story with the subsequent rise in suicides are not yet known, and cannot be precisely determined with the death certificate data under study.

Most studies on imitative suicide have been conducted along epidemiological lines. The researcher has typically examined large samples of decedents and has collected only a small amount of information per decedent. Investigations of this type are suitable for establishing the existence of an effect but not for elucidating the detailed mechanisms that produced it. In addition to more epidemiological studies, we also need psychological research conducted in a different fashion—we need to examine small samples of people, on each of whom we have collected a great deal of information. Only in this way can we learn the nature of the psychological processes which mediate the suicide story and the post-story rise in deaths.

B. Recommended data collection activities for media organizations, health professionals and governmental agencies

Many of the questions described in the previous section can not be answered with records that are currently available. This situation should be corrected as far as possible. Indices and abstracts of televised *non-fictional* news stories have been made public by various organizations (The Vanderbilt TV News Archives, CBS News, and ABC News), and these sources have been invaluable in research on the effects of suicide stories. Unfortunately, a parallel index/abstract of televised fictional stories is not available. A document of this sort would be of extraordinary value to the study of imitative suicide. Similarly, it would be extremely useful if NBC News released to the public their own ongoing index/abstract of NBC news stories. Of all the major U.S. television networks, NBC is alone in treating their index/abstract as a proprietary rather than a public resource.

Governmental agencies need to publish daily or weekly suicide statistics (not just monthly data). In addition, mortality tables should be classified by date of injury as well as by date of death in order to pinpoint the relationship between the appearance of a suicide story and a subsequent rise in suicidal behavior.

Research on imitative suicide would be greatly facilitated if suicide-prevention centers and other medical organizations could document and publish information on the number of suicidal people who contact them each day. In addition, it would be useful for health professionals to publish more information on factors which might precipitate suicidal thoughts. With data of this sort, one could estimate the effects of suicide stories, not only on suicides, but also on parasuicidal behavior. One could also discover whether other types of precipitating factors (aside from imitation) elicit thoughts of suicide.

Summary and Conclusion

Many studies indicate that heavily publicized suicide stories are followed by significant increases in imitative suicides. The more publicity given to the stories, the greater the increase in suicides thereafter. Evidence from a field experiment (Sonneck et al., 1991) strongly suggests that the incidence of suicide drops markedly after a dramatic reduction in publicity accorded to suicide stories. Censorship of suicide stories is not appropriate, but the weight of the evidence on imitative suicide has already prompted some news editors to limit voluntarily the publicity they give to stories and to change the way they report them. We have offered some guidelines for reporters which may help to diminish the harmful effects of suicide stories. In addition, we have suggested some ways in which health professionals can design anti-suicide stories and advertisements that may counteract the imitative effects of the suicide stories.

Much more research is needed before we can be sure of the precise effects of different kinds of suicide stories on different types of people. We have provided a paradigm of research topics that remain to be addressed. This research would be greatly facilitated if media organizations published more detailed information on the content of their stories, if governmental agencies published daily suicide statistics, and if health professionals published information on the suicidal clients they work with. When some of these steps are taken it seems likely that we will be able to make progress on what is now recognized as a recalcitrant public health problem in all countries: reducing the incidence of suicide.

REFERENCES

Andreoli, V. & Worchel, S. (1978). Effects of media, communicator, and message position on attitude change. Public Opinion Quarterly, 42, 59-70.

Asch, S.E. (1955). Opinions and social pressure. In Aronson, E. (Ed) (1973). *Readings about the social animal.* San Francisco: W.H. Freeman and Company.

Baron, J.N. & Reiss, P.C. (1985). Same time next year: Aggregate analyses of the mass media and violent behavior. *American Sociological Review,* 50, 347-363.

Barraclough, B., Shepherd, D. & Jennings, C. (1977). Do newspaper reports of coroners' inquests incite people to commit suicide? *British Journal of Psychiatry,* 131, 528-532.

Berman, A.L. (1988). Fictional depiction of suicide in television films and imitation effects. *American Journal of Psychiatry,* 145, 982-986.

Blumenthal, S. & Bergner, L. (1973). Suicide and newspapers: A replicated study. *American Journal of Psychiatry,* 130, 468-471.

Bogart, L. (1984). The public's use and perception of newspapers. *Public Opinion Quarterly,* 48, 709-719.

Bollen, K.A. & Phillips, D.P. (1981). Suicidal motor vehicle fatalities in Detroit: A replication. *American Journal of Sociology,* 87, 404-412.

Bollen, K.A. & Phillips, D.P. (1982). Imitative suicides: A national study of the effects of television news stories. *American Sociological Review,* 47, 802-809.

Centers for Disease Control (1988). CDC recommendations for a community plan for the prevention and containment of suicide clusters. *MMWR 1988;* 37 (Suppl. no. S-6).

Clark, D.C. (1989). Impact of television news reports. *Suicide Research Digest*, 3, 12.

Comstock, G., Chaffee, S., Katzman, N., McCombs, M. & Roberts, D. (1978). *Television and human behavior.* New York: Columbia University Press.

Dabbs, J.M. (1964). Self-esteem, communicator characteristics, and attitude change. *Journal of Abnormal and Social Psychology.* 69(2), 173-181.

Ellis, S.J. & Walsh, S. (1986). Soap may seriously damage your health. *Lancet 1986;* i:686.

Fowler, B.P. (1986). Emotional crises imitating television. *Lancet 1986;* i:1036-1037.

Ganzeboom, H.B.G. & de Haan, D. (1982). Gepubliceerde zelfmoorden en verhoging van sterfte door zelfmoord en ongelukken in Nederland 1972-1980. *Mens en Maatschappij,* 57, 55-69.

Gould, M.S. & Shaffer, D. (1986). The impact of suicide in television movies. New *England Journal of Medicine,* 315, 690-694.

Gould, M.S., Shaffer, D. & Kleinman, M. (1988). The impact of suicide in television movies: replication and commentary. *Suicide and Life-Threatening Behavior,* 18, 90-99.

Holding, T.A. (1974). The B.B.C. 'Befrienders' series and its effects. *British Journal of Psychiatry,* 124, 470-472.

Holding, T.A. (1975). Suicide and "The Befrienders". *British Journal of Psychiatry,* 3, 751-753.

Kessler, R.C., Downey, G., Milavsky, J.R. & Stipp, H. (1988). Clustering of teenage suicides after television news stories about suicide: A reconsideration. *American Journal of Psychiatry,* 145, 1379-1383.

Kessler, R.C. & Stipp, H. (1984). The impact of fictional television suicide stories on American fatalities. *American Journal of Sociology,* 90, 151-167.

Kopping, A.P., Ganzeboom, H.B.G. & Swanborn, P.G. Verhoging van suicide door navolging van kranteberichten. (unpublished paper).

Littman, S.K. (1985). Suicide epidemics and newspaper reporting. *Suicide and Life-Threatening Behavior,* 15, 43-50.

Motto, J.A. (1967). Suicide and suggestibility—The role of the press. *American Journal of Psychiatry,* 124, 252-256.

Motto, J.A. (1970). Newspaper influence on suicide. *Archives of General Psychiatry,* 23, 143-148.

Ostroff, R.B., Behrends, R.W., Lee, K. & Oliphant, J. (1985). Adolescent suicides modeled after television movie. *American Journal of Psychiatry,* 142, 989.

Ostroff, R.B. & Boyd, J.H. (1987). Television and suicide. *New England Journal of Medicine,* 316, 876-877.

Pell, B. & Watters, D. (1982). Newspaper policies on suicide stories. *Canada's Mental Health.* December 1982, 8-9.

Phillips, D.P. (1974). The influence of suggestion on suicide: Substantive and theoretical implications of the Werther effect. *American Sociological Review,* 39, 340-354.

Phillips, D.P. (1977). Motor vehicle fatalities increase just after publicized suicide stories. *Science,* 196, 1464-1465.

Phillips, D.P. (1978). Airplane accident fatalities increase just after stories about murder and suicide. Science, 201, 148-150.

Phillips, D.P. (1979). Suicide, motor vehicle fatalities, and the mass media: Evidence toward a theory of suggestion. *American Journal of Sociology,* 84, 1150-1174.

Phillips, D.P. (1980). Airplane accidents, murder, and the mass media: Towards a theory of imitation and suggestion. *Social Forces,* 58, 1001-1024.

Phillips, D.P. (1982). The impact of fictional television stories on American adult fatalities: New evidence on the effect of the mass media on violence. *American Journal of Sociology,* 87, 1340-1359.

Phillips, D.P. (1984). Teenage and adult temporal fluctuations in suicide and auto fatalities. In Sudak, H.S. et al. (Eds). *Suicide in the Young.* Boston: Wright-PSG.

Phillips, D.P. & Bollen, K.A. (1985). Same time last year: Selective data dredging for negative findings. *American Sociological Review,* 50, 364-371.

Phillips, D.P. & Carstensen, L.L. (1986). Clustering of teenage suicides after television news stories about suicide. *New England Journal of Medicine,* 315, 685-689.

Phillips, D.P. & Carstensen, L.L. (1988). The effect of suicide stories on various demographic groups, 1968-1985. *Suicide and Life-Threatening Behavior,* 18, 100-114.

Phillips, D.P. & Paight, D.J. (1987). The impact of televised movies about suicide. *New England of Medicine,* 317, 809-811.

Phillips, D.P. & Wills, J.S. (1987). A drop in suicides around major national holidays. *Suicide and Life-Threatening Behavior,* 17, 1-12.

Platt, S. (1987). The aftermath of Angie's overdose: Is soap (opera) damaging to your health? *British Medical Journal,* 294, 954-957.

Sandler, D.A., Connell, P.A., & Welsh, K. (1986). Emotional crises imitating television. *Lancet 1986*; i:856.

Shneidman, E.S. (1985). *The definition of suicide.* New York: John Wiley & Sons.

Schmidtke, A. & Häfner, H. (1988). The Werther effect after television films: New Evidence for an Old Hypothesis. *Psychological Medicine,* 18, 665-76.

Sonneck, G., Nagel - Kuess, S., Etzerdorfer, E., Smek, E. & Hauer, B. (1991) Subway suicide in Vienna: A contribution to the imitation effect in suicidal behavior (1984-1989). Forthcoming, *Crisis.*

Stack, S. (1984). The effect of suggestion on suicide: A reassessment. *Paper presented at the annual meeting of the American Sociological Association,* San Antonio, Texas, August 1984.

Stack, S. (1987). Celebrities and suicide: A taxonomy and analysis, 1948-1983. *American Sociological Review,* 52, 401-412.

Tversky, A. & Kahneman, D. (1981). The framing of decisions and the psychology of choice. *Science,* 211, 453-458.

Wasserman, I. (1984). Imitation and suicide: A reexamination of the Werther effect. *American Sociological Review,* 49, 427-436.

Weisman, A.D. & Worden, J.W. (1972). Risk-rescue rating in suicide assessment. *Archives of General Psychiatry,* 26, 553-560.

Williams, J.M.G., Lawton, C., Ellis, S.J., Walsh, S. & Reed, J. (1987). Copycat suicide attempts. *Lancet 1987*; i:102-103.

Williams, J.M.G., Lawton, C., Ellis, S.J., Walsh, S. & Reed, J. Imitative parasuicide by overdose. *Report to Research Department*, Independent Broadcasting Authority. (undated).

Note: The following two articles, kindly transmitted by Dr. A. Schmidtke, but arriving after completion of the manuscript, also provide some evidence of imitative suicide:

Schneider, V. & Hackl, A. (1988). Der Suizid nach Fernseh-Vorbild. *Kriminalistik*, 213-215.
Trubner, K. (1988). Noch einmal: Tod in der Badewanne. *Kriminalistik*, 414-418.

Subway-Suicide in Vienna (1980-1990)

A contribution to the Imitation effect in Suicidal Behavior

G. SONNECK

Introduction

Ever since the opening of the first parts of the Viennese subway system in 1978 the subway has been used as a method of committing suicide or attempting suicide. However, the number of suicides remained very low for the first years. But beginning with 1984 until mid-1987 a significant increase of suicides and suicide attempts can be registered (Table 1, Figure 1). This trend is remarkable considering that the Viennese subway system was not enlarged in this period, nor did the number of passengers rise in a comparable way (Figure 2).

Table 1: Subway-Suicides and -Attempts 1980-1990

Year	Suicides	Suicide Attempts
1980	1	0
1981	0	1
1982	1	3
1983	0	1
1984	7	0
1985	9	3
1986	14	5
1987	11	11
1988	6	1
1989	3	4
1990	4	2

The increase of 1984 was recognized also by the print media who published accordingly.

Based on the hypotheses of some authors (Phillips & Carstensen, 1986; Gould & Shaffer, 1986; Schmidtke & Häfner, 1988), that reports on suicide in media can lead to imitation, we surveyed all articles of reported suicides in general (not only subway-suicides and -attempts) in the two largest Austrian daily newspapers and analyzed them in connection with the subway-suicide-scene.

Figure 1. Subway-Suicides and -Attempts in Vienna 1980-1990

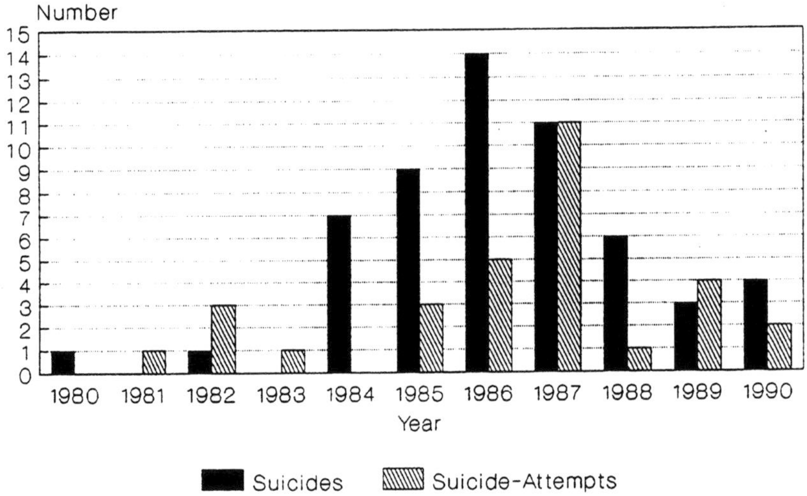

Figure 2. Public means of transportation in Vienna 1984-1989

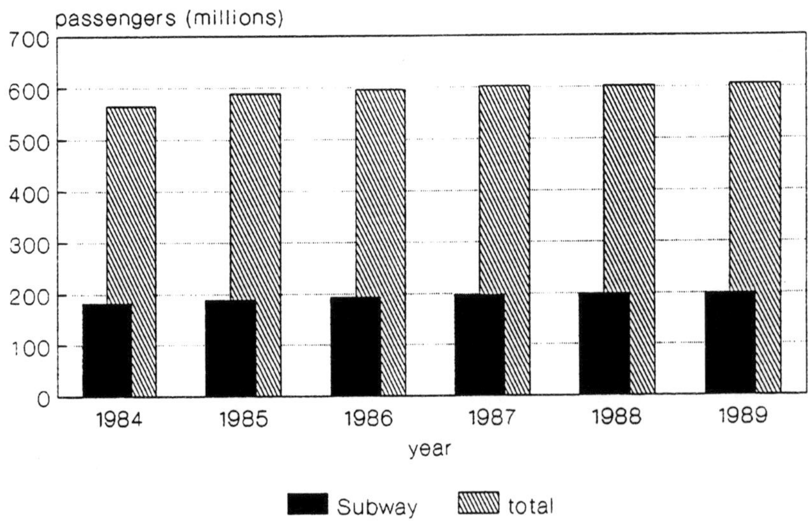

Results

1. Until 1986 the subway is increasingly used as a method to commit suicide. This trend decreases, starting with 1987, and is also evident for 1988, 1989 and 1990. The differentiation between the first and the second half of 1987 shows clearly, that the decrease starts in mid-1987 (see Figure 3). It is also then that suicide attempts, which were tremendously high in the first half of 1987, decrease dramatically (both decreases are statistically significant on the level p=0.05). Comparable changes are nowhere to be found within the total Viennese suicide rate, even though the curve might seem slightly similar (see Figure 4).

Table 2: Weekday of Subway-Suicides and -Attempts 1984-1990

	Subway-Suicides			**Subway-Suicide-Attempts**		
Day	Total	Men	Women	Total	Men	Women
Mon	15	9	6	7	4	3
Tue	8	6	2	5	3	2
Wed	5	4	1	5	2	3
Thu	10	6	4	2	2	0
Fri	6	4	2	2	1	1
Sat	5	5	0	2	0	2
Sun	5	4	1	3	1	2
Total	**54**	**38**	**16**	**26**	**13**	**13**

2. The weekday with the most subway-suicides is Monday. Nearly a third of all suicides and attempts take place on Mondays (see Table 2).

Subway-Suicides and -Suicide-Attempts which occurred on Mondays:

Suicides:	Men:23.6%	Women:37.5%	Total:27.8%
Suicide Attempts:	Men:30.8%	Women:23.1%	Total:26.9%

An emphasis on the beginning of the week can also be found with the other suicides in Vienna.

3. The average age for subway-suicides lies significantly below that of the other suicides for Vienna (see Table 3). The majority of subway-suicides are committed by the age group of 20-29 year old (the average age for subway-suicides is 37 years, whereas it lies above 55 years for all suicides in Vienna).

Figure 3. Subway-Suicides and -Attempts in Vienna 1980-1990 (half-years)

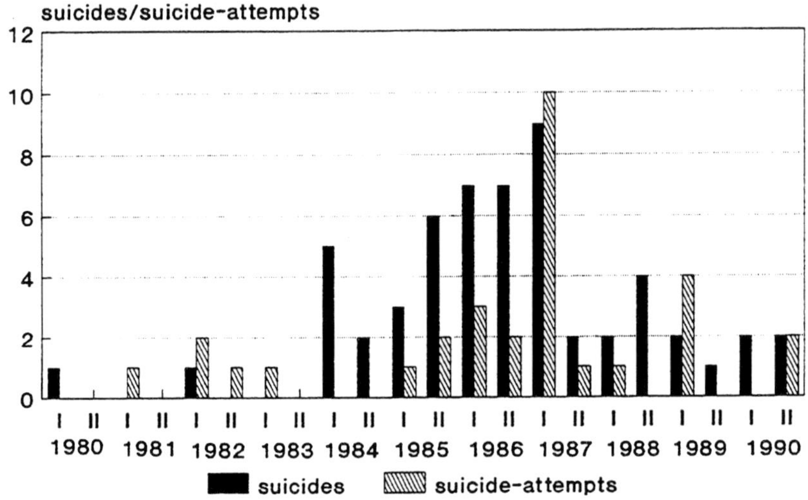

Table 3: Subway-Suicides 1984-90

Age	Total	Men	Women
under 15	0	0	0
15-19	2	1	1
20-29	18	11	7
30-39	10	8	2
40-49	14	10	4
50-59	3	3	0
60-69	2	1	1
70-79	2	1	1
80+	3	3	0
Total	**54**	**38**	**16**

4. The ratio of men to women in subway-suicides is 2.4:1 (38 men to 16 women from 1984 to 1990), whereas for the total suicides in Vienna it is 1.6:1 - a majority of men in subway suicides. The ratio for subway-suicide-attempts of 1:1 is similar to the ratio for the total in Vienna being 0.9:1 (Table 4 and 5).

Table 4: Subway-Suicides 1984-90

Year	Total	Men	Women
1984	7	4	3
1985	9	8	1
1986	14	7	7
1987	11	10	1
1988	6	4	2
1989	3	3	0
1990	4	2	2
Total	**54**	**38**	**16**

Table 5: Subway-Suicide-Attempts 1984-90

Year	Total	Men	Women
1984	0	0	0
1985	3	0	3
1986	5	2	3
1987	11	6	5
1988	1	0	1
1989	4	4	0
1990	2	1	1
Total	**26**	**13**	**13**

5. From 1984 to mid-1985 the suicides occur in rather long intervals from each other (an average of 50 days). Beginning with June 1985, groups of suicides can be distinguished where numerous suicides are committed within a short period of time (2 - 5 suicides within 1 - 7 days) followed by a longer pause. These groups are started on more often by women than by men (7 times by women, 5 times by men).

With women Mondays are more often the beginning of such groups than with men, where a tendency toward one weekday cannot be found.

6. Until June 1987 the print media reported on suicides in detail and in a very dramatic fashion (in 1986 only one case of subway-suicide had been left

uncommented). Beginning with July 1987 subway-suicides are no longer a media subject. In fact the entire "Suicide Reporting" alters to see suicides being mentioned very carefully and seldom. It is important to mention, that the "Austrian Association for Suicide Prevention, Crisis Intervention and Conflict Resolution" at this time proposed media-guidelines and asked the print medias to follow them.

These media-guidelines are based on the consideration, that a certain kind of reporting on suicide is able to work as a trigger for suicidal behavior. The hypothesis is, that reports on suicide for someone who is despaired, does not know how to go on and already is emotionally restricted, work as a proposal and produce the impression, that in this situation committing suicide is the best and maybe only way.

This trigger-effect depends on some aspects and will be the bigger:

- the more details of the special methods are reported
- the more the suicide is reported as inconceivable ("he had everything life can give")
- the more romantic the motives are reported ("to be forever united")
- the more simplifications are used ("suicide because of bad notes").

It is also suggested, that the attention will be bigger:

- if the report is printed on the front page
- if the term suicide is used in the headline
- if there is a photograph of the person, who has committed suicide
- if the attitude of the person implicitly is described as heroic and approvingly ("in this situation he had to do that").

The effect will be the smaller:

- the more alternatives are shown (where is it possible to find help in a situation like that?)
- if there are also reports on crisis, that did not end in a suicide but in a mastering
- if readers are provided with background information on suicide e.g. what to do with someone talking about suicidal ideation.

This campaign was strongly supported by a lot of psychosocial agencies. 1988 sees no subway-suicide being mentioned, with the exception of an article on a girl who apparently fell on the rails by an accident and was injured (October 8th). This case is not reflected in our numbers. Two days later, however, and again two days after this, subway-suicides were committed - the only group since June 1987.

6.1. A timely connection between media reports and occurring subway-suicides could not be safely testified. Even though groups and media reports do coincide, an explanation cannot be given for the fact that "grouped suicides" terminated, leaving long intervals (sometimes a few months) until the next suicides happened. The single report on the girl's accident in October 1988, and the two suicides following it, are, however, to be remarked.

7. Usually the number of subway-suicides exceeds the number of suicide attempts by far. 1987 shows the equal amount of attempts and completed suicides (11 suicides and 11 suicide-attempts). A closer analysis of these 22 cases of 1987 shows the following results:

7.1. Three of these suicide-attempts are attempted by the same person (male, 40 years).

7.2. The method is different: for suicides either the person jumps immediately before the subway around the beginning or the middle of the station or he/she lies on the rails either in the tunnel or in the station. Attempts happen, when the person is standing on the rails in the station. Only one suicide was completed by this method, it is usually used for attempts.

These findings correlate to that of other authors (e.g. Guggenheim and Weisman, 1972), suggesting different "types" of suicidal behavior in connection with the subway and maybe different intention.

8. Examining the data concerning the hour of the day and the stations, where these suicides and suicide-attempts did happen, it was not possible to find a peak at any time of the day. The only remarkable result was, that subway-suicide-attempts did occur more often in the second half of the day (9:17 cases 1984 to 1990). It also was not possible to find any statistically significant accumulation on a single station nor in special lines (for instance the circle line). A comparison of the ratio of the suicides related to the transportation frequency per day at the special station shows however, that the stations with the lowest frequency have the highest rates, while the crowded, bigger stations (where alcoholics and drug addicts use to stay), have the lowest rates (Figure 5). It has to be mentioned, that the last stations of the subway seem to be used less often than the others (this special investigation was done by Chr.Kienbacher).

Figure 4. Suicide and Subway-Suicides in Vienna 1980-90

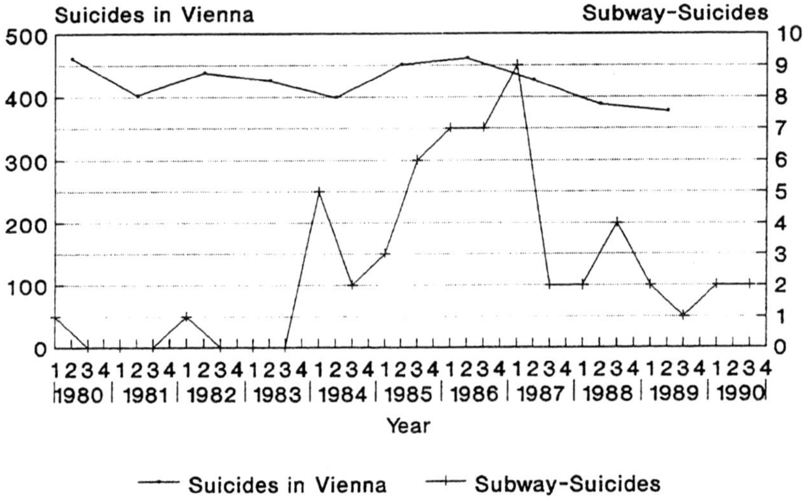

Figure 5. Relation of the Number of Passengers/Day in Subway-Stations and the Suicide Ratio

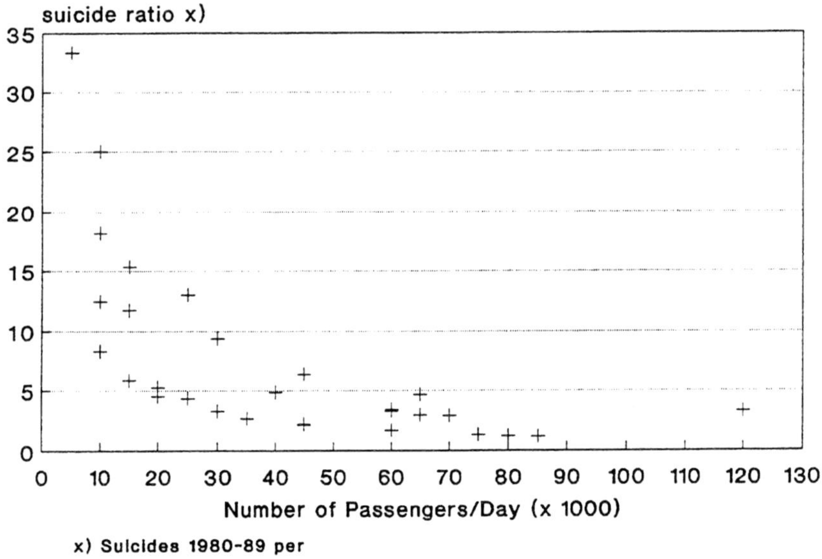

9. In 1987 the suicide rate in Vienna dropped by 10%. 1988 showed another 10% less than 1987 and 1989 another 3% less than 1988 (Figure 4). The second half of 1987, however, shows a slight increase in the total of suicides from 207 to 220 whereas the subway-suicides decreased by 60%. The second half of 1987 shows three subway-suicides and one attempt as compared to the first half of 1987 with eight suicides and ten attempts. The suicides decreased down to 40%, a figure which remains stable throughout 1988 and 1989 and also for 1990.

It is well known, that a decrease of suicides committed by a special method sometimes is substituted by other methods (e.g. Rich et al., 1990 and Sloan et al., 1990 on findings in Toronto and Vancouver, where restrictive gun laws were able to reduce firearm-suicides but not the overall-suicides). As of mid-1987 the suicide method of "Getting run over" decreases from 6% to 1% of all suicides in Vienna, perhaps this is compensated by an increase in the suicide method "Jumping from great heights" (increased from 15% to 19%) and "Hanging and Strangling" (increased from 30% to 33%).

Summary

Subway-suicides in Vienna show a dramatic increase starting 1984 to mid-1987, after which they suddenly decrease by 60%. This constant decrease, which has been lasting now for more than three years, started at the time when the medias consented to abstain from reporting on suicides. Even if a direct evidence of a connection between media-articles and suicides could not be explicitly found, the connection is apparent. The overall decrease of suicides in Vienna could be seen in context with the medias reserve to reporting on suicide in general. However, as the overall decrease is only 10%, whereas the decrease in subway-suicides sums up to 60% one could imply, that if media reports should have an influence on suicides, this is substantial only regarding special methods of committing suicide.

REFERENCES

Gould, M.S., Shaffer, D.(1986). The Impact of Suicide in Television Movies. Evidence of Imitation. *New England Journal of Medicine, 315:* 690-694.

Guggenheim, F.G., Weisman A.D.(1972). Suicide in the Subway. *The Journal of Nervous and Mental Disease, 155/6:* 404-409.

Phillips, D.P., Carstensen, L.L.(1986). Clustering of Teenage Suicides after Television News Stories about Suicide. *New England Journal of Medicine, 315:* 685-689.

Rich, C.L., et al.(1990). Guns and suicide: possible effects of some specific legislation. *American Journal of Psychiatry, 147*: 342-346.

Schmidtke, A., Häfner, H. (1988). Imitation Effects after Fictional Television Suicides in: Miller, H.J., Schmidtke, A., Welz, R. (eds.): *Current Issues on Suicidology*. Springer, Heidelberg, 341-348.

Sloan, J.H. et al.(1990). Firearm regulation and rates of suicide. *New England Journal of Medicine, 322*: 369-373.

Ethical and Legal Problems in Connection with Suicide Prevention

H.M. KUITERT

1. Introduction: Stipulations regarding Use of Terms

The increase of suicidal behavior, both fatal and non-fatal, has become quite remarkable, particularly in the industrial world. The number of successful suicides among men from the age of 15 and older increased in Hungary from 69.7 to 84.2 per 100,000 inhabitants in the period of 1974-1984, in Denmark from 40.5 to 46.7 in the same period and in Bulgaria from 21.3 to 27.1. Among women in Hungary the number increased from 27.3 to 33.6 in that same period, in Denmark from 23.4 to 25.8 and in Bulgaria from 9.1 to 10.6. It should be added, however, that not all countries show an increase. In countries such as former Czechoslovakia, Japan and Sweden the number decreased and in a number of other countries such as Finland, the former Federal Republic of Germany and Portugal the number remained virtually the same. Both in Europe and in the United States the increase in the number of adolescents who die as a result of suicide is remarkable (Diekstra and Hawton, 1987).

The reference to Western industrial countries does not imply, however, that developing countries are not faced with an increase in suicidal behavior.

The increasing number of suicidal attempts explains why suicide-prevention has become more than ever a central issue in the field of Mental Health. Prevention is, however, an act and acts have a purpose: What is the reason a society wants to prevent suicide, how far should it go in preventing suicide and what form does prevention take? In this article an answer will be sought to these and similar questions, which may serve to analyze the moral and legal implications of suicide-prevention and the underlying value-judgments. The great diversity in opinions on suicide inherent to existing cultural differences presents a problem. To resign ourselves to this fact is an all too easy solution, which moreover, does not contribute to the cooperation and understanding between the different cultures. On the other hand, the notion that the differences in normative standpoints can be bridged seems to be an illusion. Nevertheless, finding commonly accepted basic-values that hold good as transcultural constants which may eventually lead to a consensus on an acceptable strategy of suicide-prevention should not be deemed impossible.

In this chapter I understand by suicide: the intentional termination of one's own life, no matter what the conditions or precise nature of the intention or the causal route to death (Beauchamp and Childress, 1983).

By morality I mean social morality, i.e. action-guides for the social interaction which people, when asked, justify in terms of "many" and "should" (Warnock, 1971). In many instances law and social morality overlap. Morality, however, covers a much wider field: Where the law can no longer guide actions, morality continues to do so. A doctor who involves his patient in a research program without informing him does not trespass the law (which does not prohibit this), but sins against morality (which dictates him to obtain his patient's consent). On the other hand, morality is weaker as a means of regulation: it has no other sanctions but inner (through conscience) or outer (through society) commendation or blame, whereas the law is able to enforce sanctions (Leenen, 1988). It should be noted, however, that morality does not play an equally important role in all cultures. There are also societies where avoiding shame rather than avoiding guilt regulates behavior.

Whose morality is under discussion? Talking of prevention-strategies implies that we are focussing on health care services. It is their morality we are concerned about.

Suicide itself can also be discussed in terms of morality (Battin, 1982; Kuitert, 1985ab). Presently I will show that morality of prevention and moral ideas about suicide overlap: ideas about what morally permissible determine to a large extent the structure and strategy of prevention.

2. Suicide and the Value of Life

Suicide-prevention has its origin in the belief that killing oneself is an abnormal act. In every culture life is experienced as a first-rank value. First of all for its possessor, but then also in a general sense: All societies regard human life as a basic-value and seem to take this for granted. That is the reason all societies protect human life against those who wish to destroy it. "Thou shalt not kill" is a command every culture adheres to. That does not mean that killing does not take place. Every society knows forms of killings that are justified. It is, however, precisely this need to justify that shows that people are aware that killing is forbidden.

Meanwhile I purposely speak of: "a first-rank value", not the highest or first value. There are people who kill themselves. On the one hand this may mean that they have encountered something of even higher value than their own life, for example: their country or their personal honour. But the underlying reason may also be that life has become such a heavy burden for them that it lost its rank of first or highest value. Other motivations could be mentioned, for there is a large and baffling variety of reasons and motives why people commit suicide. This makes it impossible to use uniform explanations or prescriptions for prevention. The linking factor, however, between these many forms of suicide is death, which is experienced, even when deliberately chosen, as a catastrophe by the one undergoing it; an albeit that in some circumstances to continue life is evidently considered an even worse catastrophe.

For the moment this is sufficient. Life is considered a first rank-value and death the ultimate catastrophe. Against this background the choice for death is a peculiar one. This calls first of all for an explanation: why do people choose death? Secondly, it confronts us with the question: Should this death be prevented and if so, what is that conviction based on? These are the two questions which will be dealt with in this chapter.

3. Institutionalized Suicide

The question why people commit suicide takes us to the extensive field of the (explanatory) theories. This is not the place to discuss them. That will be done in other chapters of this book. I will only refer to them as far as they are necessary for describing the values and moral implications which are at stake in the case of suicide-prevention.

Generally speaking, we can distinguish between two classes of suicide. In this paragraph I will discuss the first (and smallest) one. It consists first of all of suicides based on cultural customs. By this I understand those actions which are part of a more or less accepted, sometimes even dictated, code of behavior. There are situations in which a man or a woman terminates his or her own life and regardless the amount of grief this causes to their family and friends, no one is surprised about the event. In ancient Japan, for example, suicide is an institution that offers a way out to avoid shame, loss of dignity, failure, in short: the shame of losing one's face. The procedure follows fixed rules. Until this day we do not come across suicide as a moral problem in Japanese literature. There are other cultures in which suicide is part of a more or less institutionalized code of behavior. The measure in which this holds true is connected with the diversity in the collectively accepted concepts about life, death and life-after-death (Fontaine, 1975).

The same applies more or less to what is called in terms of Western culture a "balance suicide". In this definition suicide is not a socially accepted form of behavior, but rather a rational decision on individual grounds. Both forms of suicides have, however, in common that the decision-making follows careful considerations. Suicides which take place according to this pattern—they cover a very small minority out of the total cases of suicide—do not cause alarm in a social sense. They are, so to speak, suicides which do not escape social control. With this term I do not pronounce judgment on their desirability or moral acceptability. I have only distinguished between them and that other form of suicide that will be discussed below.

Meanwhile, the fact that societies permit socially controlled suicides does not imply that for its possessor life was of little or no value. When, for example, in a country like Japan young people commit suicide, because they fail to pass their entrance examination to the university, they do on the one hand something that, to a large extent, is rooted in their culture: after having lost your face, you do away with yourself. However, on the other hand, they are really personally desperate after such a failure. So although they do something that in their culture is not a surprising action, the psychological situation in which they find themselves, is still one of profound perturbation, of which they would really like to be cured or find some other way out (Iga, 1986).

From this example it is clear that the distinction between institutionalized suicide and suicide as an expression of personal despair (see next chapter) is not always as clear as we might wish. Besides, the fact that a society recognizes socially controlled suicides does not mean that it denies life as a first-rank value. On the contrary, it is indeed the high value of life that constitutes the background of suicide as an institutionalized action. Precisely because of this fact, suicide as a conscious act receives its meaning: by giving up something of such a great value (life) an individual "pays off" the bill he still owed.

4. Suicide as Expression of personal Despair

By far the largest group of suicides cannot be classified as either a socially accepted institution or a balance-action. It can be characterized in terms of actions which escape all social control. Since these actions, too, are inspired by many different motives, I will sum them up under the following heading: suicide as expression of personal despair. The expression applies to people for whom things went wrong in their lives and who in a state of depression and confusion choose death as a way out. It often is debatable whether the agent really sought death or had in fact another intention with his action: for example, to escape from the situation in which he has imprisoned, to find rest, to get attention, to present others with the bill of their failure, etcetera. According to many researchers suicide is more often than not a means rather than an end in itself (Diekstra, 1981).

From this it follows that in this largest and most unpredictable group of suicides it is common to distinguish between suicide on the one hand and suicide-attempts on the other. A suicide-attempt should then be understood as suicidal behavior not intended to lead to actual death, hence the term "attempt". This behavior is rather aimed at drawing attention to oneself, either in terms of a "cry for help" (Farberow and Shneidman, 1961), or a challenge to the environment. By suicide, as distinguished from suicide-attempt, we should think of a deliberate choice for death. This brings up the problem—which I shall not explore—how to distinguish between attempt and deliberate choice. Since this can only be established with certainty after the event, the result is that people die who did not actually intend to and vice versa: people who deliberately sought death, sometimes do not get the chance to die. As we shall see this is an important factor when discussing prevention-strategy.

In this chapter the main focus will be on this second group: suicide as a socially uncontrolled—and uncontrollable—action of despair. In nearly all cases this form of suicide is a non-intended disaster. This datum raises some specific questions. In the case of suicide as an institutionalized action, death is a disaster chosen deliberately and intentionally; this form of suicide puts the question to us whether killing oneself is morally permissible. Suicide as an action of despair confronts us with problems of a totally different nature. What should be done if a disaster is about to take place, of which we do not even know whether it was intended or not. Is there a moral obligation which compels us to prevent someone from killing himself and, if so, what is this obligation based on? With the help of these questions we will try to establish the moral status of preventive actions: how can they be morally justified? And as a specific question: is prevention also permissible in terms of intervention?

In order to answer these questions it is necessary to take a further look at the concept of prevention: what does it imply and why do we want it?

5. Prevention

In Medical Health Care, prevention plays an important role and the concept is understood as the wish to prevent the development of certain diseases or disorders by taking certain, sometimes drastic, measures; for example, the prevention of hereditary defects in offspring by screening entire population groups for the presence of a defective gene or chromosome or compulsory vaccination of all infants against poliomyelitis. The discomfort—and in the case of compulsory vaccination even intrusion of one's privacy—such measures entail is generally accepted, since it is obvious that they are taken for the good all concerned: prevention is meant to prevent suffering.

This connotation of the concept can also be used in the case of suicide-prevention, suicide in terms of what I described above as uncontrollable suicide and for that reason a disaster. Disasters *may* be prevented. *Should* they also be prevented, if the possibility to do so exists? This can be made plausible when we look at it from the standpoint of the moral principle of beneficence, which is the basis of all social interaction. What does this principle entail?

In order to see its implications I will differentiate beforehand, as is customary in ethics (Frankena, 1973). The obligation to beneficence can be met in four (different) ways: one ought not to inflict evil or harm (1), one ought to prevent evil or harm (2), one ought to remove evil (3), one ought to do or promote good (4). The fourth possibility requires more of us than the other three. It is therefore debatable whether we should consider it an obligation for every individual. To a lesser extent this applies to number three. Number one is above all doubt an obligation for all people. This leaves the second possibility: do all people have the obligation to prevent others from being harmed or is this asking too much? If we say: too much, then suicide-prevention is condemned to ineffectiveness. If we opt for an effective way of prevention, then we apparently take the line of the obligation of beneficence in terms of: to prevent evil or harm. My starting point will be plausibility of this obligation. Suicide-prevention—apart from the way in which it is carried out—receives its moral justification from the principle of beneficence.

With that we have taken a first step: we have morally justified prevention by looking at what it should achieve: disasters may, indeed should be prevented. A second step is—and this too involves moral criteria—: what are the means a society employs in prevention? Prevention requires a strategy. A first requirement of prevention-strategies is that they should be effective: are they instrumental in achieving this goal and do they prevent suicide in practice? Effectiveness is a necessary condition when adopting a certain strategy. But we need more than that. This condition does not suffice. From a moral point of view, not all the means by which a society tries to prevent suicide are equally acceptable: obviously the end does not justify the means. These two questions: the one with respect to the morality of the means and the one about their effectiveness, are important in their own right. Means may be effective but not permissible and vice versa: what is permitted, is not always effective.

6. The traditional Western Strategy: The harsh Condemnation

The most well-known prevention-strategy is a policy of discouragement based on a moral and religious condemnation. This I call the traditional strategy, because, certainly in Western culture, religion and morality have through the ages incorporated this condemnation of suicide in their moral upbringing. I call this harsh, because it presents suicide as an unpardonable offence, a separate class of actions, which as such is to be totally rejected. Hence the almost ineradicable custom in the Western world to speak of suicide in terms of "self-murder".

The three classic arguments used in justifying this harsh No are: suicide is an offence of the individual against himself (1), against society (2), and against God (3). This is not the place to subject these arguments to an extensive examination. To put it as concisely as possible: they do not satisfy (Kuitert, 1985ab). An offence against God presumes an untenable concept of God (God as a sort of super human). An offence against oneself is only possible, if it has been established beforehand that suicide is forbidden (thus, this argument is in fact a circular reasoning) and to consider it an offence against society is only useful, if society would have by definition the authority to rule over an individual (and that is contestable to say the least).

What these arguments as counterpart of the unconditional No to suicide try to establish is an (unspoken) unconditional obligation to life. Do people have such an obligation? It seems unlikely. From the point of view of morality or philosophical anthropology it cannot be proved, unless it is already presupposed. Nor can it be deducted from the empirical datum that people prefer life to death. Religious convictions on this issue are divided. Within one and the same religion (Christianity, for instance) we often find opposing points of view, which means that a religious No only has meaning for those who attach meaning to it.

A strategy of prevention that is founded on the (non-overt) unconditional obligation to life, to sum up, makes use of a means—moral condemnation—which itself cannot be morally justified. To this we should add that it is not an effective strategy either. On the contrary, it is contra-productive, for it imposes on people an obligation they cannot fulfil. As a consequence feelings of guilt are added to the burden that life already means to them. People in the helping professions who make use of the obligation to life-argument spoil their own well-meant intentions and make victims rather than that they prevent.

To deny the existence of an unconditional obligation to life is not the same as holding a suicide not responsible for his actions. Almost everybody has a family and kin with whom he/she is related in many different ways. Life has also a social aspect: I rely on others and others rely on me. If we speak in terms of self-regarding and other-regarding acts, then suicide seldom is a self-regarding act. However, the responsibility it carries with it is a responsibility towards the environment and not an unconditional obligation to life.

This is not the place to go into the question of the origin of the harsh and in practice often cruel condemnation of suicide. Let me say this much: the background should probably be sought in the anxiety and fear related to one's own death. Seeing someone else take the step which causes one to shudder and, moreover, seeing that this step is taken deliberately without the pressure of sickness or death, causes aggression. The harsh anti-suicide morality conceals non-moral motives.

7. The Transfer to the Medical Model

However, the strategy of the harsh No is not the only strategy of prevention. Another approach replacing the moral condemnation by a medical judgment—suicide is no longer a sin or a moral offence, but rather a disease—has been presented. No more than a sick person may be held responsible for his illness should a suicide be blamed for his suicidal tendencies. He should not be put on trial, but hospitalized—as all the mentally ill.

That sounds considerably more charitable than the doctrine of the classic No and that is how it is intended. Until recently in Roman Catholic areas a "self-murderer" was not allowed to be buried in consecrated earth. However, if experts were able to determine that the agent acted in a state of temporary insanity compassion may annul this harsh condemnation. Yet another step and suicide is not only in this specific case, but always and everywhere a symptom of disease; mentally healthy people do not commit suicide (Kuitert, 1985ab).

Apart from all respect for the noble motive (compassion) behind this new approach, it still seems to me an unfortunate development. It conceals the problem that suicide poses for "helpers" and as far as I can judge that is how it is intended.

The approach according to the medical model, as I shall call it, is chosen, because it accomplishes two things simultaneously: holding on to the rigorous No of tradition and at the same time exculpating the suicide. On questioning the moral acceptability and the effectiveness of this approach, we must conclude that this strategy does not fulfill either of these conditions. Its basis still continues to be unconditional obligation to life and only in appearance is it effective: the suicide—like the sick—is put away in a clinic. That is permitted or even: imperative in cases in which the suicide is in fact mentally ill, indeed an ever-present possibility. There are, however, criteria for mental illness. It is true the opinions on these criteria differ, but by and large they are uniform. Defining suicidal individuals as mentally ill means adding an untenable criterium for mental illness on the list of criteria. Involuntary hospitalization is also permitted in cases in which a suicide is posing a danger to his environment. From the viewpoint of self-protection society is in fact obliged to do so in such a situation. Not all suicides, however, are a danger to society and should be classified as such.

Moreover, involuntary hospitalization is only effective if one is willing to lock up people forever. But does not that mean that the clinic is turned into a prison?

This is not all that can be said about involuntary hospitalization. When discussing the limits of intervention, we shall return to this subject. Our conclusion so far is: suicide is not adequately described, if we characterize it as a disease. It confines us to the level of cause and effect. Such a view is too one-sided. Suicide is also a choice, a meaningful action.

8. Strategy Corresponds with the Conception of Suicide

Not only the aim of preventive-action presupposes that the helper (the individual or the health care service) acts on the basis of values, but also the means (in terms of attitudes and the strategies), which helpers and health care services choose, have their origin in the value-judgments to which they adhere. Without values, health care is not only worthless, but also impossible.

It is therefore all the more important that the helper is aware of his own basic-values so that he may correct himself with respect to these values if necessary.

In view of this the following distinction is of importance. The value-judgment on suicide (as a human act), on which strategies of prevention are based, is a non-moral value-judgment: suicide is a disaster for all concerned. A non-moral value-judgment is not the same as a moral value-judgment; the latter views suicides as an offence against the unconditional obligation to life. To call it a disaster is, however, not the same as assessing it as an offence. Health care which defines suicide only in terms of an offence inhibits not only the suicide—as we have seen—, but also the helper. Fixation on "it is not allowed" causes him to overlook the underlying motives of the suicidal individual. The helper takes his moral principle seriously, but not the suicidal individual.

With this last remark I have come to the point where I can formulate a fundamental thesis for health care in terms of prevention: only that strategy that takes a suicide seriously can develop into a strategy that will be morally acceptable and effective at the same time. In what way can we take people with suicidal tendencies seriously?

To explain what is meant by "taking seriously" I return to the interpretation of suicidal behavior: if it is not to be considered as sinful or as a mental illness, what then is the most plausible explanation? To answer this question I will make use of the term disorder. People with suicidal tendencies are—in as far as we confine ourselves to the group we are presently discussing—normal people who find themselves in abnormal circumstances. Those abnormal circumstances can be further defined by using the term disorder. On the one hand, we should understand this as a social phenomenon: people are losing the meaningful cohesion of the world which they were part of; they become "disorganized" (Durkheim, 1897). Children lose the security of their home when parents divorce, men and women lose their jobs in an economic crisis, the elderly become lonely as their traditional contacts fall away, etcetera. On the other hand, "disorder" can also mean disintegration on a psychological level: people are in an internal state of turmoil, they lose their sense of self-esteem, they become depressive, suffer from feelings of guilt and are unable to regain that inner stability on their own (Diekstra, 1981). Social and psychological disintegration are factors which sometimes can easily be distinguished: times of economic crisis, unemployment, social deterioration of the environment, loss of jobs implying loss of status—all these are external factors.

Sometimes internal and external operate conjointly and we do not know which one comes first. Sometimes personality traits play a primary role, which means that we are evidently dealing with internal, psychological factors. Of greater importance is, however, that both groups of factors usually intensify each other. A person depressive by nature will become more depressed through loss of status than someone who has learned the art of carefree living. Apart from isolated cases which involve mental illness, neither social or psychological factors sufficiently explain the phenomenon of suicide. Not everyone who experiences disintegration will become a suicide. We must therefore reserve the order: suicide occurs under circumstances of disintegration. In other words: groups exposed to disintegration are risk groups. There must be, however, an additional factor for potential suicides to turn into actual ones. Someone's personal history, for example, which puts him in a special position, or an acute disruption of life, which the person concerned is unable to cope with. When dealing with suicide among young people we should probably pay special attention to the latter. Failure in one's own eyes, or in the eyes of someone else, disappointment in love, or what is being experienced as an irreparable loss of self-esteem, all these things may have a trigger-effect (Diekstra and Heuves, 1986).

9. Taking a Person seriously as a Strategy for Prevention

What do we gain by this interpretation? That the person with suicidal tendencies is taken seriously as a person in (acute or chronic) need. To take someone seriously implies: to recognize and to accept that a person with suicidal tendencies has reasons for his action. These may not be our reasons, but they are nevertheless reasons and as such should be taken seriously. The problems the agent faces are real problems to him or her, regardless the nature of the problems, be it loss of status, decline in social standing or a teenager's disappointment in love. To respond to these problems means that we take a suicidal person seriously. A strategy for prevention which is morally acceptable and at the same time effective can only be founded on an interpretation of suicidal behavior which does not reduce that behavior to causes—except in the case of mental illness—but does justice to the fact that suicides have their motives and reasons. This fact requires that the suicidal person be approached on different levels, which correspond to the two disintegration-areas discussed above.

1. *The communication level between helper and suicide.* People with suicidal tendencies have their motives and reasons: what are they, what is their origin, are they themselves aware of these motives, how reasonable are they, etcetera. This should be open to discussion. What the suicidal person first of all needs is to talk, to communicate: a person in need—this applies virtually always to a suicide as we have seen—wants to be taken seriously in his need, otherwise all help offered him, no matter how well-meant, will be ineffective. The helper, too, needs this kind of communication, in as far as his help is aimed at preventing a calamity. While talking over the matter, the helper, together with the suicide, looks for other solutions rather than death. How can he bring them about, if he does not take the agent's death-wish and his reason and motives seriously? The purpose of communication is—we will return to that later—: to protect a person from what he at this particular moment wishes—but which he may not really intend—and, by making use of the time that is gained by talking, to restore to the suicide the sense of life as a first-rank value.

2. *The task of the government.* Prevention is also: to prevent the rise of suicide-encouraging situations. That brings us first of all to the field of society and its social order. Every government has a responsibility in this respect: to combat loneliness and isolation of people by creating and continuing relations that integrate people in existing networks of jobs and social care. To create job opportunities, to combat or prevent pauperization, to relieve loneliness by restoring or creating intermediary relations, to stimulate everything that promotes national mental health, etcetera. By doing this suicide cannot be eradicated; what can be accomplished, however, is that the risk group will not increase.

   In connection with the above: it should be a concern of the government to provide clinical or extramural care for people with suicidal tendencies by creating facilities specifically for the purpose of suicidal care. Besides all that, it is also the responsibility of the government to draw up a policy of discouragement.

3. *The role of the community.* Prevention is not, however, exclusively a concern of professionals or a government matter. It concerns first of all the people that are close to a suicide. Of course, no one knows beforehand who will develop suicidal tendencies. In that sense vigilance is not called for. What we do know, however, is that no one can live without feeling he or she is of importance to someone else. To give people that feeling or to restore that feeling to them is the best and simplest form of prophylaxis and one need not be a professional to exercise it.

10. Prevention as Intervention

Prevention is always in one way or another a kind of interference in a person's life, or more narrowly formulated: intervention in a person's behavior. In this chapter I intend to focus explicitly on intervening in cases of acute attempts to suicide. The manner of intervention differs from case to case, but that does not alter the fact that it is bound to a fixed scenario. A person is found in a state of unconsciousness and it is suspected, or in some cases even known for sure, that we are dealing with a suicide attempt. Intervention is the next step. If there is a hospital nearby, the agent is rushed to the Emergency and everything is put in motion to save his life. If all goes well, his life spirits return and a life has been reduced from death.

The scenario, which I have sketched above, contains a large measure of (moral) plausibility. To act according to the principle of beneficence exists, among other things, of helping to prevent an evil as best as one can. Death is an evil. To prevent someone who wished to kill himself from realizing his wish means to keep him from an evil of the first order. It seems that few objections, or none at all, can be raised against prevention as intervention. I have, however, two comments to make, which will demonstrate that this is a premature conclusion.

To begin with: how much have we accomplished by the time the suicide is allowed to leave the emergency ward and return home? If the problem the suicide was facing and which motivated him to terminate his life has neither been solved nor alleviated, it means that nothing in his situation has changed. This also means that there is a considerable chance that in a few months time he will once again end up in a clinic or hospital, his life will again be rescued from death, after a while he will be released and subsequently the procedure starts all over again, until he finally succeeds in his intent. In such a case we cannot speak of a rescue from death, no act of beneficence has been carried out, on the contrary, the route to death has merely been prolonged and along with that suffering and distress have increased. Prevention in terms of intervention is, in other words, no prevention, if after his hospitalization the person concerned does not at the same time receive the care and attention he needs in precisely those circumstances which made him choose suicide. It would have been just as well (if not better), if there would not have been any intervention at all. Prevention was carried out in terms of assessment of life as an abstract value, not of life as a real person's life.

There is also another problem. Usually the agent is grateful that the helper intervened. What was intended as an act of beneficence, proved to be exactly that in retrospect. But what should be done, if this is not the case? To chose who provide health care in terms of intervention this poses a fundamental question: is someone, whose death we wrongfully prevented entitled to help in undoing the intervention, that is to say: is he entitled to assistance when committing suicide? In the last paragraph I will make some remarks on the subject.

11. Health Care and Paternalism

Following the argument mentioned above the question arises: why does a helper intervene in the case of an acute suicidal attempt? To protect a person from something he, to the best of our knowledge, does not intend to do: dying. Or to put it even more concise: to protect someone from himself. Thus formulated, the precarious nature of intervention is brought to light: we force a person to act in his own interest (Parfit, 1984). This is, however, exactly the definition of paternalism and the question is whether paternalism is morally and legally acceptable. Here we enter a much debated problem in the field of health care. I will not digress into a lengthy discussion, but restrict myself to situations that are called forth by acute suicidal attempts.

Paternalism is a problem, because the moral principle of beneficence is not the only principle with which actions in the health care field have to comply in order to be acceptable. There is another basic principle involved and that is the principle of autonomy: every human being has the right to organize his life in accordance with his own convictions (as long as they cause no immediate harm to others) and that right must be respected. This basic principle is also called: "respect for persons". If we think in terms of legal rights the concept "human rights", as laid down in the Charter of the

United Nations, is a very good description: all humans have the right to exercise their autonomy.

The problem is obvious. It is not possible from the viewpoint of the principle of beneficence to abandon intervention in the case of acute suicide-attempts. On the basis of the premise that for this person, too, life should be a first-rank value, the helper intervenes in order to keep the suicide from disaster. His intervention has a moral motive. That does not alter the fact, however, that he hinders the agent from carrying out that which he has clearly to do: terminating his life. In other words, intervention violates that other basic principle: the obligation to respect someone's right to exercise his autonomy. What should health care workers do to resolve this tension? To comply exclusively with the principle of autonomy means an unnecessary loss of life. I am referring to all those cases of suicide that were not actually intended to end in death. If, on the other hand, we comply only with the principle of beneficence, then we stand the chance of preventing people from exercising their autonomy not just for a certain period, but for life. Does this mean we are faced with an insoluble conflict? This need not be the case. Beneficence can never be: robbing someone from his freedom to self-determination. It does mean, however: helping someone restore his ability to exercise autonomy. This means that intervention can certainly be interpreted as beneficence, provided the intervention is aimed at and continues to aim at restoring a person's freedom to determine his own fate. In this way it is indeed possible to comply with both principles simultaneously.

In the Western world the individual autonomy is more valued than in other countries, whereas in non-Western cultures collectively shared values rather than individually experienced ones determine what a person thinks or feels. This should be taken into account when it comes to judging as well as designing strategies. Cultural differences co-determine the means of prevention and intervention. From a moral viewpoint, however, this consideration cannot be taken so far that it will entail forcing a person to go on living against his deepest conviction. Just as we are not allowed to do the reverse: forcing a person to die against his will.

The conclusion is: intervention in terms of interference is only morally justified as a provisional measure. In the literary sense of the word it is "first aid". It is not an end in itself, but is aimed at restoring the agent's autonomy.

To view intervention as a means aimed at restoring someone's autonomy entails, however, that those people who really want to die should have their way (and, in extreme cases, might get actual assistance in terminating their life). The reverse of the right to life is that a person also has the right to die (Speijer and Diekstra, 1980; Kuitert, 1985ab).

12. Law and Justice

Law and justice display a great diversity where suicide is concerned. They reflect the collective religious and moral concepts and beliefs, which is every nation's heritage. It is of importance that law and justice be included in the debate on suicide-prevention, as they are also instrumental in structuring health care services. On account of the great diversity, mentioned above, we shall only discuss some basic problems. We shall clarify them by discussing the legislation in a number of European countries and subsequently expose their importance for mental health care in general.

In Europe secular law usually followed clerical law, that is to say: suicide was considered an offence against criminal law. If a person was not successful in his attempt to terminate his life, he stood the chance of being condemned to death by the secular judge. This standpoint has long since been released (although in England a suicide attempt continued to be a criminal offence as late as 1961). Today suicide is no longer considered an offence anywhere. However, there is only a small number of countries that goes so far as not to mention suicide at all in their penal code: Germany, Belgium, France, Sweden, Finland and Luxembourg. This is due to the fact that in a large number of countries assistance to suicide has been brought under criminal law, even though the terms in which it is formulated as an offence differ from country to country. There may be a stipulation, for example, that penalization of assistance occurs with the success of the attempt (this applies to the Netherlands, former Yugoslavia and Turkey). The effect of this stipulation is—strangely enough—that in a number of countries not *the act* in which one assists is a penal offence, but the rendering of assistance (Simson, 1976).

The question whether the law knows of an obligation to intervene, sanctioned by criminal law, is a much debated subject. In most European countries no evidence can be established for this obligation, except in the case of careless negligence, that is to say: in the case of someone having been committed to the care of another person for the explicit purpose of keeping him from suicide. Otherwise it is assumed that in suicide cases death is sought deliberately—for whatever reasons—and subsequently no other person can be the cause of the agent's death.

In summary: people must be protected by criminal law against third parties, but criminal law is not intentioned (nor is it capable) to protect a person against himself. The altered views on suicide constitute the background of this shift in law and justice. Suicide is an act that does not belong to the realm of crime but rather to the realm of tragedy: despair and mental disorder constitute its background and not—apart from evident cases of mental illness—the wish to inflict harm. It is therefore not meaningful to classify suicide under criminal law. Criminal law is not appropriate for suicide-prevention.

The history of European legislation pertaining to suicide is of importance for mental health care in general (Curran and Harding, 1978). Most countries affiliated with the WHO have legal provisions for involuntary hospitalization on the grounds that the person concerned poses a danger to himself and/or to others. In some cases suicidal tendencies or suicide-attempts are explicitly mentioned as a specific interpretation of this danger (Brazil, Rumania, the former USSR). This is not as extreme as considering a suicide a criminal—which was custom in Europe in previous centuries—, but it does raise certain questions. The key problem lies in the usage of diagnostic labels. To consider a suicide insane or possibly even dangerous, is using an outdated interpretation and making—for that reason—the wrong diagnosis: the agent finds himself in a state of despair and disorder and is therefore in need of care and not in need of legal (or moral) condemnation. More important than involuntary hospitalization is the legal regulation of free access to treatment.

The above does not rule out, however, that in some cases a person needs to be protected from himself. This implies that custodial care may be called for in some cases; however, only in a limited way and for a limited period of time. The purpose should be to render the custody superfluous as soon as possible and to restore the agent's abilities of self-determination.

Guaranteeing specific provisions for appeal (which are lacking in a number of countries such as Brazil, for example) are essential in the legislation concerning involuntary hospitalization. An institution is not a prison and should not become one. If it does, it means that health care is in conflict with the Human Rights as proclaimed by the United Nations in 1948 (Curran and Harding, 1978). The right to life, which the Human Rights grant all people, is at least a so-called liberty, in the same sense the right to procreation is a liberty. That is to say: a person has the right to procreate, but is not obliged to. Life, too, is such a liberty. Not to make use of the right to life is also part of that right. Law and justice cannot turn life into an obligation.

Summary

Suicide is, generally speaking, for all people concerned a disaster. The implication of this is that intense efforts should be made to design strategies for prevention. The classic strategy: to threaten people who attempt suicide with moral and religious condemnations has proved to be superseded. It turns a disaster into a sin, it conflicts with more recent views on suicide as a phenomenon and as an ineffective means of prevention. The same applies to criminal sanctions against suicidal attempts: they are of no effect and overlook the distress the suicide finds himself in.

Meaningful and effective prevention begins by taking the agent seriously: in his state of despair and disorder he needs help rather than condemnation or punishment. Care and communication are the means health care services should use in order to be effective. All prevention is preceded by prophylaxis in terms of a social climate in which the individual does not feel lost, but is done full justice.

REFERENCES

Battin, M.P.(1982) *Ethical Issues in Suicide.* Prentice Hall, Englewood Cliffs, New Jersey.

Beauchamp, T.L., Childress, J.F.(1983) *Principles of Biomedical Ethics.* Second Edition. Oxford University Press, New York/Oxford ; 98.

Curran, W.J., Harding, T.W. (1978) *The Law and Mental Health: Harmonizing Objectives.* WHO, Geneva.

Diekstra, R.F.W., Hawton, K. (1987) *Suicide in adolescence.* Kluwer Academic Publisher, Dordrecht/Boston.

Diekstra, R.F.W., Heuves, W. (1986) Recent trends in suicide rates: a social learning perspective. In: Specht, F., Schmidtke, A. (eds.) *Selbstmord-handlungen bei Kindern und Jugendlichen.* Roderer Verlag, Regensburg, 50-64.

Diekstra, R.F.W. (1981) *Over suicide, zelfdestructie, zelfbehoud en hulpverlening.* Samsom Uitgeverij, Alphen aan den Rijn ; 75-77.

Durkheim, E. (1987). *Le Suicide.* Paris: Felix Alcan.

Farberow, N.L., Schneidman, E.S. (1961) *The Cry for Help.* Mc Graw-Hill, New York.

Fontaine, J. La. (1975) Anthropology. In: Perlins (ed.) *A Handbook for the Study of Suicide.* Oxford University Press, New York/London ; 77-91.

Frankena, W.K. (1973) *Ethics.* Second Edition. Prentice Hall, Englewood Cliffs, New Jersey; 47.

Hoche, A.E. (1919) *Vom Sterben.* Gustav Fisher Verlag, Jena; 28.

Iga, M. (1986) *The Thorn in the Chrysanthemum; Suicide and economic success in modern Japan.* California University Press, Berkeley/Los Angeles.

Kuitert, H.M. (1985a) *Das falsche Urteil über den Suizid. Gibt es eine Pflicht zu leben?* Kreuz Verlag, Stuttgart.

Kuitert, H.M. (1985b) *Haben Christen das Recht sichselbst zu töten?* Concilium 21, 229-233.

Leenen, H.J.J. (1988) *Gezondheidsrecht.* Tweede druk. Samsom Uitgeverij, Alphen aan den Rijn; 17-23.

Parfit, D. (1984) *Reasons and Persons.* Oxford University Press, Oxford, 321.

Simson, G. (1976) *Die Suizidtat. Eine vergleichende Betrachtung.* Beck, München; 42-70.

Speijer, N., Diekstra, R.F.W. (1980) *Hulp bij zelfdoding.* Van Lochum Slaterus, Deventer.

Warnock, G.J. (1971) *The Object of Morality.* Methuen & Co., London.

Cultural Aspects of Suicide

The case of Japanese Oyako Shinjū (parent-child suicide)

M. IGA

1. Introduction; Durkheim and an Interpretation

Most sociologists and anthropologists seem to be in accord with Durkheim's focus on the importance of social integration and value (Durkheim, 1897), as Jean La Fontaine says that anthropological analysis of suicide begins with cultural values (La Fontaine, 1975). Durkheim's typology of suicide is interpreted as a classification of suicide by cultural, interactional, and psychological indicators (see table 1; Iga, 1986).

Cultural indicators show the individual's general orientation, shared with others, to institutionalized goals and means. These include: (a) preferential values, which determine the selection of goals (e.g., group goal or self-oriented goal) and (b) obligatory values (i.e., norms), which determine the selection from available means for goal-attainment (e.g., conformity to institutionalized means or innovation). A wide goal-means discrepancy is a basic cause of suicide motivation. Suicide motivation is converted to action by interactional factors, which may be divided into (c) the degree of internalized social interactional factors, which may be divided into internalized social restraint (e.g., a sense of responsibility, shame, and guilt), (d) the degree of the individual's demands for his rights (outlet for aggression), and (e) the degree to which the individual communicates with others (social resources), together with the individual's view of life, death and suicide. The Durkheim's types of suicide may be described in light of combination of the indicators just mentioned.

Altruistic suicide is viewed as the culmination of (a) group goals that override individual goals, (b) a high degree of conformity, (c) a strong sense of responsibility, (d) strong group-goal oriented demands, and (e) substantial communication with other members of the group. Psychologically, this type of person is motivated to kill himself because of a strong sense of obligation, shame, and guilt. He may even experience a mystical joy in suicide when his death is a sacrifice for the good of the group, the most exalted of personal goals. Examples of this type are provided by elite military groups, cults, and deeply committed religious groups.

Anomic suicide, results from weak social regulation. Major features of this type include (a) compelling self-profit motive, (b) inner conflicts, involving a wish to conform to social expectations and a drive toward more effective means for self-profit, (c) a diminishing sense of shame and obligation, (d) a high degree of self expression and of self-oriented demands, and (e) a decline in meaningful communication. This type of person grapples with feelings of relative deprivation and with conflicts involving goals. To such a person, the ends justify the means. He will never be satisfied because he compares himself with other people who have more than he does. A vicious, anxiety-producing cycle maintains an inflated "ego-ideal" and dependency needs. The individual's psychological condition is characterized by greed, vanity, disillusionment, fervid imagination, and jealousy. His hostility toward others is reflected in behavior that appears accusatory, arrogant, and vengeful.

Egoistic suicide results from a marked absence of integration of the individual into society. His behavior is characterized by (a) individualistic goals overriding social ones, (b) nonconformist means of goal attainment, (c) a weak, or weakly felt, sense of shame and obligation, (d) strong self-oriented demands and self-expression, and (e) a minimum of meaningful communications. Because of the paucity of meaningful communication, the individual will have difficulty finding life meaning in a frustrating situation, since the meaning of life is obtainable only through social attachment, which he lacks. He may unconsciously experience a painful conflict between individualistic goals and his wishes for attention and appreciation from society at large. In the case of overwhelming frustration, he may lose the courage to live.

Fatalistic suicide is mentioned by Durkheim only in a footnote (on p. 276 of the 1958 edition). However, although Durkheim considered it to be only of "historical interest", this type is very important in discussing Japanese suicides. It is a reaction to "the ineluctable and inflexible nature of a rule against which there is no appeal", as in the case of slaves. Fatalistic suicide may be interpreted as characterized by the individual's (a) loss of both group and personal goals, (b) strong conformity to social norms, (c) strong sense of shame and obligation, (d) low degree of self-expression, and (e) minimum communication. Psychologically, this individual is likely to experience resentment, fear, and resignation revolving around the belief that the future will be meaningless or frightful. His passions are violently choked by oppressive discipline. He may harbour a desire to be killed, which cannot be manifest itself in acts of submission, masochism, and self-blame, concurrent with feelings of helplessness, fatigue and despair.

2. Psychocultural View of Suicide

The above interpretation of Durkheim's typology shows the importance of culture in explaining suicide. Culture greatly influences not only the environment of the suicidal victim but also, more importantly, his personality and psychology. A complex psychocultural view of suicide was proposed by George A. DeVos (1973) in terms of object cathexis and personal social polarities of situational motivation. I apply the term, however, to Durkheim's classification, simply because he used both cultural and psychological terms.

The psychocultural view deals with suicide in terms of interaction between personality and environment, especially social resources available for the individual. Personality itself is a product of interaction between human potential including Carl Roger's "inherent bodily wisdom" (Holdstock and Rogers, 1977) and potentials for reason, love, and self-expression and environments (e.g., geographic, cultural, social, situational). Once personality is formed, there is constant interaction among personality, biology and environments.

The importance of biology is exemplified by psychoanalysis of suicide e.g., "wishes to kill, to be killed, and to die" (Menninger, 1933) and by humanistic psychologist concepts as basic needs, self-development, and the hierarchy of needs (Fromm, 1941; Maslow, 1968). The significance of noncultural environments' effect upon suicide was exemplified in a study of a community in Niigata Prefecture, Japan. In that community, where a majority of youths leave home to work in big cities, the suicide rate among persons over 60 years old is very high: 317.1 (per 100,000 in 1965), 208.6 (1966), 104.4 (1967), 181.3 (1968), and 131.5 (1969) (Tamura, 1974). The fact that the rate is higher in the winter, when heavy snow hampers old people's ability to work in the fields and hinders their social interaction indicates the importance of "social integration", which Durkheim stressed.

In this chapter, suicide is regarded as produced by the interaction between social resources (cultural factors) and personality. Social resources are environmental factors which the individual can use for his tension-reduction and problem solving. They include governmental programs, social welfare services, and attitudes of family members, friends, church, etc., toward the person in need. Personality factors in suicide are given by Shneidman (1980) as:

1. Inimicality — tendency to behave against one's own interests, i.e., adaptive adjustment
2. Constriction — narrow range of perception; diminishing options and opinions ("tunnel vision")
3. Perturbation — tendency toward frightened, worried, depressed, agitated reactions to a stimulus
4. Negative view of life and accepting views of death and suicide.

Social resources and personality involved in Japanese suicide are illustrated by *oyako shinjū* ("parent-child suicides" in Japan; "murder-suicide" in the United States).

3. Oyako Shinjū

About two cases of *oyako shinjū* occurred every three days in Japan during the 1950's and 1960's. The traditional attitude of Japanese people toward it is one of acceptance. The mother involved in *oyako shinjū* is punishable by 3 to 5 years of imprisonment, according to the new law, which was enacted by the pressure from the US Occupation Forces after World War II. No mother, however, has been punished for it. Since its major cause seems to be actual or expected financial difficulty, *oyako shinjū* is expected to decrease with Japan's prosperity, but their attitude toward it has not changed. In "Oigawa Shinju" in 1978, nine persons died. The bankruptcy of a businessman and prefectural assemblyman precipitated not only his suicide but also the deaths of his family members, including a baby and an infant. One of his daughters was a third-year medical school student. With a secure future, why did she have to die with her parents?

According to the *Honolulu Star-Bulletin* (June 1, 1983), there were annually more than 400 cases of "forced suicide" in Japan in the first two years of the 1980's, and a 1982 study concluded that "family suicides seem to have increased somewhat from before World War II". Japanese *oyako shinjū* takes place in foreign countries too. In the three year period from 1985, three cases, involving Japanese mothers from Japan, occurred in Los Angeles and Anaheim, California, and Honolulu, Hawaii. The social resources and personality factors involved in *oyako shinjū* are illustrated by the case of Fumiko K.

Fumiko, a devoted mother, walked into the Pacific off Santa Monica Beach, California, taking her infant daughter and four-year old son. They were pulled from the water by passers-by; she survived but the children died. When she was pulled out of the water, she held the children tightly under her arms, as if she were protecting them. She told the police that she took them with her because she loved them. The tragedy happened ten days after Fumiko learned that her husband, a Japan-born restaurateur, had kept a mistress for three years. The mistress telephoned to let Fumiko know that she was going divorced.

Fumiko's *oyako shinjū* made headlines in the United States. The incident raised primarily three questions.

1. Why did the prospect of divorce lead to suicide?
2. Why did Fumiko kill her children "because she loved them"?
3. Why was she not socialized to American attitudes toward divorce and infanticide, when she had lived in the United States for 14 years?

A. Suicide

Fumiko's perception of social resources which she could use for tension reduction and problem solving was apparently very constricted. Divorce means the almost total loss of security for most Japanese women because there is little legal protection for the divorcee. The traditional emphasis on family solidarity in Japan is attained primarily by suppressing women's wishes. Moreover, despite the New Constitution, which is democratic, Japanese people have almost nothing to do with law in daily lives. Because of the traditional attitude of obedience to authorities, their knowledge of law is extremely poor. In 1973 only one percent of divorces was decided by legal decision. The typical solution of problems is arbitration (*chōtei*). In arbitration, however, the stronger party has an upper hand, because Japanese people "just acquiesce to the opponent's demands, if the opponent has more power" (Kawashima, 1976).

Economically, the divorcee seldom gets a respectable self-supporting job, with exception of highly educated women from an upper-class family.

Japanese prejudice against the females working outside home is indicated by the typical attitude that females should quit their jobs at marriage or pregnancy. If they work, they are more likely (in about 70 percent of the cases) to work in subcontract firms or to work part time. They are excluded from such privileges as life-time employment, promotion, or pension. In the non-agricultural sector in 1984, Japanese male workers' wages were, on the average, 48.2 percent higher than female workers'. This was the second largest after 52.5 percent for South Korea, while the discrepancy between the sexes was below 20 percent to about 30 percent for the 14 other nations studied. The pay gap leveled off or decreased from 1975 in all the countries, except Japan, where it rose from 44.2 percent. Readily available jobs for ordinary divorcees in Japan are *mizu-shōbai* (lit. "watery" business, or gay trade, e.g., waitress, barmaid, "soft-core" prostitution jobs), but their unstable income often necessitates selling sexual favors. Perception of such difficulties and language problems probably kept Fumiko from looking for a job in America.

Her despair would have been aggravated by the general attitude among Japanese that divorcees are not welcomed to their parents' home, primarily because of the strong stigma against them. Social services for the divorcees are virtually unknown in that country, where informal social control is strong enough to restrain dissatisfied wives from asking for divorce. Born and reared in Japan for about 20 years before her emigration, Fumiko probably did not know of the availability of social services for her. Moreover, even if she had known, Fumiko, like other Japanese women, would undoubtedly have avoided utilizing the services, because of the sense of shame. Japanese people generally have strong fear about revealing their own fault or misfortune to others, because of the generally cold attitude among them toward weak and poor (Nakane, 1972).

When an individual is troubled, social interaction reduces tension. However, Fumiko seems to have been handicapped in this respect, too. In Tarzana, California, where she lived, there were very few Japanese. There could have been a few *shōshaman* (employees of large Japanese firms) in the area, but generally they are not associated with non-*shōshaman*. A characteristic of Japanese communities, whether in Japan or abroad, is social segregation by socio-economic status. Even among the people working in the same organization, strict "vertical relationship" is the rule, as Nakane (1972) observed:

> A superior in one's place of work is always one's superior wherever he is met, at a restaurant, at home, in the street. When wives meet, they will

> behave toward each other in accordance with the ranks of their husbands, using honorific expressions and gestures, appropriate to the established relationship between their husbands.

With "inferior" outsiders Japanese generally have very little informal association. Fumiko's husband was a cook and co-owner of a small Japanese restaurant, who was, in the eyes of the Japanese, occupationally and educationally inferior to *shōshaman*. Therefore, Fumiko's association with other Japanese must have been very limited.

Moreover, there is a general tendency among Japanese to stay away from people in trouble. Kenshiro Ohara (1965) counts this tendency as a major factor in *oyako shinjū*. The tendency is shown even by Japanese who are sympathetic with those in need, primarily because of their lack of self-confidence in problem solving, much less in helping others. The knowledge of such a tendency probably prevented Fumiko from seeking outsider's help.

In addition to its tension-reduction function, social interaction functions as a tool of socialization. If Fumiko had had association with Americans, she might have learned much about their ways of handling problems, like divorce. However, Fumiko had very little intimate contact with Americans, even with Japanese Americans. Japanese from Japan usually have little association with Japanese Americans. The former, as a whole do not speak English well; most of the latter do not speak Japanese well.

Furthermore, there is a strong prejudice, each against the other. Japanese Americans seem to have negative feelings toward Japanese culture, which, in their eyes, is the undemocratic one of their immigrant parents or grandparents. They have an air of superiority toward those who cannot speak English well. On the other hand, the Japanese are prejudiced against Japanese Americans not only as "outsiders" but also as social inferiors. Japanese Americans are regarded as "*kimin n o ko*" (children of "forsaken people"). First-generation emigrants from Japan have been regarded as unworthy "dropouts" from Japan, although this stereotype was not true. Even Ex-Premier Yasuhiro Nakasone revealed his prejudice in the statement that Japanese-ish Japanese are respected. People, who are like *omajiri* ("mixed") are not. Japanese Americans are culturally, if not biologically, mixed.

Psychologically, the Japanese prejudice against Japanese Americans may be a displacement of their own negative self-concept upon a scapegoat. Japanese traditionally have inferiority feelings *vis-à-vis* Caucasians, primarily because of their admiration for power. Japanese Americans remind them of their "inferior" self. The hostility generated by the feeling is displaced into their look-alike, who is an object of prejudice by Americans. As was mentioned, Japanese have little sympathy for the weak and poor.

In interaction with social resources (and social interactions with them), Fumiko's personality was an important factor in her suicide attempt. The personality of Japanese women who attempted suicide was characterized by Kenshiro Ohara (1965) in terms of "compulsiveness, oversensitiveness, and high susceptibility to environmental pressure, together with a lack of effort for problem solving". The insecurity that seems to underlie these traits is shared by most Japanese females in the society, where, as Edwin Reischauer (1988) has commented, "Japanese men are blatantly male chauvinists and women seem shamefully exploited and suppressed".

Diffuse insecurity (anxiety) is a natural product of traditionally authoritarian social relationships, with emphasis on power and status difference. The society had been characterized by "Unescapable absolutism and sumptuary control of individuals" (Haring, 1956) until the end of the last war. The characteristic is much less overt today, but it is, nonetheless, functioning well as a covert potent residue. Japanese insecurity is shown by Irwin Mahler's study, using the Tennessee Self-Concept Scale. He found that Japanese university students were "highly guarded and defensive individuals, seeing themselves less adequate than the American subjects did" (Mahler, 1976).

Japan's Premier's Office (Kurihara, 1981) found in 1972 that their youth, from 18 through 24 years old, were the highest in percentage, only next to Indians, of those who saw "little hope and joy in life". Their percentage on "Man is by nature evil" was 33 in contrast to 16 for comparable Americans. The figure on "I have no friend to trust" was 23 for Japan and 10 for Americans. While 62 percent of American subjects were "satisfied with their society", only 26 percent of Japanese youth was. Fifty-one percent of American subjects thought "My country protects my welfare and rights adequately", but only 11 percent of Japanese youth did so.

Diffuse insecurity characterizes even intellectuals in Japan, when they are supposed to be the most confident of themselves in the West. Von Wolfveren (1989), President of the Association of Foreign Correspondents in Japan, cannot understand "why Japanese intellectuals just obey their authorities". John Fischer of *Harpers* (1964) characterized Japanese intellectuals with the "Dread of power", together with cliquishness and soft-edge, both of which seem to indicate insecurity.

Diffuse insecurity is not only the basic cause of conformity and group solidarity in Japan, but it also produces competitiveness among equals, because they have to fight for the favors from their social superiors. This competitiveness was mobilized skilfully by Japanese leaders. Business is often equated with war. Thus, insecurity may be regarded as a major factor in Japan's success.

If Japanese in general are insecure, women are insecure, women are expected to be much more so in that sexist society. Even their Ex-Premier Nakasone did not hesitate to show his contempt for women, stating that "I have to be careful in what I say but women remember the colour of my necktie rather than what I say" (New York Times, 1986). This is not a surprise when we know that Yukio Mishima, whom Nakasone admires, wrote that females were "decorative without much intelligence" and "something, like a watch a man takes off when he takes a bath, i.e., when he bares his real self" (in *Kinkakuji*, Golden Pavilion).

An important cause of Japanese women's insecurity is the lack of opportunity for them to develop reasoning and self-expression. Women who reason and speak up tend to be criticized as "too argumentative", which more likely places them in the list of most undesirable women in Japan. Mahler (1974) found by the use of Levinson's IPC Control Scale that Japanese women perceive things as controlled by powerful others much more than Japanese men, American men, and American women did.

For most Japanese women, marriage is their only source of security. Therefore, a great majority of them would resign themselves to the given situation with *nakineiri* ("weep and sleep") rather than risking divorce. Marriage must be guarded against any threat and when it is lost, suicide is a possible alternative to take. It may be a form of "revenge" against the husband and society.

Insecurity is combined with the traditional views of life, death and suicide. Buddhism teaches *onri-edo; gongu jōdo* (forsake the filthy world; seek after the Pure Land). "Pure Land" is the land of eternal happiness, which exists only in the afterworld. Death is a salvation. The fear of death is further alleviated by the custom of praying to ancestors' spirits through the *butsudan* (the miniature household altar). Japanese talk to the spirits and ask for protection. The deceased person's spirit can become a guardian angel to protect the remaining family members. He can even talk with them.

The sense of continuity, that this practice provides, decreases the fear of death (Lifton, Kato and Reich, 1979). There is no ban on suicide as is found in Christianity. Although suicide is not exactly "honorable", it seems to be accepted as the best way to escape from a difficulty. Sometimes suicide is even approved as an expression of sincerity, atoning for a failure, especially if it is done for a group. Sincerity in Japan means "selfless devotion to a group" rather than to a cause. In the West, if a person is sincere he should live and contribute to the fulfillment of his cause but in Japan the highest value is the group and the ultimate expression of sincerity is the literal elimination of the self, i.e., suicide.

For example, a secretary of a political leader may kill himself, assuming all responsibility for his boss's wrong-doing. He can destroy evidence, which may be used against the boss. Usually police investigation stops here, although, if the scandal is revealed to Westerners, as in the recent case of Recruit Cosmos insider stock trading and bribery, the Japanese government has to appear to operate as a democratic institution, so that Japan can maintain its honour as a modern nation. What is really important for them seems to be the national honour rather than individual life.

B. Infanticide

Several years ago, a university professor in Tokyo murdered his pregnant student mistress, and hid her body in a deep mountain. When the scandal was revealed, he was not remorseful but boasted that "she loved me and so, she must have been happy to be killed by me". He was compelled to resign from his post. A few days later, he committed suicide. His wife and two small children died with him. Why were the deaths of the wife and children necessary, when the man was unfaithful to them? An explanation is that shame and insecurity subsequent to the breadwinner's dishonorable death are inevitable in that country, and the Japanese people's hostility against the relatives of a criminal is harsh.

The child in the eyes of Japanese parents possesses no legal entitlement. Although he is not exactly a parental possession, he is the mother's *bunshin* (offshoot). Their emotional identification is so strong that the mother seems to feel that when she dies the child should naturally go with her.

Such a strong emotional identification comes from constant physical contact between an indulgent mother and her child (Caudill and Weinstein, 1969). This maternal indulgence is partly due to the usual absence of her husband from home and the generally formal, and often cold, relationship making the child the only object of her free expression of affection. Moreover, the mother's sense of achievement is gained only through rearing an obedient and successful child. The consequent symbiotic relationship is intense.

Another cause of killing the child is prejudice against the orphan. The orphan is traditionally treated as untrustworthy, because of the lack of parental love, protection, and supervision. When he is grown up, the orphan is not usually given a job at a bank or any other position that involves the handling of money. The job applicant in Japan usually has to submit the name of a *mimoto hoshōnin,* i.e., guarantor of the applicant's reliability and honesty. The sponsor summits himself to compensate any loss to the company incurred through the error made by the applicant, as the Japanese parent is responsible for his child (Kawashima, 1976). It is much more difficult for orphans to get *mimoto hoshōnin* than for others.

The job applicant also must go through pre-employment investigation (Hayashida, 1975). The most important public source of information is the family register (*koseki tōhon*), which contains basic demographic data of each household and its original area of domicile. Through this method, not only the applicant's family origin (e.g., outcast or minority group status) but also his family structure are revealed.

Because of the prejudice against orphans, it is the mother's love to save her child from expected sufferings. It is rather the woman who leaves children behind that is blamed as *oni no yōna hito* (demon like person). Moreover, like most Japanese women, Fumiko did not know of the law prohibiting infanticide involved in *oyaū*, because no woman has been punished just for it.

C. Socialization

The socialization of Japanese immigrants to American values is largely determined by verbal communication skills and international perspective. Traditionally, Japanese culture discourages verbal communication. A Kyoto University professor remarked to David Riesman and Robert Lifton (Riesman and Riesman, 1967): "Our (Japanese) language is ritualistic. There is silence in a family because there is no need to speak. Everyone knows what is going on, what is meant". Japanese people believe that sincerity will come out without words, and verbal expressions cannot be trusted.

Since Japanese are socialized to conform to social expectations, verbal self-expression is not important. Social order, the primary value in Japan, is attained by conformity rather than by understanding and cooperation. Japanese society's solidarity is "mechanical" rather than "organic", in Durkheimian terms. "Mechanical solidarity" is produced by people who think in the same way. A result is a "lack of adequate ability to communicate" (*jiko stsuusei no ketsujo*), together with "incomplete selfhood" (*jiko fukanzensei*), with which Dr. Hiroshi Inamura (1980) explains the Japanese tendency toward mental disorders and suicide in a foreign culture. "Incomplete selfhood" is indicated by an unrealistic definition of the situation, which is largely caused by a poor ability to objectively analyze one's own ability and environments, and also by a lack of self-confidence in problem solving.

The difficulty that Japanese people have in communication is due to their tradition of obscurantism. Junichiro Tanizaki, one of the most representative writers in Japan, compared Japanese language with English: (Kawashima, 1976; page 34-35),

> "In the Japanese language a few words provide and provoke the reader's imagination and make the reader himself supplement what is not really clear..... Japanese believe that as long as a person is sincere, his feeling and thinking is conveyed to another, even when they sit together without words".

The vague expression, such as "*zensho shimasu*" (I will do my best), which leaders use habitually, results in misunderstanding and mistrust in foreigners. Such a vagueness is primarily due to the lack of effort among Japanese people to define abstract terms with concrete referents. This lack makes for what Robert Lifton (1970) calls "accommodationism", compromise by juxtaposing contradictory ideas (e.g., democratic ideals and authoritarian social relations) without any effort to logically integrate them.

The lack of international perspective is based on the fact that "their primary commitment is to the well-being of their tribe rather than to ideology or religion". Probably Robert Christopher (1983) is correct when he continues, "Most Japanese don't welcome too much personal contact with foreigners, and in their hearts, feel superior to the rest of the world". The worship of tradition is called *Nihonkō*, which Isaiah Bendasan (1971) (believes to be the pseudonym of Shinchihei Yamamoto) calls the "strongest religion in the world". Shunsuke Tsurumi, one of the top intellectuals in today's Japan, reflects that "the attitude to equate criticism of the Emperor to the reaction that 'then, you are not a Japanese' is still alive in our mind" (1989). If one is a Japanese, he is, by definition, incapable of criticizing Japan.

Thus, the worship of tradition is manifest even among intellectuals, who are expected to be more internationally oriented, and critical of their own culture in the West. Allan Bloom (1987) maintains that "Man cannot remain content with what is given them by their culture, if he is to be fully human... A culture is a cave". Because of the particularistic tendency, Frank Gibney (1975), President of TBS - Britannica in Tokyo, observes:

> "Despite the tone of the big three's criticism, the press mandarins are very consciously part of the establishment. Like the bureaucracy, the professoriat, and the business statesmen, they consider themselves guardians of the state-paid critics. They are nationalists above all, as most American papers are not."

Japanese journalists are controlled by government bureaucrats through the *kisha* (correspondents) club, which screens all news. "Objectivity" in Japanese journalism means delivering reports as given by the authorities, rather than provision of reporters' interpretations tested by evidence.

Thus, the lack of adequate verbal communication skills and international perspective among general Japanese, especially among women, explains Fumiko's difficulty in socialization to American values. The difficulty seems to be shared by many other Japanese immigrants, probably more than in other Asian immigrant groups. As long as they are not confronted with a grave difficulty as Fumiko was, they seem to function adequately. Japanese function well in groups, but have difficulty alone. Suicide may be an unfortunate coping mechanism among weak-ego Japanese in a foreign culture.

Such a difficulty is transmitted to most Japanese, including Fumiko, through their education. Japanese education emphasizes rote memorization of vast amounts of unrelated facts at the sacrifice of reasoning and self-expression. Rote memorization is necessary for passing the entrance examinations in Japan, and *juku* (cram school) specializes on effective memorization. The emphasis on rote memorization at the expense of clear understanding is exemplified by their social-studies textbooks, that are marked for "studious attempt to avoid explicit interpretations and evaluations" (Rohlen, 1983). Scientific attitude is emphasized in physical and natural sciences wholeheartedly, but not so in "social sciences". It is because there are many taboos in Japan, for example, the emperor system, detailed information of World War II, or minority group relations. "Good" Japanese are not supposed to talk about these matters, and the taboos prevent Japanese from becoming fully scientific in social affairs.

The sacrifice of reasoning and self-expression is reinforced by the Japanese language, which is characterized, according to Dean Hajime Nakamura

(1964) at Tokyo University, by "indifference to logical rules, emotionality, avoidance of complex ideas, fondness of simple symbolic expression, and a lack of knowledge concerning the objective order". Education stressing rote memorization does not produce reasoning and self-confidence as much as the education emphasizing problem-solving. Reasoning and self-confidence seems to be vitally necessary for an individual to adjust to a difficulty in a foreign culture.

In short, it may be said that, although suicide is definitely an individual matter, Japanese suicide cannot be explained fully without referring to social resources and personality, which, in interaction, produce suicide. Both social resources and personality are largely determined by education and other aspects of culture.

4. Methodological Note

When we talk about cultural aspects of suicide, we immediately think about ethnographic studies, especially using the Human Relations Area File. They either compare suicide cross-culturally or relate it to institutions within a culture. Those who are interested in such ethnographic studies of suicide should read La Fontaine's excellent chapter on "Anthropology" in *A Handbook for the Study of Suicide*, published by WHO in 1975. The focus of my discussion in this chapter, however, is on suicidal definition of the situation, i.e., the selection of self-destruction as the best means for tension reduction or problem solving under certain conditions. I attempted to show that even this markedly psychological phenomenon is highly influenced by culture.

The analysis of a suicidal definition of the situation may be applied to cross-cultural studies too. For example, if detailed information on cases of divorce (setting) leading to suicide (consequence) is provided, the situations connecting them may be compared cross-culturally. The difference in situations may be explained in terms of social resources and personality, both of which are greatly influenced by education.

In such an endeavour, researchers need cooperation from native informants, who are well versed in the culture and personality to be studied. With vastly improved knowledge of different languages and cultures among Western researchers, it may be possible now to attempt an "emic" approach to studying suicide. The approach may enable researchers "to get inside the native's skin", as Malinowski proposed. This attitude is becoming increasingly more manifest with reference to Japanese culture, as shown by

William La Fleur's comments (1988): "Unlike Americans, most Japanese now see their own society as needing only some minor fine tuning. All real problems are elsewhere".

Such an approach is particularly important for studying Japanese culture, where people tend to avoid revealing seamy aspects of their society to outsiders and where foreigners who criticize Japanese culture are cut off from further cooperation by Japanese intellectuals (Von Wolfveren, 1989). When cross-cultural studies using personal documents become easier, the understanding and prevention of suicide will be greatly facilitated.

Summary

Statistical correlations studies are necessary for comparative purposes. A correlation, however, must be explained in terms of intervening factors. An analysis of Durkheim's types of suicide suggests such intervening factors as institutional goals to aspire for, institutional means to choose from, and social conditions to adjust to, together with the frequency and quality of social interaction and psychological state of the suicidal individual.

This chapter presents a case of *oyako shinjū* (parent-children suicide in Japan / murder suicide in the West), which occurred in the United States, and proposes that an explanation of Japanese suicide, within Japan or not, needs deep understanding of their culture. As Alan Bloom says 1987, culture is a system of conventions and prejudices, and prejudice is a major course of human miseries. Edwin S. Shneidman holds, "sensing the nuances of nomothetic (statistical, behavioral, cognitive) data is necessary for studying suicide in foreign culture, and this is done by ideographic, intuitive, psychological explanation". Social meanings attached to self-destructive behavior is understandable only by personological, contextualist approaches to suicide.

REFERENCES

Bendasan, I. (1971). *Nihonjin to Yudayajin (The Japanese and the Yew).* Kadokawa Shoten, Tokyo.

Bloom, A. (1987). *The Closing of the American Mind.* Simon and Schuster, New York.

Caudill W., Weinstein H. (1969). Maternal Care and Infant Behavior in Japan and America. *Psychiatry 32;* 12-43.

Christofer R.C. (1983). *The Japanese Mind; The Goliath Explained.* Linden Press/ Simon & Schuster, New York.

DeVos G.A. (1973). Role Narcissism and Japanese Suicide. In: DeVos (ed.), *Socialization and Achievement.* University of California Press, Berkeley, Los Angeles, London.

Durkheim, E. (1958). *Suicide* (First published in French in 1897). Trans. Spaulding, J. A. and Simpson G. Free Press, Glencoe Ill.

Fischer, J. (1964). The Japanese Intellectuals: Cliques, Soft Edge and the Dread of Power. In: Harpers, *The Editor's Easy Chair.*

Fromm, E. (1941). *Escape from Freedom.* Rinehart, New York.

Gibney, F., (1975). *Fragile Superpower.* W. W. Norton & Co, New York.

Haring D. (1956). Japanese National Character: Cultural Anthropology, Psychoanalysis and History. In: D.G. Haring (ed.), *Personal Character and Cultural Milieu.* Syracuse University Press, New York.

Hayashida, C. T. (1975). K shinjo and Tanteisha. Private Investigation and Detective Services. In: T. Fuse (ed.), *Modernization and Stress in Japan.* E.J. Brill, Leiden.

Holdstock, T.L. & Rogers, C. R. (1977). Person-Centered Theory. In: R. Corsini (ed.), *Current Personality Theories.* Ill. F.E. Peacock Publications, Inc., Itasca.

Iga, M. (1986). *The Thorn in the Chrysanthemum.* Berkeley, Los Angeles, London: Univeristy of California Press, Berkeley, Los Angeles, London.

Inamura, H. (1980). *Nihonjin no Kaigai Futekiō (Inadaptability of the Japanese Abroad).* Nihon Hōsō Kyōkai Press,

Kawashima, T. (1976). *Ninhonjin no Hō Ishiki (Legal consciousness of Japanese people).* Iwanami Shinsho, Tokyo.

Kurihara, A. (1981). *Gendai Seinen-ron (On Contemporary Youth)* Chikum Shobo, Tokyo.

La Fleur, W. (1988). *Through the Looking Glass of Japan.* The Los Angeles Times, Book review.

La Fontaine, J. (1975). *Anthropology.* In: A Handbook for the Study of Suicide. WHO.

Lifton, R. (1970). Individual Paterns in Historical Change: Imagery of Japanese Youth. In: N.J. Smelser and W.T. Smelser (eds.), *Peronality and Social System.* John Wiley and Sons, New York.

Lifton, R., Kato, S., and Reich, M. R. (1979). *Six Lives: Six Deaths.* Yale University Press, New Haven, London.

Mahler, I. (1974). A Comparative Study of Locus of Control. *Psychologia.* (September) 135-139.

Mahler, I. (1976). What is Self-Concept in Japan. *Psychologia.* (September) 127-133

Maslow, A. (1968). *Motivation and Personality.* Harper and Bros, New York.

Menninger, K. A. (1933). Psychoanalytics Aspects of Suicide. *The International Journal of Psychoanalysis 14;* 376-390.

Nakamura, H. (1964). *Ways of Thinking of Eastern People: India, China, Tibet, Japan.* East-West Center Press, Honolulu.

Nakane, C. (1972). *Japanese Society.* University of California Press, Berkeley, Los Angeles, London.

Ohara, K. (1965). *Ninhonjin no Jisatsu (Suicide among Japanese people).* Seishin Shobo, Tokyo.

Reischauer, E. O. (1988). *The Japanese Today.* Harvard University Press, Cambridge, Mass. & London.

Riesman, D., Riesman E.T. (1967). *Conversations in Japan.* Basic Books, New York.

Rohlen, T. P. (1983). *Japan's High Schools.* University of California Press, Berkeley, Los Angeles, London.

Shneidman, E. S. (1980). *Voices of Death.* Harpers & Row, New York.

Tamura, K. (1974). Jisatsusha no Jittai to Haikei (Actual condition and background of suicidal persons). *Bulletin of Toyo University Sociology Department,* Toyo.

Tsurumi, S. (1989). Gens no Himaku o Nuguttr massugu ni Sekai i Mitoos (See through the world by wiping out the film of illusion). *Asahi Journal:* Tenn to Nihonjin 23.

Wolfveren, K. von (1989). Naze Nihon no Chishikijin wa hitasura Kenryoku ni Tsuiju suru no ka (Why do Japanese intellectuals just obey the authorities). *Chūō Kōron 93.*

Table 1: PSYCHOCULTURAL COMPONENTS OF DURKHEIM'S TYPES OF SUICIDE

	Egoistic	**Altruistic**	**Fatalistic**	**Anomic**
A. Cultural regulation				
1. Goals	Self-oriented: with some philosophical principle	Collectivistic	Accommodation of individual goals, group goals	Self-profit oriented
2. Means	Nonconformance	Conformance	Conformance	Inconsistency between conformance and non-conformance
B. Interactional integration				
1. Social restraint; shame, obligation	Weak; effort to deny	Strong	Strong	Declining
2. Demands; self-expression	High for self-oriented goals	High for group goals	Low	High for self-profit
3. Meaningful	Low	High	Low	Declining
C. Psychological indications	Desire for meaning of life; obtainable only by social attachment (212)*; non-conforming values vs. unconscious wish for sympathy (211); loss of the will to live; depression and melancholy (214)	Sense of obligation; abnegation and the state of impersonality (223), mystical joy (233); shame and guilt	Excessive physical and moral despotism. Sense of "future pitilessly blocked and passions violently choked" (276), resentment, fear, resignation	Wilder goals-means discrepancy (246), sense of relative deprivation (253), inflated ego ideal and dependency; insecurity, greed, feverish imagination, disillusionment (256); jealousy (253)

* The numbers in the table refer to pages in Emile Durkheim's *Suicide: A Study in Sociology*, 2d ed., trans. J.A. Spaulding and G. Simpson (Glencoe, III: Free Press, 1958).

Source: Mamoru Iga, *The Thorn in the Chrysanthemum* ((Berkeley, Los Angeles, London: University of California Press, 1986) p. 10.

Biological Aspects of Suicide

Serotonergic Function in Suicide Attempters

M.L. KORN, S.L. BROWN, M. KOTLER, M. GORDON AND H.M. VAN PRAAG

1. Introduction

Much of the research in biological psychiatry has focused on the identification of biological variables corresponding to well-delineated psychiatric syndromes. Attention has primarily focused on the CNS monoamines noradrenaline (NA), dopamine (DA) and indoleamine (.i.e., 5-HT) system, they have been reported in diverse illnesses or syndromes including the affective disorders (van Praag et al., 1970), the anxiety disorders (Kahn et al., 1988b), Schizophrenia (Bleich et al., 1988) and obsessive compulsive disorder (Insel et al., 1985). Subsequently, a "5-HTergic hypothesis" has been posited for each of these disorders.

The identification of 5-HTergic disturbances in heterogeneous and seemly unrelated disorders has lead some to characterize the data as non-specific and chaotic (van Kammen, 1987). We concur that, when viewed solely through the lens of a categorical approach, the data do appear perplexing indeed. However, we have maintained that this is secondary to a methodological bias inherent in a strict adherence to a nosological/categorical viewpoint (van Praag et al., 1975). We have suggested that the nosological approach be complemented by what we have termed a functional/dimensional approach (van Praag and Leijnse, 1965; van Praag et al., 1987). The basic tenets of the functional/dimensional method are as follows: (1) The elementary units of classification in psychopathology are psychological dysfunctions (e.g., disturbances in affect, cognition, memory, etc.) rather than syndromes or nomological entities. (2) Characterization of a psychiatric disorder is a two-tired process. First, a nomological assessment is made. Subsequently, the syndrome is dissected into the constituent psychopathological dimensions. (3) Correlations between biological abnormalities and syndromal categories as well as psychological dysfunctions should be sought.

This chapter will trace the development of our understanding of 5-HTergic abnormalities first in suicide attempters, next in assaultive individuals and lastly in patients with anxiety. We will then review the interrelationships between suicide, aggression and anxiety and suggest the possibility that an underlying disturbance in CNS 5-HTergic function links these psychopathological dimensions. We will conclude by employing a functional/dimensional approach to link and integrate biological findings with psychopathological dimensions in a unified framework.

2. Serotonergic Abnormalities in Suicide Attempters

Several groups have reported that subgroups of depressed patients exhibit decreased baseline cerebral spinal fluid 5-hydroxyindoleacetic acid (5-HIAA, the primary metabolite of 5-HT) as well as diminished post-probenecid 5-HIAA accumulation in CSF, suggesting a decrease in central nervous system 5-HT metabolism in these individuals (Van Praag et al., 1970; Asberg et al., 1984; Traskman et al., 1984). Probenecid blocks the efflux of 5-HIAA from the CNS, including the CSF, to blood. The resulting accumulation of 5-HIAA in the CSF provides a crude indication of 5-HT metabolism (Van Praag et al., 1975). Patients with low CSF 5-HIAA tend to have "vital depression" (van Praag et al., 1965), a syndrome closely analogous to that of major depression, melancholic type as delineated in DSM-III. Initially, depressives with low CSF 5-HIAA could not be distinguished symptomatically from depressives with normal CSF 5-HIAA levels, although decrements in CSF 5-HIAA levels tend to be less prevalent among "neurotic" depressives and less common in mild than in severe depressives (Van Praag et al., 1975).

Asberg et al. (1976) confirmed the presence of a bimodal distribution of CSF 5-HIAA in depressed individuals. Furthermore, she and her colleagues were the first to make the important observation that the number of suicide attempts is markedly higher in patients with decreased CSF 5-HIAA as compared to depressives with normal CSF 5-HIAA levels (40% vs. 15%). Moreover, those patients attempted suicide by more "violent" means then patients attempting suicide by "non-violent" methods (e.g., drug overdose or superficial wrist cuts).

This finding has been replicated and extended by other groups. Several investigators have confirmed the presence of low CSF 5-HIAA in depressed suicide attempters. Van Praag (1982) noted an increased incidence of suicide attempts in a subgroup of depressed patients with low CSF 5-HIAA, although the incidence of violent suicides was not increased in the low CSF 5-HIAA group. Lopez-Ibor et al. (1985) studied melancholic depressed patients and found CSF 5-HIAA to be significantly decreased in those patients with a previous suicide attempt. Palaniappan et al. (1983) also noted diminished CSF 5-HIAA in depressed outpatients with either suicidal ideation or attempts. Banki et al. (1981) observed that suicidal behavior (including suicidal intent, plans and attempts) was increased in depressed female inpatients with low CSF 5-HIAA. Agren (1980) found a negative correlation between CSF 5-HIAA and the severity of suicide attempts in unipolar but not bipolar patients. Agren and Niklasson (1986) noted that CSF 5-HIAA is a significant predictor of suicidal tendencies (as measured by the SADS interview) in depressed unipolar but not bipolar patients.

Other researchers found CSF 5-HIAA to be low in non-depressed, non-psychotic suicide attempters as well as depressed individuals. Oreland et al. (1981) studied currently and previously depressed patients (some of whom had made suicide attempts) as well as non-depressed suicide attempters. Suicide attempters (most of whom were not depressed) had lower CSF 5-HIAA levels than either depressives without suicide histories or normal controls. Traskman et al. (1981) confirmed this and also noted an association between low CSF 5-HIAA and violent suicide attempts. Bank; and Arato (1983) studied a cohort of female inpatients with a variety of psychiatric diagnoses including depression, schizophrenia and alcoholism. Violent suicide attempters had diminished CSF 5-HIAA levels when compared to both non-violent suicide attempters and non-attempters. In a cohort of violent offenders and arsonists (most of whom met DSM-III criteria for a personality disorder), low CSF 5-HIAA was associated with a history of suicide attempts (Virkkunen et al., 1989).

Lastly, several studies on patients with primary psychotic diagnoses have noted similar relationships. In schizophrenics hospitalized for suicide attempts committed in response to command auditory hallucinations, CSF 5-HIAA levels in both violent and non-violent attempters were found to be low as compared to schizophrenics with no suicidal histories (Van Praag, 1983). All suicide attempters had low depression scores during hospitalization and no signs of a depressive disorder during the 3 months prior to the attempts. This was confirmed in a study by Ninan et al. (1984) in which schizophrenics with "severe" suicidal histories (i.e., violent or "well-planned" attempts) had lower CSF 5-HIAA levels than non-suicidal schizophrenic controls. Van Praag (1986), however, found that CSF 5-HIAA was normal in schizophrenics with histories of suicide attempts who were not currently suicidal when compared to normal controls. Roy et al. (1985) and Pickar et al. (1986) also noted that schizophrenics with histories of suicide attempts did not have lower CSF 5-HIAA levels than patients without such histories. The latter study, however, specifically excluded patients with histories of "seriously violent, criminal or persistent suicidal behaviors", presumably biasing the results.

Other studies have not confirmed the relationships between low CSF 5-HIAA and suicide (Berrettini et al., 1986; Vestergaard et al., 1978; Roy-Byrne et al., 1983). This discrepancy may be explained by the high number of bipolar patients in these studies, indicating that suicide attempters in this diagnostic group may have different biological substrata underlying their suicidal behavior. Secunda et al. (1986) were unable to find differences in CSF 5-HIAA in either bipolar or unipolar suicide attempters when compared to non-attempters. Roy et al. (1986) found lower levels of CSF HVA but not 5-HIAA in depressed patients (most of whom were unipolar) with recent and past suicide attempts. This latter study, however, included a small number of violent suicide attempters (3 of 19 attempters). Furthermore, CSF 5-HIAA levels in the controls were lower in this study than in the study by Asberg et al. (1976), suggesting that the control groups were not comparable.

In a prospective study, Traskman et al. (1981) followed individuals for up to 1 year after their suicide attempt. In suicide attempters with CSF 5-HIAA below the median (92.5 nmol/L), the one year mortality rate was 20%. In comparison, no attempts by suicide attempters with CSF 5-HIAA levels above 92.5 nmol/L were successful. Therefore, CSF 5-HIAA levels may have significant predictive power in the assessment of subsequent mortality risk. This was replicated by Roy et al. (1989) who found a 25% one year mortality in depressives with CSF 5-HIAA levels below 80 nmol/L. After five years, CSF 5-HIAA and HVA levels were significantly diminished in repeat attempters as compared to depressed past attempters and non-attempters.

Considering the above data, the finding of low CSF 5-HIAA in suicide attempters from diverse diagnostic categories appears to be a robust one. The general interpretation of this finding has been that a diminished level of CSF 5-HIAA is related to suicidal state (and, in particular, "violent" suicidal state) rather than to depression *per se.* Yet this conclusion cannot be drawn with certainty. As Van Praag (1985) has argued, the relationship between suicidal behavior and depression is a complex one and methodologically difficult to study. Often times depressed mood is reported to be present at the time of the suicide attempt but subsides following the event, suggestive of a "cathartic" role for this behavior (Van Praag and Plutchik, 1985). Biological parameters are measured at different times after the event when the affective state (e.g., level of dysphoria or anxiety) may be at variance from that present at the time of the attempt. A recent study by Virkkunen et al. (1989b) illustrates the potentially complex interactions existing between dysphoric mood, aggressive behavior and CSF 5-HIAA. As reviewed above, violent and impulsive individuals with histories of suicide attempts had significantly decreased CSF 5-HIAA. While most subjects met criteria for a personality disorder, 4 of 58 subjects had histories of major depression and 26 met criteria for dysthymic disorder. In a linear discrimination analysis, CSF 5-HIAA was able to correctly classify 72.4% of the subjects as to history of suicide. The percentage was increased to 79.3% after a diagnosis of dysthymia was added. Depression appears in this study to covary with aggression (both inwardly and outwardly directed) as well as with CSF 5-HIAA and may confer increased suicidal risk in patients with low 5-HT metabolite levels.

In addition, there is some evidence that the tendency of low CSF 5-HIAA levels to persist after a suicide attempt differs in patients with unipolar depression as compared to patients with schizophrenia or bipolar disorder. Van Praag (1986) found that depressives with either recent suicide attempts or histories of attempts demonstrate lowered post-probenecid CSF 5-HIAA levels. Those with only suicidal ideation had normal levels. It was concluded that in affective disorders low CSF 5-HIAA is a possible trait marker related to an increased risk of suicidal behavior. Alternatively, in this study, schizophrenics with histories of attempts have been shown to have normal CSF 5-HIAA levels.

In summary, low CSF 5-HIAA had originally been demonstrated to be present in a proportion of depressed patients. Asberg et al. (1976) noted increased suicidal behavior in some depressed patients with low CSF 5-HIAA, particularly in violent attempters. Subsequently, low CSF 5-HIAA was demonstrated in probans from other diagnostic groups with histories of suicide attempts. These findings suggest that some characteristic(s) of the suicidal state is (are) related to low 5-HT metabolism in the CNS, apparently independent of diagnostic category.

3. Serotonergic Function in Outwardly Directed Aggression

Numerous lines of evidence suggest that 5-HT is involved in the modulation and expression of outwardly directed aggressive behavior. Animal research has indicated an important role for this monoamine in particular types of aggressive behavior (for review see Eichelman, 1987). Recently, a new class of drugs possessing 5-HTergic activity called "serenics" has been developed. These drugs have been shown to be both effective and selective in their capacity to modify offensive aggression (Olivier et al., 1987). Furthermore, suicide is frequently considered to be a form of aggression directed towards the self. Disturbed 5-HT metabolism has been found repeatedly in suicidal patients, similar disturbances as in outwarding directed aggression.

Brown et al. (1979) were the first to report abnormalities of central 5-HT in aggressive individuals. In military men with personality disorders, CSF 5-HIAA correlated -0.78 with current and/or a history of aggressive behavior while 3-methoxy-4-hydroxyphenylglycol (MHPG, the primary metabolite of CSF noradrenaline) correlated +0.64 with this behavior. Individuals diagnosed with personality disorders associated with increased behavioral impulsivity (i. e., antisocial, explosive, immature and hysterical) had lower CSF 5-HIAA and higher MHPG levels than those with disorders associated with less behavioral impulsivity (i.e., passive-aggressive, passive-dependent, schizoid, obsessive-compulsive and inadequate). Histories of suicide attempts were also associated with a low CSF 5-HIAA level. Subsequently, Brown et al. (1982) studied individuals diagnosed with borderline personality disorder and found that subjects with low CSF 5-HIAA had significantly higher aggression scores. Patients with histories of suicide attempts also had significantly decreased CSF 5-HIAA as well as higher aggression scores compared to those patients without such histories of suicide attempts.

Several other studies have demonstrated significant associations between decreased CSF 5-HIAA and increased outwardly directed aggression. In 6 individuals with XYY chromosomal abnormality and histories of arson and/ or assaultive behavior, post-probenecid CSF 5-HIAA was decreased as compared to normal controls (Bioulac et al., 1980). Baseline CSF 5-HIAA was not different, however. Treatment with 5-HTP (5-hydroxytryptophan, the immediate metabolic precursor of 5-HT) resulted in decreased aggression in five of six patients. Lidberg et al. (1984) reported on three individuals manifesting violence towards family members. All three had murdered or attempted to murder one of their children, had histories of one or more suicide attempts and demonstrated low 5-HIAA levels. Lidberg et al. (1985) also found low CSF 5-HIAA levels in men who had murdered sexual partners. These levels were similar to those in suicide attempters. Interestingly, other murderers (most of whom had histories of alcoholism) did not have low levels. Since, according to case record review, the murders of the sexual partners occurred during periods of intense negative affect, the authors speculate that low CSF 5-HIAA may be related to the tendency to lose control or use violent means during periods of emotional arousal. In a study by Roy et al. (1988), a significant negative correlation was observed between CSF 5-HIAA and the "urge act out hostility" subscale of the Hostility and Direction of Hostility Questionnaire in normal volunteers.

Although there appears to be a link between outwardly directed aggression and altered 5-HT metabolism, the specific aspects of aggressive display which are linked to low CSF 5-HIAA remain to be definitely determined. Linnoila et al. (1983) attempted to separate violent from impulsive behavior and studied individuals who committed or attempted to commit murders of "unusual cruelty." Individuals committing "impulsive" (i.e., non-premeditated) violent acts had lower CSF 5-HIAA levels than those committing "non-impulsive" (i.e., premeditated) acts. Individuals who committed multiple murders had lower CSF 5-HIAA levels than those committing single murders.

Table 1: CSF 5-HIAA in aggressive and impulsive individuals

INVESTIGATORS	SUBJECTS	CSF 5-HIAA
Bioulac et al., (1980)	5 aggressive patients XYY chromosomal abnormality	Lower post-probenecid levels; normal baseline levels
Brown et al., (1979)	26 personality disorder	Negative correlation with aggression scores; lower levels also in suicide attempters
Brown et al., (1982)	12 borderline personality disorder	Lower levels in patients with high aggression scores and histories of suicide attempts
Lidberg et al., (1984)	3 individuals violent towards family members	Low levels in all 3
Lidberg et al., (1985)	77 males 16 murderers 22 suicide attempters 39 normal control	Lower levels in men who had killed a sexual partner
Linnoila et al., (1983)	21 murderers 15 individuals who attempted murder	Lower levels in "impulsive" than in "non-impulsive" murderers
Roy et al., (1988)	17 normal control	Significant negative correlation with the "urge to act out hostility"
Virkkunen et al., (1987)	20 arsonists 20 violent offenders 10 normal control	Lowest levels in arsonists
Virkkunen et al., (1989)	36 violent offenders 22 arsonists	Lower levels in recidivists

Impulsive offenders with histories of suicide attempts had the lowest levels of all. Impulsive offenders had more evidence of disturbed childhood behavior (consistent with diagnoses of attention deficit disorder or antisocial personality disorder) as well as increased histories of alcohol abuse. Virkkunen et al. (1987) also presented evidence suggesting a link between impulse control and low CSF 5-HIAA levels. Twenty individuals who committed arson (often considered an impulsive act), 19 meeting criteria for borderline personality disorder, had significantly lower CSF 5-HIAA levels than habitually violent offenders or normal controls.

As discussed above, low CSF 5-HIAA in suicide attempters has been associated with an increased incidence of future fatal suicidal behavior. Similarly, low CSF 5-HIAA in individuals manifesting outwardly directed aggression may indicate an increased probability for subsequent violent or impulsive acts. In a prospective study of violent offenders and arsonists, recidivist offenders demonstrated decreased CSF 5-HIAA as compared to non-recidivists (Virkkunen et al., 1989a). Lowered blood glucose nadir (which has also been associated with impulsive and violent behavior) in conjunction with low CSF 5-HIAA concentration was able to correctly classify 84.2% of repeat offenders.

As with suicide research, investigation of the role of biological factors in human aggression has been impeded by methodological problems. Unlike mood disorders which tend to be persistent over time, aggressive acts occur briefly, intermittently and in often unpredictable patterns. In addition, aggressive acts are strongly influenced by external factors such as social context or substance abuse. These potentially confounding variables are not only difficult to control but are also episodic, frequently inaccurately assessed or reported and usually not present at the time of biological testing. Furthermore, characterization of different types of aggressive behavior remains vague and often idiosyncratic, making the comparison of results between studies difficult.

In summary, the finding of low CSF 5-HIAA in suicide attempters (a form of auto-aggression) has been extended to individuals demonstrating increased outwardly directed aggression. Some studies have suggested a relationship between lower 5-HT metabolite levels and impulsive rather than aggressive behavior. One might conclude, therefore, that low CSF 5-HIAA (originally observed in depression) is associated with a disturbance in the ability to regulate aggressive behavior (whether inwardly or outwardly directed) and/or impulsivity rather than depression *per se*. However, several studies have suggested a complex interaction between CSF 5-HIAA and the psychopathological dimensions of aggression regulation, impulsivity and depression. Improved psychometric evaluation of this patient population is required before the interrelations can be sorted.

4. Serotonergic Function and Anxiety

The role of 5-HT in the pathogenesis of anxiety disorders was ignored until only recently. Clinical studies have demonstrated that 5-HTergic agents such as 5-HP and clomipramine (a 5-HT re-uptake inhibitor) are efficacious in the treatment of panic disorder (Kahn et al., 1987). Several newer 5-HTergic agents have also been shown to be effective anxiolytics. Both buspirone, a drug which demonstrates 5-HT-1A receptor affinity in the hippocampus and inhibits the spontaneous firing of dorsal raphe neurons (Ortiz et al., 1987), and ritanserin, a selective 5-HT-2 receptor antagonist (Gardner, 1988), have been shown to be effective in treating generalized anxiety disorder (Taylor et al., 1985; Ceulemans et al., 1985). Fluoxetine, a recently released specific 5-HT re-uptake inhibitor, has been shown to be effective in panic disorder (Gorman et al., 1987) as well as in obsessive compulsive disorder (Fontaine and Chouinard, 1986). Finally, fluvoxamine, another selective 5-HT re-uptake inhibitor, has been shown to have pronounced anxiolytic as well as anti-panic effects (Den Boer et al., 1987; Den Boer and Westenberg, 1988).

No studies measuring CSF 5-HIAA in patients with panic disorder or generalized anxiety disorder have been reported. However, there is suggestive evidence of a negative correlation between anxious affect and CSF 5-HIAA in some studies of other patient populations. Banki (1977) noted a significant inverse association between anxiety ratings and baseline as well as post-probenecid CSF 5-HIAA in unipolar depressed women ($r=-0.48$ and -0.53, respectively). This was later confirmed in another cohort of depressed women (Banki et al., 1981). Rydin et al. (1982) found increased anxiety and hostility as well as difficulties in handling interpersonal conflict in depressed and suicidal patients with low CSF 5-HIAA. Van Praag (1988) also noted a negative correlation between anxiety levels and post-probenecid CSF 5-HIAA in patients with major depression, melancholic type. This finding, however, was not replicated by Redmond et al. (1986), where a positive correlation ($r=0.65$) was noted between CSF 5-HIAA and anxiety in manic patients. No correlation between anxiety and CSF 5-HIAA was noted in depressed patients or controls in this study. Alternatively, in patients with obsessive compulsive disorder (classified with the anxiety disorders in DSM-III-R), CSF 5-HIAA has been shown to be increased (Insel et al., 1985). Thoren et al. (1980) also noted higher CSF 5-HIAA levels in these patients, although this did not reach significance. Treatment with clomipramine resulted in a significant decrement in CSF 5-HIAA which correlated with clinical improvement of the obsessive symptomatology. The finding of high rather than low CSF 5-HIAA in patients with obsessive compulsive disorder suggests differences in 5-HTergic function in this patient population as compared to depressed or suicidal patients with increased anxiety (who may tend to have diminished CSF 5-HIAA).

In order to more easily and thoroughly assess central 5-HT function in psychiatric patients, we have been employing a neuroendocrine challenge paradigm. This involves peripheral administration of an agent influencing 5-HT synthesis or function and subsequent measurement of a 5-HT-mediated function such as the release of the hormones cortisol or prolactin. When a direct postsynaptic receptor agonist is administered, the magnitude of the hormonal response is considered to be an indication of the postsynaptic receptor sensitivity.

Neuroendocrine challenge tests have resulted in much conflicting data in 5-HT research. We believe this may be due in part to the non-specificity of the agents utilized (Van Praag et al., 1987). Tryptophan, the dietary precursor of 5-HT, has been used to test the 5-HT system. While this amino acid has been shown to produce increases in central 5-HIAA, tryptophan has also been shown to significantly decrease CSF HVA and MHPG at the doses employed (Van Praag et al., 1987). Similarly, 5-HTP, the immediate precursor of 5-HT, is taken up by noradrenergic and dopaminergic nerve terminals and released as 5-HT at anatomical locations where this monoamine is not usually found, thus acting as a false neurotransmitter.

Meltzer et al. (1984) found an *increased* cortisol response to 5-HTP administration in suicide attempters. On the other hand, Coccaro et al. (1989) noted a *blunted* prolactin response to fenfluramine in patients with major affective disorders and personality disorders. Prolactin levels were particularly reduced in patients with histories of suicide attempts. In patients with personality disorders, significant inverse correlations were found between blunted prolactin response and measurements of impulsivity and aggression. Since fenfluramine has 5-HT releasing effects, blocks re-uptake and stimulates 5-HT function, the authors suggest that this agent yields a measure of overall 5-HT function (which is therefore reduced in this population). Caution should be observed, however, since the L-isomer of fenfluramine also possesses dopaminergic activity (Invernizzi et al., 1986).

As new, more specific 5-HT receptor agonists become available, more extensive and accurate delineation of 5-HT function in humans will be possible. We, as well as several other laboratories, have been employing MCPP (m chlorophenyl-piperazine), a metabolite of the antidepressant trazodone, to study 5-HT receptor function. MCPP is a post-synaptic 5-HT receptor agonist which has pronounced 5-HT1 activity as well as some 5-HT2 (Sills et al., 1984) and 5-HT3 affinity (Kilpatrick et al., 1987). This agent stimulates the release of several hormones including prolactin and cortisol. Recently, radioligand binding studies in the frontal cortex and globus pallidus of human brains have indicated equipotent binding at nanomolar concentrations at 5-HT1A, 5-HT2 as well as alpha-2 adrenergic receptor sites (Hamik and Peroutka, 1989), suggesting that MCPP may not be specific for the 5-HT system. However, studies in primates (Aloi et al., 1984) and humans (Mueller et al., 1986; Kahn et al., submitted) have demonstrated that the cortisol and prolactin response can be blocked by the 5-HT antagonist metergoline. Moreover, we demonstrated that MCPP has no effect on plasma levels of MHPG (Kahn et al., submitted). Considering these data, the fact that MCPP binds to alpha-2 receptors *in vitro* may not be functionally significant in *vivo.*

At our institution, we have employed MCPP in a challenge paradigm in patients with panic disorder. Based on clinical data indicating an initial increase in anxiety in these patients treated with 5-HTergic drugs such as clomipramine and 5-HTP, we hypothesize that these patients have a post-synaptic supersensitivity of the 5-HT receptors (Kahn et al., 1988b). We argued that a low or "threshold" dose of MCPP is required to discriminate between hypersensitive and normosensitive receptors and therefore employed 0.25 mg/kg p.o. MCPP. We demonstrated that this dose significantly elevates cortisol in normals but has no effect on behavioral variables (Kahn et al., submitted). By comparison, most other institutions have employed an oral dose of 0.5 mg/kg. If a high dose of an agent is used to challenge the receptor, maximal hormone release might be induced in both normals (with presumably normal receptor function) as well as patients with panic disorder (with hypothesized hypersensitive receptors). We demonstrated increased cortisol release (Kahn et al., 1988a) as well as increased behavioral responses (Kahn et al., 1988c) in panic disorder patients as compared to major depressives and normal controls. In addition, there was a significant correlation between cortisol response and anxiety level measured one week prior to the challenge test in both patients with panic disorder and major depression. This suggests that 5-HT receptor hypersensitivity is associated with increased anxiety in any patient rather than being specific to patients with panic disorder.

These results stand in contrast to a negative finding utilizing intravenous MCPP in panic disorder by Charney et al. (1987). However, we believe the plasma MCPP levels achieved by administration of the intravenous dose employed in this study (0.1 mg/kg) were higher than those achieved by the oral dose (0.25 mg/kg) we employed. Although blood levels were not reported by Charney et al. (1987), normal controls as well as patients with panic disorder reported anxiety and panic attacks when the intravenous dose was administered. Kahn et al. (1988) noted that a dose of 0.25 mg/kg p.o of MCPP did not induce panic attacks or significant increases in anxiety in normal controls. Since 0.1 mg/kg i.v. but not 0.25 mg/kg p.o. is anxiogenic, we presume that the i.v. dose results in a higher blood level. Since, as argued above, a high dose could obscure the ability to detect hypersensitivity of the receptor, we believe this explains the disparate findings between the two studies.

In summary, recent pharmacologic as well as experimental evidence has indicated that 5-HT plays an important role in the modulation of anxiety. Employing MCPP as a challenge agent, we have provided evidence suggestive of a role for 5-HT in panic disorder. However, it is unclear whether these results will be specific to panic disorder itself or, alternatively, whether 5-HT receptor hypersentivity is related to heightened anxiety across diagnoses. We hypothesize that, as low CSF 5-HIAA has been demonstrated to be nosologically non-specific and present in individuals demonstrating dysregulation of aggression/impulse control irrespective of diagnosis, hypersensitivity of the 5-HT receptor will follow suit in being dimensionally rather than nosologically specific.

5. Psychopathological Interrelationships Between Suicide, Aggression and Anxiety

Numerous studies have demonstrated a close association between outwardly directed and self-directed aggression. Depending on the population studied, between 7% and 48% of patients with histories of violent behavior have histories of suicide attempts. Alternatively, suicidal patients also have a high incidence of outwardly directed aggression. Inamdar et al. (1982) found a very high incidence of violent (66.7%) and suicidal behavior (43.1%) exhibited in hospitalized psychotic adolescents. Both behaviors were present in 27.5% of this cohort. Similarly, Plutchik et al. (1985) found a high incidence of suicide attempts (40%) and violent behavior (42%) among psychiatric inpatients in a municipal hospital. Suicidal and violent behavior were noted concurrently in 23% of this sample.

Both inwardly and outwardly directed aggressive behaviors have been associated with an increased level of anger as well as impulsive behavior. Weissman et al. (1973) noted increased hostility as well as interpersonal difficulties in female suicide attempters as compared to non-suicidal depressed women. Plutchik et al. (1985) found high correlations between ratings of impulsivity and measures of suicide and violence risk (+0.43 and +0.63, respectively).

The relationship between anxiety and inwardly and outwardly directed aggression has been less well studied and is more controversial. We recently found evidence that trait anxiety correlates significantly with measures of suicide risk ($r=+0.62$) and violence risk ($r=+0.48$) as well as impulsivity ratings ($r=+0.48$) in psychiatric inpatients (Apter et al., 1989). Because of the high correlations between suicide and violence risk, partial correlations were performed. Although the correlation of anxiety with suicide risk remained the same, the correlation of anxiety with violence risk became negative ($r=-0.28$, $p=0.06$), just failing to reach significance. Pfeffer et al. (1983) noted a negative relationship between assaultive behavior and history of anxiety ($r=0.29$, $r<0.01$) in children. Current anxiety did not correlate significantly with assaultive behavior, however.

The relationship between inwardly and outwardly directed aggression and anxiety remains to be clarified. There is some recent evidence of a positive relationship between trait anxiety and inwardly directed aggression and, alternatively, a negative relationship between anxiety and outwardly directed aggression. It appears that anxiety may serve to either inhibit or augment aggressive acts. Alternatively, a high anxiety level may help determine the direction of the aggressive response (i.e., inward or outward) in someone predisposed towards violence. Finally, one must question whether the observed correlation between 5-HT and suicidal and/or aggressive behavior is a "real" one or whether it is a derivative of an underlying relationship between 5-HT dysfunction and anxiety. Clearly, more rigorous delineation of the psychopathological dimensions in these populations is necessary before these questions can be answered.

Discussion

In tracing the evolution of our understanding of the relationship between 5-HT and psychiatric disorders, it was noted initially that low CSF 5-HIAA levels, an indication of diminished 5-HT metabolism, are present in depressed patients. However, subsequent identification of 5-HTergic disturbances in a wide variety of other psychiatric syndromes suggested the nonspecificity of 5-HT for depressive disorders. Asberg et al. (1976) observed that low CSF 5-HIAA in a subgroup of depressed patients was associated with suicidal behavior, particularly the violent type. Subsequently, an association between low CSF 5-HIAA and suicidality was noted in patients with schizophrenia or personality disorders who did not meet criteria for a full depressive syndrome. Thus, low CSF 5-HIAA seems to be associated with a psychopathological dimension (e.g., Major Depression). Moreover, other studies suggest a relationship between low CSF 5-HIAA and outwardly-directed aggression and/or impulsivity. Thus, decreased CSF 5-HIAA appears to correlate with the psychopathological dimension of disturbed aggression regulation, regardless of direction, rather than with a specific psychiatric diagnosis.

Recent pharmacologic and experimental data indicate the presence of 5-HT disturbances in individuals with high anxiety ratings across several diagnostic entities (as manifested by low CSF 5-HIAA and abnormal results in 5-HT challenge tests). Perhaps decreased CSF 5-HIAA correlates with the dimensions of aggression regulation and anxiety in an independent manner. Alternatively, anxiety may be a common denominator in all such patients with low CSF 5-HIAA, the relationship to aggression being secondary.

Taking into account the pattern of cerebral distribution of 5-HT, the involvement of 5-HT in several psychopathological dimensions is understandable. 5-HTergic fibers originate from cell bodies situated within the midbrain dorsal and median raphe nuclei. They primarily project via the medial forebrain bundle to multiple areas of the cerebrum including the septum, amygdala, hypothalamus, hippocampus and forebrain. These cerebral structures could be involved in the regulation of different psychological functions including anxiety, mood and aggression. Therefore, one might expect that the psychological functions regulated by these areas would covary if an overall change in 5-HT metabolism or receptor function occurred. If a pathological abnormality were confined to a particular anatomical division of the 5-HT system, a specific clustering of psychological dysfunctions might be predicted. That the 5-HT system might indeed demonstrate such neuro-anatomical variation is supported by research investigating the neurotoxic effects of the drug 3,4-methylene-dioxymethamphetamine (MDMA, a ring-substituted amphetamine structurally similar to fenfluramine). This agent, more commonly known as "Ecstasy", has been widely used in humans as a drug abuse (Barnes, 1988) and has been touted as an effective adjunctive agent in insight-oriented psychotherapy, inducing a subjective experience of heightened emotional awareness and increased interpersonal communication (Greer and Tolbert, 1986). MDMA selectively damages the dorsal but not the median raphe system when administered to non-human primates (Ricaurte et al., 1988). If toxic effects similar to those observed in animals occur in humans, we would hypothesize a selective disturbance in psychological dysfunctions that parallels the anatomical distribution of 5-HT fibers emanating from the dorsal raphe nucleus.

In order to adequately apply the functional/dimensional approach in biological psychiatry, increased rigour in the quantitative and qualitative assessment of psychological functioning through improved psychometric and behavioral analyses and measurements is required. In suicide research, for example, the degree of violence of the suicidal act or the impulsive nature of the individual is often posited as the crucial variable associated with low CSF 5-HIAA. Nevertheless, these constructs remain vague and therefore subject to varying interpretations by investigators. The impressive development of psychiatry's sophistication in identification and quantification of biological parameters has not been accompanied by a similar development in the ability to reliably and validly assess the psychological functions controlled by these neural systems. Many of the psychometric rating scales routinely employed were developed several decades ago and are frequently criticized for their lack of precision. Yet they remain widely used for reasons of historical continuity.

We have been attempting to characterize and more accurately measure various aspects of suicidal and aggressive behavior. Recently, for example, we were able to demonstrate that the strength of suicidal intent does not correlate with the seriousness of the suicidal attempt (Plutchik et al., 1985). These measures are often equated in suicide research. In addition, we recently developed a structured interview for the assessment of suicide and aggression. It is expected that this instrument will provide a comprehensive clinical evaluation of this behavior.

Modern psychiatry has benefitted considerably from the revamping of diagnostic systems that has taken place in the last several decades. The introduction of widely accepted objective criteria has allowed for more rigorous testing of hypotheses. However, specific biological "markers" for these diagnostic entities have not been identified. Rather than conclude that these findings are non-specific, we believe our efforts would be better served by complementing the nosological orientation with a functional/dimensional approach. Our understanding of the role of 5-HT dysfunction in (self)aggressive behavior supports the validity of this contention.

Summary

Attempts to understand the role of 5-HT in psychiatric disorders were originally oriented towards the identification of a diagnostic-specific association (e.g., depression). This effort met with only limited success. Asberg et al. (1976) then found that low CSF 5-HIAA correlates with suicidal behavior in depressed individuals. Other authors confirmed this finding and also found CSF 5-HIAA to be low in suicide attempters lacking primary diagnoses of depressive disorders (i.e., those with personality disorders and schizophrenia). In addition, individuals with histories of outwardly directed aggression or impulsivity were noted to have decreased CSF 5-HIAA levels. Therefore, this biological abnormality appears to be associated with a particular behavioral state of disordered aggression/impulse regulation, regardless of direction.

Recent experimental data have demonstrated that 5-HT receptor abnormalities and possibly low CSF 5-HIAA occur in patients with heightened anxiety. The relationship of anxiety to aggression and suicidal behavior has received scant attention to date. As might have been predicted considering the existing biological data linking anxiety and aggression (regardless of direction) to disordered 5-HT function, we have noted significant correlations between trait anxiety and both inwardly and outwardly directed aggression. The circumstances that determine whether anxiety serves to inhibit or facilitate the expression of aggression remain to be clarified.

In order to more clearly elucidate associations between biological parameters and psychopathological conditions, we suggest the addition of a functional/dimensional approach to the already existing nosological one. We contend that strict adherence to nosological categorization has resulted in the limitation of our ability to discern these associations. Finally, increased rigour in reliably assessing psychological dysfunctions is a necessity. Although psychological constructs such as impulsivity or violence are often posited as central to 5-HTergic disturbances, they are not uniformly defined in the literature. The resulting discrepancies can only serve to obscure any underlying relationships between biological abnormalities and psychological dimensions.

REFERENCES

Agren, H. (1980). Symptom patterns in unipolar and bipolar depression correlating with monoamine metabolites in the cerebrospinal fluid: II. Suicide. *Psychiatric Research,* 3: 211-223.

Agren, H. & Niklasson, F. (1986). Suicidal potential in depression: Focus on CSF monoamine and purine metabolites. *Psychopharmacy Bulletin,* 22: 656-660.

Aloi, J.A., Insel, T.R., Mueller, E.A. & Murphy, D.L. (1984). Neuroendocrine and behavioral effects of m-chlorophenylpiperazine administration in rhesus monkeys. *Life Science,* 34: 1325-1331.

Apter, A., van Praag, H.M., Plutchik, R., Sevy, S., Korn, M.L. & Brown, S.L. (1989). *The relationship between a serotonergically linked series of psychopathological dimensions.* Submitted.

Asberg, M., Bertilsson, L., Martensson, B., Scalia-Tomba, G.-P., Thoren, P. & Traskman, L. (1984). CSF monamine metabolites in melancholia. *Acta Psychiatrica Scandinavica.* 69: 201-219.

Asberg, M., Traskman, L. & Thoran, P. (1976). 5-HIAA in the cerebrospinal fluid: A biochemical suicide predictor? *Archives of General Psychiatry, 33:* 1183-1197.

Banki, C.M. (1977). Correlation of anxiety and related symptoms with cerebrospinal fluid 5-hydroxyindoleacetic acid in depressed women. *Journal of Neurological Transmission,* 41: 135-143.

Banki, C.M. & Arato, M. (1983). Amine metabolites, neuroendocrine findings and personality dimensions as correlates of suicidal behavior. *Psychological Research,* 10: 253-261.

Banki, C.M., Molnar, G. & Vojnik, M. (1981). Cerebrospinal fluid amine metabolites, tryptophan and clinical parameters in depresion: Part 2. Psychopathological symptoms. *Journal of Affective Disorders,* 3: 91-99.

Barnes, D.M. (1988). New data intensify the agony over ecstasy. *Science,* 239: 864-866.

Berrettini, W.H., Nurnberger, J.I., Narrow, W., Simmons-Alling, S. & Garshon, E.S. (1986). Cerebrospinal fluid studies of bipolar patients with and without a history of suicide attempts. In: J. Mann and M. Stanley (Eds.): *Psychobiology of Suicidal Behavior.* New York, N.Y.; New York Academic Science, 487: 197-201.

Bioulac, B., Benezech, M., Renaud, B., Noel, B. & Roche, D. (1980). Serotonergic functions in the 47, XYY syndrome. *Biological Psychiatry,* 15: 917-923.

Bleich, A., Brown, S-L., Kahn, R. & van Praag, H.M. (1988). The role of serotonin in schizophrenia. *Biological Psychiatry,* 14(2). 297-315.

Brown, G.L., Ebert, M.H., Goyer, P.F., Jimerson, D.C., Klein, W.J., Bunney, W.E. & Goodwin, F.K. (1982). Aggression, suicide, and serotonin: Relationships to CSF amine metabolites. *American Journal of Psychiatry,* 139: 741-746.

Brown, G.L., Goodwin, F.K., Ballenger, J.C., Goyer, P.F. & Major, L.F.(1979). Aggression in humans correlates with cerebrospinal fluid amine metabolite. *Psychiatric Research*, 1: 131-139.

Ceulemans, D.L.S., Hoppenbrouwers, M.L.J.A., Gelders, Y.G. & Reyntjens, A.J.M. (1985). The influence of ritanserin, a serotonin antagonist, in anxiety disorders: A double-blind placebo controlled study versus lorazepam. *Pharmacopsychiatric*, 18:303-305.

Charney, D.S., Woods, S.W., Goodman, W.K. & Heninger, G.R. (1987). Serotonin function in anxiety. II: Effects of the serotonin agonist MCPP in panic disorder patients and healthy subjects. *Psychopharmacy*, 92: 14-24.

Coccaro, E.F., Siever, L.J., Klar, H.M., Maurer, G., Cochrane, K., Cooper, T.B., Mohs, R.C. & Davis, K.L. (1989). Serotonergic studies in patients with affective and personality disorders: Correlates with suicidal and impulsive aggressive behavior. *Archives of General Psychiatry*, 46: 587-599.

Boer den, J.A., Westenberg, H.G.M., Kamerbeck, W.D.J., Verhoeven, V.M.A. & Kahn, R.S. (1987). Effect of serotonin uptake inhibitors in anxiety disorders; a double-blind comparison of clomipramine and fluvoxamine. *International Journal of Clinical Psychopharmacy*, 2: 21-32.

Boer den, J.A. & Westenberg, H.G.M. (1988). Effect of a serotonin and noradrenaline uptake inhibitor in panic disorders; a double-blind comparative study with fluvoxamine and maprotiline. *International Journal of Clinical Psychopharmacy*, 3: 59-74.

Eichelman, B. (1987). Neurochemical and psychopharmacologic aspects of aggressive behavior. In: H. Meltzer (Ed.). *Psychopharmacology: The Third Generation of Progress.* New York, Raven Press.

Fontaine, R. & Chouinard, G. (1986). An open trial of fluoxetine in the treatment of obsessive-compulsive disorder. *Journal of Clinical Psychopharmacology*, 6(2).98-100.

Gardner, C.R. (1988). Potential use of drugs modulating 5-HT activity in the treatment of anxiety. *General Pharmacology,* 19(3). 347-356.

Gorman, J.M., Liebowitz, M.R., Fyer, A.J., Goetz, D., Campeas, R.B., Fyer, M.R., Davies, S.O. & Klein, D. (1987). An open trial of fluoxetine in the treatment of panic attacks. *Journal of Clinical Psychopharmacology*, 7(5). 329-334.

Greer, G. & Tolbert, R. (1986). Subjective reports of the effects of MDMA in a clinical setting. *Journal of Psychoactive Drugs*, 18: 319-327.

Hamik, A. & Peroutka, S.J. (1989). 1-(m-Chlorophenyl)piperazine (mCPP) interactions with neurotransmitter receptors in human brain. *Biological Psychiatry,* 25: 569-575.

Inamdar, S.C., Lewis, D.O., Siomopoulos, G., Shanok, S.S. & Lamela, M. (1982). Violent and suicidal behavior in psychotic adolescents. *American Journal of Psychiatry,* 139: 932-935.

Insel, T.R., Mueller, E.A., Alterman, I., Linnoila, M. & Murphy, D.L. (1985). Obsessive-compulsive disorder and serotonin: Is there a connection? *Biological Psychiatry,* 20: 1174-1188.

Invernizzi, R., Berettera, C., Garattini, S. & Samanin, R. (1986). D- and L-isomers of fenfluramine differ markedly in their interaction with brain and catecholamines in the rat. *European Journal of Pharmacology*, 20: 9-15.

Kahn, R.S., Westenberg, H.G.M., Verhoeven, W.M.A., Gispen-de Wied, C.C. & Kamerbeek, W.D.J. (1987). Effect of a serotonin precursor and uptake inhibitor in anxiety disorders; a double-blind comparison of 5-hydroxytryptophan, clomipramine and placebo. *International Clinical Psychopharmacology*, 2: 33-45.

Kahn, R.S., Asnis, G.M., Wetzler, S. & van Praag, H.M. (1988a). Neuro-endocrine evidence for serotonin receptor hypersensitivity in panic disorder. *Psychopharmacology*, 96: 360-364.

Kahn, R.S., van Praag, H.M., Wetzler, S., Asnis, G.M. & Barr, G. (1988b). Serotonin and anxiety revisited. *Biological Psychiatry*, 23: 189-208.

Kahn, R.S., Wetzler, S., Asnis, G.M., Suckow, R.F. & van Praag, H.M. (Submitted).*The effects of m-chlorophenylpiperazine in normal subjects: A dose response study.*

Kahn, R.S., Wetzler, S., van Praag, H.M., Asnis, G.M. & Strauman, T. (1988c). Behavioral indications for serotonin receptor hypersensitivity in panic disorder. *Psychiatry Research*, 25: 101-104.

Kilpatrick, G.J., Jones, B.J. & Tyers, M.B. (1987). Identification and distribution of 5-HT3 receptors in rat brain using radioligand binding. *Nature*, 330: 746-748.

Lidberg, L., Asberg, M. & Sundqvuist-Stensman, U.B. (1984). 5-Hydroxyindoleacetic acid in attempted suicides who have killed their children. *Lancet* ii: 928.

Lidberg, L., Tuck, J.R., Asberg, M., Scalia-Tomba, G.P. & Bertilsson, L. (1985). Homicide, suicide and CSF 5-HIAA. *Acta Psychiatrica Scandinavica*, 71: 230-236.

Linnoila, M., Virkkunen, M., Scheinin, M., Nuutila, A., Rimon, R. & Goodwin, F.K. (1983). Low carebrospinal fluid 5-hydroxyindoleacetic acid concentration differentiates impulsive from nonimpulsive violent behavior. *Life Science*, 33: 2609-2614.

Lopez-Ibor, J.J., Jeronimo, S-R. & Perez de los Cobos, J.C. (1985). Biological correlations of suicide and aggressivity in major depressions (with melancholia). 5-Hydroxyindoleacetic acid and cortisol in cerebral spinal fluid, dexamethasone suppression test and therapeutic response to 5 hydroxytryp-tophan. *Neuropsychobiology*, 14: 67-74.

Meltzer, H.Y., Perline, R., Tricou, B.J., Lowy, M.T. & Robertson, A. (1984). Effect of 5-hydroxyptryptophan on serum cortisol levels in major affective disorders, II:Relation to suicide, psychosis, and depressive symptoms. *Archives of General Psychiatry*, 41: 379-387.

Mueller, E.A., Murphy, D.L. & Sunderland, T. (1986). Neuroendocrine effects of m-chlorophenylpiperazine, a serotonin agonist, in humans. *Journal of Clinical Endocrinology Metab.*, 61: 1-6.

Ninan, P.T., van Kammen, D.P., Scheinin, M., Linnoila, M., Bunney, W.E. & Goodwin, F.K. (1984). CSF 5-hydroxynindoleacetic acid levels in suicidal schizophranic patients. *American Journal of Psychiatry*, 141(4). 566-569.

Olivier, B., Mos, J., Heyden, J.v.d., Schipper, J., Tulp, M., Berkelmans, M. & Bevan, P. (1987). Serotonergic modulation of agonistic behavior. In: B. Olivier, J. Mos & P.F. Brain (Eds.). *Ethopharmacology of Agonistic Behavior in Animals and Humans*. Dordrecht: Martinus Nijhoff Publishers.

Oreland, L., Wiberg, A., Asberg, M., Traskman, L., Sjostrand, L., Thoren, P., Bertilsson, L. & Tybring, G. (1981). Platelet MAO activity and monoamine metabolites in cerebrospinal fluid in depressed and suicidal patients and in healthy controls. *Psychiatric Research*, 4: 21-29.

Ortiz, A., Pohl, R. & Gershon, S. (1987). Azaspirodecanediones in generalized anxiety disorder: buspirone. *Journal of Affective Disorder*, 13: 131-143.

Palaniappan, V., Ramachandran, V. & Somasundaram, O. (1983). Suicidal ideation and biogenic amines in depression. *Indian Journal of Psychiatry*, 25(4). 286-292.

Pfeffer, C.R., Plutchik, R. & Mizruchi, M. (1983). Predictors of assaultiveness in latency age children. *American Journal of Psychiatry*, 140(1). 31-35.

Pickar, D., Roy, A., Breiser, A., Doran, A., Wolkowitz, O., Colison, J. & Agren, H. (1986). Suicide and aggression in schizophrenia: Neurobiologic correlates. In: J. Mann and M. Stanely (Eds.); *Psychobiology of Suicidal Behavior*. New York, N.Y.: New York Academic Science, 487: 189-196.

Plutchik, R., van Praag, H.M. & Conte, H. (1985). Suicide and violence risk in psychiatric patients. *Biological Psychiatry*, 20: 761-763.

Redmond, D.E., Katz, M.M., Maas, J.W., Swann, A., Casper, R. & Davis, J.M. (1986). Cerebrospinal fluid amine metabolites: Relationships with behavioral measurements in depressed manic and healthy control subjects. *Archives of General Psychiatry*, 43: 938-947.

Ricaurte, G.A., Forno, L.S., Wilson, M.A., DeLanney, L.E., Irwin, I., Molliver, M.E. & Langston, J.W. (1988). 3,4-Methylenedioxymethamphetamine selectively damages central serotonergic neurons in nonhuman primates. *Journal of American Medical Association*, 260(1). 51-55.

Roy, A., Adinoff, B. & Linnoila, M. (1988). Acting out hostility in normal volunteers: Negative correlation with levels of 5-HIAA in cerebrospinal fluid. *Psychiatric Research*, 24: 187-194.

Roy, A., Agren, H., Pickar, D., Linnoila, M., Doran, A.R., Cutler, N.R. & Paul, S.M. (1986). Reduced CSF concentrations of homovanillic acid to 5-hydroxyindoleacetic acid ratios in depressed patients: relationships to suicidal behavior and dexamethasone nonsuppression. *American Journal of Psychiatry*, 143: 1539-1545.

Roy, A., DeJong, J. & Linnoila, M. (1989). Cerebrospinal fluid monoamine metabolites and suicidal behavior in depressed patients. *Archives of General Psychiatry*, 46: 609-612.

Roy, A., Ninan, P., Mazonson, A., Pickar, D., van Kammen, D., Linnoila, M. & Paul, S.M. (1985). CSF monoamine metabolites in chronic schizophrenic patients who attempt suicide. *Psychological Medicine*, 15: 335-340.

Roy-Byrne, P., Post, R., Rubinow, D., Linnoila, M., Savard, R. & Davis, D. (1983). CSF 5-HIAA and personal and family history of suicide in affectively ill patients: A negative study. *Psychiatric Research*, 10: 263-274.

Rydin, E., Schalling, D. & Asberg, M. (1982). Rorschach ratings in depressed and suicidal patients with low levels of 5-hydroxyindoleacetic acid in cerebrospinal fluid. *Psychological Research*, 7: 229-243.

Secunda, S.K., Cross, C.K., Koslow, S., Katz, M.M., Kocsis, J., Maas, J.W. & Landis, H. (1986). Biochemistry and suicidal behavior in depressed patients. *Biological Psychiatry*, 21: 756-767.

Sills, M.A., Wolfe, B.A. & Frazer, A. (1984). Determination of selective and nonselective compounds for the 5-HT1A and 5-HT1B receptor subtypes in rat frontal cortex. *Journal of Pharmacology Exp. Therapy,* 231(3). 480-387.

Taylor, D.P., Eison, M.S., Riblet, L.A. & Vandermaelen, C.P. (1985). Pharmacological and clinical effects of buspirone. *Pharmacology Biochemical Behavior,* 23: 687-694.

Thoren, P., Asberg, M., Bertilsson, L., Mellstrom, B., Sjoqvist, F. & Traskman, L. (1980). Clomipramine treatment of obsessive compulsive disorder. II. Biochemical aspects. *Archives of General Psychiatry,* 37: 1289-1294.

Traskman, L., Asberg, M., Bertilsson, L. & Sjostrand, L. (1981). Monoamine metabolites in CSF and suicidal behavior. *Archives of General Psychology,* 38: 631-636.

Traskman, L., Asberg, M., Bertilsson, L. & Thoren, P. (1984). CSF monamine metabolites of depressed patients during illness and after recovery. *Acta Psychiatrica Scandinavica,* 69: 333-342.

Van Kammen (1987). 5-HT, a neurotransmitter for all seasons? *Biological Psychiatry,* 22: 1-3.

Van Praag, H.M. (1982). Depression, suicide and the metabolism of serotonin in the brain. *Journal of Affective Disorder,* 4: 275-290.

Van Praag, H.M. (1983). CSF 5-HIAA and suicide in non-depressed schizophrenics. Lancet, II: 977-978.

Van Praag, H.M. (1985). Indoleamines in affective disorder and suicide. In: A. Villeneuve (Ed.): Brain Neurotransmitters and Psychiatry. *Acta Pharmaceuticals* Canada, Ltd. .

Van Praag, H.M. (1986). (Auto)aggression and CSF 5-HIAA in depression and schizophrenia. *Psychopharmaca Bulletin*, 22(3). 669-673.

Van Praag, H.M. (1988). Serotonergic mechanisms and suicidal behavior. *Psychiatry and Psychobiology*, 3: 335-346.

Van Praag, H.M., Kahn, R.S., Asnis, G.M., Wetzler, S., Brown, S.L., Bleich, A. & Korn, M.L. (1987). Denosologization of biological psychiatry or the specificity of 5HT disturbances in psychiatric disorders. *Journal of Affective Disorder*, 13: 1-8.

Van Praag, H.M., Kahn, R., Asnis, G.M., Wetzler, S., Brown, S., Bleich, A. & Korn, M. (1988). Beyond nosology in biological psychiatry. 5-HT disturbances in mood, aggression and anxiety disorders. In: M. Briley & J.Fillion (Eds.): *New Concepts in Depression.* London: Mcmillan Press.

Van Praag, H.M., Korf, J., Lakke, J.P.W.F. & Schut, T. (1975). Dopamine metabolism in depression, psychoses and parkinson's disease: The problem of the specificity of biological variables in behavior disorders. *Psychological Medicine,* 5: 138-146.

Van Praag, H.M., Korf, J. & Puite, J. (1970). 5-Hydroxyindoleacetic acid levels in the cerebrospinal fluid of depressive patients treated with probenecid. *Nature,* 225: 1259-1260.

Van Praag, H.M., Korf, J. & Schut, D. (1973). Cerebral monoamines and depression: An investigation with the probenecid technique. *Archives of General Psychiatry,* 28: 827-831.

Van Praag, H.M. & Leijnse, B. (1965). Neubewertung des dyndroms. Skizze einer funktionellen pathologie. *Psychiatrie, Neurologie, Neurochirurgie*, 68: 50-56.

Van Praag, H.M., Lemus, C. & Kahn, R. (1987). Hormonal probes of central serotonergic activity. Do they really exist? *Biological Psychiatry*, 22: 86-98.

Van Praag, H.M. & Plutchik, R. (1985). An empirical study on the cathartic effect of attempted suicide. *Psychiatry Research*, 16: 123.

Van Praag, H.M., Uleman, A.M. & Spitz, J.C. (1965). The vital syndrome interview. A structured standard interview for the recognition and registration of the vital depressive symptom complex. *Psychiatrie, Neurologie, Neurochirurgie*, 68: 329-346.

Vestergaard, P., Sorensen, T., Hoppe, E., Rafaelsen, O.J., Yates, C.M. & Nicolaou, N. (1978). Biogenic amine metabolites in cerebrospinal fluid of patients with affective disorders. *Acta Psychiatrica Scandinavica*, 58: 88-96.

Virkkunen, M., Nuutila, A., Goodwin, F.K. & Linnoila, M. (1987). Cerebrospinal fluid monamine metabolite levels in male arsonists. *Archives of General Psychiatry*, 44: 241-247.

Virkkunen, M., DeJong, J., Bartko, J., Goodwin, F.K. & Linnoila, M. (1989a). Relationship of psychobiological variables to recidivism in violent offenders and impulsive fire setters. *Archives of General Psychiatry*, 46: 600-603.

Virkkunen, M., DeJong, J., Bartko, J. & Linnoila, M. (1989b). Psychobiological concomitants of history of suicide attempts among violent offenders and impulsive fire setters. *Archives of General Psychiatry*, 46: 604-606.

Weissman, M., Fox, K. & Klerman, G.L. (1973). Hostility and depression associated with suicide attempts. *American Journal of Psychiatry*, 130: 450-455.

Glossary of terms

Adrenergic receptor;
A receptor located on cell membranes that binds the catecholamine noradrenaline. There are several subtypes of receptors which have been identified including alpha-1, alpha-2 and beta receptors which are located in different anatomical areas and have varying physiological effects.

Blood glucose nadir;
The lowest level of blood glucose.

CNS monoamines;
Neurotransmittors having only one amino group. Included in this class aredopamine, norepinephrine and serotonine.

Cortisol;
A steroid hormone which is secreted by adrenal cortex. The synthesis and releases of this hormone is regulated by a pituitary peptide which is partly under serotonergic control.

Dopamine (DA);
A monoamine neurotransmitter with limbic as well as stratial connections.

Fenfluramine;
A ring-substituted amphetamine which releases and blocks the re-uptake of serotonin receptors.

Homovanillic acid (HVA);
The primary metabolite or breakdown product of dopamine. Measurement of this substance in CFS provides an indication of CNS dopamine metabolism.

5-hydroxyindoleactetic acid (5-HIAA);
The primary metabolite or breakdown product of serotonin. Measurement of this substance in CSF provides an indication of CNS serotonin metabolism.

5-hydroxytryptophan (5-HTP);
The direct precursor of serotonin.

L-isomer;
Molecules may exist in several forms and these forms may be classified according to various physical characteristics. One means of classification is based on the tendency of molecule to rotate light to the left (i.e. L-isomer) or right (i.e. D-isomer).

M-chlorophenylpiperazine (MCPP);
A metabolite of antidepressant trazodone and a 5-HT receptor antagonist. This agent stimulates the release of several hormones including prolactine and cortisol and is utilized as a neuroendocrine challenge agent.

3-methoxy-4-hydroxyphenylglycol (MHPG);
The primary metabolite or breakdown product of noradrenaline. Measurement of this substance in CSF provides an indication of CNS noradrenaline metabolism.

3,4-methylene-dioxymethamphetamine (MDMA);
This chemical is a ring-substituted amphetamine structurally similar to fenfluramine. It is more commonly known as "Ecstasy" and has been used as a drug of abuse as well as an adjunctive agent in insight-oriented psychotherapy. MDMA selectively damages the dorsal but not the medianraphe system when administered to non-human primates.

Noradrenaline (NA);
This monoamine acts on many areas of the CNS and is thought to be involved in the pathogenesis of depression and anxiety.

Prolactine;
A pituitary hormone which is partially regulated by serotonin.

Radioligand binding studies;
A laboratory technique which allows the investigator to characterize and localize receptors.

Receptor;
A molecule usually attached to the cell membrane which then produces intracellular effects after binding to another molecule (i.e., ligand).

Serotonin (5-hydroxytryptamine or 5-HT);
This indoleamine originates from the raphe nuclei and acts on many areas of the limbic system and neocortex. It has been implicated in the pathogenesis of depression, anxiety, suicide and violence.
Serotonin stimulates several hypothalamic-pituitary hormones including cortisol and prolactin.

Serotonergic (5-HTergic) hypothesis;
The hypothesis that a particular syndrome is caused by an underlying disturbance in serotonergic function.

Serotonin receptor;
A molecule located on cell membranes which is stimulated by serotonin. There are several subtypes of receptors which have been identified including 5-HT-1A, 5-HT-2 etc., which are located in different anatomical areas and have varying physiological effects.

Schedule of Affective Disorders and Schizophrenia (SADS);
A widely used semi-structured interview which allows the researcher to reliably diagnose Psychiatric syndromes.

Tryptophan;
An essential amino acid which is the dietary precursor for serotonin.

XYY chromosomal abnormality;
A genetic abnormality in males often resulting in behavioral abnormalities and a tendency to be tall in stature. There is an increased incidence of this abnormality in prison population.

Clinical Applications of Biological Aspects of Suicide

J.A. MOTTO

Introduction

New information continues to emerge at a steady pace in most aspects of the behavioral sciences, but the rate at which new biological data have been reported in recent years has been bewildering. Not only has a flood of hard-science observations been presented to the clinician, but most of it has been couched in the not-so-familiar languages of psychopharmacology, neurochemistry, neuroanatomy and psycho-endocrinology. Even a superficial understanding of current reports in many leading psychiatric journals requires some familiarity with such concepts as adrenergic, serotonergic, and dopaminergic systems and their metabolites; agonists, antagonists and ligands; and chlorine and calcium channels and their significance.

The challenge to the clinician has entailed both the effort to remain abreast of this rapidly growing body of technical information and, more important, to determine its usefulness in the everyday task of patient evaluation, treatment and management. The present discussion addresses this question of the practical application of suicide-related biological observations at our present state of knowledge.

Background

The idea of biochemical measures as predictors of behavior has threaded through the history of modern psychiatry. The first with clear implications for suicide was probably the "anger in—anger out" hypothesis of Funkenstein et al. (1954), who presented evidence that a high urinary norepinephrine-to-epinephrine ratio is related to a tendency to turn anger outward (assaultiveness), and low ratio to directing anger inward (depression and self-destructiveness).

More specific indicators of suicide risk subsequently emerged from the scrutiny of biologic compounds in the course of studying the biology of depression. In prospective studies of depressed inpatients, those subjects who were found to have committed suicide after discharge were reviewed to determine if their previously observed levels of various biological measures differed significantly from those of subjects who had survived. This serendipitous sequence was first reported by Bunney and Fawcett (1965), who observed elevated 17-hydroxycorticosteroids in the urine of the suicides in their sample of depressed patients studied at the National Institute of Mental Health. Increasing interest in this approach was evident through the 1970s, and by the end of the next decade biologic observations related to suicide had increased from a few scattered reports to a relative torrent of information.

Several issues cloud the clinical scene. One is that some observations appear so esoteric as to have a remote, if any, specificity for suicide at this time. A second is that much available data regarding suicide is of great interest to researchers, and thus gets to the media, but has no present relevance to clinical practice. Third, pertinent studies have focused on correlates of a wide array of suicide-related phenomena, such as a past history of suicide attempts or suicidal ideas, a tendency toward violence, or a future suicide attempt or complete suicide by means other than drug ingestion or a single wrist cut. The range of possible implications of various biological markers had led clinicians outside the research arena to take a generally watchful but passive stance as regards the application of these observations to clinical work. The ever present question, of course, is at what point is it appropriate to change that stance to a more active use of biological measures in the service of suicide prevention and optimal clinical care.

Biological Measures with Potential Clinical Use

5-Hydroxyindoleacetic Acid (5-HIAA) in the cerebrospinal fluid (CSF)

Though not the first potential biological marker of suicide risk to be identified, CSF 5-HIAA has completely dominated the field during the past decade both in research reports and in popular interest. Its role as the leading candidate over this period stemmed from two considerations. First, it is a major metabolite of the neurotransmitter serotonin (5-hydroxytryptamine, 5-HT), which has played a prominent role in current studies of the biology of depression. It was in the course of such a study that Asberg et al. (1976) unexpectedly found that depressed subjects with low concentrations of CSF 5-HIAA made more suicide attempts than other depressed subjects. The traditional association of depressive and suicidal states give this connection between altered serotonin turnover and suicidal behavior was seen as a "formidable question" because of our limited knowledge of serotonergic function.

Second, the previously observed association (in experimental animals) of reduced serotonin synthesis with increased sensitivity to pain and increased aggressive behavior became an immediate focus of attention. Asberg and her co-workers pointed out that the observed low CSF 5-HIAA may not be directly related to depression and suicidal behavior, but rather an epiphenomenon to other, more important processes, and that its clinical value as an indicator of suicide potential remained to be proven. In a subsequent support to the initial observations about low CSF 5-HIAA and suicidal behavior, the investigators reiterate that routine 5-HIAA determinations to assist the evaluation of suicide would be premature.

In the past decade a steady flow of reports has provided additional findings consistent with the earlier results. These have extended the scope of inquiry beyond adult depressed inpatients to samples of such populations as homicide offenders (Lindberg, 1985), suicidal schizophrenic patients (Ninan et al., 1984), brain tissue of completed suicides (Arora & Meltzer, 1989; Arango et al., 1990), repeated suicide attempters (Roy et al., 1989a), elderly suicide attempters (Jones et al., 1990), alcoholic suicide attempters (Roy et al., 1990), and inpatients with mixed diagnoses (Apter et al., 1990). They represent studies of depression from research centers around the world, including Sweden (Traskman et al., 1981), the Netherlands (Van Praag, 1982), England (Montgomery & Montgomery, 1982), India (Palaniappan et al., 1983), Hungary (Banki et al., 1984), and Spain (Lopez-Ibor et al., 1985). The findings with few exceptions are consistent with the initial observations of lower CSF 5-HIAA in persons who exhibit suicidal, homicidal, assaultive, aggressive or impulsive behaviors.

In spite of the number and agreement of those findings, no recommendation for the clinical application of CSF 5-HIAA levels has been made. Asberg (1989) points out that while such determinations might help in the assessment of suicide risk, that there are problems in using them in a clinical setting. Firstly, the range of values is such that a large number of "false positives" would be found. Second, there are so many factors that influence CSF concentrations of 5-HIAA (age, sex, height, physical illness, drug treatment, diet, technical aspects of obtaining and analyzing the CSF) that the spinal tap procedure would have to be standardized "to an extent that is rarely practical in a busy clinic". Third, overnight hospitalization is required, and finally, the patient must have been off all antidepressant and neuroleptic drugs or lithium for several weeks before the spinal tap. In spite of these points, Asberg allows that routine taps may nevertheless be a real help in clinical management, while acknowledging that there is a need for further prospective studies.

It seems clear that while the determination of CSF 5-HIAA remains an intriguing window for the observation of serotonin metabolism in a research setting, it is not yet a usable clinical tool as regards suicide risk assessment. Detailed reviews of this approach have been provided by Van Praag (1986), Asberg (1989), Ricci and Wellman (1990), and Brown and Linnoila (1990).

Tritiated Imipramine binding

The complexities of obtaining spinal fluid to measure serotonin activity in the brain makes it desirable to find a simpler method. Since the receptor sites of blood platelets and of brain tissue possess virtually identical binding characteristics, and since there is evidence that tritiated imipramine binding is associated with the neuronal uptake mechanism for serotonin, it could be predicted that the platelets of depressed persons would show decreased binding sites for this compound. Extending this to suicidal states, Stanley, Virgilio and Gershon (1982) demonstrated that the brain tissue of persons who had committed suicide showed reduced binding as compared with brains of persons who died of other causes. The implied marker for suicide risk, therefore, would be a determination of tritiated imipramine binding in platelets in the peripheral blood as an indicator of the level of serotonin transmission activity in the brain. A lower level would imply a higher suicide risk. The simplicity of such a blood test would certainly be appealing if a valid cutoff point could be established. Recent work, however, (Gross-Isseroff, Israeli, & Biegon, 1989) suggests that different areas of the brain show different changes in imipramine binding in persons who committed suicide, and that the correspondence between brain and platelets is still inconclusive (DeLeo & Marazziti, 1988). Clinical application of this biological approach to understanding suicide is not yet at hand.

Urinary 17-Hydroxycorticosteroids

Urinary 17-hydroxycorticosteroids (17-OHCS) provided the first model for the identification of biological markers for suicide (Bunney & Fawcett, 1965). When 3 of 36 depressed research subjects committed suicide during or shortly after a period of inpatient study and treatment, it was recognized that their levels of urinary 17-hydroxycorticosteroids had been among the highest in the entire sample. Of special clinical interest was the fact that twice daily estimates of suicide risk had ranked all three of these subjects below the group mean. The findings were interpreted cautiously with the postulate that 17-OHCS levels might reflect the intensity of psychic pain in a certain subgroup of depressed patients with limited psychological defenses, pointing out that a low 17-OHCS level in other patients (less than 9mg/24hr for women, and less than 14mg/24hr for men) should offer no reassurance regarding suicide.

A second report four years later (Bunney et al., 1969) provided an enlarged sample and added the refinement of "long-term" and "short-term" patterns of elevated 17-OHCS. The investigators reiterated that low levels should not be considered an indication of low suicide risk, and commented that the clinical significance of their data remained uncertain. Meanwhile, a few scattered contrary reports appeared, based—as was the original report—on very small samples, and pointing out the confounding effects of body size, psychotropic drugs, and the difficulty of obtaining a complete 24-hour urine sample.

The simplicity and logic of measuring a stress-related compound by a non-invasive technique retains its early appeal, but replication studies have not been forthcoming, and the use of urinary 17-OHCS determinations has not been widely adopted in the clinical setting.

Urinary Norepinephrine-to-Epinephrine ratio

The prospect of using urinary compounds for suicide risk assessment received renewed interest with an investigation of the hypothesis that a high urinary norepinephrine-to-epinephrine ratio is indicative of a tendency to turn anger outward, and a low ratio to directing it inward (Ostroff et al., 1982). This revived an idea explored much earlier in a widely publicized laboratory experiment (Funkenstein, King, & Drolette, 1954). The new report was prompted by finding a low ratio in two suicides and one serious suicide attempter among 22 male research subjects, which was consistent with the anticipation that a low ratio would suggest risk of suicide and a high ratio would indicate risk of assault. Earlier findings consistent with this had been reported by Woodman (1979), who found a positive relationship between a consistently high ratio and assaultiveness in prison inmates. A later effort to demonstrate a low ratio in persons with a history of suicide attempt produced statistically significant differences in mean values, but the overlap was so great that the clinical usefulness of the observation is questionable (Ostroff et al., 1985).

Roy et al. (1989a) examined the relationship of suicidal behavior and noradrenergic activity, including norepinephrine concentration, as reflected by indices in the cerebrospinal fluid and blood plasma as well as in urine. A lower level of noradrenergic function in suicidal subjects would support the concept of a low norepinephrine-to-epinephrine ratio as a marker for suicide. No consistent pattern was found, which was interpreted as indicating that the noradrenergic system is probably not a major determinant of suicidal behavior in depressed patients.

In spite of the lack of confirmation that low norepinephrine or a low norepinephrine-to-epinephrine ratio are related to suicide, the dynamic appeal of an "anger in" versus "anger out" measurement is still intriguing. Its clinical role, however, is yet to be demonstrated.

Cortisol levels in plasma and cerebrospinal fluid

Elevated levels of cortisol have long been observed in states of depression and in conditions of increased psychological or physical arousal. Krieger (1974) first focused attention on cortisol as a possible indicator of suicide risk by pointing out that this precursor of 17-OHCS was not only simpler to determine than its urinary metabolite, but would more accurately reflect the intensity of emotional distress experienced by the subject. He noted that 13 patients who committed suicide within two years of the test had a significantly higher mean serum cortisol level (21.08 ìg%) than did 39 suicide-risk matched patients who did not commit suicide (16.5 ìg%). He postulated an elevated "set point" in the hypothalamus of some individuals, resulting from genetic influence or from early emotional stress, that leads to a higher than normal basal level of cortisol. This could make the person more vulnerable to suicide in the presence of added stress in their lives. He pointed out further that various clinical states involving similar steroids, such as Cushing's disease or treatment with steroid medications, are known to be associated with depressive and suicidal states.

Krieger (1975) later offered a clear clinical application of the test for serum cortisol concentration by suggesting that if a patient recognized to be at risk for suicide has a level above 20 ìg%, in the absence of other causes for such a high level, special suicide prevention measures were indicated. These would include more protective precautions, more frequent therapist contact, and prolonged aftercare following discharge. Trials of the usefulness of this risk indicator have not been reported, to our knowledge, though a recent observation by Meltzer and Lowy (1989) showed that while 18 suicide attempters had a higher mean serum cortisol (14.3 ± ìg%), than 76 non-attempters (11.6 ì% ± 4.8 ì%), the 20.0 ìg% cut-off point (as suggested by Krieger) did not effectively differentiate the two samples.

Most of the attention to serum cortisol has been in the use of the dexamethasone suppression test (DST) for the diagnosis of depression. Very widely used 5-10 years ago, questions of validity have gradually led to its relatively infrequent use at present. Its potential value as a suicide risk indicator has appeared to be mixed at best, as noted in reviews by Motto (1986) and Meltzer and Lowy (1989).

We have probably not heard the last of cortisol as a marker of suicide risk, but it does not yet have a place in our clinical armamentarium.

Homovannillic Acid (HVA) and 3-Methoxy-4-Hydroxyphenolglycol (MPHG)

The examination of neurotransmitters as possible indicators of suicide risk has included, in addition to serotonin, dopamine and its metabolite homovanillic acid, and norepinephrine and its metabolite 3-methoxy-4-hydroxyphenologlycol. Numerous efforts to relate these compounds to suicidal thinking or behavior have thus far been relatively unproductive, hence their somewhat low visibility in the suicide prevention literature. They are included here for the sake of completeness.

Roy et al. (1986) pointed out that in a sample of depressed patients with a prior suicide attempt, three of the four who committed suicide within one year of evaluation were melancholic subjects who had shown a CSF-HVA level below 75 pmol/ml and were DST nonsuppressors. Similarly, in a sample of elderly depressed patients, those who attempted suicide showed significantly lower CSF 5-HIAA and HVA than those who had not made a suicide attempt (Jones et al., 1990). This is consistent with the observation of Asberg (1989) that in studies relating CSF metabolites to personality features of high vitality, self-reported impulsivity and psychopathy-related features, correlations with HVA tend to parallel those with 5-HIAA, though they are weaker.

In an effort to relate suicidal behavior, depression and noradrenergic function, Roy et al. (1989a) found no consistent pattern of norepinephrine or MHPG-levels in urine, CSF or plasma in depressed patients who had attempted suicide. In another attempt to find suicide-related characteristics in a specific clinical subgroup, Roy et al. (1990) examined alcoholic patients who had attempted suicide. They found no significant differences between attempters, non-attempters, or normal controls as measured by CSF 5-HIAA, HVA, or MHPG.

Though still of much theoretical interest, it seems clear that at this point practical application of what is known of HVA and MHPG is not yet feasible.

Thyroid-Stimulating Hormone (TSH) response to Thyrotropin-Releasing Hormone (TRH)

The study of the hypothalamic-pituitary-adrenal (HPA) axis in suicidal behavior was recapitulated with the hypothalamic-pituitary-thyroid (HPT) axis, in that dysregulation of the latter was initially suggested as a marker for depression. Specifically, evidence was found of a reduced response of thyroid-stimulating hormone, from the anterior pituitary, to thyrotropin-releasing hormone from the hypothalamus in depressed subjects.

The next step, encountering suicides in a sample of depressed subjects whose TSH response to TRH had previously been determined, was reported from Brussels by Linkowski et al. (1983). They observed that all four suicides in a 5-year follow-up of 51 depressed women had shown an absence of TSH response (less than one microunit/ml) when first evaluated, with three natural deaths all showing greater responses than the suicides. Recognizing that this might provide a biological indicator of high suicide risk in depressed female patients, an expanded sample was subsequently reported to show that in a mean follow-up of 8 years, five of seven suicides had very low TSH responses compared with the non-suicidal deaths and controls (Linkowsky et al., 1984). Even among suicide attempters, subjects with a history of "violent" suicide attempts showed significantly lower responses than those with no history of suicidal behavior. In view of a decreased TSH response in normal men over 40, the test was suggested only for depressed women.

Efforts to replicate these observations have led to inconsistent and contradictory findings, though they have primarily involved suicide attempts (Banki et al., 1984; Banki, 1985; Van Praag & Plutchik, 1984; Kjellman et al., 1985) and suicide ideation (Maes et al., 1989) rather than completed suicides. Though the test is relatively simple and inexpensive, it has not been widely reported in either clinical or research settings, so we are still awaiting clarifying information and definitive guidelines for its use.

It seems that while enormous strides have been made in biochemical knowledge, measurement of biological compounds, and technological resources, the underlying concepts of physical-emotional-behavioral interplay is fairly constant. In this regard, a psychiatric study of seven depressed women that was carried out 60 years ago, noted a tendency toward low basal metabolic rates in the sample. This led to the comment that "organotherapy" with thyroid and -pituitary compounds "obviously suggests itself" (Bowman & Bender, 1932). It seems that the puzzling role of the hypothalamic-pituitary-thyroid axis in depression and its complications is not a new challenge to the researcher.

Cerebrospinal Fluid Corticotropin-Releasing Factor (CRF)

In a persistent scrutiny of the role of the hypothalamic-pituitary-adrenal axis in completed suicide, Arato et al. (1986) in Budapest have provided a promising lead. Using a "new research tool in the investigation of completed suicides", specifically, post mortem CSF analyses, they found no differences between suicides and controls in CSF cortisol, reflecting adrenal activity, or in CSF adrenocorticotrophic hormone (ACTH), reflecting pituitary activity. Pursuing this one step further, they subsequently did find evidence of increased hypothalamic stimulation of the pituitary in the form of increased CRF levels in the CSF of suicide victims (Arato et al., 1989). This is consistent with findings in depressed patients, who also show elevated CSF CRF concentrations (Banki et al., 1987; Roy et al., 1987). It is also consistent with the finding of decreased CRF receptor density in the frontal cortex of suicide victims, attributed to the down-regulation of CRF binding sites induced by CRF hypersecretion by the hypothalamus (Nemeroff et al., 1988).

The hypothesis is advanced that severe, prolonged stress could lead to a breakdown of psychological defenses and eventually to suicide. In that case, the measurement of CRF would be a better indicator of stress than either ACTH or cortisol, as secondary changes at the pituitary and adrenal levels could conceal any hyperactivity of the HPA axis. The investigators assume, however, that the elevated CRF concentrations found suicides are due primarily to their underlying depression, as suicidal and non-suicidal depressed subjects show no differences in CSF CRF (Banki et al., 1987). It remains to be seen whether there are differences between depressed suicides and suicides without depression.

In any case, this arena clearly remains in the realm of research. At present, clinicians can only watch with intense interest.

Cerebrospinal Fluid Magnesium

After Banki et al. (1985) reported that low CSF magnesium concentrations were highly correlated with suicide attempts in 11 of their 56 female patients, this simple element was added to the growing list of potential indicators of suicide risk. The subjects represented a mixture of depressive states, schizophrenia, and adjustment disorders, and the correlation of suicide attempts with a lower mean CSF magnesium was found regardless of diagnosis. Magnesium levels correlated significantly with CSF 5-HIAA, especially after correction for height and age, and even showed a stronger correlation with suicide attempts than 5-HIAA.

Confirming studies have not appeared to our knowledge, so in spite of its intriguing potential as a simple chemical test with a possible relationship to peripheral blood levels, it remains clinically just an interesting observation.

Genetics

So many human characteristics tend to cluster in families that it is not surprising that suicide does as well. Much evidence exists to support a genetic factor in major psychotic and affective disorders, but the role of genetics in suicide itself remains less clear. Twin studies have been inconclusive, and family and adoption studies have not yet satisfactorily separated a genetic risk for suicide from the genetic risk for depression or schizophrenia. A practical application of this situation is suggested by Roy (1989b) in the form of giving added attention to a depressed or suicidal adolescent with a family history of suicide. This would give recognition to the possibility that the young person may be developing a treatable recurrent affective disorder.

The most recent evidence (Roy et al., 1991) based on 176 twin pairs, finds a clear preponderance of concordance for suicide in the monozygotic (identical) twin pairs (11.3%), as compared to the dizygotic (non-identical) twin pairs (1.8%). When treatment for psychiatric disorders in the twins and their first or second-degree relatives was considered as well, the conclusion was that "genetic factors related to suicide may largely represent a genetic predisposition for the psychiatric disorders associated with suicide".

While the precise role of genetics remains to be clarified, we can and should address the issue of suicides in family members with a grasp of the potential psychological and social implications of such a pattern. The biological implications, however, cannot yet be put to clinical use.

Other Biological Considerations

Electroencephalogram (EEG)

The recognition by Struve et al. (1972) of a significant association of paroxysmal EEGs with suicidal ideation, suicide attempts, and assaultive-destructive behavior raised hopes of a non-invasive biological indicator of risk for these behaviors. Efforts to explore this relationship further led to "a paucity of positive findings", though suicidal persons of high emotional "reactivity" did show paroxysmal EEGs, while those with a more detailed suicide plan had normal records (Struve et al., 1977).

A recent approach to this question examined sleep EEG patterns in suicidal and non-suicidal adolescents with major depressive disorder (Dahl et al., 1990). The suicidal subgroup showed significantly longer sleep latency than the non-suicidal subgroup or the controls, though other sleep-related EEG characteristics were similar.

The use of the EEG for suicide risk assessment has the considerable advantages of minimum discomfort for the subject, non-invasiveness, outpatient applicability, and a rich context for interpretation. Its imprecision and lack of specificity are also great, and at present it is not a very active arena of investigation.

Growth Hormone (GH) response to Desipramine

Another biological function explored in depressed adolescents is the response of growth hormone to desipramine. This response was found to be significantly decreased in depressed adolescents with suicidal ideation or attempts as compared with those who showed no suicidal manifestations. The difference was attributed to differences in central nervous system beta-adrenergic and/or serotonergic function associated with suicidality (Ryan et al., 1988). These findings were interpreted as supporting the idea that "suicidality per se is the important variable in growth hormone secretion", a far-reaching interpretation that will require more testing before it is a candidate for clinical application.

Thyroid dysfunction

Mood disorders are a well-known aspect of thyroid dysfunction, whether hypo- or hyperthyroid states are considered. Though suicide is always an issue with disordered mood, a special clinical consideration was introduced by the identification of early symptomless autoimmune thyroiditis (SAT) (Gold, Pottash & Extein, 1982). This syndrome, apparently related to atrophic changes in the thyroid gland, reveals no clear thyroid symptoms or laboratory abnormalities, but presents in the form of anergia, difficulty concentrating, and depression that can reach suicidal intensity. The patient's despair may be increased if the clinician misinterprets the symptoms as a major depressive disorder that does not respond to treatment.

The investigators point out that this condition is characterized by an exaggerated TSH response to TRH (in contrast to a blunted or absent response in depression), combined with a positive test for antithyroid microsomal antibodies. The TSH response is recommended as a screening test for patients who present with anergia or depression and do not respond to traditional treatment. If the TSH response is exaggerated, a complete thyroid evaluation would be indicated, and finding antithyroid antibodies for the thyroid microsome would serve as a marker for SAT. The recognition of SAT and other thyroid disorders is especially important because relatively simple treatment, for example thyroid medication, may provide relief of symptoms.

Electroconvulsive Therapy (ECT)

Electroconvulsive therapy deserved to be mentioned because of its prominent role in the treatment of mood disorders, which in turn are closely associated with suicide. Though clinical and methodological considerations prevent a controlled study of the potential of ECT to prevent suicide, efforts to explore the question have been made. For example, Avery and Winokur (1978) reported a one-year follow-up of 519 depressed inpatients, of whom 257 received ECT. None of the subsequent four suicides had received ECT, and the rate of suicide attempts during the first six months of treatment was 0.85% in the ECT group compared to 7.0% in the "adequate antidepressant treatment" group.

As with many procedures, the key to effectiveness with ECT is patient selection. The best results have been seen in primary endogenous depression, but a number of clinical patterns have been seen to respond, even when the disorder has appeared to be intractable. Patients with personality disorders are less likely to show improvement, but if a superimposed depression is present, the suicide risk may be reduced even though some symptoms persist. An excellent review of the clinical issues involved in the use of ECT with suicidal patients is provided by Frankel (1984).

Suicide related medications and drugs

The metabolic correlates of suicide discussed above have been considered as possible endogenous biological "markers" or indicators of increased suicide risk when their concentrations are within a specified range. It is also the case that some medications used as therapeutic agents in various physical disorders can induce suicidal states, which may present unexpectedly in persons with no prior evidence of emotional difficulty.

Not surprisingly, in view of the compounds noted above, the best known of the exogenous agents associated with suicide is steroids. An advantage here, of course, is that with the onset of cognitive, mood, thought, or behavioral dysfunction, the steroids can be reduced or eliminated till normal nervous system function is restored. What sometimes occurs, however, is that the person does not report early signs of toxicity, or may manifest only mild intermittent evidence of confusion, despondency, euphoria, or disordered thinking. If the steroid intake is not reduced, a suicidal outcome may result (Brauning et al., 1989).

Another source of steroids in the contemporary world is self-administered anabolic compounds in athletes and weight lifters. If not monitored very closely, such misuse of steroids may lead to a suicidal episode, especially during the first 3 months following abrupt discontinuation of such use (Pope & Katz, 1988). Brower et al. (1989) point out that patients may be reluctant to volunteer information about steroid use, and that urine testing may be a useful check in the case of a depressed athlete or body builder.

Interferon alfa-2b, an agent used in the treatment of a number of neoplastic and infectious disorders, has been found to cause depression in a significant proportion of patients. Though a number of medications may induce depressive symptoms (e.g., propranolol), the affective disturbance observed with interferon has in some instances been so intense and unresponsive to any anti-depressant measures that the medication had to be stopped to avoid an impending suicide (Fenster, 1990).

An active controversy presently creating concern in the clinical community involves the potential of the widely-used antidepressant, fluoxetine, to induce or intensify both suicidal and homicidal thoughts and behavior. Sparked primarily by a report of six depressed patients who developed intense, violent suicidal preoccupation from two to seven weeks after starting treatment with fluoxetine (Teicher et al., 1990a), the broad issue of "antidepressants" paradoxically triggering suicidal states is coming to the fore.

The observation is not new. Alprazolam has been seen to produce a dramatic increase in aggression, self-mutilation, and suicidal behavior (Gardner and Cowdry, 1985), presumably by a process of disinhibition. Fifteen of 28 borderline patients treated with amitriptyline were reported to show increased suicide threats and assaultiveness (Soloff et al., 1986). One suicidal patient with desipramine (Dalmuji & Ferguson, 1988), One suicidal patient on fluoxetine recovered on a tricyclic agent, and two suicidal patients on desipramine recovered when switched to fluoxetine. A detailed critique of the Teicher et al. (1990a) report by Tollefson (1990) met an equally detailed rebuttal (Teicher et al., 1990b), and a large study by Fava and Rosenbaum (1990) which showed no greater suicidality in fluoxetine treated patients than in other antidepressants, is cited by Teicher et al (1990b) as supporting an opposite view when only those patients without suicidal thoughts prior to treatment are considered.

In view of the present popularity of fluoxetine, a clinician might best take note of what most observers agree on, specifically, that essentially all psychotropic drugs can produce atypical and unexpected effects, and that watching closely for that possibility is a routine aspect of pharmacological treatment.

Discussion

The current flood of biological information as regards suicidal persons shows no signs of abating as researchers continue to pursue an exhaustive search of the body and brain to identify new associations between organic observations and self-destructive behaviors. Although the most frequent paradigm is suicide attempts, correlates of past or present suicidal thoughts, violent or non-violent suicide attempts, a range of impulsive/aggressive/assaultive characteristics, suicide threats, completed suicides, and various combinations of these behaviors are also reported. Post-mortem studies provide an additional dimension by revealing different findings in various areas of the brain. The newest investigative technique, post-mortem CSF studies, compares CSF samples from different points in the central nervous system. Still another dimension is represented by specific diagnostic categories such as depression, mania, or schizophrenia, that may account for some biological manifestations independently of suicidal behaviors. Though much of what we have learned about the biology of suicide was derived from studies of depressive states, the value of neuroendocrine tests even in major depression remains controversial (Rubin, 1990).

It is tempting to cite several hundred references to document the many intriguing investigations that have been carried out to explore the questions raised in this area. At present, this would not further our search for practical applications. In view of the frequent methodological problems of small samples, multiple paradigms, and retrospective design, the present body of biological information can best be characterized as reflecting an area of ongoing active research rather than a source of new clinical tools.

The most consistent and promising biological data relate low CSF 5-HIAA levels to a variety of suicidal, impulsive, or disinhibited behavior patterns. Although there are some inconsistent findings, so many confirmatory reports have appeared that they have been said to constitute "one of the most highly replicated set of findings in biological psychiatry" (Brown & Goodwin, 1986). Yet, in spite of the general agreement among researchers that serotonin is somehow related to aggressive behavior, no clinical guidelines have been suggested to translate that observation into a practical clinical tool. A clinician might ask whether such a tool is needed to recognize vulnerability to aggressive behavior, in view of its accessibility by clinical inquiry. Such inquiry makes it possible to assess the person's capacity to control aggressive impulses as well, which may be the determining factor as regards outcome.

We might anticipate that one of the next biological systems to become prominent as a possible suicide marker will involve the pineal gland and melatonin, which in the CSF has been found to correlate with CSF magnesium, and in nocturnal serum to be decreased in depression (Claustrat et al., 1984; Milin et al., 1990). Serotonin is a precursor of melatonin, although little is known of any correlation between the concentrations of the two compounds in humans (Asberg, 1989).

Another compound found unexpectedly to be indirectly associated with suicide and not yet studied regarding its links to suicidal behavior is cholesterol. In examining the cardiovascular effects of this substance in a long-term mortality study, subjects with lowered serum cholesterol levels showed a reduced mortality rate from heart disease but a significantly higher rate of death from accidents, suicide and violence (Muldoon et al., 1990). That the finding was consistent across all of the six studies analyzed creates inevitable questions as to the mechanisms involved, especially whether there is some link to serotonin metabolism.

The list of still-unexplored potential markers for suicide seems almost endless. Those on the immediate horizon include changes in the ì and ä opioid receptors in the brain, altered skin conductivity, reduced prolactin response to fenfluramine, and structural characteristics of the hippocampus.

A source of confusion that may complicate the practical application of new biological data is the difference between clinical significance and statistical significance. The widespread use of the p value for judging the importance or merit of a given outcome, and adhering to the arbitrary .05 levels as the guide to acceptance of new findings, can be misleading.

While the search for a clinically useful role for biological markers continues, we are reminded by Stanley (1986) of serious ethical issues involved in such investigations. These are especially pertinent to the danger of prematurely identifying a finding as indicative of high risk. For example, what should a person with a positive finding be told? Could a self-fulfilling prophesy emerge? What effect might it have on health or life insurance, sensitive jobs, or public office? The unsettled state of the field is acknowledged in this thoughtful reminder by granting that these are not immediate concerns, but clinicians have been appropriately cautioned.

Investigators and clinicians alike seem to agree that in spite of many advances, the search for biological markers of suicide risk is still in a tentative stage. Secunda et al. (1986) express it succinctly: "It is clear that no unitary clinical or biochemical relationship exists between a clinical diagnosis, e.g., depression, and a behavior-suicide. The most recent work attempting to define the impact of alterations in the biogenic amine system on aggression and impulsivity is interesting and invites much speculation as regards one final common pathway behavior-suicide. However, the work remains too sketchy and it must be for future authors to provide the necessary linkage".

Summary

Biological correlates of suicide emerged over the past twenty-five years as an incidental finding in the course of investigating the biology of depression. The most consistent candidate for potential clinical use as an indicator of suicide risk has been serotonin and its metabolite 5-hydroxyindoleacetic acid. The relationship of these compounds to suicidal acts appears to be their role in a broad range of aggressive, impulsive and anxiety-related behaviors. Although some tentative ideas have been expressed as regards possible clinical applications, there is general agreement that such use at present would be premature. There have been no published reports to our knowledge of the non-investigative utilization of any biological correlates of suicide, a reflection of the absence of clear guidelines for doing so.

A new standard of care has not been created by the expansion of knowledge about neurochemical and endocrine functions related to suicidal behavior. Contemporary literature and professional meetings devote increasing attention to the issue, but presentations are still couched more in terms of supporting evidence than confirmation of hypotheses.

Although new information continues to be reported at a remarkable rate, the psychobiology of suicide remains an area of exciting ongoing research rather than a source of practical clinical tools. None of the measurements developed to date have a clear and present role in suicide risk assessment.

REFERENCES

Apter, A., Praag, H. van, Plutchik, R., Sevy, A., Korn, M., & Brown, S. (1990). Interrelationships among anxiety, aggression, impulsivity, and mood: A serotonergically linked cluster? *Psychiatry Research, 32*, 191-199.

Arango, V., Ernsberger, P., Marzuk, P., Chen, J., Tierney, H., Stanley, M., Reis, D., & Mann, J. (1990). Autoradiographic demonstration of increased serotonin $5HT_{22}$ and beta-adrenergic receptor binding sites in the brain of suicide victims. *Archives General Psychiatry, 47*, 1038-1047.

Arato, M., Banki, C., Tothfalusi, L., Nemeroff, C., Bissette, G., Akil, H., & Watson, S. (1986). Postmortem CSF measurements as a new research tool. *Clinical Neuropharmacology, 9* (suppl. 4), 578-580.

Arato, M., Banki, C., Bissett, G., & Nemeroff, C. (1989). Elevated CSF CRF in suicide victims. *Biological Psychiatry, 35*, 355-359.

Arora, R., & Meltzer, H. (1989). Serotonergic measures in the brains of suicide victims: $5HT_2$ binding sites in the frontal cortex of suicide victims and control subjects. *American Journal of Psychiatry, 146*, 730-736.

Asberg, M. (1989). Neurotransmitter monoamine metabolites in the cerebrospinal fluid as risk factors for suicidal behavior. In L. Davidson & M. Linnoila (Eds.), *Report of the Secretary's task force on youth suicide, Vol. 2* (pp. 193-212). DHHS Pub. no. (ADM) 89-1622.

Asberg, M., Traskman, L., & Sjostrand, L. (1976). Monoamine metabolites in CSF and suicidal behavior. *Archives of General Psychiatry, 33*, 1193-1197.

Avery, D., & Winokur, G. (1978). Suicide, attempted suicide, and relapse rates in depression: Occurrence after ECT and antidepressant therapy. *Archives of General Psychiatry, 35*, 749-753.

Banki, C. (1985). Biochemical markers for suicidal behavior. *American Journal of Psychiatry, 142*, 147-148.

Banki, C., Arato, M., Papp, Z., & Kurcz, M. (1984). Biochemical markers in suicidal patients. *Journal of Affective Disorders, 6*, 341-350.

Banki, C., Bissette, J., Arato, M., O'Conner, L., & Nemeroff, C. (1987). CSF corticotropin-releasing factor-like immunoreactivity in depression and schizophrenia. *American Journal of Psychiatry, 144*, 873-877.

Banki, C., Vojnik, M., Papp, Z., Balla, K., & Arato, M. (1985). Cerebrospinal fluid magnesium and calcium related to amine metabolites, diagnosis, and suicide attempts. *Biological Psychiatry, 20*, 163-171.

Bowman, K., & Bender, L. (1932). The treatment of involution melancholia with ovarian hormone. *American Journal of Psychiatry, 11*, 867-892.

Braunig, P., Bleistein, J., & Rao, M. (1989). Suicidality and corticosteroid-induced psychosis (letter). *Biological Psychiatry, 26*, 209-210.

Brower, K., Blow, F., Eliopulos, G., & Beresford, T. (1989). Anabolic androgenic steroids and suicide (letter). *American Journal of Psychiatry, 146*, 1075.

Brown, G., & Goodwin, F. (1986). Human aggression and suicide. *Suicide and Life-Threatening Behavior, 16*, 223-243.

Brown, G., & Linnoila, M. (1990). CSF serotonin metabolite (5-HIAA) studies in depression, impulsivity, and violence. *Journal of Clinical Psychiatry, 51* (suppl.), 31-41.

Bunney, W., & Fawcett, J. (1965). Possibility of a biochemical test for suicide potential. *Archives of General Psychiatry, 13*, 232-239.

Bunney, W., Fawcett, J., Davis, J., & Gifford, S. (1969). Further evaluation of urinary 17-hydroxycorticosteroids in suicidal patients. *Archives of General Psychiatry, 21*, 138-150.

Claustrat, B., Chazot, G., Brun, J., Jordan, D., & Sassoias, G. (1984). A chronobiological study of melatonin and cortisol secretion in depressed subjects: Plasma melatonin, a biochemical marker in major depression. *Biological Psychiatry, 19*, 1215-1228.

Dahl, R., Puig-Antich, J., Ryan, N., Nelson, B., Dachille, S., Cunningham, S., Trubnick, L., & Klepper, T. (1990). EEG sleep in adolescents with major depression: The role of suicidality and inpatient status. *Journal of Affective Disorders, 19*, 63-75.

Dalmugi, N., & Ferguson, J. (1988). Paradoxical worsening of depressive symptomatology caused by antidepressants. *Journal of Clinical Psychopharmacology, 8*, 347-349.

DeLeo, D., & Marazziti, D. (1988). Biological prediction of suicide: The role of serotonin. *Crisis, 9*, 109-118.

Fava, M., & Rosenbaum, J. (1990). *Suicidality and fluoxetine: Is there a relationship?* In New Research Program and Abstracts, 143rd Annual Meeting, American Psychiatric Association. Washington, DC: APA.

Fenster, L. (1990). *Gastroenterology update*. Lecture at Virginia Mason Medical Center. Seattle, November 9.

Frankel, F. (1984). The use of electroconvulsive therapy in suicidal patients. *American Journal of Psychotherapy, 38*, 384-391.

Funkenstein, D., King, S., & Drolette, M. (1954). The direction of anger during a laboratory stress-inducing situation. *Psychosomatic Medicine, 16*, 404-413.

Gardner, D., & Cowdry, R. (1985). Alprazolam-induced dyscontrol in borderline personality disorder. *American Journal of Psychiatry, 142*, 98-100.

Gold, M., Pottash, A., & Extein, I. (1982). "Symptomless" autoimmune thyroiditis in depression. *Psychiatry Research, 6*, 261-269.

Gross-Isseroff, R., Israeli, M., & Biegon, A. (1989). Autoradiographic analysis of tritiated imipramine binding in the human brain post mortem: Effects of suicide. *Archives of General Psychiatry, 46*, 237-241.

Jones, J., Stanley, B., Mann, J., Frances, A., Guido, J., Traskman-Benz, L., Winchel, R., Brown, R., & Stanley, M. (1990). CSF 5-HIAA and HVA concentrations in elderly depressed patients who attempted suicide. *American Journal of Psychiatry, 147*, 1225-1227.

Kjellman, B., Ljunggren, J-G., Beck-Fries, J., & Wetterberg, L. (1985). Effect of TRH on TSH and prolactin levels in affective disorders. *Psychiatry Research, 14*, 353-363.

Krieger, G. (1974). The plasma level of cortisol as a predictor of suicide. *Diseases of the Nervous System, 35*, 237-240.

Krieger, G. (1975). Is there a biochemical predictor of suicide? *Suicide and Life-Threatening Behavior, 5*, 228-231.

Lidberg, L., Tuck, J., Asberg, M., Scalia-Tomba, G-P., & Bertilsson, L. (1985). Homicide, suicide and CSF 5-HIAA. *Acta Psychiatrica Scandinavica, 71*, 230-236.

Linkowski, P., Wettere, J. van, Kerkhofs, M., Brauman, H., & Mendlewicz, J. (1983). Thyrotrophin response to thyrostimulin in affectively ill women: Relationship to suicidal behavior. *British Journal of Psychiatry, 143*, 401-405.

Linkowski, P., Wettere, J. van, Kerkhofs, M., Gregoire, F., & Brauman, H. (1984). Violent suicidal behavior and the thyrotrophin releasing hormone-thyroid stimulating hormone test: A clinical outcome study. *Neuropsychobiology, 12*, 19-22.

Lopez-Ibor, J. Jr., Saiz-Ruiz, J., & Perez do los Cobos, J. (1985). Biological correlations of suicide and aggressivity in major depressions (with melancholia): 5-hydroxyindoleacetic acid and cortisol in cerebral spinal fluid, dexamethasone suppression test and therapeutic response to 5-hydroxytryptophan. *Neuropsychobiology, 14*, 67-74.

Maes, M., Vandewoude, M., Schotte, C., Martin, M., Block, P., Scharpe, S., & Cosyns, P. (1989). Hypothalamic-pituitary-adrenal and thyroid axis dysfunctions and decrements in the availability of L-Tryptophan as biological markers of suicidal ideation in major depressed females. *Acta Psychiatrica Scandinavica, 80*, 13-17.

Meltzer, H., & Lowy, M. (1989). *The neuroendocrine system and suicide*. In L. Davidson & M. Linnoila (Eds.) (pp. 235-246). DHSS Pub. No. (ADM) 89-1622.

Milin, J., Previtera, L., Sovljanski, M., Previtera, M., & Milin, R. (1990). The pineal gland morphofunctional disorder: A risk factor of suicidality? In G. Ferreri, M. Bellini, P. Crepet (Eds.), *Suicidal behaviors and risk factors* (pp. 693-689). Bologna, Italy: Monduzzi Editore.

Montgomery, S., & Montgomery, D. (1982). Pharmacological prevention of suicidal behaviors. *Journal of Affective Disorders, 4*, 291-298.

Motto, J. (1986). Clinical considerations of biological correlates of suicide. *Suicide and Life-Threatening Behavior, 16*, 83-102.

Muldoon, M., Manuck, S., & Matthews, K. (1990). Lowering cholesterol concentrations and mortality: A quantitative review of primary prevention trials. *British Medical Journal, 301*, 309-314.

Nemeroff, C., Owens, M., Bissette, G., Andorn, A., & Stanley, M. (1988). Reduced corticotropin releasing factor binding sites in the frontal cortex of suicide victims. *Archives of General Psychiatry, 45*, 577-579.

Ninan, P., Kammen, D. van, Scheinen, M., Linnoila, M., Bunney, W., & Goodwin, F. (1984). CSF 5-hydroxyindoleacetic acid levels in suicidal schizophrenic patients. *American Journal of Psychiatry, 141*, 566-569.

Ostroff, R., Giller, E., Bonese, K., Ebersole, E., Harkness, L., & Mason, J. (1982). Neuroendocrine risk factors of suicidal behavior. *American Journal of Psychiatry, 139*, 1332-1325.

Ostroff, R., Giller, E., Harkness, L., & Mason, J. (1985). The norepinephrine-to-epinephrine ratio in patients with a history of suicide attempts. *American Journal of Psychiatry, 142*, 224-227.

Palaniappan, C., Ramachandran, V., & Somasundaram, O. (1983). Suicidal ideation and biogenic amines in depression. *Indian Journal of Psychiatry, 25*, 286-292.

Pope, H., & Katz, D. (1988). Affective and psychotic symptoms associated with anabolic steroid use. *American Journal of Psychiatry, 145*, 487-490.

Ricci, L., & Wellman, M. (1990). Monamines: Biochemical markers of suicide? *Journal of Clinical Psychology, 46*, 106-116.

Roy, A. (1989b). Genetics and suicidal behavior. In L. Davidson & M. Linnoila (Eds.), *Report of the Secretary's task force on youth suicide, Vol. 2*. (pp. 247-262). DHHS Pub. No. (ADM) 89-1622.

Roy, A., Agren, H., Pickar, D., Linnoila, M., Doran, A., Cutler, N., & Paul, S. (1986). Reduced CSF concentrations of homovanillic acid and homovanillic acid to 5-hydroxyindoleacetic acid ratios in depressed patients: Relationship to suicidal behavior and dexamethasone nonsuppression. *American Journal of Psychiatry, 143*, 1539-1545.

Roy, A., Lamparski, D., DeJong, J., Adinoff, B., Ravitz, B., George, D., Nutt, D., & Linnoila, M. (1990). CSF monomine metabolites in alcoholic patients who attempt suicide. *Acta Psychiatrica Scandinavica, 81*, 58-61.

Roy, A., Pickar, D., DeJong, J., Karoum, F., & Linnoila, M. (1987). Suicidal behavior in depression: Relationship to noradreneergic function. *Biological Psychiatry, 25*, 341-350.

Roy, A., Pickar, D., Linnoila, M., Crousos, P., & Gold, P. (1987). Cerebrospinal fluid corticotropin-releasing hormone in depression: Relationship to noradrenergic function. *Psychiatry Research, 20*, 229-237.

Roy, A., Sega, N., Centerwall, B., & Robinette, D. (1991). Suicide in twins. *Archives of General Psychiatry, 48*, 29-32.

Rubin, R. (1990). Value of neuroendocrine tests in major depression remains controversial. *Psychiatric Times,* (Aug.), p. 42.

Ryan, N., Puig-Antich, J., Rabinovich, H., Ambrosini, P., Robinson, D., Nelson, B., & Navacenko, H. (1988). Growth hormone response to desmethylimipramine in depressed and suicidal adolescents. *Journal of Affective Disorders, 15*, 323-337.

Secunda, S., Cross, C., Koslow, S., Katz, M., Kocsis, J., & Maas, J. (1986). Studies of amine metabolites in depressed patients. In J. Mann & M. Stanley (Eds.), *Psychobiology of suicidal behavior* (pp. 231-241). Annals of the New York Academy of Sciences, 487.

Soloff, P., George, A., Nathan, R., Schultz, P., & Perel, J. (1986). Paradoxical effects of amitriptyline on borderline patients. *American Journal of Psychiatry, 142*, 1603-1605.

Stanley, B. (1986). Ethical considerations in biological research on suicide. In J. Mann & M. Stanley (Eds.), *Psychogiology of suicidal behavior* (pp. 42-46). Annals of the New York Academy of Sciences 1986, 478.

Stanley, M., Virgilio, J., & Gershon, S. (1982). Tritiated imipramine binding sites are decreased in the frontal cortex of suicides. *Science, 216*, 1337-1339.

Struve, F., Klein, D., & Saraf, K. (1972). Electroencephalographic correlates of suicide ideation and attempts. *Archives of General Psychiatry, 27*, 363-365.

Struve, F., Saraf, K., Arko, R., Klein, D., Becka, D. (1977). Relationship between paroxysmal electroencephalographic dysrythmia and suicide ideation and attempts in psychiatric patients. In C. Shagass, S. Gershon & A. Friedhoff (Eds.), *Psychopathology and brain dysfunctions* (pp. 199-221). New York: Raven Press.

Teicher, M., Glod, C., & Cole, J. (1990a). Emergence of intense suicidal preoccupation during fluoxetine treatment. *American Journal of Psychiatry, 147*, 207-210.

Teicher, M., Glod, C., & Cole, J. (1990b). Dr. Teicher and associates reply (letter). *American Journal of Psychiatry, 47*, 1692-1693.

Tollefson, G. (1990). Fluoxetine and suicidal ideation (letter). *American Journal of Psychiatry, 147*, 1691-1692.

Traskman, L., Asberg, M., Bertilsson, L., Sjostrand, L. (1981). Monoamine metabolites in CSF and suicidal behavior. *Archives of General Psychiatry, 38*, 631-636.

Van Praag, H. (1986). Biological suicide research: Outcome and limitations. *Biological Psychiatry, 21*, 1305-1323.

Van Praag, H. (1982). Depression, suicide and the metabolism of serotonin in the brain. *Journal of Affective Disorders, 4*, 275-290.

Van Praag, H., & Plutchik, R. (1984). Depression type and depression severity in relation to risk of violent suicide attempt. *Psychiatric Research, 12*, 333-338.

Woodman, D. (1979). Evidence of a permanent imbalance in catecholamine secretions in violent social deviants. *Journal of Psychomatic Research, 23*, 155-157.

Index of Subjects

Index of Names